TROTSKYISTS ON TRIAL

CULTURE, LABOR, HISTORY SERIES
General Editors: Daniel Bender and Kimberley L. Phillips

Trotskyists on Trial

*Free Speech and Political
Persecution since the
Age of FDR*

Donna T. Haverty-Stacke

NEW YORK UNIVERSITY PRESS
New York and London

NEW YORK UNIVERSITY PRESS
New York and London
www.nyupress.org

© 2015 by New York University
All rights reserved

References to Internet websites (URLs) were accurate at the time of writing. Neither the author nor New York University Press is responsible for URLs that may have expired or changed since the manuscript was prepared.

ISBN: 978-1-4798-5194-2

For Library of Congress Cataloging-in-Publication data, please contact the Library of Congress.

New York University Press books are printed on acid-free paper, and their binding materials are chosen for strength and durability. We strive to use environmentally responsible suppliers and materials to the greatest extent possible in publishing our books.

Manufactured in the United States of America

10 9 8 7 6 5 4 3 2 1

Also available as an ebook

For Michael Kammen, who taught us so much and inspired so many

CONTENTS

ACKNOWLEDGMENTS

Many people helped make this a better book. I first would like to thank my fellow historians Daniel J. Walkowitz, Richard Polenberg, Ken and Elizabeth Fones-Wolf, Jennifer Luff, Eric Arnesen, the members of the DC Working-Class History Group, Jonathan Rosenberg, Benjamin Hett, and (before his passing) Michael Kammen, who gave me valuable feedback on chapters as I revised them. I would especially like to thank Ellen Schrecker and Bryan Palmer, who generously read the entire manuscript in an earlier form and provided helpful comments.

I want to thank Joe Allen, for sharing his work on the Trotskyists, and David Riehle, for sending along wonderful photos and oral histories that have enriched the manuscript. Vincent Tobin also generously shared his personal research on the case and his memories of his grandfather. Thanks, too, to my editor at NYU Press, Clara Platter, and to the series editor, Daniel Bender, whose excitement for my work and strong support guided it smoothly into press.

Good historians also know the value of great librarians and archivists. I would like to express my appreciation to the teams at the National Archives and Records Administration in College Park, Maryland, and in Kansas City, Missouri; the Franklin D. Roosevelt Presidential Library in Hyde Park, New York; the Minnesota Historical Society; the Wisconsin Historical Society; the Hennepin County Library; the Cornell University Law Library; and the Tamiment Library and Robert F. Wagner Labor Archives at New York University. In addition, I am grateful to the research assistance provided by Patrick Dixon, Shaun S. Nichols, John Kunicki, and Martha V. Miller. I also want to thank Hunter College for the Presidential Travel Award that supported a portion of my research and for the Presidential Fund for Faculty Advancement Grant that defrayed the cost of preparing the index.

Portions of chapters 1 and 2 have appeared, in somewhat different form, in my article "'Punishment of Mere Political Advocacy': The FBI, Teamsters Local 544, and the Origins of the 1941 Smith Act Case," *Journal of American History* 100, no. 1 (June 2013): 68–93. I would like to thank Oxford University Press for permission to reprint this material.

Finally, I must thank my family and friends, especially my loving husband, Dylan, and our beautiful daughter, Josephine, for the laughter and the love.

Introduction

On June 27, 1941, FBI agents and U.S. marshals raided the offices of the Socialist Workers Party (SWP) in Minneapolis and in St. Paul. Following orders from the Department of Justice, they confiscated party files and literature, two red flags, and several pictures of Leon Trotsky. Three weeks later, twenty-nine party members, fifteen of whom also belonged to the militant Teamsters Local 544, were arrested. In July, a federal grand jury indicted them for violating the 1940 Smith Act, specifically for conspiring to advocate the overthrow of the government. As Socialist Workers, these men and women openly opposed the war in Europe and supported the creation of a socialist commonwealth through proletarian revolution. The Roosevelt administration deemed them a threat to the nation because of their advocacy of these beliefs. These twenty-nine Trotskyists became the first Americans to be indicted under the Smith Act.

Among the twenty-nine defendants were organizers and officers from Local 544, including the locally infamous Dunne brothers, Grant, Miles, and Vincent, who led the epic 1934 Teamsters strikes in Minneapolis. First in the coal yards and then among the truck drivers, these men coordinated three separate walkouts over six months that ground the city's business to a halt and ultimately transformed what had been one of the nation's most committed open-shop cities into one in which strong unions had a significant presence.[1] Other defendants in the 1941 Smith Act case included activists from the Federal Workers Section (FWS) of Local 544, an auxiliary dedicated to organizing the unemployed and those who worked on various Works Progress Administration (WPA) projects during the Great Depression. The feisty young Max Geldman and his SWP comrade Edward Palmquist, who helped lead the 1939 WPA strike in Minneapolis, were among those targeted for prosecution under the Smith Act.[2] And then there were the national leaders of the SWP, including James P. Cannon, the titular and spiritual head of the American organization; Farrell Dobbs, the party's chief labor strategist, whose roots were deeply planted in the soil of the Minneapolis Teamsters' struggles; and Albert Goldman, the party's legal counsel who represented, in part, its New York intellectual wing.[3]

Leading SWP figures from Minneapolis and St. Paul were also included in the federal government's prosecution. Grace Holmes Carlson and her sister

Dorothy Holmes Schultz, two of the three women defendants, were active SWP members. Carlson in particular had become a leading public figure in the movement by 1940; that year she both worked as a state organizer and ran for U.S. Senate as a Trotskyist.[4] The federal government thus targeted for prosecution the Trotskyist leaders of Local 544, their supporters in the FWS, their high-ranking comrades in the SWP in New York, and those who had public profiles in the party in Minneapolis and St. Paul.

Not all of the twenty-nine defendants were ultimately convicted. In a tragic turn of events, Grant Dunne committed suicide on October 4 before the trial convened on October 27. Judge Matthew M. Joyce issued a directed verdict of not guilty on November 18 for five defendants, including Dorothy Schultz, citing insufficient evidence of their knowledge of the conspiracy in question. On December 1 the jury found all remaining twenty-three defendants not guilty on the first count of the indictment (organizing armed revolution against the government). It also found five other defendants not guilty on the second count, the sedition and conspiracy charge. The remaining eighteen defendants, however, including Vincent Dunne, Farrell Dobbs, James Cannon, Max Geldman, and Grace Carlson, were found guilty on the second count, of violating the Smith Act, and were sentenced to prison for twelve to sixteen months.[5]

By exploring the social, political, and legal history of the first Smith Act case, I chart the compromise many Americans were willing to make between free speech and national security during wartime and probe the implications of that choice for dissent and democracy in American society during the middle to late twentieth century. With the benefit of declassified government documents and recently opened archival sources, I explore the social and political history of the first Smith Act case from its roots in intra-union rivalry during the mid-1930s to its role in shaping the parameters of free speech law during the Second Red Scare of the late 1940s and early 1950s. I also consider the ongoing efforts of the Trotskyists to defend their civil liberties throughout these decades and beyond, including their landmark 1981 lawsuit against the FBI. Until relatively recently, such a comprehensive history of the experiences of the Minneapolis twenty-nine has not been possible.[6] Access to newly available sources allows for a fuller and more historically grounded story that explains the implications of the first Smith Act case for organized labor and civil liberties in wartime and postwar America.[7]

Passed in June 1940, the Smith Act was a peacetime antisedition law that marked a dramatic shift in the legal definition of free speech protection in America. The Smith Act criminalized advocacy of disloyalty in the armed forces and of the overthrow of the government by force. It also criminalized the acts of printing, publishing, or distributing any materials advocating such sedition and made it illegal to organize or belong to any association that did the same.[8] Although such provisions were not unprecedented in federal law (the World War I era Sedition Act contained similar prohibitions), their being enshrined in legislation and applied in prosecutions during peacetime were realities not seen in the United States since the Alien and Sedition Acts of 1798. In 1940, as in 1798, fear of an impending war, and of domestic dissent against the administration in power preparing for that war, fueled the legislation's passage.[9] The Smith Act found strong supporters among the nation's military leaders and patriotic organizations (including the American Legion) but faced vocal opposition from the American Civil Liberties Union (ACLU).[10] In defending the bill, its sponsor, Virginia congressman Howard Smith, stoked fears of possible fascist or communist attacks from within.[11] At the height of what historians have called the "little red scare," with the war in Europe raging under Hitler's blitzkrieg, President Roosevelt signed the Smith Act into law on June 29, 1940, seven days after the fall of France.

The defendants' opposition to the war was not the only reason they were prosecuted under this new law, but it does help explain why they were targeted when Communists were not. By late June 1941, with the German invasion of the Soviet Union, the Communist Party's volte-face positioned it squarely in support of the Allied war effort. On the political left, only the SWP remained opposed to the war, and its members' alleged plans to take advantage of the wartime crisis to advocate a proletarian revolution placed them in the crosshairs of the Smith Act. The strong Trotskyist presence among the leadership of Teamsters Local 544 in Minneapolis, a radical stewardship that successfully guided drivers and thousands of their supporters in a bloody fight against the open shop during the momentous 1934 strikes, was already well known to the FBI and made it an object of concern to the bureau. With the added statutory authority provided to it by the Smith Act, J. Edgar Hoover's agency intensified its domestic surveillance of SWP members and their affiliates in Local 544, seeing both groups as possible agents of internal subversion.

Because the origins of this case can be found partly in the actions of a rank-and-file opposition movement formed in late 1940 against Local 544's Trotskyist-dominated leadership, its history fits within the story of early labor anticommunism—opposition to communism within the ranks of labor during the 1930s and early 1940s. Several historians have charted this territory, exploring how internal union factionalism often followed the contours of anticommunist sentiment that was at times sincerely felt for ideological, faith-based, partisan, or moral reasons (i.e., among liberals, Catholics, Socialists, or anti-Stalinists), and at other times was embraced for more practical ones (e.g., Walter Reuther's shifting alliances within the United Auto Workers).[12] These historians have noted how workers' opposition to communism, whatever the motive, became more intense by 1939. With the announcement of the Nazi-Soviet Pact that August and with the outbreak of the war in Europe that September, anticommunism among the ranks of labor became an important sign of respectability and conformity.

These attributes became valuable to unions confronting both the new political reality of what historians have called the "little red scare" of 1939–1941 and the nation's shift to wartime preparedness.[13] This tense political context made union militancy impractical; any interruptions in production—including those legitimately based on workers' grievances—could now be perceived as internal subversion, as was the case at North American Aviation. When workers struck at the plant in Inglewood, California, that June, shutting down "25 percent of all fighter aircraft production" in a maneuver that "appeared to be . . . Communist-led," the president authorized the military seizure of the factory that broke the strike. Even though America was not at war, supporting its allies created a sense of emergency in which drastic action in the name of national security went virtually uncriticized.[14] American workers and their union leaders were beginning to appreciate what Roosevelt's shift from Dr. New Deal to Dr. Win-the-War would come to mean for them.

But changes also took place within the house of labor because of the growing international crisis: both the no-strike pledge and the proliferation of anticommunist resolutions and bans on communists serving as union leaders were, in part, manifestations of workers' responses to the wartime emergency.[15] And such responses were not necessarily markers of conservative political tendencies within the ranks of labor. Similar "Communazi" resolutions were supported in left and liberal organizations at the time, including the ACLU.[16] The rank-and-file opposition to the Trotskyist leadership of Minneapolis Teamsters Local 544 was one manifestation of this type of early, liberal anticommunism.

What sets this case apart are those ties between the local rank-and-file opposition and the FBI, something that has been less thoroughly probed in the scholarship on early labor anticommunism.[17] The hostility certain Teamsters felt toward the Trotskyists in their midst dovetailed with the Justice Department's independent concerns about national security risks in the transportation industry on the eve of America's entry into World War II, leading it to seek these first Smith Act indictments in July 1941. But unlike the situation at North American Aviation, when the federal government intervened after a strike had begun to disrupt defense production, in the Minneapolis case the prosecution was based on what might happen at some unspecified time in the future because of the advocacy of certain beliefs. The defendants' alleged statements regarding their plans to overthrow the government by force, to undermine morale in the armed forces, and to disrupt the nation's freight transportation networks were first brought to the attention of the attorney general by the FBI through its lengthy and extensive secret investigations, aided by informants within the union.

Because the 1941 Smith Act case originated, in part, out of that cooperation between the Trotskyists' rank-and-file opponents and federal agents, this book provides a case study of the relationship between such early labor anticommunists and the developing security state. It demonstrates how some working-class Americans welcomed federal investigations into their internal union disputes, a disquieting reality not yet fully explored by labor historians.[18] Labor and radical factionalism have been well documented, but the cooperation of rank-and-file workers with the mechanisms of government repression has not, especially for this earlier period.[19] Yet in Minneapolis men like Thomas Williams, James Bartlett, and their supporters in the opposition group they formed rebelled against Vincent Dunne and the other Trotskyist leaders of Local 544 in part because of the radical political activities of those leaders within the union. Williams, Bartlett, and their Committee of 100, as it became known, cooperated with the FBI's investigation of the SWP, transforming the struggle for control of the union from a local squabble into a federal criminal case.

The origins of the 1941 case also reveal the extensive involvement of the FBI in investigating targets under the Smith Act and in pressuring both union and federal government officials into supporting a case against those targets. By encouraging the first prosecution under the Smith Act through his communications with the attorney general and the U.S. attorneys, J. Edgar Hoover tapped into the statutory authority of the new sedition law to legitimize the FBI's investigation of subversives. And, as with investigations of other alleged subversive groups during the war, he expanded the bureau's inquiries to include more proactive domestic intelligence work: the use of informants and plants to disrupt the internal workings of targeted organizations, as well as the promotion of prosecutions based on such work.[20] His agents' presence in Minneapolis played a role in fueling the grassroots opposition to the Trotskyists by emboldening it and contributing to its sense of self-importance in what was perceived as a struggle against fifth columnists. As a result, the bureau's agents raised the stakes in what otherwise was a run-of-the-mill intra-union factional fight mired in the politics of early labor anticommunism. And what followed—the prosecution of the Trotskyists under the new peacetime sedition law—silenced the voices of skilled organizers within the Teamsters and undermined the Trotskyist adventure in trade union work.

In addition to deepening our understanding of early labor and liberal anticommunism (illuminating in particular the role of the FBI), this study of the 1941 Smith Act case engages with the broader issue of how the state balanced the competing claims of civil liberties and national security just before and during World War II. Specifically, it explores the role of the Roosevelt administration in restricting free speech at home while it supported the fight to save democracy abroad. Under Acting Attorney General Francis Biddle, the administration prosecuted the Trotskyists beginning in July 1941. This action was the first time since 1798 that the United States put defendants on trial for sedition while the nation was not at war. The decision to go ahead with the case illuminates how even self-described civil libertarians participated in curtailing free speech. As such, this study complements existing works on the civil liberties violations that took place under the Roosevelt administration.[21] The Minneapolis case, however, shows how far the administration went to prosecute political dissent—even to the point of targeting the labor-liberal left. The history of the case reveals how strong fear of fifth column activity became on the eve of war and how figures like Biddle allowed that fear to trump their defense of free speech rights.

This study of the Minneapolis case also complements the works of scholars who have begun to explore the links between the wartime growth of the FBI and its domestic security programs. They have grappled with the convergence of spreading fears of the fifth column, shifting attitudes toward the Communist Party, deepening hostility aimed against anti-interventionists, and growing support for the Smith Act in the summer of 1940 on the eve of America's entry into World War II. And they have probed some of the ways civil liberties were eroded during the war.[22] It was during the wartime emergency that the framework of the nation's postwar security state was constructed. The Trotskyists were among that state's first victims, and their case had critical legal consequences for those—on the right and the left—who would follow.

Most significantly, their case legitimized the Smith Act itself and, as one contemporary observer noted, its "punishment of mere political advocacy."[23] The government's prosecution of the Trotskyists marked a turning point in First Amendment litigation. During the trial, and throughout the appeals process, the defense team unsuccessfully urged the courts to apply the clear and present danger test to federal restrictions on free speech. Challenging the validity of such application, the prosecution interpreted its mandate as merely having to prove a conspiracy to advocate the violent overthrow of the government. As was the case in the infamous Haymarket trial in 1886 (albeit on the state level) and as would be the case in the prosecution of the Communist Party leadership in 1949, the government constructed an argument based, in part, on literary evidence. The Marxist classics, along with party publications, were interpreted as proof of the movement's crimes in which the indicted party members conspired. Any question of the evident or imminent threat that their beliefs posed to the nation was disregarded as the argument for the criminality of their political associations and utterances was forcefully advanced and upheld by the courts.[24]

First implemented in this way in 1941, the Smith Act remained in full force for the next sixteen years.[25] It served as the statutory basis for many of the prosecutions of the Second Red Scare, most notably that of the Communist Party leadership in 1949. The Trotskyists protested this, even though the Communists, adhering to their doctrinaire ways, had supported the SWP's prosecution under the "Gag" Act in 1941.[26] While it remained unchallenged by the Supreme Court until 1957, that law contributed to the chilling of political dissent during the early Cold War years. For the anticommunist opposition within Local 544 during the summer of 1941, however, the immediate internecine union fight was all that mattered, and the alliance with the FBI that led to this first Smith Act prosecution seemed worth it. The Minneapolis defendants paid the price that year, but the cost, in terms of free speech and the expansion of the nation's domestic security state, was something that many more Americans would bear in the postwar years.

The central issue of how Americans have tolerated (or suppressed) dissent during moments of national crisis not only is important to our understanding of the period around World War II but also remains a pressing concern in the post-9/11 world. Americans were willing in the past to place limits on First Amendment rights in the context of perceived grave and imminent threats to the nation's security, and they have been willing to do so again now with the PATRIOT Act as the country finds itself in a state of perpetual war on terror. This study traces some of the implications of this compromise between rights and security that was made in the middle to late twentieth century, offering historical context for some of the consequences of such bargains struck today.

1

Militancy and Fear

May 1934–June 1940

The first Smith Act trial originated, in part, in the personal histories of the defendants. The ties between certain members of Teamsters Local 544 and the Socialist Workers Party shaped their union militancy and made them targets of government concern as early as the mid-1930s. The political history of the Smith Act's passage also informed the background to the case. As World War II spread throughout Europe and Asia, anxieties deepened in America over the fate of its own security in a dangerous world. In 1940, the fear of subversion at home fueled an antiradical mood that supported the passage of the Smith Act, the most restrictive peacetime sedition measure in more than 140 years. Many Americans argued that to preserve democracy, the civil liberties of those deemed a threat to national security had to be suspended. In 1941, such thinking made possible the arrest and trial of twenty-nine Trotskyists, eighteen of whom were convicted for conspiring to advocate the violent overthrow of the government.

Past as Prologue: Trotskyist Militancy in Minneapolis during the 1930s

Max Geldman, one of the twenty-nine, reflected later in life on something James Cannon, a fellow defendant and leader of the SWP, once told him: that ardent revolutionaries were able "to live with the music of one's youth."[1] They remained committed to beliefs forged early in life, even during trying times. That, to Geldman, was the mark of a true member of the movement—in his case, the Socialist Workers Party. The description could be applied to most of Geldman's fellow defendants in the 1941 case. Each came to the SWP, and for some also to Local 544, from different backgrounds, but each came to share a commitment to Trotskyist politics and militant union organizing during the depths of the Great Depression. Most carried those commitments with them for the rest of their lives. Before being challenged during the 1941 trial, those beliefs sustained these revolutionaries through the turbulent events of the 1930s in Minneapolis: the 1934 Teamsters strikes; the 1939 Federal Workers

Section strike; and their Union Defense Guard's confrontation with fascist Silver Shirts in 1938.

Vincent Raymond Dunne, one of the leading defendants in the 1941 trial, certainly remained true to the music of his youth during his long life. Born in Kansas City, Kansas, in 1889, he moved to Minnesota to live on his grandfather's farm after his father was seriously injured on the job in a streetcar accident. One of nine children, Vincent learned the hard lessons of survival in America's expanding industrial economy not only from the trauma that his father's workplace injuries caused his family, but also from his having to work to support that family when he turned fourteen. Dunne, once described as resembling Humphrey Bogart with his "cool blue eyes" and long, dark face,[2] labored as a lumberjack in Minnesota and Montana and as a grain harvester in North Dakota, where he first heard of the Industrial Workers of the World (IWW). After being laid off the job in Montana, he hoboed his way to Seattle, where he was drawn further into the Wobbly orbit and was arrested six times for speaking publicly about industrial unionism. While he was working in Montana, he had briefly become a member of the Western Federation of Miners (WFM), but it was through the IWW that Dunne first became a self-identified socialist. Although he respected the sincerity of the Debsian socialists in the Wobbly movement, he preferred the more syndicalist approach of the WFM branch.[3] Dunne's commitment to militant union organizing as the core of workers' self-liberation remained at the heart of his radical politics for the rest of his life.

Returning to Minneapolis after his years tramping around the Northwest, Dunne "got a job teaming" and soon "worked himself into the class of express drivers." Over coffee at the lunch counter of the Union Depot he met a young Swedish waitress named Jennie Holm. They married in 1914 and had two children, but that did not slow down Dunne's political activism or union organizing.[4] He became a delegate and the financial secretary of the city's Central Labor Union in the early 1920s. And he soon found an ally and mentor when he became a weigh master in the coal yards.[5] Carl Skoglund, who would become known as a "grand old working-class leader," immigrated to Minneapolis from Sweden in 1911 and, after surviving a near-debilitating accident while working for a cement contractor, tried his hand at a variety of jobs until becoming a coal yard truck driver in 1928.[6] There he became an organizer for the Teamsters Local 574 and forged a close friendship with the militant Dunne, becoming his "first real teacher . . . as a revolutionary socialist."[7] The two men held true to their shared sense of militancy and drew on their friendship for support as they organized workers in the coal yards in the mid-1930s and, later, when they faced the Smith Act prosecution in 1941.

Both Dunne and Skoglund not only believed in industrial unionism but also were drawn into the ranks of the nascent Workers (Communist) Party during the early 1920s. In this political commitment they were joined by several others who would share their fate as defendants in the first Smith Act trial. James Cannon, like Dunne, was born in Kansas, experienced the difficulties of life as an industrial worker firsthand in the meatpacking, railroad, and printing industries, and first became drawn into the revolutionary wing of the Socialist Party and the IWW. After 1918, Cannon became a leader of the new Workers (Communist) Party in America. He was instrumental in the party's shift from its underground and divided posture (between the foreign language sections and the native-born American labor-based wing) into a united entity by 1922. In these early years, Cannon was supported in his work by Vincent Dunne's brother William.[8] But it was not just personal ties that drew workers like Vincent Dunne and Skoglund into the early manifestation of the Communist Party. It was the revolutionary nature of the new party that attracted them and several others in the city's coal yards, like Harry DeBoer and Farrell Dobbs. Born in 1907 in Crookston, Minnesota, DeBoer had to leave school after the eighth grade to earn a living. He worked as a truck driver "his entire adult life" and served as an organizer for his Teamsters local from 1934 to 1941. Dobbs, who was born in Queen City, Missouri, in 1907, graduated from high school and was employed "as a wire man for Western Electric" until the Depression hit, when he lost his job and took up work in the coal yards. There he was drawn into the growing community of Trotskyist labor organizers, joining their ranks in March 1934.[9] Each of these militant workers and political radicals remained true to the music of his youth and paid the price when later targeted by the Justice Department for advocating those beliefs.

Cannon, Dunne, and Skoglund believed they first paid a price for remaining true to their beliefs in 1928. That September the Sixth World Congress of the Communist International met in Moscow and laid bare the divisions that had been forming within the movement during the previous few years. It quickly became apparent that dissent from Stalin's rule would not be tolerated and any interpretations of the party's agenda, other than his focus on building "socialism in one country" (the prioritizing of the Soviet state), would be definitively rejected. Leon Trotsky, who criticized Stalin's position, had been banished from the movement. Those who agreed with Trotsky were likewise expelled. James Cannon and William Dunne found themselves on opposite sides of this fight, with Cannon in the ousted Trotskyist camp. Along with him went other future Smith Act defendants in Minneapolis, including Vincent Dunne, Carl Skoglund, and Oscar Coover.[10] Coover, a "quiet-spoken, warm-hearted and friendly" electrician, had belonged to the International Brotherhood of Electrical Workers since 1906 and by the late 1920s had come to support the Trotskyists in Minneapolis.[11] To these exiles their expulsion signaled that their work had just begun: they would (re)build what they believed to be a true Marxist party, a Left Opposition, which advocated world proletarian revolution. As Dunne saw it, that commitment to global socialist revolution was the real manifestation of Marxism. In his mind, he and his fellow Trotskyists did not leave the Communist Party so much as it had left them.[12]

By the early 1930s, the Trotskyists had created their own organization, officially called the Communist League of America, Left Opposition of the Communist Party, and issued their own newspaper, the *Militant*. Headquartered in New York, centered on a group of leftist intellectuals, it had a committed branch in the Minneapolis contingent that was connected to that city's labor movement via the small Teamsters Local 574.[13] The Trotskyists in Minneapolis were devoted to using their Left Opposition (what would become the SWP) as a vanguard party to "unite the working class in struggle."[14] They also believed that democratic, industrial unions were central to this revolutionary commitment as vehicles through which workers could "resist oppression" and as forums in which to educate workers in the ideas of the party.[15] Their approach thus essentially married the lessons that Dunne, Skoglund, Cannon, and others had learned in their younger years struggling though hardscrabble lives in America's expanding industrial heartland with the radical Marxist politics they accessed first via the IWW and later the Communist Party, now having taken a unique Trotskyist turn. In Minneapolis the body that they would focus on transforming into the democratic, industrial union for this revolutionary cause was Teamsters Local 574.

A fledgling craft union with about 200 members by 1933, Local 574 was at that time a "small, cautious and conservative" union. Its leaders, facing the hostility of Minneapolis employers and the city's reactionary Citizens Alliance, were wary of launching bold organizing drives for fear of losing what little ground they had gained. The infamous alliance deployed labor spies, kept files on activists, and cooperated with the FBI in order to maintain an open-shop town.[16] Confronting such opposition, the leaders of 574 instead remained committed to defending workers they had organized and supported the craft unionism generally advanced by their parent bodies, the International Brotherhood of Teamsters (IBT) and American Federation of Labor (AFL).[17]

As radical socialists and labor militants, Dunne and Skoglund supported the industrial union approach and dismissed the fears of their more wary

Teamster brothers. In order for them to lead a successful organizing drive among all coal yard workers, they would have to overcome both the hesitancy within Local 574 and the hostility of the city's employers. The first step Dunne and Skoglund took was to organize all the coal yard truck drivers into 574, including independent owner-operators as well as men who drove trucks owned by the coal companies; in 1933 the local represented workers in only nine of the city's sixty-two yards. Although 574's council did not initially support this effort, the two men moved ahead with their plan anyway, building on the trust the men had in them as fellow workers and on the support of 574's president, William Brown, who shared their industrial union vision. Personal connections aided these alliances. Dunne's brother Miles, a "dashing young bachelor" who was fond of "prize fights, football, hunting and fishing," was a "bosom drinking companion" of Brown's. Vincent Dunne, as a weigh master, knew almost all the men who came through the yards. And Skoglund, the "old Swede," became a father figure to many of the younger men, including DeBoer, who were drawn to his call for solidarity in the fight for better wages, shorter hours, and safer working conditions. Over the years, Dunne and Skoglund built up the ranks, more than doubling the size of the local. By November 1933, they felt it was time to demand that all the city's coal yard employers recognize these workers within Local 574.[18]

Not surprisingly, given Minneapolis's history as an open-shop town, the employers refused. But Dunne and Skoglund did not give up. Sustained by the backing of the men and aided by the organizing skills of Miles Dunne, they took advantage of a sudden cold spell and the increased demand for home heating coal in early February to call a strike. Seven hundred men walked off the job on February 7, bolstered in their commitment to the cause by the tactics that their Trotskyist leaders had the foresight to implement, including nightly meetings to boost morale and the use of "flying squadrons" (groups of three or four strikers who patrolled the yards) to intercept trucks driven by "scabbing drivers."[19] By February 10, the men returned to work, confident in their ability to gain union recognition. On February 14 and 15, elections were held across the city in the yards, with Local 574 winning support from approximately 77 percent of the voting men.[20]

But the elections were not a total victory. Under pressure from the Regional Labor Board, the coal yard employers recognized the existence of Local 574, but they did not promise to recognize it for exclusive collective bargaining. Its struggle for the closed shop became one of the driving forces behind Local 574's next round of confrontations with Minneapolis employers. By the spring of 1934, the Dunnes and Skoglund were focused on utilizing the momentum they had built in the coal yard organizing drive. That effort had rapidly expanded the ranks of the union to almost 3,000 workers by the end of April.[21] Cognizant of the vital role trucking played in Minneapolis's economy, being the main form of transportation for goods into and throughout the city, and eager to secure the bread-and-butter demands that were of concern to the workers, they decided to take action.

With the support of President William Brown and Vice President George Frosig, Local 574 issued its demands on April 30 for "'the closed shop, shorter hours, an average wage of $27.50 a week, and extra pay for overtime.'" Immediately it was confronted with the concerted opposition of the 11 major trucking firms to which it presented these demands, and soon thereafter, of the more than 150 other companies in the city. Continued employer resistance led the union to vote for a strike, which began on May 16.[22]

Of the many major strikes that took place around the United States during 1934, the Teamsters strikes in Minneapolis were among the bloodier. Girding themselves for the struggle, members of the union's strike committee set up special headquarters with a field hospital and a commissary staffed by a women's auxiliary. Almost as soon as the workers took to the streets, their pickets were met with fierce resistance. Striking truck drivers clashed with police in the city's market district on May 19 and May 21, resulting in the injury of thirty-seven people. On May 22, strikers and their sympathizers— some 20,000 to 30,000 strong, including workers from the city's building trades who had declared a sympathy strike with the Teamsters—faced the police and close to 2,000 special deputies. With the numerical tables turned against them, and facing the fury of the Minneapolis working class, two of those special deputies were killed. With Governor Floyd Olson's intervention a truce was called and an agreement finally reached on May 31 that guaranteed members' representation by the union. But it remained unclear if the so-called inside workers in warehouses and loading bays were included in this guarantee.[23] The agreement left room for employers to deny certain of their employees the right to be represented by the union.

As a result, Local 574 voted to strike again at midnight on July 16. During this walkout the Trotskyist leaders built on tactics that had proved successful during the May strike, including the flying squadrons and nightly meetings. They now also organized a special rally to reinforce the drivers' alliance with the local unemployed that drew 12,000 participants and circulated the *Organizer* to 10,000 readers in an effort to combat employers' propaganda.[24] By halting all trucking into and out of the city, the striking Teamsters effectively closed it down. In their attempt to reopen the streets, the police responded with a heavy hand: on "Bloody Friday," July 20, they shot at the pickets, wounding 67 workers and killing 2. More than 40,000 workers turned out to

Figure 1.1 Vincent R. Dunne, strike committee member, was arrested and held at the provost guard stockade at the Minnesota State Fairgrounds in St. Paul, on August 1, 1934, reinforcing his reputation early in his career as a militant and radical organizer. Photo HG3.18T p79, negative number 7632, Minnesota Historical Society. Courtesy Minnesota Historical Society.

mourn Henry Ness, one of the victims, in a demonstration of solidarity with the strikers. Governor Olson, fearful that popular anger over police brutality might fuel more violence, and eager to end the strike, declared martial law on July 26.[25]

After several rounds of failed arbitration, employers and the union finally agreed to a settlement on August 21. It included major concessions for the union, namely, recognition of the Teamsters and a minimum wage. Local 574 ended up representing 724 workers (53 percent of those voting) across seventy-seven firms.[26] Though organized by just a handful of Trotskyists at the start, the 1934 strikes developed into a popular uprising of tens of thousands of supporters, in which the mighty Citizens Alliance was defeated and union recognition secured. For many observers, the 1934 Minneapolis strikes became a harbinger of what militant class struggle could achieve: the breaking of an open-shop city in a process that inspired some (like United Mine Workers president John L. Lewis) and troubled others (like IBT president Daniel Tobin).[27]

The militant guidance of the Trotskyists was vindicated with the strikes' gains and rewarded in the next union elections. Local 574's new executive board reflected what Farrell Dobbs would later describe as "a synthesis of Trotskyist militants who had won authority in the battle and incumbent officials who had conducted themselves well." Brown and Frosig were reelected as president and vice president. Grant Dunne, who had been instrumental on the strike committee with his brothers Vincent and Miles, was elected recording secretary. Dobbs was elected secretary-treasurer, and Vincent Dunne and Harry DeBoer were voted trustees.[28] Emil Hansen, known as "the big Dane" because of his large frame, was a longtime supporter of the Dunnes. He brought the cab drivers into solidarity with the 1934 strike and became one of 574's trusted organizers.[29]

The Trotskyists on the new executive board moved Local 574 into a more aggressive organizing posture after the 1934 strike, building up the membership in the General Drivers Union and providing support to workers in other unions too. These included not only others in the "driving trades" (like the ice drivers, the milk wagon drivers, and the sanitation drivers) but also workers in trades with weak or nonexistent unions (like the city's garment workers and dry cleaners). Local 574, with its mission of organizing the unorganized, became influential in supporting unionization throughout the city, providing pickets to striking candy workers and carpenters in 1935, for example, and helping to bring some 17,000 members into the Teamsters Joint Council by the end of 1937.[30] The new board also created an auxiliary, the Federal Workers Section, for the city's unemployed and those receiving relief under the Works Progress Administration and sent delegates to additional cities to share their organizing skills with other Teamsters.[31]

For the time being, the rank-and-file Teamsters in Minneapolis seemed to accept their leadership's Trotskyism, especially since it did not directly interfere with the workings of the union. Some of this tolerance came from the city's unique political culture that drew both from native-born "itinerant farmworkers, lumberjacks, miners, and railroad workers" who formed the old IWW presence in the city, and from immigrants consisting of "large numbers of Norwegians, Swedes, Finns, Danes, and Germans who brought collectivist principles with them from Europe."[32] As Grace Carlson, an SWP member and defendant in the 1941 Smith Act case, later noted, most of the rank and file "didn't really have a truly basic interest in Marxism; their interest was what the Marxists could do for them in the trade union movement."[33] So while the Minneapolis drivers were not all Trotskyists, most of them tolerated their leaders' political commitments, especially when they helped to secure union recognition and better wages. And this they did: by October 1934, Local

574 "had under contract ninety-one percent of Minneapolis transfer firms, ninety-five percent of market houses and ninety-eight percent of the coal companies." By 1940, the union secured an increase in the average driver's wage from nineteen dollars per week to more than thirty. Most of the rank and file were satisfied with this delivery of the goods.[34]

That was not the case when it came to the Teamsters' international leadership, which was concerned with the militant tactics of 574 and its Trotskyist leaders. Local 574 weathered a major challenge in 1935 when the IBT executive board stripped it of its charter and backed a new, nonradical rival, Local 500. The international justified the revocation on technical grounds (nonpayment of the per capita tax), but its actions were also tied to Tobin's contempt for the local leadership's socialist politics, its support for industrial unionism, and its coordinating the 1934 strikes without explicit IBT authorization.[35] The Irish-born, Catholic Tobin, who began his career driving a delivery wagon in 1900, rose through the ranks of the IBT to become its president in 1908, a position he held for forty-five years. His socially conservative background cultivated his deep distrust of socialists and communists, and his experience in the cut-throat teaming industry contributed to his defense of craft-based union organizing.[36] But in confronting the situation in Minneapolis in 1935, he faced continued defiance from the leadership of Local 574, which maintained its rank-and-file support. Tobin and the IBT executive board backed down from their challenge and restored the charter to what became known as General Drivers Union Local 544-IBT in 1936.[37] But the relationship between Tobin and the Minneapolis Teamsters remained an uneasy one.

The executive board of the new Local 544 consisted of leaders from both the dissolved Locals 574 and 500.[38] The presence of Trotskyists in the local's leadership contributed to its militant industrial posture during the late 1930s. Dobbs became secretary-treasurer, and Skoglund a trustee. Vincent, Miles, and Grant Dunne, Harry DeBoer, Carl Skoglund, and other veterans of the 1934 strikes remained active members and would be elected as officers in the coming years.[39]

These workers remained committed to building a democratic, militant industrial union in Local 544 as a foundation for the workers' revolution that their Trotskyist politics demanded. For them, organizing the working class into strong unions that won concessions from employers was important. So too was organizing the unskilled, most notably the over-the-road drivers, whom Farrell Dobbs guided into the North Central District Drivers Council in 1937. Through that organization he helped secure contracts covering thousands of men over eleven states by 1939.[40] But these Trotskyists also believed that bringing workers into self-governing organizations was the first step in what would be the worldwide proletarian revolution. To realize that, potential workers needed guidance from a revolutionary party: the SWP. In this sense, Dunne, Skoglund, Dobbs, and the other Trotskyists recognized a deeper calling in their union work: growing the party through the union, and thereby advancing the revolution.[41]

To recruit members into the party, Trotskyist laborers sought leadership positions within the Teamsters' locals and the joint councils. While the grassroots concerns of the workers drove much of what these militant trade unionists did, so too did the advice of the national SWP leadership. The ties among Vincent Dunne (a 544 organizer), Farrell Dobbs (who in early 1940 left the Teamsters to work full-time as SWP labor secretary), and James P. Cannon (the party's national leader) were close and intense; these men had gone through the fires of Communist Party factional fights together and had forged trusted bonds in their work as strategists during the 1934 strikes.[42] They consulted each other regularly in correspondence, discussing topics ranging from the latest organizational gains in the local to the party's maneuverings with respect to advancing its favored candidates in union elections.[43]

These men stood firmly not only with each other but also with their Trotskyist political movement as it underwent several changes in affiliation between 1933 and 1938, from the short-lived Workers Party (WP) of the United States in 1934–1935, to the ill-fated "entry" into the Socialist Party in 1936, to the creation of the independent Trotskyist Socialist Workers Party in 1938.[44] The SWP was officially founded at a convention in Chicago held from December 31, 1937, to January 1, 1938. At this gathering, delegates denounced the popular front, having attempted, unsuccessfully, to form alliances with others on the left one too many times. And they pledged loyalty to their new party, which firmly embraced Trotskyist principles: the doctrine of permanent revolution; the law of combined or uneven development; the recognition of the need to "bore from within" in trade union work; the rejection of pacifism and the acceptance of violence to achieve ends, if necessary; and the acknowledgment that the Soviet Union "needed a restoration of revolutionary purity."[45]

The proletarian wing of the party remained quite strong, with Cannon as its national advocate. The Local 544 activists in Minneapolis formed the solid core of this wing. But there were others in the city who were drawn into the SWP orbit who did not initially have direct union ties. Grace Carlson was born in 1906 in St. Paul to an Irish and German Catholic working-class family. Her Irish father's participation in the 1922 shopmen's strike was Carlson's first introduction to union militancy, but she later claimed that she also "picked up [her early] pro-union and pro-radical ideas" from her German uncle who read the *Daily Worker* and the nuns at her Catholic school who, as Irish nationalists, "tended to be kind of anti-government."[46] Carlson earned her PhD in psychology in 1933 from the University of Minnesota and was working for the Minnesota Department of Education when she first encountered the Trotskyists in the Twin Cities. Her sister and brother-in-law, Dorothy and Henry Schultz, had ties to the local Teamsters union and the Workers Party. Dorothy, who earned a master's degree in political science from the University of Minnesota, was introduced to the local Trotskyist community by her professors and by her future husband, Henry, who was an organizer for Local 574. Carlson began attending the WP's political meetings with Dorothy and Henry in 1934.

Carlson was impressed with the group's political program and its leaders, finding them "much stronger political characters" than those in the Farmer-Labor Party (FLP).[47] She was not alone in this estimation of the FLP; while the Trotskyist leaders of 544 affiliated the union with the county Farmer-Labor Association in 1936, their proposal for the unemployed to take over and operate idle factories was deemed too radical by the more moderate reformers in that movement and their Communist Party–influenced union backers who, at that time, were supporting the New Deal as part of the popular front. Indeed, by 1937, the Trotskyist leaders of 544 and other anti-Stalinists left the Farmer-Labor Association altogether, deeming it an inexpedient vehicle for change. They would pursue their political agenda via the Socialist Party (SP) and, after its creation, the SWP.[48] Carlson joined the Trotskyist movement when it was a part of the SP in 1936 and was present in Chicago in 1938 when it reconstituted itself into the SWP.[49]

Carlson became one of the "most prominent women in the SWP," largely bucking the trend in union and party circles that placed women in subordinate positions. Prior to 1941, "no woman sat on either the large, elected national committee or the smaller, appointed political committee" of the SWP.[50] In the Minneapolis labor movement, while women's activism ranged from militant manning of pickets to essential staffing of strike kitchens, makeshift hospitals, and fund-raising centers, their participation was also "basically seen as supportive"; women were "excluded from participation in decision making."[51] The Teamsters union, as a male-only preserve, left no room for women in its inner circle. Local 544 could not provide Carlson with the chance to become a "'militant trade unionist.'" As a state employee, however, she honed her organizing skills by becoming a charter member and serving on the executive board of the American Federation of State, County and Municipal Employees (AFSCME) Local 10. And Carlson asserted herself within the SWP by becoming a state organizer and running for Senate in

1940, making a "coast-to-coast speaking tour" for the party in 1941 and 1945, and, later, twice standing as its vice presidential nominee. Respected by her male Trotskyist colleagues for her hard work and intelligence, Carlson carved out a uniquely influential career for herself in the party. Unlike most of her female counterparts who contributed behind the scenes, Carlson never had any children, and so was freed from the binding ties of the familial household to pursue her devotion to the party more publicly.[52] She, along with her sister Dorothy and friend Rose Seiler (a social worker and business agent for the Stenographers, Bookkeepers and Tax Accountants Local 17611),[53] joined the ranks of the twenty-nine Smith Act defendants in 1941. All three women had become active supporters of the SWP, but Carlson had the most prominent public and national profile.

Other defendants included two more SWP activists with ties to Local 544: Max Geldman and Edward Palmquist.[54] Geldman, who was born in a Warsaw ghetto in 1905, came to America as a child with his parents and grew up in Brooklyn. He attended City College and "tried his hand at selling and teaching" in New York before moving to Minneapolis, where he became "a fighting leader of the unemployed." Palmquist, the son of a carpenter, was born in Minneapolis and graduated from Hopkins High School before working "as a machinist in a steel plant until the depression years, when he became unemployed." He then "plunged into the unemployed struggle."[55] Geldman and Palmquist became leading organizers in Local 544's union's auxiliary, the Federal Workers Section, which had been created in 1934 to organize the city's unemployed and those receiving relief benefits. The effort was motivated both by the practical logic of undermining employers' use of the unemployed as scabs and by the Marxist ideal of uniting all workers—including those without jobs—in a common front.[56] After a six-week struggle in April 1937, the FWS succeeded in convincing the Board of Public Welfare to make permanent the supplemental aid that had been granted "as a temporary concession during the winter months."[57] But its most notable work in Minneapolis took place in 1939, when the FWS supported a massive strike of relief workers employed by the WPA. Those workers were protesting the cuts in hourly wages and the increase in monthly hours announced in July in the Emergency Appropriation Act (Woodrum Relief Act). These and other cuts to New Deal programs were introduced because of the improvement in the economy measurable by early 1937, but the spending reductions were met with both widespread protests, including the WPA strikes, and the "Roosevelt Recession" of 1938–1939.[58]

The WPA strikes began as spontaneous walkouts upon workers' hearing the news of the cuts on July 5. Strikes took place around the country, with

32,000 people walking off their jobs in New York and 18,000 in Minnesota. In Minneapolis and St. Paul, 10,000 people went on strike. Building trades' projects were affected, as were the predominantly female sewing projects. By the sixth day of the strike, white-collar workers began to join the ranks of the protesters so that there were an estimated 125,000 WPA workers on strike around the nation.

In Minneapolis, the FWS of Local 544, along with the Communist-dominated Workers Alliance, gave its support to the walkout.[59] The city became the location of one of the most pointed confrontations between government representatives and protesting workers. The state WPA administrator, Linus Glotzbach, announced on July 6 that workers who did not return to their jobs by July 10 would be fired and replaced; the local police chief promised protection for those replacements. Such threats did not dissuade the strikers, who remained on the picket lines. But the tensions between protesters and police mounted in the coming days when a series of confrontations ended with the death of one police officer, the shooting of one relief officer, injuries to seventeen other persons, and the stabbing of a striker. Although in each case the violence perpetrated was not instigated by the strikers, the press quickly blamed the bloodshed on the protesters.[60]

Pressure mounted for a resolution to the crisis, especially after Glotzbach shut down all relief projects in response to the violent encounters. Finally, on July 21, an agreement was reached between the strike committee and the WPA administrator, mediated by Governor Harold Stassen. It allowed for the return to relief work of those who had gone out on strike, as long as they signed an affidavit stating "that they had not engaged in illegal activities in violation of the federal relief law." But the wages and conditions of the new act remained.[61] And more disturbing, for the protesters and for the Trotskyist organizers in the FWS who supported the strikers, was the federal investigation of supposed violations of the Woodrum law that followed. That law made it a felony for anyone to deprive "any person of any of the benefits to which he may be entitled under any such appropriations, or attempts to do so, or assists in so doing." The Justice Department authorized a grand jury investigation. Max Geldman and Edward Palmquist of the FWS were among those targeted. U.S. Attorney Victor Anderson (who would later prosecute the 1941 Smith Act trial) convened the grand jury hearings in St. Paul on July 24.[62]

The hearings lasted several weeks, during which Anderson called to the stand close to 200 witnesses, including policemen, FBI agents who had worked undercover as strikers, WPA officials, and laborers who had "scabbed" during the walkout. On August 18, the grand jury handed down 103 indictments and, in the coming days, 63 more after hearing from subpoenaed witnesses.

Anderson authorized nighttime raids of private homes for most of the arrests. And at the bail hearings in federal court, "monstrously high bond was then set—a total of more than a quarter of a million dollars."[63] The demonstration of federal authority in the response to the WPA strikes was under way.

Because Anderson and other Justice Department officials interpreted the WPA strikes as constituting an upheaval against the government, they decided to prosecute a mass of alleged perpetrators in federal court on conspiracy charges, rather than put the few who were directly involved in the episodes of violence on trial in police court.[64] The Woodrum law provided the shield for this legal attack on what was deemed a nefarious plot to challenge an individual's right to work, the federal relief project, and ultimately, the authority of the federal government.

Minneapolis's disgruntled workers did not see their strike in the same way that the Justice Department did. While Trotskyists like Geldman and Palmquist viewed the upheaval as a political protest,[65] most workers were probably just angry at the relief cuts and believed they had a right to express that frustration by withholding their labor. Local labor organizations, including the Central Labor Union, the Building Trades Council, the Teamsters Joint Council, and the FWS, supported the defendants by quickly mobilizing a defense movement, successfully petitioning for a reduction in their bail, and raising funds to pay their bond.[66] The defendants, who were arraigned en masse before a federal judge, pleaded not guilty.

Yet several of them were soon convicted in court before federal Judge Matthew M. Joyce. Joyce, who earned his law degree at the University of Michigan in 1900, had been the general solicitor and then general counsel for the Minneapolis and St. Louis Railroad from 1917 until 1932, when he was appointed to the U.S. District Court by then president Herbert Hoover.[67] Like Anderson, he would play an important role in the 1941 Smith Act trial, presiding over that case as well. He too was eager to demonstrate the authority of the federal government against perceived subversive threats. Joyce was on the bench for the first WPA trial, which began on October 2, 1939, and which ended with five FWS members being convicted of interference with WPA workers. Four of those five FWS members were also convicted of the more serious charge of conspiracy in violation of the Woodrum law. The three other defendants in this first trial were acquitted. In the second trial, also presided over by Joyce, three of the four defendants (all FWS members) were convicted of conspiracy and of committing overt acts of violence in preventing workers from engaging in WPA projects.

In the third trial, begun on October 31, twenty-five defendants faced Judge Joyce and a jury that—as had been the case in the first two trials—did not

contain a single union member. Geldman, Palmquist, and several other leading activists in the FWS were among those tried in this third group. During
the testimony of several witnesses, the extent of FBI involvement in the case
became clear. For example, when asked by the defense about his testimony,
police sergeant John Finn admitted that he had "merely rehearsed" it with
Agent Roy Noonan. Other witnesses, who were seen chatting with agents
outside the courtroom, provided stories that sounded coached in their "pat"
manner.[68] The bureau's involvement in the WPA trials was a further sign that
the Justice Department considered the 1939 events harbingers of something
much more serious than just a run-of-the-mill walkout. Anderson in particular seemed fixated on the role of the FWS, seeing behind what was a spontaneous protest of spending cuts a radical communist conspiracy to destroy the
city. In his closing statement the U.S. attorney thundered, "Minneapolis, so
long as I am here, is not going to become the Moscow of America!"[69] With the
aid of both the FBI and the Woodrum Relief Act, he planned to crush what he
believed was a foreign-inspired proletarian uprising.

The jury found all twenty-five defendants in this third trial guilty of conspiracy to violate the Woodrum law. Geldman and Palmquist, described as
the "'very fountainhead of the Minneapolis WPA strike conspiracy,'" were
sentenced to a year and a day in prison. As cochairs of the FWS, the two
men had been very active in the strike. They served their time in the federal
penitentiary at Sandstone, Minnesota, where they would be imprisoned again
after their convictions in the 1941 trial. Geldman later recalled how the experience "wasn't good." When he and Palmquist first arrived at Sandstone, the
warden threatened them, saying, "We know your reputation and we know
you consider yourself [sic] tough guys . . . but we'll be watching you and the
first misstep you'll see that we can maintain control."[70] The other convicted
WPA defendants faced prison terms of as long as seven months and as short
as thirty days, with a few granted suspended sentences and probation.[71]

With those the federal government deemed the main conspirators now
tried and convicted, and in the face of increasing criticism of the mass trials
from labor and liberal corners, the Justice Department decided to bring the
confrontation with the accused to an end. By the end of the year, Assistant
U.S. Attorney General O. John Rogge moved to dismiss 120 of the 125 remaining cases. The last five defendants—all FWS members—pleaded nolo
contendere (no defense) to the conspiracy charges. The 1939 prosecutions
finally came to a close.[72]

But the effects of the prosecutions were felt well beyond 1939 and had significant ramifications for the Trotskyists and their militant industrial organizing. First, two members of the party, Geldman and Palmquist, were now

convicted felons. And they had been convicted of conspiracy in a trial that essentially equated criticism of government policy—the protests of relief cuts—with subversion. Furthermore, Anderson and Joyce had sustained this equation and had advanced the notion that union militancy could be integral to such subversive plots. While Joyce was careful to assert that workers had the right to strike, the 1939 action supported the notion that political radicals (in this case Trotskyists in the FWS) could manipulate such legitimate worker activism for illegal ends.[73] Similar arguments, made by the same men, would come back to haunt Local 544 and the SWP in 1941.

So too would the Trotskyists' commitment to self-defense. Even before some of them became involved in the 1939 WPA strikes, others found themselves active in the creation of the Union Defense Guard (UDG). Formed in 1938, the UDG was intended to protect union members and Local 544's property from the Silver Shirts, a fascist organization founded by William Dudley Pelley in 1933. Pelley founded the Silver Legion as "an organization dedicated to bringing fascism to the United States" and made up of the nation's "'cream'" of white, Protestant men. The Silver Shirts—who wore a uniform of dark slacks with a silver shirt and dark tie—were intended to be Pelley's "version of Hitler's SS." In the depths of the Great Depression, his message of anti-Semitic hatred and anticommunist hysteria found some resonance among those who looked for easy targets to blame for the nation's economic woes. According to Geoffrey Stone, "By 1934, there were 15,000 Silver Shirts and [Pelley's weekly newsletter] *Liberation* had attained a circulation of 50,000."[74] In 1938, Pelley sent Roy Zachary to Minneapolis to establish a branch of the organization. Local 544 members quickly became aware of the rumors that they were prime targets for the Silver Shirts' rhetorical and physical violence.[75]

Soon after arriving in Minneapolis, Zachary held two rallies "in quick succession on July 29 and August 2." Although the rallies were by "invitation only," Farrell Dobbs later claimed that Local 544 sent someone undercover to discover what took place there. It became clear that Pelley's newly formed contingent had forged links with the head of the city's Associated Industries (AI) (the same employers' group that had been known as the Minneapolis Citizens Alliance before it changed its name in 1936).[76] To Dobbs and the Trotskyists in Local 544, this development proved to be a "dire threat against the Teamsters." In order to meet that threat, they encouraged Local 544 to organize the Union Defense Guard in August 1938.[77]

Just as the creation of the FWS reflected the Trotskyists' belief in the need to bring all workers into the industrial union orbit through militant organizing, so too did the UDG reflect a Trotskyist tenet: the priority of workers' self-defense when faced with antilabor and fascist threats. The *Northwest Or-*

ganizer, Local 544's newspaper, prominently announced the creation of the UDG as a body formed for the "'defense of the union's picket lines, headquarters and members against anti-labor violence.'"[78] The guard's ranks were filled by union members, many of whom either were military veterans or had experience in previous strikes. Growing to a total of almost 600 men, the UDG was organized into squads of five, each with its own captain. As Dobbs recounted, "Members of the guard were issued small lapel emblems bearing the legend '544 UDG,' which they were encouraged to wear at all times. When on duty they used large armbands prominently marked '544 Union Defense Guard' to identify themselves."[79] Like the bold announcement in the union's newspaper about the creation of the UDG, the regalia were intended to publicize the presence of the organization so as to intimidate the Silver Shirts. The UDG also purchased "two .22 caliber target pistols and two .22 caliber rifles to give guard members a way to improve their ability to shoot straight." It hosted target practice drills for its members, many of whom already owned hunting guns, in displays also intended to deter the Silver Shirts.[80]

While the idea of the UDG originated among Trotskyists in Local 544, non-party-affiliated members gave their support to the guard because they too felt that their union was under siege and that they could not rely on the police for the protection they needed. Vern Bennyhoff, for example, would later testify to the FBI about his participation in the guard, noting that, even though he was not a member of the Trotskyist group, he believed the UDG was a legitimate response to threats from the Silver Shirts.[81] And Ray Rainbolt, who had left the party in January 1938, was elected commander of the guard and played a major role in the UDG's activities.[82]

Whether the UDG had any effect on deterring the Silver Shirts, or whether the fascist group fizzled out of its own accord, is debatable. Dobbs certainly gives credit to the guard for having stymied at least one Silver Shirt gathering in Minneapolis by its mere intimidating presence outside the fascists' meeting hall.[83] But beyond that, the guard did not seem to be much of a threat to anyone; indeed, by late 1939, it had essentially devolved into a social group that provided ushers for local union gatherings, including the annual children's Christmas party.[84] Perhaps one of the more remarkable things about the guard was Rainbolt's leadership and what it said about his fellow Minneapolis teamsters. As Jack Barnes later noted, "For workers in the mid-1930s to choose a Sioux Indian to lead them in combat—to issue them orders, to discipline them if necessary—was far, far from an everyday occurrence in this country, especially in the Upper Midwest or Western United States."[85] The men's respect for Rainbolt as a union brother trumped any racially based hostility that may have existed; it also represented the strength of progressive attitudes among some on the Minneapolis labor scene, especially the men in Local 544 associated with the SWP.[86]

At no time, however, did the guard pose a real a danger to the public. But that did not prevent local and federal government officials from perceiving Local 544's UDG as a threat precisely because it was a workers' militia organized by Trotskyists.[87] Armed workers were nothing new in American history; both unionized and unorganized workers used guns to defend themselves during the Great Railroad Strike in 1877, at Homestead in 1892, and at Blair Mountain in 1921. More organized proletarian militias or armed union branches existed in cities during the 1870s and 1880s, including the German and Bohemian Lehr und Wehr Verein in Chicago. But in response to those efforts in the past, the government essentially disarmed workers by rewriting state militia laws or confronted them with federal troops,[88] whereas in the context of the "little red scare" of the late 1930s and early 1940s, it pursued a slightly more nuanced counterattack through the legal prosecution of insurrection.

During the 1941 Smith Act trial, the existence of the UDG, and especially a public mobilization that it had coordinated in the fall of 1938, became a focal point for the prosecution as it tried to make the case for the Trotskyists' attempt to overthrow the government by force.[89] On September 29, 1938, the UDG had published a notice in the *Northwest Organizer* calling on all captains and members to be ready for a full-scale mobilization at a moment's notice, an announcement that was intended to intimidate the Silver Shirts into leaving Minneapolis. One month later, when it was clear that the fascist group was not backing down, the UDG launched its emergency mobilization. Using a phone tree, the guard successfully gathered 300 men in one hour in an open lot near the center of the city. Once they made this public display of strength, the men disbanded and headed to the Gayety, a downtown burlesque theater, revealing the particular masculine, working-class subculture that pervaded Local 544 and of which the UDG was also a part. That subculture included the hunting and fishing excursions that men like Miles Dunne enjoyed as often as they could, as well as the hard drinking sessions they engaged in at local bars where they built and sustained their camaraderie in the union and SWP.[90] Dobbs later described the 1938 mobilization as a serious showing of UDG solidarity that contributed to the fading out of the Silver Shirts in Minneapolis. That may be true, but it seems a far cry from this local display of bravado to the first step in the mobilization of a proletarian army intent on overthrowing the U.S. government. Indeed, when assistant to the U.S. attorney general, Henry Schweinhaut, advanced the latter theory, I. F. Stone quipped in the *Nation*, "I have heard of the Gunpowder Plot. Maybe this will go down in history as the G-string Conspiracy."[91]

The Justice Department did not find the event as amusing as Stone did. Like the 1934 and 1939 strikes, the existence of the UDG and its October 1938 mobilization would come back to haunt the Trotskyists in Local 544. By being true to the music of their youth, those Trotskyists unwittingly drew the attention of the FBI to their activities and engaged in behavior that would be used to justify their criminal prosecution in 1941.

Loading the Revolver: Roosevelt, the FBI, and Congress during the "Little Red Scare"

That prosecution was based on the alleged violation of two laws: a Civil War era statute that criminalized overt acts of rebellion, which the activities of the UDG were alleged to be in count one of the 1941 indictment; and the 1940 Smith Act, which prohibited the advocacy of the overthrow of the government by force or violence and which constituted count two. How this more restrictive sedition bill became law forms another important part of the background to the 1941 case. The emergency wartime context of the late 1930s and early 1940s nurtured latent fears that political radicals and disloyal immigrant aliens could carry out acts of internal subversion.[92] This potent mix of national security concerns and revived nativism in the context of a world war enabled those who favored more restrictive immigration and sedition statutes to trump those who supported the preservation of civil liberties.

Though defenders of civil liberties emerged from the First Red Scare insisting on the expansion of free speech as the antidote to the abuses of that period, by the late 1930s, as events around the globe undermined freedom and as episodes at home seemed to imperil national security, many argued for federal regulation of speech in order to protect democracy. They trusted that the Justice Department and the FBI, as centralized, professional bodies, would administer such regulations wisely. It was hoped that they would avoid the kind of "popular intolerance" and local vigilantism that marked the First Red Scare. Many Americans, especially leaders in Washington, came to believe that the threats to democracy posed by fascism and communism were great enough to warrant this arrangement.[93] The Smith Act was a product of this bargain.

Peacetime sedition bills similar to the Smith Act had been introduced in Congress well before 1940. During the First Red Scare, seventy such bills were introduced and enjoyed the backing of then attorney general A. Mitchell Palmer. But the press, the AFL, and civil liberties proponents, like Harvard professor Zechariah Chafee, strongly opposed these measures. As the heat of the scare cooled by 1921, such proposed laws lost momentum.[94] It would not be until the 1930s, with the outbreak of the Great Depression and the growth of the Communist Party in the United States, that support for antiradical and antisubversive legislation revived. The creation of the Fish Committee in the House in 1930 by Congressman Hamilton Fish was one manifestation of this revival. Its recommendations included the outlawing of the Communist Party and the banning of its written materials from the mails.[95] The McCormack-Dickstein Committee, established in 1934 by Congressmen John McCormack and Samuel Dickstein, was created to "investigate 'un-American' activities" on both the communist left and the fascist right. It called for the restriction of seditious speech, specifically the advocacy of political change that "might incite violent overthrow of government authority."[96] And it wanted to criminalize speech that influenced members of the armed forces to reject military regulations. Although the army, navy, American Legion, Veterans of Foreign Wars, and Reserve Officers Training Corps (ROTC) got squarely behind such proposals, there was considerable opposition from the American Civil Liberties Union (ACLU) and other civil rights advocates. Like the Fish Committee's recommendations, the McCormack-Dickstein proposals represented the stirring of antiradical and antisubversive sentiment in early-1930s America, but one that was not strong enough to prevail against the liberal political tide that had swept FDR into office and that was then sustaining New Deal legislation. Neither committee's recommendations became law at this point.[97]

Behind closed doors at the White House, however, President Roosevelt became increasingly concerned about the threats that fascist elements in America posed to the nation's safety. Pelley's Silver Shirts were just one manifestation of these kinds of pro-fascist groups. There were several others, including the Friends of Nazi Germany, the German American Bund, and the Black Legion.[98] Wanting to know how strong were the ties (if any) to Germany and how much of a threat these organizations posed to the country, Roosevelt met with Attorney General Homer Cummings, Secretary of Labor Frances Perkins, and FBI chief J. Edgar Hoover in May 1934. In that meeting, Roosevelt "ordered the FBI to monitor American Nazis and their sympathizers and to determine the extent to which Germany had influenced domestic groups." The FBI readily accepted the assignment.[99]

Two years later, Roosevelt remained concerned about the activities of fascist groups, but now, with the political ferment being expressed on the left over the Spanish Civil War, he was also increasingly worried about communist organizations. The president expressed his apprehension to Hoover in a private meeting held at the White House in August 1936. He asked the bureau chief to investigate how the activities of both right-wing and left-wing organizations in America might "'affect the economic and political life of the coun-

Figure 1.2 J. Edgar Hoover, head of the Federal
Bureau of Investigation, leaving the White House.
Hoover met often with FDR, who increased the
power of the FBI during his presidency. LC-
USCZ62-123127, New York World-Telegram and the
Sun Newspaper Photograph Collection, Prints and
Photographs Division, Library of Congress.

try as a whole.'"[100] Hoover took full advantage of this confidential and verbal
order, launching investigations around the country and dispatching reports
to the White House.[101] This new approach constituted a reversal of former
attorney general Harlan Fiske Stone's 1924 prohibition of purely political (and
noncriminal) investigations. In his interpretation of the 1936 order, Hoover
also looked beyond "foreign-directed activities against the national interest,"
as was the purview of the appropriation's authorization, to include any groups

perceived to be engaged in subversive activities.[102] By late 1939, both Teamsters Local 544 in Minneapolis and the Socialist Workers Party headquartered in New York became targets of the bureau's investigations.

The American public came to share Roosevelt's and Hoover's concerns about internal subversives in early 1938, after the FBI revealed the presence of a German spy ring centered in New York led by a Nazi agent named Guenther Gustav Rumrich. The ring had plotted to acquire naval blueprints for two aircraft carriers and the army's mobilization plans for the East Coast. Even though the ring was "for all intents and purposes, rather inept," its presence, and the press coverage of its discovery by the FBI, fueled the public's fear of infiltrators.[103] As Francis MacDonnell has argued, the Rumrich spy case "was key to the emergence of a Fifth Column scare," as the "elaborate web of intrigue which the government unmasked in 1938 seemed to prove Hitler's commitment to offensive action against the United States." The exposure of such intrigue revived old fears of German subversion that were rooted in acts of sabotage during World War I, the most infamous of which was the July 1916 explosion that resulted in $20 million in damages on Black Tom Island, the "enormous powder and munitions depot" in New York Harbor from which shipments were made to the Allies. The mass media's "saturation coverage" of the 1938 case kept the popular anxiety over such infiltration alive through the end of the year, when the trial and sentencing of the spies took place.[104]

As a result, support grew in Congress for another committee to investigate subversion, specifically un-American propaganda and more broadly all so-called un-American activities. For Democratic congressman Martin Dies of Texas, who introduced the resolution in the House to establish such a committee, the motivation stemmed more from his desire to "dig into Communist infiltration of the CIO and the New Deal programs he hated" than it did from any fear of Nazi fifth columnists. But he took advantage of the political atmosphere created by the Rumrich case to steer his motion to approval in May 1938, creating the special House Committee Investigating Un-American Activities. Dies investigated more than 600 organizations, 400 newspapers, and 200 labor unions with alleged communist ties. Swept up by the fifth column fear, the House approved the committee's extension into 1939; 79 percent of the public expressed support for Dies's work.[105]

It was in this heightened antiradical, antisubversive atmosphere that antiimmigrant sentiment in the United States dovetailed with the growing fear of the fifth column to sustain the Smith Act of 1940. The association many nativists made between foreigners and subversives was not new to 1939. The vigilante violence aimed at immigrant radicals during the First Red Scare and the prejudice surrounding the Sacco and Vanzetti case were notorious fruits of that connection.[106] But it returned with a vengeance in America on the eve of the outbreak of the war in Europe. The bill, H.R. 5138, introduced by Democratic representative Howard Smith of Virginia in April 1939, reflected this reprise, incorporating both immigrant registration requirements and the peacetime criminalization of sedition in its five titles.[107]

In Title I, the bill outlawed the advocacy of the overthrow of the government by force or violence, banned the issuing and circulation of printed matter that encouraged the overthrow of the government by force or violence, and criminalized membership in any association that advanced such an agenda. Reflecting concerns over fascist and left-wing paramilitary organizations, Title II outlawed membership in any "civilian military organization" unless that organization had a permit from the secretary of war. Title III, which addressed the fear of immigrant subversives, banned the naturalization of anyone who advocated (or was a member of an organization that advocated) the overthrow of the U.S. government, and it amended existing grounds for deportation to include those offenses. Title III also called for aliens eighteen years or older to register every six months (with a federal court official) and for every alien to be registered and fingerprinted upon entry to the United States. In addition, this title stipulated that if an immigrant did not become a citizen within five years of the bill's passage or five years of his or her entry, he or she may be "taken into custody and deported."[108]

Title IV made it illegal to "attempt to commit or to conspire to commit any of the acts prohibited by any of the provisions of this Act" and established fines (of not more than $10,000), prison terms (of not more than ten years), and deportation (for aliens) for violating those provisions. Furthermore, Title IV stipulated that if any country refused to take back an alien deported under this law, that country's immigration quota would be "suspended and revoked." Finally, Title V dealt with the sticky issue of what to do with aliens who were to be deported but whose home countries would not or could not take them back because of the wartime crisis. Those individuals were to be taken "to such a place of detention as may be designated by the Secretary of Labor" and held there until the home country agreed to take them, or the secretary of labor agreed to release them. This last draconian provision essentially called for the creation of concentration camps in America.[109]

On April 12, 1939, the House opened hearings on H.R. 5138 before a subcommittee of the judiciary committee. Eighteen people testified during the two days of hearings, twelve of whom were in favor of the bill. Those who supported it included a number of representatives from the military, certain congressmen, and leaders of self-described patriotic organizations. Among the military personnel who urged passage of the bill was Lieutenant

Ira Nunn of the navy's Judge Advocate General's Office. Speaking specifically with reference to Title II, he reminded the committee that the navy had supported such sedition provisions for some time, but that now, with the increased presence of subversives at home (like the Rumrich ring), "affairs had grown to the acute stage where it was . . . almost essential, that the Navy Department make, as part of its legislative program, a measure which would give us . . . the legal machinery for preventing the circulation of certain subversive . . . material to our armed forces."[110] While he acknowledged that the Espionage Act of 1917 stipulated penalties for interference with the armed forces, Nunn reminded the committee that it only applied when the nation was at war. H.R. 5138, as a peacetime sedition law, would plug that hole.[111] The other military commanders who testified agreed.[112] As far as they were concerned, Title II was something that had become necessary to the security of the armed forces by 1939.

Leaders of a handful of self-described patriotic organizations also spoke in support of H.R. 5138, but they engaged with the bill more comprehensively than the military's limited focus on Title II. During the first day of the hearings, John Thomas Taylor, director of the American Legion's National Legislative Committee, argued that H.R. 5138 in all of its five titles was "a long step in the right direction" dealing with both native insurgents and troublesome aliens.[113] James H. Patten, a representative from the General Sons of America, likewise spoke of his organization's agreement with the bill's provisions. Rejecting the ACLU's argument made in testimony earlier that day that aliens should have the rights of citizens, Patten sniped, "Aliens are merely guests and should act as guests, and be shown the door if they abuse our hospitality, or have the impudence and impertinence to try to tell us what kind of house we shall live in or the kind of government we shall have."[114] Patten also dismissed the concerns voiced by some opponents of the bill that the fingerprinting and registration of aliens would be a violation of their liberties by claiming that "no alien that has not something to conceal ought to object to it."[115] He saw nothing un-American about immigrants having to show their papers.

John B. Trevor, president of the American Coalition, which "represents delegates from 115 of the leading patriotic societies of the country," also spoke in support of H.R. 5138 but emphasized the national security justifications for the bill. Speaking before the committee on April 13, Trevor echoed Nunn, arguing that the Espionage Act was insufficient to deal with the subversive threats America faced in peacetime. Instead, the bill before the committee was "eminently desirable" because it was much more akin to New York State's criminal anarchy act, which had been upheld by the Supreme Court in the 1925 *Gitlow* decision.[116] Because of this, Trevor insisted that any concerns over the constitutionality of the bill should be put aside. Because of the "subversive moment" in which America found itself, he argued, H.R. 5138 was necessary for the nation's safety.[117]

But what price should be paid for that safety? Opponents of the bill, who conceded that the nation faced real subversive dangers, posed this question in their testimony before the committee on April 12. Osmund Fraenkel of the ACLU spearheaded the attack by first targeting Title I, the sedition provision, as an unjustified violation of First Amendment rights. He argued to the committee that "if you enact legislation of this kind, you encourage informers, you encourage persecution, you encourage hysteria; and above all things, now is the time for us to keep our heads clear and cool."[118] In such precarious times, Fraenkel argued, draconian legislation would only make things worse by inciting panic. The violation of First Amendment rights that Title II represented to Fraenkel was, to him, unwarranted and dangerous.

Fraenkel also expressed the ACLU's concern over Titles III, IV, and V as potentially undermining immigrants' rights to free speech and freedom of movement. Title III, for example, which prevented the naturalization of any alien who *advocated* change in the government, was worded so broadly that he feared it would intimidate immigrants from engaging in any kind of political discussion. And Title V's proposed detention camps were particularly problematic. "The fact that [the detention] is not to be at hard labor is a mitigating circumstance, which I suppose is some benefit," Fraenkel argued, "but freedom is the essential thing, the freedom to work and live and love, and a person who has served his time, should not be perpetually kept in jail because he is an alien, and only because he is an alien."[119] He deemed such indefinite detention of anyone for any reason unconstitutional and inhumane.

Read Lewis of the Foreign Language Information Service joined Fraenkel in opposing H.R. 5138. Lewis did not speak to the sedition measures in Titles I and II ("since they are not within the direct field of work of our organization"), but he did echo the ACLU's concerns about the rescinding of immigration quotas as punishment for nations that refused to accept deportees (Title IV) and the creation of the holding camps (Title V). Identifying the anti-Semitic implications of the bill in the context of European events in 1940, Lewis argued that "it would work a great injustice, if we closed our doors, say, in the case of Germany, at the present time, to all the refugees and others seeking admission under our quota." And he denounced the "concentration camps for aliens" that the bill proposed to establish.[120] Ralph Emerson of the Maritime Unions, CIO, also spoke out quite forcefully against the camps, observing that "we would hate to see this country adopt a law that would in any way follow the example of Nazi Germany."[121] Paul Scharrenberg, legislative representative of the AFL, agreed.[122] As the communication sent to Congress by the American Committee for the Protection of the Foreign Born insisted, the bill "attack[s] the very foundation of our American institutions and directly threatens the welfare and well-being—the democratic rights—of the American people."[123]

For the defenders of H.R. 5138, however, it was the American people and their democratic form of government that the bill was intended to protect. Representative Howard Smith insisted that "the country is demanding" this kind of legislation to stop subversives and to "provide for the deportation of aliens who are here wrongfully, and will restrict those who are coming unlawfully." He appealed to his fellow lawmakers to "listen to the voice of those who believe that such legislation has really become a matter not only of desirability but of necessity."[124] Named "Man of the Hour" by the *Nation* that summer for best embodying the "frightened atmosphere in Washington," Smith refused to back down from doing what he argued was what the American people wanted.[125] Although he was willing to tweak the bill in response to some points raised in the committee, Smith refused to adjust the compulsory naturalization or sedition provisions. He argued that Americans and their Congress "do not desire to put up with any such doctrines that aliens may come here and advocate openly revolution and bloodshed in this country without any restraining force at all."[126] Smith took advantage of the fifth column scare in America to argue that it was high time for the United States to protect itself from subversion.

Smith's argument persuaded his colleagues in the House. After the Judiciary Committee reported the bill to the full chamber on June 27, it passed the measure 272 to 40 and sent it to the Senate on June 29. Aside from a strong denunciation published in the *Daily Worker,* there was limited coverage of these events in the press.[127] The White House did not voice opposition either, perhaps because it had already begun to increase its control over subversives within the United States.

Three days before the House sent H.R. 5138, now known as the Alien Registration Bill, to the Senate, President Roosevelt issued a secret order "placing all domestic investigations [of espionage, counterespionage, and sabotage] under the FBI, Military Intelligence Division, and Office of Naval Intelligence," with the FBI as the central coordinating agency. Roosevelt was influenced by Hoover's argument that such centralization would prevent the kind of abuses that had taken place at the local level during and immediately after World War I.[128] While this argument was commonly made within civil libertarian circles by the summer of 1939,[129] Hoover's use of it was self-serving. As Douglas Charles has noted, the FBI director "now had almost exclusive control over domestic surveillance, and his power and influence would increase

Figure 1.3 Representative Howard Smith, author of the 1940 Alien Registration (Smith) Act, which took his name. LC-H22-D-8531, Harris and Ewing Collection, Prints and Photographs Division, Library of Congress.

as the Second World War developed."[130] There would be no objection from Hoover or Roosevelt to the alien registration and sedition measures making their way through Congress that summer.

By late summer 1939 the sense of danger the nation faced from fascist and communist threats—and corresponding support for the Alien Registration Bill—increased with the shocking news of the Nazi-Soviet Pact. Signed on August 23, 1939, between Germany and the Soviet Union, this nonaggression pact not only ruptured the political left in America, creating even deeper divisions between Old Guard socialists and Communists, but also reinforced the perceptions of those on the right that there was essentially no difference between fascism and communism. The pact signaled the Soviets' about-face, as they appeased fascists, whom they had for so long declared their enemy.[131] The agreement also further inflamed anticommunist sentiment in America, which contributed to the "little red scare" and increased congressional backing for the Alien Registration Bill.

The revelations of Soviet spy defector Walter Krivitsky during the spring and summer of 1939 and the outbreak of the war in Europe in September 1939 added to the sense of crisis and, correspondingly, to support for the bill. Krivitsky's "sensational series of articles for the *Saturday Evening Post*" had "exposed Soviet intrigue in Europe and America," confirming many Americans' worst fears of a communist fifth column.[132] The German invasion of Poland in the fall led them to worry even more than before about Nazi aggression and perfidy.

In response to the eruption of war abroad, J. Edgar Hoover quickly established a secret Custodial Detention list that kept track of those with "strong communist [or Nazi] tendencies" and categorized them according to their level of dangerousness; those deemed the most threatening were identified as eligible for detention if America entered the war.[133] The bureau's power was expanded, and its mandate to investigate subversives made public, when on September 6, 1939, Roosevelt issued a press release calling on all local law enforcement officials to share with the FBI any information they had on subversive activities. It would continue to take the lead in such investigations as it had been doing secretly since June. The president also issued an executive order increasing the bureau's manpower so that it could better respond to the national emergency.[134]

Using the Custodial Detention program and stepped-up investigations of subversives, Hoover made the most of the antiradical, antisubversive sentiment that was deepening across the nation, especially in Washington. As someone who had always shared the conviction that enemy aliens and political radicals of all stripes were a threat to America's security, Hoover had the additional motive of a partly nativist belief that such draconian measures were necessary for the nation's well-being, not just for the FBI's. His perception was rooted in his past experiences as a member of the Alien Enemy Bureau in the Department of Justice during World War I and as head of the Radical Division of the Bureau of Investigation from 1919 to 1924, during which he helped coordinate with Palmer the federal raids, arrests, and deportations of the First Red Scare. Hoover thus had been eager for some time to see a restrictive peacetime sedition act that applied to both aliens and citizens.[135] By the summer of 1940, as head of the FBI, his convictions remained the same; the difference was that now more Americans, especially leaders in Washington, were coming to share his views.

Conservative senators who, like Hoover, had long been anxious to see the passage of tougher alien registration and sedition provisions, decided to take action. As the "phony war" of late 1939 turned into the blitzkrieg of April and May 1940, the wartime crisis provided them with even greater political justification for the passage of what was now being referred to as the Smith bill. H.R. 5138 was brought before a subcommittee of the Senate's Judiciary Committee on May 17, 1940.

The bill, which had been redrafted by the House before its final vote in 1939, still contained five titles, but the content of each title was amended to reflect feedback from the House hearings. Title I criminalized the advocacy of disloyalty in the armed forces (through the spoken word or written text), including the attempt or conspiracy to carry out such advocacy, establishing a penalty of not more than ten years in prison, a $10,000 fine, or both. Title II encompassed the more general sedition law, making it unlawful to "knowingly or willfully advocate, abet, advise, or teach the duty, necessity, desirability, or propriety of overthrowing or destroying" the government by force or violence. It also criminalized the acts of printing, publishing, or distributing any materials advocating such sedition and made it illegal to organize or belong to any association that did the same.[136] Titles III, IV, and V dealt with the deportation of immigrants, the banning of immigration, and the fingerprinting of aliens. Title III tightened the original bill's language to stipulate that aliens must be "convicted" of espionage or sabotage before they could be deported, whereas Title IV expanded the law's reach to include for deportation those anarchists who held radical views "no matter how short the duration or how far in the past." Title V pulled back from the first draft of the bill, requiring fingerprinting only for recent immigrants, not longtime residents, and making no provision for detention camps.[137] Some of the strongest concerns voiced against provisions in the original bill had registered with lawmakers. Even though in the same month that the Senate took up the legislation such camps were being created in Britain that would house 27,000 German, Austrian, and Italian nationals by the summer of 1941, American legislators turned away from doing the same, for the time being.[138]

Howard Smith spoke forcefully for the amended bill before the Senate committee, using the spreading war in Europe to bolster his case. He argued that, given "recent developments . . . , it is most desirable and necessary now that we look to the stranger within our gates."[139] For Smith, Title I of the bill provided warranted protection for the military from saboteurs, while Title II guarded the federal and state governments from subversives. He believed so strongly in the need for the sedition statutes laid out in the bill that when asked by Senator John Danaher of Connecticut if he saw any violation of the First Amendment in its broad restrictions, Smith boldly answered, "I do not think so. If it does, I think we ought to change the Constitution."[140]

Smith's brazen reply captured one of the fundamental questions about the bill. The sparring in the Senate hearings between opponents and supporters of the bill heated up over whether the sedition titles (I and II) violated the Constitution's free speech protections. Representative of these verbal clashes was that which took place between Mary Bodkin, secretary of the national legislative committee of the Descendants of the American Revolution, and Democratic senator Tom Connally of Texas. Bodkin's organization had recently been created by liberals in Boston as a progressive alternative to both the Daughters of the American Revolution and the Sons of the American Revolution; in particular, the newer organization welcomed African American members and criticized the discriminatory practices of its rival organizations.[141] Bodkin opposed Title II's "federal criminal syndicalism clause" that attached criminality to *advocacy* because she, like others, saw it as a clear violation of First Amendment rights. But when she tried to explain why, Connally all but accused her wanting to overthrow the government by daring to question the bill before them.[142]

Although she quickly became aware that she and the senator were speaking at cross-purposes, Bodkin pressed her position, arguing that the bill as now written infringed on "absolute freedom of expression, assembly, and the press," and that as such it "might serve as an entering wedge to infringe upon those basic rights." Her point, one built on the logic of contemporary free speech scholars, made a distinction between expression and provocation: "It is the difference between treason, a crime already punishable by statute, and mere expression of opinion." And, Bodkin continued, "Unless the advocacy of the overthrow of the Government by force and violence constitutes a 'clear and present danger' . . . it is not treasonable," and therefore "past affiliations would be of no significance, and present ones would be of significance only insofar as they constituted this 'clear and present' danger."[143] Thus, she insisted, Title II's provisions (and the deportation provision in Title IV for past allegiances) were unnecessary and constitutionally questionable.[144] As a civil libertarian who wanted to secure greater protections for speech from government prosecution, she invoked the clear and present danger test established by Oliver Wendell Holmes in the Supreme Court's 1919 *Schenck* decision, even though it had not yet been used by a court majority to strike down a federal law. But Bodkin and those like her disturbed by the bill looked to Holmes's test, as applied in his *Abrams* dissent as speech protective, as a vital safeguard against government attacks on First Amendment rights.[145]

Connally's response to Bodkin's argument was to red-bait her. He grilled her about the nature of her organization, how it was funded, what programs it sponsored, and so forth.[146] During his testimony in the House the previous year, Fraenkel had faced similar accusations from Representative John J. Dempsey about the ACLU. Now Bodkin and others who came before the Senate found their patriotism questioned and themselves all but accused outright of being communists for challenging the Smith Act. For the civil libertarians, the bill's hearings seemed to portend the very dangerous implications they feared from such a "gag" act. Although the nation faced subversive threats by the summer of 1940, risking its cherished democratic freedoms for security through the implementation of such questionable provisions—in terms of both their legal legitimacy and their practical effectiveness—was of concern to these opponents of the bill.

Despite the very real dangers the nation faced, these free speech advocates were right to be wary of the bill and the political trend of which it was a part. The Smith bill gained support as a result of the fifth column fear and "little red scare" that had gripped the nation since 1938 and 1939, respectively. But it also resulted from the backing of conservative southern Democrats and Republicans, who had begun to form an alliance on various issues—the alien registration and sedition measures of this bill being just two. That alliance was part of a broader political backlash against the social democratic elements of the New Deal. Men like Smith and Connally, with their powerful positions of seniority in the House and Senate, worked with Republicans to create a bulwark against any significant economic or racial reordering of society in either the creation or the implementation of programs like Social Security and the Works Progress Administration. And they struck directly at labor too, cosponsoring the War Labor Disputes Act (Smith-Connally Act) in 1943 that placed limitations on strikes and authorized the president to "seize and operate struck plants."[147] The 1940 Smith Act was a part of this reactionary legislative initiative.

But as Bodkin, Fraenkel, and others demonstrated during the hearings, not everyone embraced this agenda. Speaking out most boldly against the Smith Act in the Senate hearing was Stanley Nowak, a state senator from Michigan who was also a United Auto Workers organizer and representative of the Civil Rights Federation of Detroit. Nowak argued that in dangerous times Congress had the duty to protect the nation, but he insisted it also had a duty to safeguard civil liberties that were "greatly endangered" because of the "stress" of the times. "When everyone is anxious to protect the country there is a tendency to stretch that fear and to suppress people unjustly, deny them their rights unjustly," he explained, "and I am of the opinion that that bill expresses that fear; in fact, I see that it is to be stretched too far; that it may deny rights that are very honorable to us, and rights that we all cherish."[148] Nowak was not willing to trade the freedoms guaranteed in the Constitution for the sake of national security.

Despite Nowak's impassioned plea, the bill made its way out of the subcommittee to the full Judiciary Committee at the end of May and was reported to the Senate on June 15. The "little red scare" and the fifth column fears that persisted as the war expanded in Europe altered the atmosphere on

Capitol Hill so as to deafen legislators to the cries of the nation's civil libertarians. In the Senate, Connally was able to persuade his colleagues of the need for the bill and secured a voice vote on June 15 for its passage. After a conference committee met to reconcile the House and Senate versions of the bill, it was brought back to the House floor on June 22 for a final vote.[149]

Before that vote, a few technical alterations made by the joint committee were announced, and one last discussion of the bill ensued among the representatives. Sam Hobbs, C. E. Hancock, and Howard Smith defended the bill by emphasizing what they believed was a clear and present danger facing the country at that time: subversion by either a Nazi or a communist fifth column. Referencing the popular (if incorrect) view that the Nazis' ability to move so quickly through the Low Countries and France was due to internal subversives, Hancock noted how "a year ago this provision [for fingerprinting and registering of immigrants] . . . might have been rejected, but we now know that the modern technique of war involves 'fifth columns.'" He and the other supporters of the bill therefore regarded alien registration "as a measure of self-defense."[150] Smith insisted that the government needed to know who any "alien within our gates" was and "something about" him lest he be beholden to a foreign enemy.[151]

Not everyone agreed with Hancock and Smith, but these dissenters were in a decided minority, and only one was bold enough to speak out passionately against the bill on the House floor. Vito Marcantonio, American Labor Party congressman from New York, argued against the spirit and letter of the proposed law. Recognizing the dangerous world America found itself in by the summer of 1940, Marcantonio insisted, "It seems to me that in a period as trying as is this period the test of a democracy lies in the ability of that democracy to maintain its liberties, to preserve those liberties, and to have more freedom rather than less freedom during the period of crisis." If it did not, he argued, America risked destroying the very liberty it wanted to preserve. Acknowledging that "spies and saboteurs and anybody who engages in any illegal activity should be immediately apprehended and severely punished," Marcantonio insisted that this bill did "not accomplish that end." Spies would never register, and instead, innocent immigrants would be compelled to sign their names to a watch list. The proposed law was to him both ineffective and dangerous. "What I am fearful of is that under the guise of supporting and maintaining our American way of life, by this type of legislation," he argued, "we are taking steps with seven-league boots toward establishing in America, in free America, the slavelike institutions of Nazi Germany."[152]

In this dissent, Marcantonio was a "lone voice in the wilderness" of Congress. He would later argue that the act had been "'blitzkrieged' through

Congress as part of the so-called national defense program," which "was another legitimate offspring of the present-day war hysteria."[153] Only one other representative—Emanuel Celler of New York—voiced concerns over the bill, but they were mostly technical. He ended up supporting the bill as a "bitter pill to swallow" but the "best [bill] to be had under the circumstances."[154] When the final vote was called, there were only four nays; Celler voted yea along with 381 of his colleagues.[155]

The Alien Registration Act, which quickly became known as the Smith Act after its chief sponsor, was passed the same day that France fell to the Nazis. Although the ACLU and the Communist Party deluged the White House with communications urging President Roosevelt not to sign the bill, the support expressed by the Justice Department and the military—and recent events in Europe—reinforced FDR's conviction to support it.[156] Roosevelt's signing statement of June 29 laid out his official position and expressed his concern that the registration of loyal aliens be conducted without stigma and as "smoothly, quickly and in a friendly manner" as possible. Yet it also communicated Roosevelt's resolve for dealing with the disloyal and with "those who are bent on harm to this country" when he insisted that the government, "through its law enforcement agencies, can and will deal vigorously" with them.[157] Hoping to strike a balance between a benevolent implementation of the registration provisions and a firm enforcement of the sedition statutes, Roosevelt trusted that the Smith Act would give his administration the authority it needed to protect the innocent and prosecute the guilty. His experience as Woodrow Wilson's assistant secretary of the navy during World War I allowed him to "see the extent of German intrigue in America and made him aware of the nation's vulnerability to foreign penetration." But it also led him to want to avoid the "hysteria that had transpired between 1917 and 1918." As a result, when the German menace seemed to emerge once again by the late 1930s, FDR hoped to safeguard the nation from internal subversion, but to do it in a way that prevented the abuses perpetrated during and after the Great War. Establishing tight federal control over domestic security threats was seen as the way to achieve both these ends.[158]

Because of the secret reports of domestic subversives that his White House had been receiving from the FBI since 1936, Roosevelt believed the time had come for such statutory authority.[159] How the Smith Act would be used would depend greatly on the hands into which it was entrusted. Much of this hinged on the attorney general and the temper of the Justice Department. In this respect, as Richard Steele has noted, Zechariah Chafee described the Smith Act as a "loaded revolver": "If it was handed over to the U.S. attorneys, 'some of them may start sniping at soapbox orators by the front gate,' but if the attorney general kept it in his desk lest a 'burglar ever shows up,' it was unlikely to be misused."[160]

When it came to the registration of aliens, Attorney General Robert Jackson, who delegated the oversight of the process to his solicitor general, Francis Biddle, held that revolver carefully by his side. Under the new law almost 5 million aliens were registered. After the attack on Pearl Harbor, that registration information was used to categorize the 900,000 Italian, German, and Japanese nationals as enemy aliens eligible (under the 1798 Alien Enemies Act) for detention and deportation.[161] Biddle, who had replaced Jackson as attorney general at this point, used the information gathered from the registration process in as targeted a fashion as possible and insisted on hearings for those taken into custody before they could be detained or deported. When it came to Japanese nationals and American citizens of Japanese descent, however, Biddle met his match in California's governor, Culbert Olson; the state's attorney general, Earl Warren; and the West Coast army commander, General John DeWitt, who convinced President Roosevelt of the need for exclusion. Neither Biddle nor Hoover agreed, each arguing that the existing process of targeted arrests—a process made possible by the FBI's secret Custodial Detention program and by the registration information gathered under the Smith Act—had already dealt with true threats to the nation. Their protest that Roosevelt's Executive Order 9066, which allowed for the exclusion from the West Coast of 120,000 Japanese Americans, was unnecessary and unwise was dismissed in the deafening silence of the angry American public.[162]

When it came to targeted sedition prosecutions, however, Hoover was much more enthusiastic and Biddle more compliant. What Chafee perhaps did not count on in his assessment of the danger posed by the Smith Act was the pressure that the FBI would apply to the attorney general for investigations and prosecutions of sedition under this new law. The bureau not only had the bureaucratic charge to conduct such investigations (from the 1936 and 1939 presidential orders) but now also had the statutory authority of the Smith Act. It would make use of this power in its investigations around the country, including that of the SWP headquarters in New York and the Teamsters Local 544 in Minneapolis.

2

Dissent Becomes a Federal Case

September 1940–June 1941

The FBI's investigation of the Trotskyists in Local 544 was aided by a rank-and-file workers' movement that coalesced in the months after the Smith Act's passage. James Bartlett and Tommy Williams, leaders of this group, accused the Dunne brothers, Harry DeBoer, Emil Hansen, and other SWP-affiliated union leaders of sacrificing the local's interests to those of the party. The accused union leaders disagreed, arguing that Bartlett and Williams's opposition was based not on a concern for democracy but on a naked desire to seize control of the local.[1] Such internal union squabbling is not uncommon; this one became the nucleus of a federal case because of the existence of the Smith Act, the FBI's interest in the Minneapolis situation, and the opposition's willingness to partner with the government in its crusade against the Trotskyists. Hoover and his agents welcomed testimony from Bartlett and the others and compiled it in reports for the attorney general.[2] Those reports contributed to Biddle's decision to indict the Trotskyists under the Smith Act; in June 1941, he metaphorically removed Chafee's revolver from his desk drawer and fired it for the first time at the SWP.

Rank-and-File Fear and Anger: The Committee of 100

By 1941 the association between the SWP and Local 544 was well known throughout Minneapolis. Since the 1934 strikes, the Dunne brothers, Carl Skoglund, Farrell Dobbs, Emil Hansen, and others had secured significant gains for the local, while hiding neither their political affiliation nor their vision for a socialist future. These men included Kelly Postal, who became secretary-treasurer of Local 544 after Dobbs.[3] While some workers embraced the SWP's ties to the union, and many others passively accepted them, there were some who came to oppose the connection vehemently. This opposition intensified as the Trotskyists in Local 544 dominated the elected offices after William Brown's death in 1937[4] and stepped up their party work within the union during the summer of 1940. By selling party literature at union headquarters and asking their Teamster brothers for regular donations to the SWP,

Vincent Dunne, DeBoer, Hansen, Postal, and others made it harder for many rank-and-file members to tolerate their radical politics.[5] James Bartlett and Tommy Williams spearheaded the opposition movement to protest what they believed was the Trotskyists' misuse of Local 544's leadership positions and headquarters. Along with this concern for the integrity of the union, personal animosity and professional jealousy contributed to Bartlett's and Williams's criticism of the Trotskyists.

Bartlett's history suggests such mixed motives. Born in Connecticut, Bartlett moved between New York and Minneapolis as a teen before settling in Minnesota in 1930. As the Depression deepened, he found himself on relief hanging around Bridge Square with other down-and-out workers, joining the local Unemployed Council and the Communist Party in 1932. He switched political allegiance in 1936 to the Left Opposition, claiming that he made the shift with the help of Vincent Dunne in exchange for the Trotskyists' aid in organizing Minneapolis's warehouse workers.[6] Bartlett then became business manager for Teamsters Local 359. When he ran for union president in January 1941, however, he faced opposition from an SWP-backed candidate.[7] By late December 1940, it had become clear to Dunne and Dobbs that Bartlett was not really "a party man" anymore but someone who had been following "an opportunistic deviation" in his joining the progressive, but not revolutionary, Farmer-Labor Club, running for alderman in Ward 10, and purchasing a bowling alley. To the Trotskyists, Bartlett had lapsed as a committed party member and had neglected his union organizing duties in favor of personal and professional aggrandizement, and so they opposed him in the coming elections.[8] Bartlett did not see things this way. While he would later admit that he was certainly "no longer sympathetic" to the party by early 1940, he cited a political "change of heart" based on his disagreement with the party's "revolutionary cause" as the reason.[9]

Like many of the rank and file who had been recruited into the SWP after the 1934 strikes, Bartlett seems to have been less concerned with the finer points of Marxism than with what the party could do for him and his union. Bartlett later explained that when he was a member, he only attended party meetings "on and off." And even though he visited Trotsky while on vacation in Mexico in February 1940 at Dunne's request, Bartlett began to have reservations as he became fully aware of the party's revolutionary agenda.[10] At that point, those goals became disagreeable to Bartlett either because he truly felt they posed a threat to the integrity of the union (as he claimed to the FBI and during the trial), or because he saw their usefulness as a tool to criticize his opponents in the upcoming union elections (as Dobbs claimed). Once his attack on the Trotskyists was fully under way, he seemed eager to expand his power in the Teamsters at their expense.[11]

Tommy Williams, the leader of the movement against the Trotskyists in Local 544, also came to believe that the SWP was a threat to the union. Williams, like Bartlett, had once been party member. A cab driver, he became an organizer for Local 544 in 1937 and joined the Trotskyists that same year, later claiming he did so only to secure a job as a union organizer.[12] Williams, if he had ever been faithful to the cause, did not remain so for long: he stopped paying his dues and attended his last meeting sometime in the spring of 1939. He later claimed that after sixteen months in the party he "began to smell a rat," believing that the Trotskyists were using the union to expand the size and coffers of the SWP rather than prioritizing the interests of union members.[13] His outright rejection of the radical leadership of Local 544 began in late 1940—around the time when the Trotskyists became more aggressive in conducting party activities within the union. In those same months, Williams started hosting meetings in his home for those who shared his criticism of the Trotskyists.[14]

This internal union opposition did not seem to center on social differences given the relatively homogeneous nature of Minneapolis's population.[15] While there were Catholic anticommunists among the rank-and-file opposition forming around Williams, they would have contributed to a broader antiradical coalition. When it came to union organizing tactics, there also does not seem to have been as big a divide between the local opposition movement and 544's leaders as there was between 544's leaders and the executive board of the IBT. Militant industrial unionism was something Bartlett supported; he had organized the unskilled warehouse workers into Local 359 with the aid of the Trotskyists. The opposition was thus fueled mainly by ideological and personal disputes.[16]

Ideological opposition was tied to practical concerns. Dissidents who came together in late 1940 feared that 544's executive board had turned the union into a tool of the SWP by requesting that officers contribute 10 percent of their weekly earnings to the party, promoting the sale of party literature at union headquarters, and speaking there about the need for workers to seize control of industry and the government.[17] Such concerns were a response to activities in the union that had increased in the weeks before the assassination of Trotsky in August 1940.[18] They also resulted from the changed national mood: the fear of fifth column threats also shaped the men's opposition. Bartlett and Williams articulated their complaints about the abuses they saw taking place within their union in staunch anticommunist terms, making the Trotskyists' politics central to their protest.

Williams, Bartlett, and other Teamsters who coalesced in late 1940 found legitimacy for their grievance in the IBT's ban on communists serving as union leaders. That ban had been added to the union's constitution at its September 1940 convention. As Bartlett later testified, groups of 20 to 30 workers (allegedly reaching up to a total of 800 individuals) met nightly at Williams's home to discuss removing "those elements which were violating the Constitution and by-laws of the Teamsters International."[19] Among the disenchanted workers were an undercover special agent and an unnamed confidential FBI informant. Alfred Blair, the state labor conciliator, claims in his memoir that Sidney Brennan, an ambitious 544 job steward and a "good Roman Catholic," admitted to being one of the FBI's informants.[20] How much influence the informants and agents had in promoting the split within the union is difficult to ascertain, but it is clear that they filtered back to the bureau information about members' discontent and the actions of the Trotskyist leadership.[21]

Williams built up the rank-and-file opposition to the Trotskyists through these initial meetings in his home. By early 1941, he, Bartlett, and Brennan designated the opposition the Committee of 100. A minority voice within Local 544, which had more than 6,000 members, it held an inaugural meeting at the Nicollet Hotel in February.[22] Shortly after attending this gathering, however, Williams was dismissed as an organizer for Local 544 on the grounds of "indiscipline and disloyalty."[23] Furious, Williams challenged his expulsion.[24] Local 544's executive board held a hearing to consider the matter but refused to reinstate him, arguing that Williams did not have the "ability, principles or honor to hold the job."[25]

Williams struck back by issuing an open letter to the membership in which he "announced he would lead [the] movement to have the leadership [of 544] investigated by the union's international"[26] because of its "subversive" politics.[27] The Committee of 100, which met a second time on March 1, supported Williams in this effort by drafting a telegram to Daniel Tobin asking him to "investigate 'an intolerable situation' in the local."[28] Meeting again on Friday, March 7 (when at least one FBI agent was present among them), the committee passed a resolution stating, "These persons such as V. R. Dunne, Miles Dunne, Emil Hansen, Kelly Postal, Harry DeBoer and others have and are using the labor movement to screen their activities to develop a Communist movement within our ranks, the doctrines of which we are opposed to."[29] The battle lines were now clearly drawn between the two groups, with the politics of Local 544's leadership at the center of the fight.

The tensions between 544's executive board and the growing opposition movement deepened even further with the sudden death of Tommy Williams on March 10, 1941. That day he, Brennan, and Bartlett met to draw up the Committee of 100's formal charges against 544's executive board. That morning, the three men went to the Nicollet Hotel, where a stenographer prepared copies to be sent to the membership. Bartlett later told police that he spent the rest of the afternoon with Williams, staying with him at his house until four thirty. Bartlett noted that once they had sent out the charges, Williams was "in good spirits and remarked, 'Jim, I think we have got them licked.'" It seemed as though the opposition was on the way to unseating the executive board.

After having dinner at home, Williams left for the union hall, where he met up with Bartlett again around eight o'clock. Immediately, however, Bartlett noticed that Williams did not look well. Williams "mumbled to [him], 'Jim, please call a doctor, I'm sick.'" While waiting for the ambulance, Bartlett and another member of the opposition took Williams back to his home, where he slipped into a coma. The ambulance arrived there to take him to the hospital, but Williams died on the way of a massive heart attack, evidently the fifth and worst of such attacks he had sustained over the previous few months.[30]

Williams's death was followed by a dramatic reaction at the hospital and in the union hall. At St. Barnabas, members of the opposition group guarded Williams's body until a doctor from the University of Minnesota came to perform the autopsy. With the memory of William Brown's murder on their minds, they did not trust the doctor sent by the union. The former Local 544 president had been shot in 1937, four months after securing the office in a contested vote, leading to rumors that his killing may have been politically motivated and carried out by the Trotskyists. These were explosive allegations that were never substantiated.[31] But Williams's death on the very night he was to present the charges against the SWP leaders was considered suspicious by many of his supporters.[32] Their anxieties, however, were based on irrational fears that were themselves rooted in the unfounded rumors and political hatreds that fueled the growing opposition movement in the local. Those fears may have been shared by some of the 1,500 union members who were gathered for the meeting at 257 Plymouth Avenue. In the confusion that evening, Bartlett had returned to the union hall after seeing Williams safely onto the ambulance. He then received the news of Williams's death by phone. Overcome with emotion, Bartlett ran to the microphone and shouted, "Tommy Williams is dead!" "Many men leaped to their feet and startled cries were raised" in reaction to the shocking news. The men knew that the opposition was planning to present its charges that night and realized that with Williams's untimely demise it would now be temporarily silenced. But Bartlett calmed down the members as quickly as he had roused them by explaining that Williams had died of a heart attack.[33] Miles Dunne and Ray Rainbolt also moved to reassure those gathered that there had been no foul play, calling for a moment of silence to commemorate their lost union brother.[34] The meeting was then hastily disbanded, and the executive committee went into conference.

Miles Dunne subsequently announced that the board would make "no statement" about Williams's death, while Tobin told the press that at this stage the dispute in Minneapolis was "strictly private within the organization."[35] Both the leadership of Local 544 and the IBT wanted to keep a lid on the situation and find a peaceful way to defuse it. The anger and frustration felt by those in the opposition, however, continued to simmer in the days after Williams's death. John Geary, an IBT vice president from St. Paul who was sent to Minneapolis to speak with Miles Dunne, reported back to Tobin on March 14 that "this committee of 100 representing the Williams and Bartlett outfit is still raising Cain." Geary had heard that "they are bringing men around the headquarters carrying guns" but that "so far no trouble has happened." Because Local 544's leaders stayed away from Williams's funeral, "everything went off nice."[36] Five hundred mourners gathered that Thursday to say their last good-byes. Williams quickly became a martyr to the cause of the renamed Committee of 99, now headed by Brennan and Bartlett.[37]

The group invoked Williams's name in an "open letter to the members of Local 544 and other Teamster's unions" sent on March 23. In it the committee complained that "the Dunnes and their stooges have not in one single instance answered the charges made by Tommy Williams." The committee reiterated its accusation that the leaders had turned the General Drivers Union into a "screen to build their Communist machine," but now also claimed that those radicals had "set up a system of patronage around the union headquarters that gives preference to members of their party."[38] Both concerns—the alleged capturing of the local for SWP business and the spoils system in the local—undergirded their litany of complaints.

Although consisting of, at most, 1.6 percent of the local's membership, the Committee of 99 claimed to be the voice of the "real sentiments of the rank and file of our memberships" that was ready to oppose what it termed the "small handful of un-American elements": the SWP "machine controlling" the union.[39] By focusing on the specific ties between Local 544's leaders and the SWP, the opposition drew the attention of those outside of Minneapolis to the local struggle. As the presence of the special agent and informer inside 544 attests, the FBI was already following the situation. It would deepen its investigation in the coming months. The IBT's executive board also decided that it was time to intervene.

Tobin and the FBI "Step In"

Daniel Tobin had been keeping tabs on events in Minneapolis before the March 23 letter publicly exposed the opposition's charges. The day after Williams's death, John Geary, an IBT vice president, visited Local 544's head-quarters, indicating to Vincent Dunne that Tobin wanted to investigate the opposition's allegations.[40] On the afternoon of March 14, Geary visited again and met with Miles Dunne for three hours.[41] The following week Geary met once more with Miles and pushed him to have the 544 leaders "sever connections with the Socialist Labor [sic] Party if possible." Geary tried to "convince them that if they would quit this party, everything would work itself out all right."[42]

Within two weeks after Williams's death, however, the opposition continued its noisy offensive against the Trotskyists, culminating in the March 23 letter. Geary also faced a "steady stream of visitors coming [to him in St. Paul] from Minneapolis," which was looking for help from the International.[43] The charge that 544's leaders had turned the local into an arm of the SWP was now harder to silence. Although he initially tried to contain the situation in Minneapolis through Geary's private meetings with Miles Dunne, Tobin soon found the pressure coming from the rank and file too much to ignore. Geary's visits had not produced a resolution. In addition, Tobin quickly recognized that there was another party that had caught wind of the dispute and made it difficult for him to handle the situation discreetly: the FBI.

FBI agents had been investigating the relationship between the SWP and Local 544 for several years.[44] By March 1941 they began a more aggressive campaign and reached out for information to Geary, who reported to Tobin that "the FBI men stepped into the game. How they got started, I don't know."[45] Recommending that Geary "not show any disrespect for the representatives of the F.B.I.," Tobin advised him to "answer their questions as best you can."[46] For now Tobin seemed willing to trust the FBI.

Tobin's cognizance of the FBI's interest in the Minneapolis situation was reinforced by the information he received from a rank-and-file member of Local 544, Robert Hawn, in April 1941. Hawn told Tobin all about his trouble over the past few years finding work and confessed to having worked for the FBI in order to make ends meet. He detailed how in August 1940, after losing a job as an extra driver for the Werner Transportation Company, he "got a chance to work here in Mpls for a Mr. Ed Notesteen who is with the F.B.I." Hawn explained how his job "was to investigate as much as possible all communist activitys [sic] here in Mpls so of course [his] investigating did concern some of the officers of Local #544."[47]

Hawn's communication to Tobin reveals that the FBI in Minneapolis was investigating the leadership of Local 544 as early as August 1940, even before Williams coordinated the opposition meetings in his home. By the spring of 1941, once the Committee of 99 was active, the FBI would find many more willing informants in Minneapolis. Brennan and Bartlett became two of the bureau's most cooperative contacts.[48] Well before the agents turned up on Geary's doorstep in March 1941, then, the atmosphere within Local 544 had been affected by the presence of the FBI and its informants. That presence intensified the animosity against the Trotskyist leadership felt by the rank-and-file members like Hawn (or if he were an FBI plant, on the part of the members he could rally against the leadership under his cover as an angry member).[49] It also turned up the heat on Tobin.

Hawn's story reveals how Local 544 was caught in an FBI probe. The bureau initiated its investigation of the union partly on its own, based on its mandate to scrutinize domestic "communist activity." Local 544 and its Trotskyist leaders were an obvious target given that they had drawn national attention to themselves when they shut down Minneapolis during the 1934 strikes.[50] With Dobbs's organization of the over-the-road drivers into the eleven-state agreement in 1939, the SWP's influence seemed to expand beyond the streets and warehouses of Minneapolis. And in the context of the anxieties over fifth column sabotage generated by the "little red scare," that influence was worrisome to the FBI. By early 1941, Hoover believed that with their opposition to the war and their position at the helm of a union at the center of the nation's domestic transportation network, the leaders of 544 posed a domestic security risk.

Hoover's concerns stemmed from the FBI's early surveillance of Local 544's leaders. In September 1940, the bureau issued a Custodial Detention card on Vincent Dunne.[51] By January 1941, it began a file on him based on a November 1940 letter from military intelligence claiming Dunne instructed Local 544's Union Defense Guard "to hold itself in readiness for war."[52] Dobbs in particular came under FBI scrutiny, even after he left the Teamsters in January 1940 to devote himself full-time to the party. In December 1940, Hoover requested that the Special Agent in Charge (SAC) in New York begin an investigation of Dobbs,[53] and in March 1941 he recommended that Dobbs be "considered for custodial detention in the event of a national emergency."[54] By the spring of 1941, the investigation thus had broadened out beyond the Teamsters in Minneapolis to mesh with the existing investigations of national SWP leaders in New York.[55]

By April 1941, members of the Justice Department became concerned about the FBI reports coming out of Minneapolis. Of particular interest was

Agent Thomas Perrin's dispatch filed on April 5. Perrin had gathered signed statements that alleged the SWP-affiliated leadership of Local 544 not only had repeatedly spoken about the violent overthrow of the government and the undermining of morale in the armed forces but also had a stash of guns ready for "the revolution." Having first contacted Tommy Williams in February, Perrin later gathered testimony from Bartlett, Brennan, Eugene Williams (Tommy's brother), Violet Williams (Tommy's widow), and several others. They claimed they had heard the 544 leaders, especially Vincent Dunne and Farrell Dobbs, speak often of plans to overthrow the government by force, and they alleged that these leaders presented 544's Union Defense Guard as having been inspired by Trotsky to serve as the vehicle for proletarian revolution. In addition, the informants argued that Dunne "would talk for hours [about] how we could work out things by sabotaging our government by armed force, by getting a member into every branch of private industry and to spread 'the word' around, as he called it." The informants reported that it was supposedly through the party's infiltration in "key positions in industries, power plants, etc." that the revolution would be initiated by "paralyz[ing] all forms of communication, power, industry." And to carry out such revolution, both Eugene Williams and another member of the 544 opposition, Roy Wieneke, claimed that "Emil Hansen has bought a bunch of guns for the SWP and keeps them in the basement under his garage."[56]

Perrin's shocking report was first sent to U.S. Attorney Victor Anderson in St. Paul, who quickly referred the matter to the attorney general, Robert Jackson, in Washington. After hearing about the situation in Minneapolis, Special Assistant to the U.S. Attorney General Henry Schweinhaut requested more information. Hoover gladly sent along a copy of Perrin's full report, emphasizing in his cover letter the alleged guns stored in Hansen's basement. He undoubtedly understood that in the context of the nation's fears of saboteurs and spies the testimony of the disgruntled 544 opposition would reinforce the notion that the Trotskyists in Local 544 posed a threat to national security. Accepting those statements uncritically—statements that came from relatives of the deceased Tommy Williams and others associated with the opposition movement within Local 544—the FBI, and now the Department of Justice, convinced themselves that there might have been a real fifth column in Minneapolis.[57] Although a search warrant was never issued for Hansen's home and no guns were presented as evidence during the trial that fall,[58] at this early stage of the investigation Perrin's report and the testimony it contained were worrisome enough for Hoover to push for a prosecution. Local 544 leadership's ties to the SWP, its alleged desire to paralyze the transportation network of the Midwest, its supposed talk of disrupting the armed forces, and the allegations of its having stored weapons for the fight made it an easy and, to the FBI, a clear target for prosecution under the nation's new peacetime antisubversive statute: the Smith Act.

Seeing the Writing on the Wall: The IBT's Crackdown and Local 544's "Bolt" to the CIO

It was not only the Justice Department that was concerned about the goings-on in Minneapolis; the IBT's disapproval of the antiwar radicals in its own ranks deepened as the national political climate changed. By late March 1941, Trotskyists in Local 544 and their comrades in the SWP began to see the writing on the wall, sensing that Tobin and the IBT executive board were becoming even less accepting of them as the FBI's investigation intensified. After he and the other Local 544 leaders had been summoned by Tobin to a meeting in Chicago on April 8, Vincent Dunne concluded that "Tobin views the situation here as more serious than we had at first supposed." He and the others would later discover that the complaints of the opposition and the FBI's investigation encouraged Tobin (who had long despised the Trotskyists) to crack down on their political affiliation. At the time, however, without that information, they planned to attend the conference "with a stiff committee prepared to be on the offensive from start to finish," ready to defend themselves and their record as militant and successful union leaders against the grievances of an opposition they deemed to be composed of power-hungry men who had failed at organizing. They remained hopeful that Tobin and the IBT would accept their position.[59]

Cannon was a bit more wary. Using his SWP code name "Martin," he sent a letter to Dunne and Dobbs expressing his belief that the "general political situation and the winds from Washington" seemed to be the only explanation for why Tobin chose this moment to make a fuss over their political affiliation. Tobin had known about and disapproved of their ties to the SWP for some time; he had even tried to oust them from control of Local 574 after the 1934 strikes, but he backed down once it became clear that the membership supported them as skilled union leaders. In the changed context of the spreading war in Europe, however, what limited tolerance Tobin had for the Trotskyists completely evaporated.[60] Cannon's observation was apt, but what he did not admit was that part of the reason Tobin had lost patience with the Trotskyists was that they had increased the profile of their party activity within Local 544 over the course of the previous year, which in turn contributed to the emergence of the Williams-Bartlett opposition movement. If they had kept their party activities out of the union hall, the conflict may not have occurred, or at least it would not have allowed Tobin to intervene again. But for revolutionaries like Cannon, Dunne, and Dobbs, such distinctions were false and misguided: their trade union work was essential to their party work and vice versa, and therefore could not be separated.

In order to protect that relationship, however, Cannon recommended drastic action. He believed that Trotskyist leaders in Local 544 should officially resign from the SWP, remaining only as sympathizers, so the issue of party affiliation could be taken off the table at the April 8 conference. The focus of the discussion in Chicago over the conflict within Local 544 could then be put "on its proper basis of trade union practices," since, Cannon argued, the "attempt to rest your case on your alleged political association is obviously an attempt to divert attention from the real issue": Local 544's militant industrial unionism. Though officially leaving the SWP was not an easy concession to make, Dunne understood what was at stake and followed Cannon's advice.[61]

The Committee of 99's allegations that the leaders of Local 544 were using the union to sustain the SWP were aired formally at the April 8 meeting. Gathering at the Sherman House Hotel in Chicago were three representatives from 544 (Miles Dunne, Kelly Postal, and Ray Rainbolt), two from the Committee of 99 (James Bartlett and Sidney Brennan), and representatives from the IBT's executive board, who were led in the proceedings by Tobin's assistant, John Gillespie. The IBT president was not in attendance.[62] At the start of the meeting, Gillespie explained that the IBT was responding to charges made by Tommy Williams and "a large number of members" who were all "in good standing" that "some officers and members of both Local 544 and the Joint Council" were running the SWP from inside the union, and that this party was "as nearly Communistic in its principles and aspirations as if it were a part of the Communist Party." Because the SWP "has as its aims and object" the creation of "'a revolutionary workers' government'" to replace the current political and economic system (aims set out in the SWP's Declaration of Principles), the IBT decided it needed to investigate.

In addition, Gillespie revealed that the opposition movement had also asked the IBT to impose a trustee over the local "for the benefit of the membership, on the ground that the local union is not now being conducted in the best interests of the International Union . . . or in harmony with the principles and declarations of the American government."[63] It was now clear that what Dunne and the other leaders of 544 feared was true: Tobin had taken the complaints of the Committee of 99 seriously and was going to challenge their work as union leaders because of their politics, not their organizing abilities.

Bartlett's and Brennan's testimony at the April 8 meeting repeated the familiar allegations of the Committee of 99. As Dobbs later recounted, Miles

Dunne, Postal, and Rainbolt responded by going on the offensive, laying out their evidence for Bartlett's and Brennan's inefficiency as union leaders and their "unprincipled conduct" as proof that they "could not possibly have the best interests of the union in mind." The Trotskyists also "denied for the record" that they were formal members of the SWP. By the end of the meeting, Gillespie called for a truce.[64] The opposition's complaints had been officially aired and Local 544's leadership had responded, denying the charges and asserting that they were no longer formally members of the SWP. For now, things were left at that. Initially Vincent Dunne was hopeful that Miles, Postal, and Rainbolt had quieted the concerns of the IBT. He noted how a few days later Gillespie chatted amiably with him, Miles and Grant Dunne, and Harry DeBoer at an over-the-road conference, telling the men that "hell . . . we didn't do anything to you fellows, we just listened to a lot of stuff," betraying, perhaps, the ambivalence with which some IBT officials pursued the charges of the Bartlett opposition group.[65] Dobbs later noted, however, that he was wary of the truce, accepting it only for the time being. Even though the April 8 meeting may have restored order within the IBT temporarily, neither side was fully satisfied with the papering over of the central issue dividing the ranks: the Trotskyist politics of Local 544's leaders and their alleged use of the union to advance the cause of the SWP.

While Tobin's assistant was busy working to defuse the situation in Minneapolis, the Department of Justice built its case against the 544 leaders. By April 29, Wendell Berge, assistant to the attorney general, had read Perrin's report and concluded in a memo to Hoover that "a violation of various sections of Title I of the Alien Registration Act [Smith Act], 1940" had taken place.[66] On that same day, Berge also wrote to Anderson explaining that "the Department is considering the question of prosecution of this case."[67] Special Agent Roy T. Noonan, who had been involved in the 1939 WPA strike trials, issued his own damning report on May 2. It spoke most directly to the allegations of subversive speech, including accusations that Dunne, Skoglund, and others specifically called for the overthrow of the government by force and violence on numerous occasions.[68] Such information reinforced Berge's sense that prosecution was urgently needed to defend national security.

The essence of Berge's concern was soon appropriated by Tobin, who took a much harder line against the Socialist Workers in his union's ranks. In May 1941 the IBT president issued a stern warning in the *Minnesota Teamster* to those who were members of the SWP: cut party ties or face expulsion from the union. Arguing that he now had "information at hand that the Socialist Workers Party is about as radical as the Communist Party of Russia" and is of "a dangerous revolutionary character," Tobin made the case for its inclusion within the union's constitutional ban on communists.[69] The intelligence Tobin referred to had been supplied to him by the Justice Department upon his request and may have been a summary of Perrin's inflammatory report. It reinforced Tobin's long-standing contempt for the radicals and emboldened him to take this public stand on the heretofore internal union dispute.

Cannon characterized Tobin's May ultimatum as "a clear threat of a new attack against the teamsters' movement in the Northwest." He felt it undermined the best interests of the nation's workers, which he believed must ultimately be served by a revolutionary workers' movement. "This may well develop into the central struggle between war-mongering reactionaries and class struggle militants in the American labor movement," Cannon warned, "as the country moves daily nearer to the actual participation in the war."[70] It certainly would put the Trotskyist presence in trade union work to the test.

Cannon was right when he cited the deepening war in Europe as a factor in the IBT "attack" on the SWP. Tobin was most immediately concerned with the FBI investigations of Local 544, but he also was cognizant of the national political climate when he issued his ultimatum in the *Minneapolis Teamster*. The federal investigation of the local in Minneapolis was proceeding apace,[71] but there also loomed the possibility of federal intervention in the IBT throughout the entire Northwest if the disruption in Minneapolis portended a larger disturbance in that region's transportation networks. Such intervention was something Tobin wanted to avoid.

The federal government's intrusion into industrial and labor relations had become more likely in early 1941 as America's ally, Great Britain, struggled to fend off German assaults. Roosevelt's dispatching of federal troops on June 9 to reopen the North American Aviation plant in California where workers had gone on strike demonstrated the fullest extent of such intervention. The importance of maintaining uninterrupted lines of industrial production, especially for defense, had been heightened with the passage of the Lend-Lease Act in March. When President Roosevelt signed the bill into law, he reminded Americans that they would now be the "great arsenal of democracy," aiding Britain as it stood alone against the Nazi menace.[72] Claiming even broader executive powers to ensure that America's support for Britain and preparation of its own defenses would take place at maximum capacity, Roosevelt declared an "unlimited national emergency" on May 27.

This emergency status gave the president the power to "increase the size of the regular army or navy, to place compulsory defense orders in factories or plants, and to assign priority rating to producers and suppliers, directing them to fill defense orders ahead of private orders." Roosevelt warned Americans that they could not wait until the Nazis were "'in our front yard'" to prepare their defenses and called for more air and sea power to support patrols convoying supplies to Britain. The national defense effort required strengthening, Roosevelt insisted, "'to the extreme limit of our national power and authority.'"[73] Industry and labor were expected to comply fully with the intensified war preparedness program. Disruptions—like the one possibly brewing in Minneapolis—would not be tolerated.

The AFL's executive council understood the implications of this national emergency climate. It responded to the president's message by declaring its unswerving support for national preparedness and for supplying Britain in the fight against fascism.[74] Accepting that America was "now actually and officially in a grave emergency," the federation's executive council called upon "all its members to serve the cause of American democracy" by supporting its new no-strike policy and warned that any local union in its jurisdiction that violated the new policy would face disciplinary actions.[75]

As an affiliate of the AFL, the IBT was subject to this commitment. For Tobin, the Teamsters' executive board, and many of the union's members, this was an easy pledge to make. And it was one they reinforced publicly when, on June 5, the board sent a letter to President Roosevelt "solemnly" pledging the IBT's support to him and the nation "in this dark and fateful hour."[76] This position of support stood in direct contrast to the anti-interventionism of the Trotskyists and further alienated Local 544's leaders within the Teamsters union.

The IBT's letter, the AFL's pro-war "no strike" pledge, and the intensifying national wartime political climate created an inhospitable environment for Local 544's leaders. Dunne and the others tried to focus on impending contract negotiations in Minneapolis, but they faced opposition from employers who used the intra-union fight as an excuse to refuse to come to the bargaining table. By dividing the local and making it vulnerable in this way, the Committee of 99—in the Trotskyists' view—proved it did not have the workers' best interests at heart, but merely desired to grab control of the union at any cost. Remaining true to their militancy, 544's leaders did not allow this vulnerability to impede their work on behalf of the members; when talks stalled, they issued strike notices against 370 trucking companies.[77]

But the distraction of the intra-union conflict became overwhelming when the IBT's executive board requested that Local 544's leaders appear before it on June 3 in Washington, DC, on charges of violating the IBT's constitution with their radical associations.[78] Local 544's executive board chose Kelly Postal, Ray Rainbolt, and Vincent Dunne to make the trip. There, before Tobin and the IBT's executive board, they were, as Dunne would later recount, "humiliated and insulted." By contrast, Bartlett and the representatives from the Committee of 99 were received "warmly" and allowed to speak at length. Tobin spoke last and quoted from an FBI report, emphasizing passages that spoke of the 544 leaders' continuing ties to the SWP.[79] Tobin was reported to have argued that because the 544 board members subscribed to teachings of a subversive organization that planned to overthrow the government, "in these critical times such a situation cannot be tolerated."[80] The truce that had been reached at the April meeting had collapsed.

Convening a private meeting with Dunne, Postal, and Rainbolt the next morning, Tobin presented his solution: to impose a receiver over Local 544. With the approval of the IBT's executive board, Tobin was granted the authority under the IBT constitution to impose receiverships (or trusteeships) over locals that the IBT deemed to be in the hands of "dishonest or incompetent" leaders or whose "organization [it believed was] not being conducted for the benefit of the entire membership." Under the receivership, "whomever Tobin appointed as trustee enjoyed complete power over the daily affairs of the local, subject to oversight by Tobin."[81] Control of the local would be taken out of the hands of its elected leaders. Tobin wanted the representatives from Minneapolis to agree to the arrangement on the spot, but Dunne, Postal, and Rainbolt refused, arguing that 544 "was a democratic union, that [their] committee [of Dunne, Postal, and Rainbolt] had no power to make any [such] decision."[82]

Instead, Dunne and the others pursued a course of action that would allow them to maintain the SWP's ties to Local 544: they planned to call on John Lewis, past president of the CIO and head of the UMW, who happened to share their opposition to Roosevelt's war policy, albeit for different reasons. At the time Lewis and his brother, Denny, had been organizing drivers and warehouse workers in the construction and retail industries via the United Construction Workers Organizing Committee (UCWOC) and United Retail, Wholesale, and Department Store Employees as a part of their vision to create industry-wide unions in the CIO. Such efforts were a direct threat to the AFL's presence among those same workers and to the federation's attempts to stabilize through closed-shop agreements the construction industry that was then feeling the pressure of the new wartime preparedness demands. When Dunne, Rainbolt, and Postal presented their request to have Local 544 make the switch from the IBT-AFL to the CIO, Denny Lewis was happy to oblige.[83]

The 544 representatives then returned to Minneapolis with both Tobin's proposal for the imposition of a receiver and the knowledge that Denny Lewis was moving ahead to secure them a charter with UCWOC. Local 544's board quickly reached a consensus and contacted Tobin that Saturday with its decision: it had unanimously rejected his proposal for the receivership.[84] Instead, it prepared for the general meeting on Monday, June 9, when it planned to inform the rank and file of what happened in Washington and of its decision to reject the receivership. On Monday evening about 6,000 members jammed the headquarters at 257 Plymouth Avenue, eager to weigh in on how their union should proceed.[85]

Although the Trotskyist leaders had essentially taken it upon themselves at the level of the executive board to decide what to do, they at least moved to secure the support of the members for that choice through an open vote, which was more than Tobin had been willing to do with his proposal. Once the meeting was called to order, Vincent Dunne presented his report. Arguing that Tobin's proposal amounted to the stripping away of 544's autonomy, Dunne thundered, "This union is not going to permit itself to be handled with rough hands, . . . it is not going to accept a dictatorship, no matter from whom." Dobbs then stepped up to the microphone and, echoing Dunne's comparison of Tobin to a dictator, asserted, "This union has concluded there must be no appeasers of dictators. We are not Chamberlains. We don't carry an umbrella, even when it rains!"[86] Miles Dunne then drove home the executive board's position. Having heard back from Denny Lewis by telegram just a few hours before the membership meeting, Dunne knew that he could present the opportunity for Local 544 to join the CIO under a charter issued by UCWOC.[87] He called upon those gathered to support the move away from "the dead hand of a reactionary dictator" and into "a more progressive section of the American labor movement," where "liberalism, militancy and progress will be rewarded rather than punished."[88] The majority of Local 544's membership found these arguments convincing; at the June 9 meeting it voted to approve a resolution calling for the disaffiliation of the local from the AFL and for its acceptance of the UCWOC charter. Local 544 had "bolted" from the IBT-AFL for the CIO.

Tobin's June 12 Telegram and Biddle's Decision to Prosecute

While Denny Lewis welcomed the truck drivers into their new national organizing body, designated now as the Motor Transport and Allied Workers Industrial Union, Local 544-CIO, the disgruntled members of the original General Drivers Union, Local 544-AFL, were outraged.[89] The news from 544 was quickly followed by Ice and Coal Drivers Local 221's announcing that it too would be leaving the AFL for the CIO. Tobin sent Dave Beck, an IBT vice president from the Pacific coast, to salvage the AFL hold on 544. Neither Tobin nor the Committee of 99 was willing to accept the secession of the General Drivers Union, which they considered the result of union raiding.[90]

Given John Lewis's vocal opposition to the war—and to Roosevelt's third run for president the previous November—Tobin found this turn of events particularly galling. Not only had the Trotskyists angered him by bolting with the drivers, but so too had Lewis, his trade union and political nemesis, infuriated him with his behind-the-scenes machinations.[91]

Others shared Tobin's outrage. AFL president William Green, Minnesota state labor conciliator Alfred Blair, Governor Harold Stassen, and the FBI aided Tobin in his efforts to maintain control of the drivers union. Bureau agent Perrin met with Blair on June 7, after Sidney Brennan and representatives from the Committee of 99 admitted to him that they had been informing for the FBI. Blair had already "had many meetings with Brennan and his followers" in April and May of that year and had come to side with them in their dispute against the Trotskyist leadership of Local 544, seeing those leaders as a threat to the union and to national security. Blair claimed that Green was convinced of the threat too and supported Tobin's desire to place a receiver over Local 544. According to Blair, Green planned to discuss the matter with President Roosevelt.[92] When Blair, Brennan, Dave Beck, Isadore Goldberg (counsel for the AFL and IBT), and George Sjoselius (assistant attorney general) gathered in a secret meeting at the Nicollet Hotel on June 11, Blair communicated Green's assurance that Roosevelt "will issue the order through the Department of Justice to pick up those advocating the overthrow of the government, and it will happen as soon as search warrants are prepared and their staff is implemented." If Blair's account is accurate, Green's communication reinforced what Roosevelt had come to believe from the FBI reports and Justice Department memos that had already crossed his desk: that it was time to move against the Trotskyists under the Smith Act.[93] The men who gathered at the Nicollet Hotel on June 11 also discussed the IBT's plans to place Beck as receiver and for the International to "foot the bill." And Blair reported that he had been in discussions with Stassen about "preparing for a mobilization of a National Guard unit to implement [sic] the Minneapolis Police force, if necessary."[94] It was to be a no-holds-barred counterattack on Local 544-CIO launched on the local, state, and federal levels.

At this point Tobin also reached out directly to President Roosevelt. The two men had become personal friends after Tobin worked as chairman of the Labor Division of the Democratic Party during Roosevelt's presidential campaigns. Roosevelt began his run in 1940 with a speech at the IBT's convention, and Tobin worked the radio to help pull in the labor vote.[95] Tobin thus felt comfortable turning to the president with his concerns and, by the summer of 1941, felt it was necessary. He had already met with Roosevelt on June 5 to reinforce the IBT's support for the president's war preparedness program.[96]

Figure 2.1 President Franklin D. Roosevelt and Daniel
Tobin, president of the International Brotherhood of
Teamsters, ca. 1944, seated before a bank of micro-
phones. The friendship between the two men led the
Trotskyists to accuse Tobin of using that personal connection to get the Justice Department to indict them
under the Smith Act as punishment for Trotskyist-led
Local 544's withdrawal from the IBT-AFL in June
1941. Courtesy International Brotherhood of Teamsters Labor Archives, George Washington University.

But it was not until June 12, 1941, after Local 544 "bolted" from the IBT, that
he sent a telegram to the White House in which he specifically outlined the
danger he believed the Trotskyists posed. Tobin argued that the Trotskyists,
who had succeeded in organizing drivers across the central states,[97] were in
a position to disrupt the nation's commercial transportation networks and, if
they took advantage of the war crisis, could overthrow the government and
set up a socialist state. He pointed to their opposition to the war in Europe
and their Union Defense Guard to sustain his accusations.[98]

Because of this telegram, Tobin has been accused of setting in motion the chain of events that led to the arrest of twenty-nine members of the SWP and Local 544. At the time of those arrests and during the trial, the defense argued that Tobin called in a political favor from Roosevelt and that the president intervened in an internal union dispute, launching the first Smith Act prosecution.[99] This "political debt" argument has survived in varying degrees in the limited scholarly literature on the case and has informed the popular memory of the prosecution within the SWP.[100] The Department of Justice, however, had already been seriously considering such prosecution as early as April 1941, based on the independent investigation of the FBI dating back to the fall of 1940.[101] And the White House was already privy to Hoover's concerns. On June 9, the FBI chief had sent to both Edwin M. Watson, secretary to President Roosevelt, and the attorney general "information received from a confidential source" about the June 3 and 4 IBT meetings in Washington, DC, from someone who was there, most likely either Bartlett or Brennan, given their cooperation with the FBI at the time.[102] Like Tobin's telegram, which was to follow in three days, Hoover's memo to Watson placed special emphasis on the dangers that Local 544 presented to national security. The June 9 memo, however, remained classified until 1975, so it was impossible for the defendants at the time of the trial and scholars studying the case before its release to understand the extent of the federal government's investigation prior to the June 12 telegram.

The full trajectory of the first Smith Act case reveals how the prosecution of the Trotskyists in 1941 was the product of the convergence of multiple historical forces. Tobin's contempt for the radical union leaders certainly played a part, but so too did the indigenous anticommunism of the rank-and-file opposition movement that formed in Minneapolis in late 1940 and the independent FBI investigations of Trotskyists within Local 544. The relationships among the local opposition movement, the bureau's agents, the IBT's international leadership, and ultimately the U.S. attorney and attorney general mutually reinforced the growing sense that the SWP-affiliated leaders of Local 544 presented a danger not only to the integrity of the union but also to the nation on the brink of war. The origins of the 1941 prosecution thus reveal the extensive nature of such early labor anticommunist networks and shed light on how the FBI and the Justice Department engaged in such early domestic security work. Tobin had his own motives for wanting to purge the Trotskyists from Local 544, but he was neither the lone nor the primary instigator of that ouster.[103]

By early June 1941, pressure for action on the case also came from Victor Anderson and Wendell Berge. Anderson telegrammed Berge saying that the matter in Minneapolis was in "urgent need [of] immediate action."[104] Hoover kept up the heat as well. On June 19 he sent a confidential memo to the solicitor general and to President Roosevelt expressing his fears that the situation unfolding in Minneapolis could lead to strikes that might "cause a tie-up of materials flowing to and from plants in that vicinity having National Defense contracts."[105] Minnesota governor Harold Stassen also pushed for something to be done, asking Acting Attorney General Francis Biddle to go after the Trotskyists. Feeling the pressure from all sides now, Biddle authorized the prosecution.[106]

At this stage, however, Biddle still wanted to keep things out of the press.[107] Until his agency agreed that there was a violation of the Smith Act, Biddle wanted to play things close to the vest. Biddle's desire to tread carefully may have stemmed from the unease with which he considered the Smith Act. As a civil libertarian he was uncomfortable with this law, which restricted free speech. He claims in his autobiography that he only reluctantly agreed to the prosecution of the twenty-nine under the Smith Act "so that the law would be tested at the threshold, and taken to the Supreme Court, where it would, [he] hoped and believed, be knocked out." And he sent Schweinhaut to St. Paul "to supervise the Dunne trial, to see that the United States Attorney did not let his patriotism run away with him." Biddle also wanted Schweinhaut to "say quietly to the trial judge that the Attorney General was anxious that the trial be narrowed as much as possible."[108] Through such measures Biddle tried to prevent an abusive implementation of the act; he attempted to prevent Anderson from engaging in Chafee's proverbial "sniping at soapbox orators by the front gate" and repeating the abuses of the First Red Scare.

It is difficult to know if Biddle's decision to prosecute was due to any other reasons because there are missing pages in his personal papers in the section that deals with this case. Among several spiral-bound notebooks in which he kept handwritten notes for his autobiography, In Brief Authority, there were two that dealt with the sedition cases he handled as solicitor general, acting attorney general, and attorney general. Notebook "AG V" begins in midsentence with Biddle referring briefly to the case: "led by Dunne brothers, which I had authorized as Acting Solicitor General . . . to test the constitutionality of the act." Biddle is clear about his reason for supporting the prosecution: to test the new law. But that is all he says about the case. The next sentence moves on to a discussion of another sedition case. And notebook AG IV, which would presumably have the beginning of the story that finishes in notebook V (and perhaps a lengthier discussion of the 1941 case), is missing entirely from the collection.[109] What is preserved in these notebooks, then, does not provide any more insight into Biddle's thinking than what appears in the published autobiography: that is, Biddle pursued the case to test the constitutionality of the Smith Act. One wonders what, if anything, may have been in notebook IV to shed additional light on Biddle's feelings about the origins of the case or about the pressures that may have been placed on him to prosecute.

Although Biddle may have been conflicted about authorizing the prosecution, Henry Schweinhaut and Wendell Berge seemed eager to gear up for the case. In mid-June, Schweinhaut suggested to Hoover that the FBI place a plant in the SWP headquarters in New York to gather more information for the trial.[110] Berge backed up Schweinhaut's suggestion, telling him that "if you think there is information which, from the investigative standpoint, can be best secured by the method you discussed with me on the telephone, you are authorized to order such an investigation," noting that he and his advisers "agree that it would not amount to entrapment so long as the government agents do not inspire the doing of illegal acts merely for the purpose of getting evidence."[111] The enthusiasm for such methods, however, was not shared by Hoover, who worried about the "serious possibility of embarrassment to the Bureau" and the Department of Justice "if the agent were later used as a witness and required to testify in open court." He wanted firmer legal assurances from the attorney general's office before proceeding and so refused to send an agent to New York to work undercover.[112] It was not so much the method of using plants that Hoover balked at—he had undercover agents in place in Minneapolis for some time—but rather Schweinhaut's interest in having them testify in court, a step that would expose one of the bureau's tactics to a scrutiny that might undermine its future effectiveness.

Despite Hoover's hesitancy to adopt Schweinhaut's aggressive techniques against the SWP in New York at this stage in the investigation, the wheels at the Justice Department were in motion based on the evidence it had already received from the FBI's work in Minneapolis. By mid-June, with Biddle's authorization, it officially began to build a case against the Trotskyists for violating the Smith Act.

Teamsters Divided: The Fight for Minneapolis

While the Justice Department in Washington geared up for the first Smith Act prosecution, chaos erupted back in Minneapolis in the wake of Local 544's withdrawal from the IBT-AFL. The repercussions of the June 9 "bolt" quickly became apparent, as an all-out turf war over 544's union headquarters, funds, and members ensued between the rump Local 544-AFL and the new Local 544-CIO. Confusion over which group constituted the bargaining agent for the workers encouraged employers to stall the contract negotiations that had begun in May. The AFL's accusations that the CIO embraced subversive radicals in its ranks (by welcoming the secessionist 544 faction) and the CIO's charges that the AFL engaged in undemocratic and violent rule (by imposing a receiver on 544 and sending in teams of men to "persuade" members to remain loyal to the IBT) added fuel to the already hot fire ignited by the June 9 vote.

In the immediate wake of 544's break with the IBT, Tobin sent Dave Beck into Minneapolis to move ahead with the receivership and dispatched Joseph Casey from San Francisco to oversee the transition process.[113] Beck's first step was to get up to speed with events in Minneapolis by meeting at the Nicollet Hotel with AFL and IBT general counsel, Judge Joseph Padway, and IBT international district organizers, T. T. Neal and H. L. Woxberg. After the meeting, Padway announced to the press that the IBT would "resort to all legal steps necessary to recover property of 544, if that property has been taken over by seceding and disloyal members." And Tobin made it clear that the rump local would receive a new IBT charter within a few days. Neither he nor those who remained loyal to him and the Teamsters were willing to give up Local 544 without a fight. While the new Local 544-CIO asserted its public presence in the city by issuing distinct badges to its members (a button displaying "C.I.O. 544 JUNE 1941"), Tobin kept up his condemnation of the seceding body, charging that the rival group was led by radicals who were themselves "directed by undercover secret organizations which are helping the dictators of Germany and Russia."[114] It was going to be an ugly fight.

The stakes were high for all involved. For the IBT, there was the loss of members that resulted from Local 544's withdrawal and from the disaffiliation of Local 221 (the Ice and Coal Drivers Union) and Local 778 (the Construction Workers Drivers Union), which followed on June 10 and June 15, respectively. What began as a dispute within the General Drivers Union spread to workers in various trucking and allied trades. Tobin and his allies feared the mass secession of workers from the AFL in the region that could follow.[115] For the Dunnes and the other SWP members on the executive board of Local 544, their union's militancy and democracy were at stake. In their eyes, the local's integrity was threatened by Tobin's receivership plan, especially since it was proposed in the midst of the contract negotiations with employers. For Denny Lewis, there was an opening in the middle of this upheaval to launch an industrial organizing campaign across the Midwest—precisely what Tobin feared. Lewis traveled to Minneapolis along with William K. Thomas, a representative of the CIO's general counsel, to oversee the program.[116] As both sides struggled to win the loyalty of Minneapolis teamsters, employers saw what was at stake for them: a chance to take advantage of the chaos in the current round of contract negotiations and weaken the position of all unions.

Figure 2.2 Motor Transport and Allied Workers Union (Local 544, Congress of Industrial Organizations), 1328 Second Street North, Minneapolis. Photo MH5.9MP5.3p76, negative number 43915, Minnesota Historical Society. Courtesy Minnesota Historical Society.

When it came to holding on to the IBT locals, Padway, Casey, Neal, and Woxburg led the fight. Woxburg told the press that the IBT "'would shoot the works' to fight back and keep its northwest locals in the AFL," noting defiantly that "we've got $6,000,000 in our international defense fund, and if we have to spend it all to keep our locals in the AFL we're going to do it."[117] The Teamsters' first line of attack was the heart of the current crisis—Local 544—and the need to regain control over its executive board and union headquarters. On June 16 they served a formal court order on Miles Dunne and the other board members notifying them that they had been suspended as officers of 544-IBT and demanding that "all moneys, books and property" of the union be turned over to T. T. Neal, trustee of Local 544 and its new receiver.[118] Dunne and the other defectors were to vacate the union headquarters on Plymouth Avenue, where all door locks and safe combinations would be changed.[119]

Anticipating such an attack, Dunne and the others had already made arrangements for an alternate headquarters. Complying with the court order on June 17, they moved from 257 Plymouth Avenue to new offices around the corner at 1328 Second Street North. Characterizing the transfer as their having been "illegally dispossessed by police" when "T. T. ('Raw Deal') Neal" seized the property of their union, the 544 board members carried on their work under the auspices of the CIO's Motor Transport Local. Defying the spirit of the court order, they signaled their intent to carry on their organizing work, noting how the hall in the new office building was big enough to serve as a strike headquarters. And, just as Padway, Woxburg, and the IBT representatives used the press to get out their side of the story, members of the 544 board projected their take on the situation in the *Northwest Organizer*, which since the local's split had become the official organ of 544-CIO. They argued that because the move to the CIO had been agreed to by a majority of members, the property of the union (including the headquarters, funds, and books) still belonged to that membership. They insisted, therefore, that Tobin's court order amounted to theft and was a renunciation of the union's vote.[120]

Padway, Casey, Neal, and Woxburg refuted this interpretation of events. Instead, they argued that they were fighting for those teamsters who did not agree to the AFL disaffiliation and who saw the June 9 vote as a coup launched by a minority radical fringe in the name of a subversive political agenda that directly threatened national security and President Roosevelt's war effort. The IBT representatives insisted that Local 544 was still affiliated with the IBT-AFL because they considered the June 9 vote illegitimate. In a mass meeting held with the Committee of 99 on June 19, these men made their position clear. Gathering at Eagles Hall, "about 2,000 AFL drivers who have refused to join CIO" cheered on the IBT officials. Woxburg talked about the Committee of 99's loyalty to the union and the nation, characterizing its members as believing in American democracy and standing courageously in opposition to "a group of subversive radicals who want to promote a revolution and use their union members as guinea pigs." James Bartlett, Sidney Brennan, Myer Lewis, and others also took to the stage to drive home the same argument: that they were the victims of a radical SWP plot to undermine the union, that they had been marginalized at the June 9 meeting, that their union had been hijacked by subversive forces, and that they now were seeking to set things right by salvaging Local 544-AFL as the body that represented its members' wishes.[121] Later that night, Casey reported back to Tobin that the meeting "was [a] real success" in terms of the number of attendees and the positive reception of their message. He believed that the program to take back Local 544 was "well underway."[122]

Part of the program to take control of the representation of the Minneapolis drivers was to undermine 544-CIO's independent contract negotiations with employers in the city. On June 17, the same day Local 544-CIO involuntarily moved to its new headquarters, it moved ahead with the strike it had declared on more than a dozen of the city's furniture companies. Emil Hansen had delivered the strike notice the day before to Lloyd McAloon, representative of the furniture dealer employers. Because the dealers did not provide an "acceptable proposition" by 8:00 p.m., Local 544-CIO led the drivers and helpers out on strike on the morning of June 17. Yet employers quickly stymied their efforts by securing a court order halting the strike and banning pickets. The employers argued that 544-CIO had violated the ten-day notice for calling strikes required under Minnesota's Labor Relations Act (1939) and, more significantly, that due to the recent split in the local between the forces loyal to Tobin and those that had "bolted" with the Dunnes, they did not know who was the legitimate bargaining agent.[123] At the same time that the Dunnes presented their group as the voice of the Teamsters in Minneapolis, sending Hansen to the furniture dealers with their demands, Casey and Neal (with the backing of Tobin) had continued to insist in communications with McAloon and other employer representatives that all contract negotiations and renewals would be handled by the AFL.[124]

With the strike weapon taken away from them and the AFL forces challenging their legitimacy, the leaders of 544-CIO decided to call the employers' bluff and to face off directly with Padway, Neal, and Tobin. They demanded employee elections certified by the National Labor Relations Board (NLRB), arguing that they would "put an end to the confusion which has been created by the contention of the employers that they do not know who represents their workers."[125] For the Dunnes and the other radical leaders of 544-CIO, the answer was clear: they were the legitimate representatives of the majority of the drivers in the city, as evidenced by the June 9 vote. As Farrell Dobbs later noted, the call for the NLRB elections was not just a demonstration of that confidence "in the real sentiments of the workers" but also a tactic to expose what he believed was the antidemocratic tendency of the 544-AFL forces, "since they were bound to oppose a democratic solution to the conflict."[126] Casey objected to 544-CIO's call for elections, deeming them unnecessary because he believed, as did Tobin, that the legitimate agent had been and always would be the AFL. Despite this objection—which was then used by the Dunnes to reinforce their argument that the "imported agents of Tobin" were "attempting to circumvent the democratic choice of the workers"—the demand was filed. As they awaited word from the NLRB, the 544-CIO workers called off their strike and returned to work, hopeful that the democratic process would vindicate them.[127]

Casey, Neal, and the organizers sent in to oversee the preservation of 544-AFL did not sit back and wait for those elections to take place. They instead took action to influence the drivers in Minneapolis to support the IBT. They not only held the morale-boosting meeting on June 19 with the Committee of 99 but also supported a boycott on materials transported by members of 544-CIO. At stake for the AFL were both the membership of the General Drivers Union in Minneapolis and the fate of the other IBT unions throughout the Midwest that Denny Lewis threatened with his regional organizing drive.[128] On June 18, Casey met with more than fifty representatives from the Central States Drivers Council and issued the order: "No trucks driven by CIO drivers will be permitted to go through," and AFL over-the-road drivers would not be allowed to drive trucks that had been handled by CIO drivers.[129] The disruptions began the next day, with the first "report of truck stoppage" coming from St. Paul. Casey explained to the press that the AFL-IBT had "150 to 200 agents at various transfer points in the northwest to carry out the boycott" and that they planned to "stop trucks at transfer points" but would not "do anything violent."[130]

Despite Casey's promises, violence erupted among the men on the streets. The boycott added pressure to an already tense environment, and the pending NLRB elections strained things even further. In a desperate attempt to shore up support for the AFL in those possible upcoming elections, some of the men loyal to 544-AFL cruised around the city looking to sign up workers. In many cases, the encounters were marked by anything but diplomatic persuasion. Local AFL supporters were bolstered by organizers the IBT sent from Detroit, including the young Jimmy Hoffa, who did not shy from physically attacking men who demonstrated support for the new CIO local. Things got so bad by June 21 that 544-CIO leaders sought a court order "restraining the AFL-544 from 'acts of violence' in signing up truck drivers and allied workers."[131]

Among those testifying before the court was Frank Kolinski, who told of how, as he was bringing a load of potatoes from a warehouse basement, he was surrounded by a group of men demanding to see his union button. When they realized Kolinski was wearing a CIO badge, the men ordered him to put on an AFL button, pulled him to the ground, kicked him, threatened him with a knife, and warned that "he would 'get it'" if he did not sign in support of the AFL. Kolinski said he agreed to sign but only because he was threatened. Edmund Gilmore testified to being followed by a group of men in a car who pulled him out of his truck and hit him when he stopped at a red light. And Frank Norman spoke of being surrounded at his workplace by a group of thirty-five to forty men who demanded he sign up, saying, "'This will be an AFL plant or you won't work.'" He managed to flee out a back door with several other workers who sought safety at the nearby CIO headquarters.[132]

Jake Cooper was not so lucky. Surrounded at his job on the loading dock of the Werner Transportation Company by fifty AFL men, including Gene Williams, who attempted to intimidate him into quitting if he did not leave the CIO, Cooper attempted to walk away but was beaten so badly he ended up spending six days in the hospital.[133] The struggle for control of the drivers in Minneapolis had taken a nasty turn.

It was because of these attacks on their members that the CIO representatives appealed to the court for a restraining order against the AFL men. But they also launched a campaign in the local press condemning the violence. Frank Barnhart, CIO director for the United Construction Workers Organizing Committee, claimed that "mobs of imported hoodlums [sent by Tobin] are raiding local truck terminals and warehouses, and at the point of knife and gun forcing CIO employes [sic] to wear AFL teamsters buttons and sign AFL pledge cards."[134] He also charged Minneapolis employers with working in "open collusion" with the AFL in the attempt to break the CIO's presence in the city. The local SWP branch agreed with Barnhart, reporting in the *Northwest Organizer* that "several CIO members were refused their pay-checks this week-end by their bosses until they had signed AFL cards."[135] And Miles Dunne and Farrell Dobbs, editors of the *Northwest Organizer*, denounced the "foul, slimy picture" and "brutal crimes" of "Tobin's Hitlerite Invasion of This City," arguing that the "rank and file cannot be forced into line with violence."[136] The 544-CIO contingent defended themselves as best they could when attacked by AFL "organizers" in the streets, but they never engaged in such violence directly. The Trotskyists in particular condemned such thuggery as unethical and unproductive: winning men to a union by force was a false victory in their eyes, for only through education and persuasion could loyal and dedicated members be won. They waged this battle for the union in the courts and in the press instead.

The NLRB-certified elections were all the more urgent now if 544-CIO was to survive. Yet 544-AFL's fate was not secure either. The violence ripping at the seams of the teamster community had created a volatile situation that no one seemed fully able to control. Tobin fretted about the IBT's reputation as the press broadcast the men's rough street tactics.[137] And Casey reported back to IBT headquarters about the difficulty of maintaining the allegiance of the drivers. He noted that "these fellows are like a pendulum on a clock which swings back and forth—CIO—AFL—CIO—AFL, depending entirely on who was the last group that talked to them." Casey found out that "the boys have two buttons—CIO in one pocket and AFL in the other, and they don't wear any button, but when an AFL comes up they start putting on the AFL button." It had become clear to him that "this thing is not at all won," and that just because they had some dues coming in did not mean they had the bulk of the nearly 6,000 members "solidly with us."[138] The optimism he had expressed after the June 19 mass meeting at Eagle's Hall waned, as fierce attacks continued in the city's streets. There was still no clear victor. Local 544-CIO gained the official backing of Philip Murray, and 544-AFL made strange bedfellows with the Communist-dominated Minneapolis Central Labor Union. But even as each side received significant endorsements from these other labor representatives, the fate of the drivers was still uncertain.[139] The NLRB dragged its feet in response to 544-CIO's request for elections, claiming that the "matter 'needed careful study.'" In the meantime, Minnesota state labor conciliator Alfred Blair responded to a request made by the IBT for "industry-wide certification as bargaining agent." He scheduled "blanket hearings" to begin June 30.[140] As Casey observed, the situation was far from settled.

Biddle under Fire: Proceeding with the Peacetime Sedition Case

While the situation in Minneapolis was becoming more chaotic, the thinking at the Justice Department in Washington about what to do with the Trotskyists became increasingly clear. By June 23, Biddle deemed it practical to proceed with the case. Hoover had already communicated to him his fears that the situation in the city could lead to strikes that would be harmful to the nation's defense preparations throughout the Midwest. And the turf war between the AFL and the CIO that resulted from the June 9 "bolt" certainly did not foster stability. With the German invasion of the Soviet Union on June 22, the SWP remained the sole voice on the political left protesting the war, which meant its adherents—including the leaders of 544-CIO—were now even more vulnerable to accusations of disloyalty and sedition. In this context, the attorney general took seriously the charges of subversion that had been made by the Committee of 99 for more than five months, by Tobin in his June 12 telegram to the president, and by Hoover in his internal reports to members of the administration throughout the spring and early summer of 1941.

On June 27, 1941, the Department of Justice took action. Armed with search warrants, four federal officials raided the SWP offices at 919 Marquette Avenue in Minneapolis and 138 East Sixth Street in St. Paul. Henry Schweinhaut had arrived from Washington to oversee the raids. As described by the sensational coverage in the local press, Schweinhaut and his men gathered up cartons of papers and hauled them out to waiting trucks. Photos of the marshals clearing out boxes from the party headquarters and carrying out "2 red flags and Trotzky [sic] photo" were splashed across the front page of the *Minneapolis Morning Tribune* under the screaming headline "Socialist Workers Party Offices Here Raided by U.S. Marshals. Leadership Faces Conspiracy Charges."[141]

Dismissing accusations made by the CIO and SWP that the raids were an "attack on organized labor" by the government taking sides in the 544 dispute, Biddle insisted that the prosecution was "brought under the criminal code of the United States against persons who have been engaged in criminal seditious activities."[142] But not everyone agreed with Biddle's explanation. Miles and Vincent Dunne, Kelly Postal, Ray Rainbolt, and the other 544-CIO executive board members rejected Biddle's argument that the union dispute had nothing to do with why the Justice Department targeted the Trotskyists in Minneapolis. Barnhart agreed and issued a joint statement with the 544 leaders. They pointed out that Tobin had known about the politics of the Dunnes and others in Local 544 for years but only took action against them when it became clear that he could not control the fate of the local. Protesting what they saw as a blatant attempt on the part of Tobin and the Roosevelt administration to quash their free speech rights, they argued, "This is not Hitler-Germany. . . . The people of this country still have a right to express their opinion about the policies of both Tobin and Roosevelt."[143] Rhetorically positioning themselves against the "tyranny" of Tobin, they vowed to "press [the CIO's] fight to win for the motor transport and allied workers of Minneapolis their democratic right to belong to an organization of their own choosing."[144]

The SWP also girded itself for battle. On June 28, in a confidential letter to all locals and branches, James Cannon put the raids in Minneapolis into perspective. "This is the beginning of a persecution and prosecution that we all expected," he announced. "We have not been caught by surprise." Rather than retreating from the attack, Cannon counseled action. "There is now available to us an unparalleled opportunity," he insisted, "to make more workers acquainted with our program and our activities than has hitherto been possible." The answer to the raids was not panic, "not even excitement," but "intensified work." It was "absolutely essential that all activities of the branches continue as hitherto" and that party members "hasten the collection of the War Chest fund." Although indictments had not yet been handed down, he insisted that "we shall need a huge amount of money to fight them."[145]

True to form, the Trotskyists continued to protest what they considered an unwarranted political prosecution as they awaited the indictments. On July 1, Carlson publicized a telegram sent to Biddle on June 30 from Cannon and Albert Goldman, the SWP attorney and party member from New York. In it they articulated the party's main objections to the raids and impending

Figure 2.3 Left to right: Major Lemuel B. Schofield (at the time of his appointment to the Immigration and Naturalization Service), Solicitor General Francis Biddle, and Attorney General Robert Jackson, Washington, DC, June 14, 1940. Biddle became attorney general the summer after this photo was taken. LC-DIG-hec-28807, Harris and Ewing Collection, Prints and Photographs Division, Library of Congress.

prosecution under the Smith Act. They refuted Biddle's claim that the union dispute had nothing to do with the decision to move ahead with legal action and argued that the looming prosecution was instead intended "to prevent thousands of workers from carrying out their democratically expressed desire to change from the AFL to the CIO. Your purpose in this prosecution is to give aid to the Minneapolis employers and to Tobin."[146] As such, Cannon and Goldman concluded, "the prosecution is a violation of the elementary principles of democracy for which this government claims to be fighting against the German Nazis"; they demanded that Biddle cease the action.[147] The next evening, July 1, members and leaders of 544-CIO turned out at a mass rally at the Lyceum Theater to voice a similar condemnation and vowed they were not going to stop their organizing or their struggle to win bargaining rights under the CIO because of the recent raids.[148]

In authorizing these raids, Biddle was criticized not only by the Trotsky-ists but also by civil libertarians. He had, after all, just authorized the first peacetime sedition indictments in more than 140 years. On the same day Biddle received the telegram from Cannon and Goldman condemning the raids, he found one waiting from the Reverend John Haynes Holmes. Holmes expressed how "greatly concerned" the ACLU was upon hearing the news of the impending indictments "under statutes penalizing mere opinions and advocacies apart from overt acts." Echoing Cannon and Goldman's reference to the wartime fight for democracy, he argued that "in these days particularly prosecutions for opinions or non-criminal activities are obviously dangerous to preservation of democracy." Questioning the constitutionality of the Smith Act, Holmes urged Biddle to reconsider the planned prosecution.[149]

Biddle responded to Holmes on July 10 in a tone that balanced reassurance with assertiveness. Positioning himself as a civil libertarian, Biddle reminded Holmes of "my own feelings with respect to the protection of constitutional guarantees" and assured him "that in the Minneapolis case the civil rights of no one have been interfered with." Referencing but not revealing his FBI sources, Biddle told Holmes that "persons there are being charged with con-spiring to overthrow the Government of the United States by armed force, and it is our considered judgment that there is abundant proof of such a con-spiracy." Furthermore, Biddle explained, "The 'raids' to which you refer were the execution of search warrants procured pursuant to law, and in all respects agreeable to constitutional requirements."[150] As someone who prided himself in his defense of civil liberties, Biddle tried to explain his position by pointing to the evidence that had led him to authorize the prosecution. The "abundant proof" of the conspiracy to violently overthrow the U.S. government during a wartime emergency had pushed Biddle to take action. Although he otherwise generally held back from going after seditionists—and took flack from Roos-evelt for months because of his hesitancy—Biddle made the move in this case largely because of the intelligence he received from the FBI.[151]

Despite Biddle's explanations, his detractors abounded. One of the stron-gest critics of Biddle's decision to prosecute under the Smith Act came from inside the Justice Department, revealing concerns within the Roosevelt ad-ministration over the use of the new legislation. In a July 14 memo to Biddle, Edward F. Prichard, special assistant to the attorney general, vehemently pro-tested the impending indictments, arguing that they constituted "a clear de-parture from that aversion to the repression of unpopular political opinions to which the defenders of constitutional liberty have always clung." The new law allowed for "punishment of mere political advocacy in the absence of some clear and present danger that the advocacy would incite unlawful action" and thus flouted the limited free speech safeguards that had been derived from the Supreme Court's *Schenck* decision since Holmes's protective application in his *Abrams* dissent. Hinting at his fear that the law, once implemented, would abet the growth of the domestic security state, Prichard warned that "if there is no imminent danger, the suppression of unpopular political opinion becomes a threat to the liberty not only of the political pariah and the outcast, but to the liberty of all those thousands of good democrats and progressives whose activities are suspicious . . . to agencies not far distant from your own august office." Prichard advised Biddle "not to institute proceedings under Title I of the Smith Act" lest we become a "pallid reflection" of Hitler in our attempt to defeat him.[152] Despite Prichard's warnings and the protestations of Holmes, Cannon, Goldman, and others, Biddle stood firmly behind his decision to move ahead with the case. In the balance between civil liberties and national security, the acting attorney general placed his weight with the latter and moved to indict.

3

"Socialism on Trial"

July 1–November 18, 1941

After authorizing the raids on the SWP offices in Minneapolis and St. Paul, the Justice Department was prepared to convene a grand jury in order to secure indictments against the twenty-nine. From the time those indictments were handed down on July 15, through the duration of the trial, which took place from October 27 through November 29, the SWP and 544-CIO protested what they believed was a wanton violation of civil liberties, as did the ACLU, progressive trade unions, concerned citizens, and the left-liberal press. At a time when the United States was standing up for democracy against fascist aggression abroad, it seemed to these critics a tragedy for their nation to sacrifice free speech rights in the name of national security. But the prosecution rejected their calls to apply the clear and present danger test as a protection for subversive speech and instead built its case on the grounds that the SWP was an illegal conspiracy. "The darling of the modern prosecutor's nursery," as Learned Hand described it, the conspiracy charge had been used against unions during the nineteenth century, as well as against political dissenters during the World War I era,[1] and so it made sense that the government would prosecute the Trotskyists in this way, especially since the nature of the Smith Act's advocacy provisions supported this kind of blanket conspiracy proceeding. Proving that the SWP and its members in Local 544 constituted an illegal conspiracy and had advocated fifth column activities became the focus of the prosecution's case during the trial that began in October.

Indicting the Twenty-Nine: The Blanket Conspiracy Charge Criticized and Defended

Before it could make its case in court, the government had to secure indictments. Convened in Minneapolis on July 1, 1941, the grand jury proceedings were veiled in "air-tight secrecy." Although the proceedings remain sealed, details of the testimony gathered for the hearings can be found in the report that federal agent Roy T. Noonan filed with the FBI on July 26. His account outlined the specifics of the interview process and included the affidavits of most of the forty-nine witnesses who appeared in court between July 1 and July 14.[2]

Certain themes emerged in the accounts of the witnesses who testified. First, there was the assertion that specific figures in Local 544 had clear ties to the SWP and that those figures either actively tried to recruit other union members into the party or gave preferential treatment in terms of job opportunities to those who joined the SWP and gave it 10 percent of their income. Likewise, some witnesses testified to their having lost work for not supporting the Trotskyists in the union.[3] Then there were the allegations of more dangerous things: revolutionary speech and actions on the part of certain 544 and SWP leaders. For example, Peter Bove testified that "on one occasion Grant Dunne said 'We believe we cannot gain our ends through legislation. Revolution is the only method'"; Franklin Page claimed he heard Grace Carlson insist, "'Armed seizure of power is the only possible means of overcoming our present capitalist system.'"[4]

Even more disturbing allegations were made by other witnesses who, like those interviewed by Perrin in April, swore that the Trotskyists were stockpiling weapons in anticipation of such armed revolt. John Novack claimed that Oscar Coover told him, "'We even have ammunition planted between the walls of churches and it is better than the Army's. It will go through an inch thick of armed plate.'" Ed Blixt testified that when he was a member of the Union Defense Guard, he saw "at least three boxes of ammunition and three boxes of tear gas," as well as "several rifles and pistols" stored by the group. Price Amo described an even larger cache among the guard, claiming "they must have had 600 or more guns at one time as all of the guards had at least one," and that he had heard a "rumor to the effect that the guns were kept on a farm near New Brighton." Several other witnesses also described the potential danger of the UDG.[5]

What the grand jury did not hear, however, was testimony from a handful of other witnesses who claimed never to have seen stockpiles of weapons or to have heard any of the 544 leaders speak of the violent overthrow of the government. James Morris, Grant Dunne's neighbor, told the agent who interviewed him that although he had never been in Dunne's home, he had no reason to think an arsenal was stored there. Anthony Seinco stated in his interview that "as far as he knew Postal only had two guns" that he used to hunt "gophers and rabbits."[6] Three other witnesses told the FBI that they knew the Dunne brothers and other 544 leaders and never heard any of them make revolutionary statements or mix their party politics with union business.[7] Although the FBI had taken their statements too, the government did not call these witnesses.[8]

The strategy proved successful. On July 15, the grand jury returned indictments against twenty-nine individuals: James Cannon, Grace Carlson, Jake Cooper, Oscar Coover, Harry DeBoer, Farrell Dobbs, Grant Dunne, Miles Dunne, Vincent Ray Dunne, George Frosig, Max Geldman, Albert Goldman, Walter Hagstrom, Clarence Hamel, Emil Hansen, Carlos Hudson, Karl Kuehn, Felix Morrow, Roy Orgon, Edward Palmquist, Kelly Postal, Ray Rainbolt, Alfred Russell, Oscar Schoenfeld, Dorothy Schultz, Rose Seiler, Carl Skoglund, Harold Swanson, and Nick Wagner. Bench warrants were issued for all twenty-nine, with bond fixed at $5,000 each.[9]

There were two counts to the indictments. Count one charged that those named had engaged in an "unlawful conspiracy from and before July 18, 1938, to date of the indictment" in Minneapolis, St. Paul, and New York, "to destroy by force the government of the United States" in violation of Section 6 of Title 18 of the U.S. Code (a Civil War era insurrection statute).[10] It charged that the accused had encouraged members of the SWP and others to join them in an impending uprising against the government by teaching that workers and farmers needed to take control of the country. It claimed that the accused had placed themselves in "key positions in all major industries" and in trade unions so that they could paralyze the nation's economy as the first step in that revolution. And it alleged that they had infiltrated the army to undermine its effectiveness and had created an armed Union Defense Guard to act as the nucleus of a proletarian army "to overthrow, destroy, and put down by force the duly constituted, Constitutional Government of the United States." It also charged that the defendants had stockpiled weapons for this fight and took their orders from the teachings of Lenin and Trotsky.[11]

Under count two (the Smith Act violation), the accused allegedly "advised insubordination in the armed forces with intent and distributed literature to the same effect," and "knowingly and willfully would, and they did, advocate, abet, advise and teach the duty, necessity, desirability and propriety of overthrowing and destroying the government of the United States by force and violence." In addition, count two charged that the accused did "print, publish, edit, write, circulate etc. literature with same intent," had "organize[d] societies and groups to teach the overthrow of the government," and had become "members of such groups, knowing the purpose thereof."[12] This was a broad condemnation, then, of alleged seditious speech, publications, and association.

The twenty-nine accused had six days to present themselves voluntarily to the authorities. William Thomas and D. J. Sharma acted as counsel for the Local 544 defendants along with Gilbert Carlson, Grace Carlson's husband, from whom she was estranged at the time.[13] They worked in conjunction with Albert Goldman and Arthur LeSuer, the attorneys for the other SWP defendants, to reduce the bail for each of the accused from $5,000 to $3,500.[14] On Saturday, July 19, Kelly Postal surrendered, followed on Monday, July 21, by the remaining fifteen of the defendants associated with Local 544. All but Carl Skoglund posted bail and were released on July 22.

Skoglund, who had applied for citizenship but was not yet naturalized, was incarcerated on July 18 on a separate deportation charge. Allegedly FBI agent Perrin had approached him earlier that year with the promise of a fast track to citizenship if he joined the Committee of 99 and informed on his fellow Trotskyists, but Skoglund had refused. When the sedition indictment was handed down, immigration officers stepped in and arrested him first. It was only after vehement protests from his friends and allies in the labor movement that his bail was reduced from $25,000 to $3,500. The CIO posted his bond, and Skoglund was finally released on July 25.[15] The other defendants in the sedition case—some of whom, like James Cannon, came to Minneapolis from New York—surrendered in the days after the July 15 indictment and either posted bail or, in the case of Goldman, Seiler, and Schultz, were released on their own recognizance.[16]

Although they surrendered their bodies to the authorities, the defendants refused to admit their guilt or to accept the validity of the indictments. From the very moment the grand jury's conclusions were announced, Cannon, Carlson, Goldman, Dunne, Dobbs, and others issued statements to the press, penned editorials, and delivered speeches condemning the indictments. They saw the SWP and Local 544-CIO as victims of an unjust political prosecution meant to quash the free speech rights of the Trotskyists because they opposed the war and to overturn the union's June 9 vote to leave the AFL.[17]

Indeed, at the time the grand jury hearings took place, the struggle over bargaining rights for drivers between 544-CIO and 544-AFL continued to rage. In early July, when the NLRB refused to act, 544-CIO filed its own petitions with the state's labor conciliator, Alfred Blair, calling for employee elections to settle the dispute.[18] In response, Blair held a series of hearings that ran concurrently with the federal government's convening of the grand jury in pursuit of sedition charges.[19] By the end of July, Blair's decision on these series of hearings was still pending. But he weighed the testimony from them in the context of the recently issued federal indictments and arrest warrants for most of Local 544's leadership.[20] That put those leaders in a weak position. To them, the timing of the indictment was no coincidence but yet another facet in the IBT's (and Tobin's) attack on their attempt to establish a militant industrial union affiliated with the CIO.[21]

The public response of the Communist Party USA (CPUSA) to the indictments reinforced the defendants' perception that theirs was a politically motivated prosecution, which was linked both to Local 544's decision to leave the AFL for the CIO and to their opposition to the war. Since the invasion of the Soviet Union in June, the Communists' volte-face made them staunch supporters of the fight against fascism; they viciously attacked anyone who opposed to the war, especially the SWP. At first, the CPUSA ignored the Trotskyists' plight: there was not a single article on the case in the *Daily Worker* at the time of the raids or indictment. It was not until August 16 that an article appeared, which supported the prosecution.[22] Although Milton Howard was critical of the Smith Act and of the FBI's intrusion into Local 544's business, he insisted that no one should defend the "Trotskyites," whom he deemed "a fascist fifth column" that "deserve no more support from labor and friends of national security than do the Nazis" because of their continued opposition to the war. Viewed in this light, he argued, the Smith Act prosecution was justified.[23] And in New York, a group of Communists within the Teamsters denounced the CIO's organizing drive—which by implication included Local 544's June 9 "bolt"—as a threat to national security.[24] Now that it supported the war, the CPUSA used it to skewer its political opponents within the trade union movement. Although the Communists did not have any influence over the government's decision to prosecute, the CPUSA's attack on the Trotskyists reinforced the defendants' belief that their opposition to the war and Local 544's internal union fight were the reasons for the prosecution.

They were not alone in this estimation. The CIO's Labor's Non-Partisan League (LNPL) noted how it was not until three years after the formation of the UDG that the Justice Department moved "against these allegedly subversive persons" in an action that harkened back to the days of the Palmer raids. It believed that not just "labor's basic rights" were at stake but also "fundamental civil liberties."[25] The American Civil Liberties Union agreed. Immediately after the indictments were handed down, Arthur Garfield Hays, the ACLU's general counsel, announced that his organization "would seek a test of the constitutionality" of the Smith Act. Because its provisions "penalize opinions and advocacies even in the absence of overt acts," Hays argued that they were "a violation of constitutional guarantees" and that they constituted "a political instrument of oppression against unpopular minorities and organized labor."[26] The editors of the *New Republic* shared the ACLU's concerns.[27] And I. F. Stone, in an acerbically worded essay in the *Nation*, expressed similar criticism of the indictments, noting that "for the first time in peace since the Alien and Sedition Laws of John Adams a mere expression of opinion is made a federal crime." Noting how only "1/260 of 1 per cent of the people of this country belong to the Socialist Workers Party," he also wondered if "the courts will find it possible to equate the faint cannonading of Trotskyist popguns with the firing on Fort Sumter."[28] Stone did not see the SWP's activities as being on a par with the insurrection launched by Confederacy and considered the application of the Civil War era statute grievously misplaced.

Other critics of the indictments communicated privately with Biddle to register their complaints.[29] Bruce Bliven of the New Republic was "a good deal disturbed" by the indictment because he did not see the clear and present danger in the case if the issue was mere advocacy of unpopular ideas.[30] Biddle's retort underscored what he and the Justice Department had come to believe was the real and pressing threat presented by the accused. Because "such conduct is forbidden by statute"—the Smith Act—Biddle insisted that he did not "have any alternative but to require the prosecution to go forward."[31]

What Biddle did not admit in his response to Bliven was that his sense of having "no choice" but to move ahead with the case may have come not just from his commitment to uphold the law but also from a much more practical concern. When he authorized the raids in June and backed the grand jury hearings in July, Biddle was acting attorney general: President Roosevelt had not yet decided who would officially replace Robert Jackson, who had risen to the Supreme Court on June 12. During those summer months, Roosevelt actively courted other candidates for the position of attorney general. Biddle may have moved against the Trotskyists, in part, to demonstrate he was tough on the anti-interventionists and worthy of replacing Jackson. In late August, he received the nomination. Although Biddle never admitted that this concern influenced his decision to prosecute, it may have been a factor that weighed against the Trotskyists.[32]

In his correspondence and in statements to the press at the time of the indictments, Henry Schweinhaut echoed Biddle's public explanation for the prosecution. Responding to criticism from Ira Latimer of the Chicago Civil Liberties Committee, Schweinhaut insisted that the "prosecution was not lightly considered" and was "instituted only after an extensive investigation had demonstrated that the leaders of the Socialist Workers Party actually envisaged and laid plans for the overthrow of our present form of government ... by armed force."[33] The day after the indictments were handed down, the Minneapolis Daily Times noted how Schweinhaut "said the story seemed fantastic to him when first reports drifted into Washington; but further study, and accumulation of more reports, convinced him leaders of the party were 'serious in their intent.'"[34] As former head of the Justice Department's Civil Liberties Unit under Attorney General Frank Murphy, Schweinhaut had spent two years working to protect Americans' basic rights.[35] But, like Biddle, the unsettling FBI reports, along with the climate of the times (and perhaps, too, a desire to heighten his professional profile) persuaded him that it was right to take action.[36] When Biddle ordered Schweinhaut to go out to Minneapolis to oversee the case, he did not hesitate.[37]

Girding for the Fight: The Prosecution and Defense Square Off before the Trial

Despite the government's attempt to justify the prosecution of the Trotsky-ists, detractors continued to insist that the grounds upon which the case was built were unconstitutional. The ACLU argued that in the absence of "any overt acts or even of any 'clear and present danger,'" the charges that certain of the accused's utterances or publications were illegal—charges that rested on the new statute of the Smith Act "not previously applied"—violated the First Amendment of the Constitution. In August the organization not only once again urged Biddle to drop the case but also now promised "to engage in the defense with a view to testing [the law] in the Supreme Court."[38]

The question of the constitutionality of the Smith Act was of concern to the prosecution insofar as it wanted to be prepared to head off such a chal-lenge in court. In the weeks before the trial, Anderson and Berge drafted memos arguing for the constitutionality of the law and for the inapplicabil-ity of the clear and present danger test to the case.[39] Anderson wanted to make sure he took a position consistent with the attorney general's office in eliminating the need to question at trial whether the clear and present danger test applied to the defendants.[40] Berge supported this approach, arguing that such constitutional questions were not valid before juries and that Congress's enacting of the Smith Act "made certain definite and specific acts offensive in and of themselves." Thus, Berge assured Anderson, "there is no need to set up a barrier which must be hurdled before a guilty verdict is returned such as is a necessity when passing on the criminality of acts which become criminal only under certain circumstances." The law assumed the context of a clear and present danger, and so the test need not be applied to the defendants indicted under its statutes.[41]

Anderson and Berge's interpretation of the Smith Act and inapplicability of the clear and present danger test echoed, in some ways, attitudes other Americans held with respect to the nation's wartime crisis atmosphere and what that meant for civil liberties. In particular, legal scholars took up this question in a series of articles that appeared in the fall, winter, and spring volumes of the *Bill of Rights Review*, a quarterly published by the Bill of Rights Committee of the American Bar Association. Struggling with the challenge of how to strike that balance between liberty and security during times of national crisis—like the one America found itself in since the outbreak of the war in 1939 and the fifth column scare that accompanied it—these legal thinkers offered various solutions. While some wrote about the need to protect those liberties no matter what the alleged threat to national security, others expressed a willingness to sacrifice them.[42]

By the fall of 1941, Biddle fell into the latter camp. As the case against the Trotskyists unfolded in court, Biddle published an article for the *Review* in which he implicitly supported the constitutionality of the Smith Act and dismissed the applicability of the clear and present danger test in cases dealing with national security. He argued that "in times of stress" when "the life of the nation is at stake," it was more important to safeguard that life than "temporary individual considerations." In a play on Holmes's dissent in the *Abrams* case, Biddle asserted that "swift preparation for war cannot be achieved in the leisurely decisions which come from the free competition of ideas in ordinary times." Although he recognized that the United States was not at war, he believed that "we are in a curious twilight zone in which, on account of the war in Europe and its threat to us it may be necessary at any time to take steps which would not be considered in ordinary times." Biddle argued that in such extraordinary times, like war or the "twilight" state America found itself in, some rights had to be sacrificed in order to preserve democracy, lest democracy itself—and all the rights it guaranteed—be lost forever.[43]

Such a Faustian bargain was not one all Americans were willing to make. Left-wing and liberal-minded individuals around the country became increasingly aware of the case as it developed over the late summer and early fall of 1941, both through media reports (like the stories in the *Nation* and the *New Republic*) and by direct appeals made by the SWP and the Civil Rights Defense Committee (CRDC). The CRDC, created in July 1941, raised funds for the defendants' bail and counsel but also sent out mass mailings to individuals and groups around the nation to gain public support for its campaign against the prosecution.[44] Some individuals who heard about the case from either the CRDC or the SWP wrote directly to Biddle with their concerns, arguing, for example, that "if we are not respectful of all people's opinions, no matter how mistaken they may be, in war, we will lose the ends for which the fighting is undertaken."[45]

Such criticism, though perhaps uncomfortable for Biddle, who prided himself on being a defender of civil liberties,[46] did not influence him to drop the case. The defendants were arraigned as planned on August 11. Although defense counsel requested ninety days to prepare motions and demurrers, the prosecution protested. Anderson and Schweinhaut pushed to have the case brought to court as soon as possible. Despite the defense's best pleas, the Court decided "that any attack upon the indictments must be in writing and filed in the Clerk's office not later than September 1" so that the case could be added to the top of the docket when the court reconvened on September 23.[47]

The defendants considered this development part of the government's attempt to "railroad" them to trial. It was presented by the *Industrial Organizer*, the official organ of 544-CIO, and the *Militant*, the SWP's newspaper, as yet further evidence of the "Tobin-Roosevelt machine['s]" desire to crush the rebellious union local.[48] And James Cannon, in a speech delivered at the party's Trotsky memorial meeting in New York that August, described the entire case, including the rush to trial, as a government "frame-up" in the sad tradition of earlier labor prosecutions, like the Haymarket trial, and of political suits, like the Sacco and Vanzetti case. Repeating his long-standing argument that he and the other defendants were targeted because of their opposition to the war and as a political favor to Tobin, Cannon cast the defendants as victims of capitalist injustice and as fighters in a heroic struggle for labor and free speech rights.[49]

The defendants' sense of abuse at the hands of the government was reinforced on September 25, when Judge Joyce rejected all of their pretrial motions. Their demurrers to the indictments were rejected, as were their motions for severance, for a bill of particulars, and for the application of the clear and present danger test to the Smith Act.[50] Joyce also turned down the defense attorneys' request to have at least three months to prepare their case, setting the date for the opening of the trial on October 20.[51] Anticipating a lengthy and costly proceeding, Cannon instructed SWP members to carry on their party work and remain active at their posts, so that the money that would have been used to defray the cost of party members' attending the proceedings could be spent on the defense. Since the government was "showing every determination to rush the case through," Cannon communicated the urgency of having the party close ranks behind the defendants.[52]

As if having their motions denied was not bad enough, the defendants also had to grapple with the disappointing findings of the state labor conciliator, Alfred Blair. He had decided on September 18 to certify 544-AFL instead of 544-CIO as the bargaining agent for drivers in Minneapolis. In many ways, this decision was a foregone conclusion given Blair's opposition to the Trotskyists and his alliance with Brennan, the FBI, Goldberg, and Green that dated back to April. The elections that 544-CIO requested were denied, and 544-IBT AFL was granted bargaining rights.[53] Claiming to have 4,215 men as members in good standing, Local 544-AFL convinced Blair it was the legitimate bargaining voice for the drivers in Minneapolis, despite evidence presented in the hearing that such numbers were padded by 544-AFL's claiming men to its ranks who had not paid dues to its union since the June 9 bolt.[54] Local 544-CIO's representatives smelled a dirty deal not only in the cozy relationship Blair had with AFL and IBT leaders but also in his failure to reflect in his decision any of the extensive CIO testimony that called into question the legitimacy of the support for 544-AFL that was won through intimidation and violence.[55] The 544-CIO and its SWP supporters blasted the decision and vowed to appeal. But no matter how defiant they remained, they also could not help but recognize how devastating the developing sedition trial had been to their attempts to organize the workers in Minneapolis. If the prosecution was pursued as a political favor to Tobin, it was now paying off in the systematic undermining of the rebellious 544-CIO.[56]

But things truly went from bad to worse for the defendants in early October, when they were confronted with the shocking and tragic news that one of their own, Grant Dunne, had committed suicide. The *Militant* reported how "shortly after 6 p.m." on October 4, Dunne was "found fatally wounded on the floor of a bedroom in the apartment in which he lived with his wife and two of their four sons." Also discovered was "a 22-target pistol . . . at his side. He had been shot through the right temple."[57] His wife, Clara, told police that she had been concerned about him for some time and had recently urged him to get out of the house to visit his brother Miles. She had left clothes out for him and was in the kitchen with their ten-year-old son when she heard the shots.[58] In trying to make sense of this awful tragedy, the party's newspaper cited Dunne's poor health related to the "shell-shock" he had suffered during the Great War. His wounds sustained fighting in the Battle of the Argonne Forest were both physical and mental and had haunted him since his return in 1919. Although he eventually found work alongside his brothers Miles and Vincent in the coal yards of Minneapolis, and played a significant leadership role in the 1934 strikes, Grant "never made a full recovery." And the recent pressures of both the sedition prosecution and the attacks on 544-CIO seemed to have become too much for him to bear.[59]

Yet as the *Industrial Organizer* noted, "Ironically, the federal government (which has charged Grant together with 28 other members of Local 544-CIO and the Socialist Workers Party, with 'subversive conspiracy') found itself honoring Brother Dunne with military services in the national cemetery at Fort Snelling."[60] Hundreds of mourners gathered there on October 7. His brothers, Vincent, Miles, Fenton, and Paul Dunne, along with his friends Carl Skoglund and George Frosig, served as pallbearers.[61] Farrell Dobbs delivered a moving and passionate eulogy.

Figure 3.1 Grant Dunne, Harry DeBoer, and Gilbert Carlson (left to right) entering the courthouse in Minneapolis, late summer 1941, during the time of the indictments. Grant Dunne committed suicide in October before the trial began. Courtesy Hennepin County Library Special Collections.

In his remarks Dobbs described Grant's remarkable life, noting how, like his brother Vincent, he also had to go to work at a young age to help support the family. Many years later, after surviving his injuries in the war, Grant educated himself in math to secure a job as an estimator in a construction company to feed his wife and four sons. With the Depression, Grant lost that job and threw himself into the working-class political struggle in Minneapolis. Dobbs explained how Grant's efforts at union organizing, first in the coal yards and then among the drivers, were made "under the severe handicap of his physical infirmity as a result of his war wounds," and yet he never complained. And Dobbs acknowledged that it was Grant who "picked me out from behind a coal pile—where I labored daily—bewildered and confused by the maelstrom of events. And he set my feet on the high-road of the working class (political) movement."[62] Dobbs mourned not only a man he so loved and admired as a friend but also the comrade who brought him, and many others, into the movement.

Dobbs then launched into an attack on the Roosevelt administration, which he implicitly blamed for his friend's untimely death. Noting how the government had gone after those who opposed the war, Dobbs argued that "Grant Dunne was caught up in the vortex of this whirlpool of persecution indicted by the federal government for alleged seditious conspiracy, made a victim of this witch hunt because he was against Roosevelt's war program." And, Dobbs pointed out, "This they did to a man who was himself a victim of the last war." Such troubles weighed heavily on Grant's mind, as did his worries that his own sons may have to go fight in the war then raging in Europe. The combined pressures became too much for him, Dobbs argued, calling on his fellow defendants, SWP members, and 544-CIO brothers to remember Grant and honor his memory by continuing his fight:

> Let us bury him with the honors of a soldier, in the liberation war of the workers. Write his name on the banner—of his union—and his party—and here at his funeral—let us strike up once again—the forward march—to carry that banner forward—in spite of everything—to the final victory of the workers—and the free world of emancipated labor.[63]

Dobbs's fellow defendants and their supporters in the party and the union took up his call and girded for the fight. Cannon in particular continued to speak out against the prosecution, delivering a speech at a mass meeting in Chicago on October 10 in which he declared that he and his fellow Socialist Workers would not be cowed by the government's case against them. Cannon argued that "when we go on trial they will not drag us in there like repentant slaves to repudiate what we have said and what we have done." Instead, "We will go into that court room not as defendants at all, but as accusers of the prosecutors and the system they represent."[64] He voiced this defiance once again in his political report to the plenum on October 11, remarking that "the real test of a workers party is its ability to stand up under the attempts of the class enemy to intimidate it and scare it out of existence." When facing the sedition charges, he insisted that the policy will be "not to renounce, not to water down the revolutionary doctrines of our Party, but to defend them openly and militantly in court." And he argued that outside of the courtroom the party also had to "struggle to function legally as long as possible."[65] Cannon practiced what he preached and forged ahead with his candidacy for mayor of New York, even as he remained in Minneapolis for the sedition trial.[66]

Grace Carlson shared Cannon's commitment to continuing the party's work even as it suffered the costs of the sedition trial. She also embraced his assertion—one that was approved in a resolution at the plenum—that the defendants would not back down from their commitment to the party's revolutionary doctrine, "but on the contrary, [would] defend it militantly." In a letter to her friend, mentor, and regular correspondent Natalia Sedova (Trotsky's widow), Carlson explained that for the SWP members "the court room will be a forum from which we shall speak to the American workers about the evils of the corrupt capitalist system and the necessity for a revolutionary overthrow."[67] Undaunted, the Trotskyists continued to advocate their provocative beliefs on the eve of the trial.

While Cannon and Carlson focused their energies in the weeks before the trial on clarifying the party's position to its members, the CRDC and the ACLU tried to reach out to the general public on behalf of the defendants. Each organization published its own pamphlet in which it criticized the impending trial. In *Witch Hunt in Minnesota*, James T. Farrell, the CRDC's chairman, penned an impassioned foreword in which he argued that "freedom of speech is meaningless if it is freedom to agree with those who are in power." He declared that as Americans "it is our highest duty to remain free in a world of the most brutal oppression and tyranny. And we remain free men by defending the liberty of others, as well as of ourselves, whether or not we agree with them."[68] The ACLU similarly emphasized the consequences of the case for the civil liberties of all Americans. In the pamphlet it issued in October, entitled *Sedition! The First Federal Peacetime Prosecution for Utterances and Publications since the Alien and Sedition Act of 1798*, the ACLU reprinted the written exchange between Hays, Holmes, Baldwin, and Biddle from earlier that year. The ACLU allowed itself to have the final word in the pamphlet, insisting that the origins of the case were rooted in Roosevelt's political debt to Tobin; there was no clear and present danger involved. As such, the civil rights organization argued, "In order to prevent its establishing a precedent it is essential that the case should be vigorously defended and that any conviction obtained should be appealed to the highest courts."[69]

On the eve of the opening of the trial there was thus a clear divide between the defense (and its supporters) and the government prosecution (and its backers) over the origins, nature, and significance of the case. Perhaps the one thing both sides could agree on was the seriousness of the matter: in the eyes of the defense, civil liberties were on the line; for the prosecution, national security was at stake. In the atmosphere of the deepening war crisis abroad, how to strike the balance between these two issues vital to American public life would be fought out in a criminal courtroom in Minneapolis.

The Trial Begins: Opening Statements

The first Smith Act trial opened in the Minneapolis federal courthouse before Judge Matthew Joyce on October 27, 1941, at 10:00 a.m. The proceedings had been postponed a week to accommodate Joyce, whose mother was ill. In the relatively small thirty-by-fifty-foot chamber the preliminary examination of the jurors took place on the first day of the proceedings.[70] Made up of eleven men and one woman with two female alternates, the jury was impaneled on October 28.[71] To the dismay of the defense, not one of the jurors was a trade union member. Instead, the jury was composed of a janitor's wife (Dora Peterson), a newspaper publisher (B. A. Gimstead), a plumbing laborer (Elmer Peterson), two store clerks (Duane Reese and Oscar Anderson), two farmers (Anton Anderson and Charles Barta), a lumber salesman (Glenn Ross), two small-business owners (Stanley Speltz and Lloyd Nelson), a retired garage manager (Louis Christenson), and a bank executive (Joseph Downes). Only one of the jurors lived in Minneapolis (Downes); the remainder came from surrounding rural counties.[72] As the *Industrial Organizer* explained, "The defense attorneys, after they got through striking off the names of some of the bankers and corporation executives, did not have any challenges left and had to be satisfied with the jury as it was."[73]

Later that day, Victor Anderson addressed the jury with the prosecution's opening statement. After outlining the two counts of the indictment, Anderson explained the government's understanding of the criminal conspiracy in question. He insisted that in this case, under the relevant statutes, there was no need for the prosecution to prove the accused had committed an overt act because "the conspiracy itself is made unlawful." Despite defense counsel Albert Goldman's objection that this was a legal question upon which the jury should be instructed after it heard the evidence, Anderson was allowed to push ahead by claiming that in defining conspiracy in this way, he was merely trying to establish what the government needed to prove for a guilty verdict. In a rather bold assertion, Anderson insisted that the conspiracy "can be established by circumstantial evidence" and that the very plan and purpose of the SWP was the conspiracy.[74] Hence the prosecution's focus would be on proving the defendants' membership in the party and their knowledge of the conspiracy such membership allegedly constituted. The trappings of the party—including its dues, membership books, meetings and other gatherings, and forms of discipline that constituted its structure as an organization— would thus be subjected to probing during the trial.[75]

The specific conspiracy that the party was alleged to have entered into was to overthrow the U.S. government by force. Anderson explained to the jury how the SWP viewed all governments outside of Soviet Russia as imperialistic and in need of overthrow and that it planned to do this in the United States in a number of ways, which had been outlined in the specific charges under each count of the indictment. Party members would effect this revolution by winning to the SWP workers and farmers in key positions, so that even if party members were a numerical minority in the country at large, "their people" would be located where they could most efficiently disrupt society and trigger the violent overthrow of the government. Allegedly they would use trade unions as part of this plot. Those party members eligible to enter the military would also "kick" in the army to disrupt its morale and undermine its mission, so that when the time came for the revolution, the soldiers would "turn their weapons against their officers." In addition to these far-reaching tactics, Anderson asserted that the SWP had been behind the creation of the Union Defense Guard in Minneapolis, which, the government contended, was "established for the sole purpose of forming the nucleus of a military organization to be used against the armed forces of the United States."[76] In each of these ways, and in all of them combined, it was alleged that the SWP was engaged in the conspiracy to violently overthrow the government of the United States.

Anderson further informed the jury that the prosecution would show how the party urged its members to secure firearms to carry out their program and that ultimately they were following the orders of Leon Trotsky in planning their evil deeds. Because of that connection, Anderson argued, the prosecution would lay out Trotsky's ideas for the jury, showing how they encouraged revolution as a carefully managed program, not as a single, violent mass uprising dependent upon large numbers of supporters. The U.S. attorney claimed that the government would show the court how one of the defendants brought part of this revolutionary plan back to America after visiting Trotsky in Mexico (the notion of setting up a military operation in Minneapolis under the guise of Local 544's Union Defense Guard) and how the party as a whole spread its revolutionary ideas via the *Appeal*, the *Militant*, and other publications.

Ultimately, Anderson declared, the government planned to demonstrate that the accused advocated Marxist ideas that were in themselves inherently unlawful because, according to Anderson, they depended on the advocacy of violent revolution.[77] Thus the crux of the government's argument was that the party and the Marxist ideas it was founded upon were illegal. In this sense, socialism itself was put on trial. The prosecution deemed the SWP a revolutionary party that would use force to achieve its program, be that through the infiltration of the armed forces or the creation of special union defense corps, and thus, it contended that any of the defendants knowingly connected with it was guilty of conspiring to violate the laws under which they had been indicted.[78]

The link between the SWP and Local 544 was also an essential component of this conspiracy, according to the prosecution. Anderson explained to the jury that the government would demonstrate how the SWP came to control Local 544 in Minneapolis, as a way to achieve its revolutionary ends. Part of the evidence it would present also included testimony from workers who felt pressured by their union leaders to join the SWP in order to keep their jobs. Through such tactics of intimidation, Anderson alleged, the party gained control of the union, which was one step in implementing its larger revolutionary program.[79]

While much of Anderson's opening statement focused on explaining the substance of the government's case, it was also a carefully constructed speech that was intended to trigger an emotional reaction from the jurors. At certain points in his discussion of the SWP's activities, Anderson played on popular fears of alien infiltration by emphasizing how the radical organization had ties to a leader located in a foreign land, displayed only red flags in its meeting hall, and conducted its business under the shadow of portraits of Lenin and Trotsky. And although he stated in his explication of the conspiracy charge that the SWP's adherence to the Marxist principles of redistribution of property was not part of the charges in question, Anderson raised the specter of class warfare to demonize the defendants and to alienate the jurors further from the accused. In closing, Anderson commented confidently that if the prosecution proved what it contended, he was sure the jury would return a verdict of guilty.[80]

The defense vehemently disagreed. Albert Goldman rose and began his opening statement by reminding the jury that not all of the accused were members of the SWP. Some had been members in the past but were no longer, and others had never joined the ranks of the party. Such distinctions, he argued, were important, especially given the way the prosecution defined the ties of the conspiracy, a definition the defense, nonetheless, planned to refute. And even more important, Goldman insisted, were the larger issues that were at stake in the trial: the liberties of the accused, as well as the great principles of freedom of speech, press, and assembly upon which the nation was founded.[81]

Those freedoms were at risk, Goldman argued, because of the nature of the prosecution's case, specifically its reliance on the conspiracy charge. Goldman urged the jurors to "know the difference between . . . a political movement . . . and a conspiracy hatched in the darkness of night for the purpose of committing a crime." The SWP was created in the open, he explained, and although it was based on principles with which Anderson and the jury may not agree, that did not make it an illegal conspiracy. The position of the defense, Goldman told the jury, was that the accused had a First Amendment right to free speech that allowed them to hold and advocate their beliefs, however unpopular they may be.[82]

Goldman thereby adhered to the strategy that Cannon and Carlson had outlined before the opening of the trial. He did not deny that their beliefs were revolutionary, but he explained that the defense would show how the SWP's understanding of revolution was not what Anderson claimed it to be: the party predicted that violence would be a part of future change (as capitalists would resort to violence to oppose the rise of socialism), but it never advocated the use of violence to bring about that change. In order to demonstrate this to the jury, the defense would share with it details of the party's business, in terms of its dues structure, meetings, forums, and publications. Confident in the innocence of the accused with respect to the conspiracy charges, he also promised that the defense would "try to recollect for the benefit of the Jury and for the benefit of the prosecution, what the speakers said at those mass meetings and let you judge whether or not they advocated the violent overthrow of the Government of the United States."[83] In addition, Goldman explained that he would demonstrate to the jury, through witness testimony and exhibits, how the SWP engaged in legitimate political campaigns, including Carlson's recent run for Senate in Minnesota and Cannon's race for mayor of New York City. Such evidence, he argued, would show that the objective of the party was to win a majority to its ideas through education and the ballot box, not to organize a conspiracy to overthrow the government by force.[84]

Likewise, Goldman asserted, the party's interest in trade unions—and the fact that many of its members were active in Minneapolis Local 544—did not indicate a conspiracy to control those unions. Instead, Goldman insisted, Trotskyist union activism had secured the best kind of democracy in the ranks, since SWP members honored the principle of majority rule. Such had been the case in Local 544, he argued, where the real opponents to democracy were the likes of Daniel Tobin, who had tried to impose a receiver on the local when its members voted to affiliate with the CIO. When Goldman tried to expand on this point—his attempt to introduce at trial the "political debt" theory of the origin of the case—Anderson jumped to his feet and protested.

Judge Joyce upheld the U.S. attorney's objection and instructed the jury to disregard the statement.[85] This would not be the last time Goldman would find his attempt to discuss this theory muzzled by the court.

Turning his attention to the prosecution's other accusations, Goldman admitted that the defendants were opposed to the war but insisted that there was no evidence that they had or would sabotage the war effort. Again, he insisted, there had to be a distinction between political beliefs and illegal acts. And in its support for military training under trade union control, Goldman explained, the party demonstrated its distrust of elite generals in the capitalist system and its belief that workers needed to defend themselves—not to overthrow government but to protect the "interests of the soldiering masses" against capitalist abuses.[86]

Interrupted at this point so that the court could adjourn for the day, Goldman resumed his opening statement at ten o'clock the next morning. He turned his attention to refuting several more of the prosecution's accusations. First he explained that because of the Voorhis Act (1940), which made "it illegal for a party to be part of an international organization," the SWP had officially severed its ties to the Fourth International and gave up its original Declaration of Principles, and so, he insisted, the prosecution should bring neither into the courtroom as evidence against it. Next, Goldman tackled the question of Local 544's Union Defense Guard, which the prosecution pointed to as evidence of the defendants' overt act of rebellion. Rejecting that interpretation, Goldman promised that the defense would show the real reason for the UDG's creation as a response to the Silver Shirts' threat. Any attempt to make this more than it was, he insisted, betrayed what the defense claimed was a government "frame-up" of the accused.[87]

Finally, Goldman turned to the issue of the defendants' Marxists beliefs. While the party defended the Soviet Union, it distinguished between the workers' state and the Soviet government, and so too should the jury, he argued, if it were to understand the SWP. Likewise, while some of the defendants admired Trotsky and believed in his ideas as the best hope for mankind, some did not, and that was something else the jury needed to distinguish. And although the party supported the idea of the Russian Revolution of 1917, that did not mean that it advocated the same for the United States at this time. Ultimately, Goldman argued, these beliefs were not relevant to the case. The real issues, he insisted, were "Did we advocate the overthrow of the Government by force and violence? Did we incite people for the violent overthrow of the government? That is the heart of the question." The party's prediction that there would be violent class struggle at some time in the future did not constitute such advocacy, he argued, because the SWP's followers could not create something that would come about of its own volition (class struggle) and because they actually preferred a peaceful transition to socialism.[88] The prosecution's accusations to the contrary, he claimed, not only represented a clear violation of the defendants' First Amendment rights to free speech but also embodied a fundamental misunderstanding of the political beliefs it condemned. Goldman closed by insisting that the evidence the defense would bring forth during the trial would show that the defendants had a constitutional right to express their beliefs—a position he hoped the jury would support with a verdict of not guilty.[89]

Goldman and Anderson had presented the jury with two very different versions of events and two very different interpretations of the law. The defense contended that the SWP was a legitimate political party and that its members, including those in Local 544, had a protected First Amendment right to advocate their beliefs. Denying that they had engaged in overt acts of rebellion or had advocated such illegal behavior, Goldman insisted that the defendants were innocent and intended to use the clear and present danger test to make his case. The prosecution rejected the notion that the SWP was a legal political party, contending that it constituted an illegal conspiracy whose stated objections included overthrowing the government by force. Anderson insisted that the defendants not only took up arms once in their creation of the UDG but also were prepared, through their influence over Local 544, to sabotage the nation's war effort and advocate revolution in the context of the current wartime crisis. In sifting through these consequential legal and constitutional questions, it would be up to the jury to decide which side presented the more convincing case

"Socialism on Trial": The Prosecution's Case

With the opening statements concluded, it was time for the prosecution to make its case. Anderson called the government's first witness, James Bartlett, on October 29. This would be the first of seven times Bartlett would be called to the stand. Before he was sworn in, Goldman moved that the other witnesses—of which there were more than three dozen for the prosecution—not be allowed in the courtroom during Bartlett's testimony for fear that they would echo his version of certain encounters and events. Judge Joyce, unconvinced by this argument, denied the motion and allowed all the witnesses to remain in the room, privy to each other's testimony.[90]

As the prosecution's lead witness, Bartlett was asked about a number of topics. All were focused on proving the government's position that the SWP was an illegal conspiracy to overthrow the government by force and that those who were connected to it were guilty under the two counts of the indictment. To prove these links, Bartlett was asked to name who among the defendants were members of the SWP, who were the most active in attending party meetings, what was included in the party's Declaration of Principles, and how the SWP membership cards were used. On his first day of testimony, Bartlett positively identified Vincent Dunne, Miles Dunne, Dobbs, Skoglund, DeBoer, Coover, Cooper, Hudson, Palmquist, Hansen, Postal, and Kuehn as members of the party. He also painted a picture of a disciplined organization with its own headquarters, membership cards, and publications that advocated the revolutionary principles laid out in the party's founding declaration.[91]

Anderson followed up on Bartlett's testimony about the SWP's founding ideals by reading excerpts from its Declaration of Principles. Goldman objected on the grounds that the original version of the document was no longer binding on party members, but Joyce overruled. Anderson carried on, reading passages that emphasized the revolutionary agenda of the SWP, the role of working-class militias, the party's relationship to workers, and its internationalist perspective and loyalties.[92] The U.S. attorney thus used the SWP's own words against it; he laid the groundwork for his conspiracy argument by identifying what he believed was the criminal revolutionary agenda within the party's original founding document. Anderson then asked the court for permission to recall Bartlett[93] and called two more witnesses to the stand: FBI agents Thomas Perrin and Roy Noonan.

Perrin's testimony was intended to demonstrate to the jury the SWP's foreign and radical commitments. He told of having confiscated a red flag and a framed picture of Trotsky when he raided the party's headquarters in June. Both items were dramatically presented before the jury as government exhibits while he spoke.[94] Noonan's testimony echoed Perrin's, describing the facts of the June raids in sensational fashion. But while Anderson attempted to use both men's accounts to demonize the SWP as an underground organization loyal to a foreign communist power, Goldman was able to pull out on cross-examination testimony to the contrary. Just because the party's headquarters were raided did not necessarily make the organization criminal, and the fact that the agents were freely admitted to the premises where the literature they subsequently seized was publicly displayed worked against the argument that the SWP was a hidden conspiracy.[95] Whether the jury would be convinced of the relevance of the party's openness, or whether it would be swayed more by the agents' dramatic recounting of the materials seized in the June raid, was unclear at this point. For the time being, the first full day of testimony had drawn to a close, and court was adjourned.

The next day Anderson called Bartlett to the stand again. This time he asked his star witness to recount the content of speeches made and conversations had during certain party meetings held at 919 Marquette Avenue (the SWP's offices in Minneapolis) with an eye to drawing out evidence of the defendants' seditious utterances. Having been a member of the SWP for a short time in the past, Bartlett alleged that at one meeting in 1938 there was a conversation about the differences between the Socialist Party and the SWP during which, Bartlett claimed, those at the meeting said that unlike the SP, the SWP believed in armed overthrow of the capitalist form of government in order to establish a dictatorship of the proletariat. Although he did not identify specific defendants as having uttered these revolutionary statements, Bartlett was allowed to describe this recollection, over Goldman's objection, clearing the way for additional allegations of party members' sedition and their shared revolutionary program.[96]

During the remainder of his testimony that second day on the stand, Bartlett spoke about the links between the SWP and Local 544, in terms of specific defendants (who were members of both organizations) and in terms of the influence of the party's broader revolutionary agenda over the union. He named Vincent Dunne, Clarence Hamel, and Emil Hansen as party members who pressured 544's rank and file to contribute 10 percent of their salary to the party, allegedly so that the SWP could build a base in the trade union movement. And he explained how he had heard Vincent Dunne, along with Carl Skoglund, Max Geldman, Carlos Hudson, and Emil Hansen, discuss how the party would use the trade union movement to foment a general strike in order to create a revolutionary situation, from which it could overthrow the government.[97] During this line of questioning, Anderson also entered into evidence the SWP pamphlets *What Is Trotskyism?* and *Trade Union Problems* to substantiate Bartlett's claims about the purpose of the SWP's takeover of Local 544. But, as with the Declaration of Principles, Anderson only read into the record selected excerpts that supported his star witnesses' interpretation of the party's agenda. Despite Goldman's objections, Bartlett was allowed to testify that class warfare was the "gist" of the latter pamphlet's argument.[98]

In an attempt to draw out what it believed were the defendants' desire to replicate the Russian Revolution on U.S. soil and their loyalty to Trotsky's instructions for fomenting that revolution, the prosecution also entered into evidence the pamphlet *Lessons of October* and a photograph showing Bartlett and his wife (along with Harry DeBoer and his wife) meeting with Trotsky in Mexico in early 1940. The photo in particular was used to dramatic effect, passed slowly by the jury as Anderson questioned Bartlett about the ties between the SWP members in Local 544 and this foreign communist leader. Specifically, Bartlett was asked about the relationship between Trotsky and the UDG. Bartlett testified that Trotsky told him during his trip to Mexico that he had instructed Vincent Dunne and James Cannon, via Emil Hansen, to establish such a force as the "nucleus of a workers army." To drive home these accusations, Bartlett spoke about the UDG's formation and its use of armbands and badges, which were then also placed into evidence by Anderson, as the martial trappings of this allegedly insidious force.[99] Through the combined effect of Bartlett's testimony and the physical evidence passed before the jury, the U.S. attorney hoped to drive home his point that the UDG was a foreign-inspired but domestically manifested dangerous fifth column in America. Despite Goldman's objection that because Trotsky was not named in the indictment he therefore could not be considered part of the conspiracy, Anderson insisted that he could: the government included Trotsky as a co-conspirator even though he had been dead for more than a year. Joyce allowed Bartlett to testify about Trotsky's connection with the defendants and his alleged role in the creation of the UDG.[100]

Bartlett's lengthy testimony continued on November 3, interrupted briefly by Anderson's calling two additional witnesses: Thomas Smith and Malcolm Love. Both men were members of an Omaha Teamsters local and were used by Anderson to demonstrate how Dobbs, Dunne, and Al Russell allegedly tried to impose the influence of the SWP over that city's trade union as well. Although Smith testified that Dobbs gave him party literature (samples of which were placed into evidence), he also stated during his cross-examination by Goldman that he never heard Dobbs or Russell advocate the overthrow of the government in any of their speeches or in any private conversations. Smith admitted that he joined the SWP not because he was pressured to or because he feared he would not have access to jobs otherwise but because he admired the work of its members on behalf of laborers. Love's explanation for why he temporarily joined the SWP was the same as Smith's, and he too insisted that he was never told of any plan to overthrow the government.[101] These two prosecution witnesses, then, were not the most forceful advocates of the government's case.

In order to recover from the minor setback that Smith's and Love's testimony represented, Anderson entered additional inflammatory excerpts from SWP pamphlets into evidence and recalled Bartlett to the stand. In order to prove one of the government's main contentions—that the defendants, through their involvement in the SWP, constituted an illegal conspiracy to teach the overthrow of the government by force—Anderson questioned Bartlett about the party's dissemination of *The Communist Manifesto*. Bartlett

Figure 3.2 James Bartlett (far right) and his wife pose with Leon Trotsky and Harry DeBoer (far left) and his wife in Mexico, ca. 1940. Bartlett would later break with the SWP and become the government's star witness at the Smith Act trial of his former comrades (including DeBoer). This photo was placed in evidence during that trial. Folder 7256 U.S. v. Dunne 201–220, box 195: Exhibits, Minnesota, Fourth Division, Minneapolis, 1890–1983, Records of the District Courts of the United States, RG 21 (National Archives at Kansas City, Kansas City, Missouri). Courtesy National Archives.

claimed that Dunne, Geldman, Hudson, and Coover had spoken to him many times about the publication, recommending it to him as embodying the same revolutionary principles as the SWP. Goldman tried to have this line of questioning thrown out, arguing that the *Manifesto* was written in 1848 and therefore could not be seen as an expression of the party's current principles. But Joyce allowed it. Schweinhaut defended the government's position from the prosecution's table, arguing that "the second count of the indictment charges conspiracy to, among other things, advocate, or I mean to distribute and disseminate literature which advocates the overthrow of the Government by armed force. We say this one does. It is just another link in the complete chain and another part of the whole picture."[102] Despite Goldman's continued objections to the government's use of radical literature, particularly selected excerpts or titles not penned by any of the specific defendants, the prosecution repeatedly advanced its link-in-the-chain logic to implicate the accused in the alleged seditious conspiracy. And that logic convinced Joyce, who allowed the prosecution free rein in such exchanges with witnesses.

In addition to helping it establish the advocacy of revolutionary ideas on the part of some of the defendants, Bartlett's testimony was used by the prosecution to amplify the characterization of the SWP made by Anderson in his opening statement. Raising the specter of the party as an international communist body, Bartlett described how the two red flags and the framed portrait of Trotsky seized in the June raids normally hung just above where speakers sat in the meeting hall of the SWP's Minneapolis offices. In yet another theatrical flourish, Anderson had Bartlett point out the exact location of these radical, international trappings on a map of the party's headquarters. Demonstrating the SWP's alleged dominance of Local 544, Bartlett explained how Trotskyists in union office gave preferential treatment, including better access to jobs, to those in the SWP. And revealing how the party tried to recruit additional workers to the revolutionary cause, Bartlett claimed that certain defendants had asked him to distribute party literature in the form of pamphlets to "as many sympathetic members as there were in the union." He also stated that he was familiar with several issues of the SWP *Internal Bulletin*. These included one from April 1940, from which Anderson, in melodramatic fashion, then read an excerpt that spoke of the overthrow of capitalism and the existence of class struggle, even during times of war.[103]

During this part of his direct examination by Anderson, Bartlett also admitted to his role in the Committee of 99 and to having cooperated with the FBI. He spoke of meeting with Agents Perrin and Noonan in late February and early March, linking that cooperation with what he described as a sincere concern about the revolutionary agenda of the Trotskyist leaders of Local 544, a concern that had led him to leave the party in 1940. He argued that at that time he "did not like their attitude towards the questions that were discussed, and I quit of my own volition. . . . The questions discussed related to the overthrow of the United States form of Government, and I did not believe that was right, and I quit."[104] The prosecution knew that the defense would try to discredit Bartlett because of his role in the intra-union fight and attempted to head them off by having Bartlett offer an independent reason for his cooperation with the FBI.

The defense team was not convinced by this story. During his cross-examination of Bartlett, Goldman attempted to demonstrate how the witness had long harbored animosity toward the Dunne brothers and other Trotskyists, citing an incident during an unemployment relief rally in 1934 when Bartlett, then a Communist active in Minneapolis's Unemployed Council, had publicly denounced some of the defendants as "Trots" who "sold out the workers."[105] Bartlett denied Goldman's allegations. While he admitted that some of the defendants might have come under fire in the CPUSA's press, "all I know is that I never attacked them."[106] It would seem that for the time being it was Goldman's word against Bartlett's on the issue of the 1934 rally. And for a jury of average Minnesota citizens with no associations with trade unions or the political left, Goldman's attempt to draw out Bartlett's alleged Communist bias most likely fell on deaf ears. For those well versed in the internecine conflicts on the political left, the suggestion that Bartlett had been active in the Communist Party during the early 1930s was intriguing, but the evidence for any continued Communist commitment by 1941 was lacking.

Goldman then tried another approach, asking Bartlett about his jealously over losing the union election in January 1941.[107] Goldman's line of questioning was intended to discredit Bartlett and to show that the results of the union elections were determined not by the SWP but by the wishes of the rank and file.[108] Bartlett stuck to his guns, however, insisting that he did not need to wait until the results of the January elections or for the FBI's aid to confront the union leaders. He asserted that by November 1940 "I was already openly criticizing and attacking the Socialist Workers Party. I was not afraid of making public my hostility to them. I had already stopped paying my ten percent contribution to the party. . . . It was open warfare."[109] Again, Bartlett did not hide his opposition to the Trotskyists but presented it as authentic, independent of the FBI, and rooted in his political disagreement with the party's revolutionary agenda, not the product of his election defeat.

Goldman struggled to undermine Bartlett's credibility. At times it even seemed like the defense attorney was making the prosecution's case. When Goldman pushed Bartlett to detail what he had been told about fomenting a revolution, for example, Bartlett claimed that Dunne told him the SWP "would undertake the revolutionary overthrow of the Government by force and violence either when there was a depression period or a war situation or a political scandal, or any one of two or all three of them." Although Goldman managed to push Bartlett to admit that the SWP's plan to win over a majority to its agenda was based on education, not force, and that the violence of the revolution would come first from capitalist resistance, not the party or the workers, he allowed the witness to testify again to the defendants' talk of revolution.[110] After hearing Bartlett's assertion that certain defendants made statements "as late as January and February, 1941, in which they advocated the armed overthrow of the government," could the jury follow the distinctions Goldman was trying to draw?[111] Goldman seemed willing to take the risk. His refusal to deny that the defendants engaged in such speech—he only wanted to clarify the specifics of the kind of revolution the SWP supported—reflected the Trotskyists' plan to maintain its radical principles even when under fire in the federal courthouse. Though perhaps an honorable position, it may not have been the most effective as a defense.

Bartlett finished this round of testimony on November 5. Later that day the prosecution called Agent Noonan to the stand again to address the question of how the case originated. Aware of the defense's contention that the investigation was tied to the struggles internal to Local 544—something that Goldman had tried to draw out in his cross-examination of Bartlett—Schweinhaut asked the FBI agent about the origins of the investigation. In testimony that implicitly rejected the notion that the prosecution resulted from Tobin's June telegram, Noonan asserted that the FBI "had several investigations of the Socialist Workers Party in their files for the past years," and that it was "in the latter part of 1940" when "there were two or three specific investigations, and in this case it was intensified in February of this year." When Goldman tried to introduce the "political debt" theory on his cross-examination of Noonan—asking the agent if he knew that his superiors in Washington had been instructed to get an indictment after receiving Tobin's telegram—Anderson's objection was upheld and the line of questioning suspended.[112] For the second time the court blocked the defense's attempt to present the Tobin connection to the jury, thereby denying it the ability to build a convincing case for its charge that the prosecution was a politically motivated reprisal that reached all the way to Washington, DC. Anderson and Joyce rejected the legitimacy of such claims, but they also presumably knew what the implications would be had they allowed their airing in open court: the case would be seen as a gross miscarriage of justice fabricated by President Roosevelt and the attorney general to protect the war preparedness program from those who opposed it. That interpretation of events was something neither Anderson nor Joyce was willing to allow the jury to hear.

At this point in the proceedings, the prosecution had spent almost six days presenting its case. It was to carry on for eight more, bringing to the stand thirty-three new witnesses, recalling Bartlett twice, and introducing close to 250 exhibits. Most of those who testified named specific defendants as having been associated with the SWP and alleged to have heard some of them engage in talk of violent revolution. Others spoke about the stockpiling of guns and the alleged revolutionary purpose of the UDG. And still others linked the defendants' opposition to the war to their supposed plans to interfere with the armed forces and spur a proletarian revolution. All would add to the picture of the seditious conspiracy the government wanted the jury to see.

Both Walter Stultz and Franklin Page contributed to this image. On November 6, the prosecution questioned Stultz, a teamster from Omaha who was then serving time at Sandstone prison for interference in interstate commerce. He named Al Russell and several other members of his local, Local 554, as members of the SWP. More damningly, Stultz also claimed that in one conversation with Russell (the time and place of which he could not recall) the defendant proclaimed that in order for workers to secure control over industry and the government, "'We have got to grab a rifle and go get it.'"[113] Page, a former student at the University of Minnesota, testified to having heard Grace Carlson make seditious comments when she spoke before the Socialist Club in November 1940. He claimed that when she spoke of how workers were to achieve political power, there was "no discussion of legal means, balloting of any kind." Instead, "She advised her listeners to accept willingly their training in the armed forces under the Selective Service Act because as she pointed out, it would train them in the use of weapons they would have to have when the time for that seizure of power came."[114] Page's testimony, like Stultz's, condemned a specific defendant but also indicated what the prosecution contended were the contours of the alleged illegal conspiracy engaged in by all the accused: advocating the violent overthrow of the government.

Roy Wieneke, a member of Local 544-AFL, also gave testimony damaging to the defense, claiming that Vincent Dunne told him during a UDG meeting in 1939 that "the idea for a Union Defense Guard had come from Trotsky and that masquerading under the object of fighting fascism or the Silver Shirts, it would in reality be the first part of the militia for the Socialist Workers Party."[115] Wieneke then claimed that he heard Dunne and Geldman in early 1939 say that since the United States "was about to enter the war this would be a very good time to start knocking at the back door, as they said, to start agitating for the revolution."[116] And he repeated a story similar to that already made by other witnesses when he alleged that Jake Cooper had told him he would need to join the SWP if he were to get a good job in Minneapolis because the party controlled the local union.[117] Wieneke thus offered testimony that sustained several of the prosecution's main contentions about the defense. Goldman, however, was somewhat successful in casting doubt on his statements. He clarified for the jury Wieneke's ties to the original Committee of 100 and the current 544-AFL, thus linking him to the intra-union fight, which the defense contended was the real reason for the prosecution. He also revealed how rote Wieneke's statements were with regard to the defendants' alleged advocacy of revolution: when pushed, he could not give details and tripped up on certain inconsistencies in his own testimony.[118]

But that did not stop Anderson and Schweinhaut from continuing to make their case. When Wieneke stepped down, they called to the stand John Novack, a member of Local 544 who never joined the SWP, despite the entreaties of Geldman, Palmquist, Orgon, and Coover (who, he claimed, used the union hall to conduct party business).[119] Repeating much of the sensational testimony he offered before the grand jury in July, Novack alleged that Palmquist said the process of selective service would provide "a good time for these members of the Socialist Workers Party—that is, the ones that are drafted will spread dissention and misunderstandings in the army." He claimed that Palmquist argued that party members "'amongst the draftees [could] cause dissatisfaction, complain about food, etc., and of course, talk about the Socialist Workers Party and things like that.'"[120] In addition to substantiating the allegations that Trotskyists intended to interfere with the armed forces, Novack testified to their alleged revolutionary plans. He claimed that Coover said the principles of the party called for the armed overthrow of the government and that during one conversation with Coover, a man named Rube (who was not one of the defendants) boasted, "'We have guns and ammunition planted in the walls of churches. We have bullets that will go through an inch and a half or two inches of armored plate, which is better than the United States army.'"[121] Although Goldman objected to this testimony because Rube was not one of the accused, the court allowed it. Once again, government witnesses voiced before the jury lurid details of the Trotskyists' alleged plans for armed revolution.

During his cross-examination of Novack, Goldman tried to connect the witness to Tommy Williams and James Bartlett to establish prejudice and thereby discredit him. Although Novack insistently denied such ties, when pressed by Goldman he admitted that he was not entirely convinced by Rube's boasting about the Trotskyists' stockpile of weapons, believing it was an exaggeration born of bravado.[122] And significantly for the defense, the prosecution had uncovered no weapons in its search of the two party offices and offered none into evidence during the trial.

Despite this failure to uncover a hidden stash of guns, Anderson and Schweinhaut called additional witnesses to drive home the ways in which the defendants allegedly advocated the violent overthrow of the government and actively prepared for the day of revolution (thereby bolstering the case for the Smith Act violation). A parade of men and women were brought to the stand to testify to their having heard certain defendants call for the armed overthrow of the government, for the spread of the SWP's influence in trade unions to help achieve that revolutionary end, and for the exploitation of the wartime emergency to sow dissension in the ranks of the armed forces and thereby speed the workers' takeover of society.[123] Some also spoke of the defendants' direct involvement in the UDG's target practices and the 1938 "mobilization," evoking images of an armed corps of laborers led by SWP radicals.[124]

Goldman pushed some of these witnesses to admit that they could not recall much about the teachings of the SWP aside from the party's alleged desire to overthrow the government by force.[125] He thereby cast some doubt on their reliability by raising the possibility that their statements may have been coached. But those statements, even if rote, were also ultimately quite sensational and constituted the more memorable moments of these witnesses' time on the stand. They also reinforced the evidence given by Bartlett and the others in the preceding days.

Similar testimony was given by the prosecution's remaining twenty witnesses over the last five days the government spent making its case. Although Goldman was occasionally able to cast doubt on some of this testimony, as he had done with a few of the earlier witnesses, the sheer number of those who paraded to the stand to hammer away at the same arguments was overwhelming. Among them were many who had testified before the grand jury in July, including Violet Williams, Harry Holstein, Eugene Williams, and Ed Blixt. One by one they came and spoke of their knowing which defendants were affiliated with the SWP, and which had spoken out about the need for armed revolution through the use of the UDG or by the infiltration of the armed forces. Dunne, Coover, Geldman, Skoglund, Cooper, Cannon, Carlson, De-Boer, Hansen, Dobbs, Palmquist, and select others were pointed to again and again as advocates of a grand revolutionary plan.[126] When Goldman succeeded in pushing one witness to admit that he or she had not actually heard any of the defendants explicitly call for violence,[127] Schweinhaut and Anderson came back with another who could certify that they had. Such was the case with Sidney Brennan, one of the original participants in the Committee of 99, who claimed that he had heard Skoglund, Dunne, and others call for the overthrow of the government by force and that he heard Carlos Hudson explain how SWP members would infiltrate the army "and that when the time came the workers would have guns and they could turn them around on the different governments."[128]

To reinforce their case further, Anderson and Schweinhaut continued to offer into evidence dozens and dozens of exhibits—almost all of them pieces of SWP literature that had been seized in the June raids. While the extensive witness testimony formed one flank of the prosecution's attack on the defense, the use of the party members' own written words against them constituted the other. It was in these moments of the prosecution's work that the contention that this was a trial of political ideas seemed most viable. Proving the conspiracy charges by putting the ideas of an unpopular political movement on trial through the introduction of literature associated with (but often not penned by) those in the movement was not a new government strategy, as the 1886 trial of the Haymarket anarchists attests; it also would not be the last time such a strategy was used, as the 1949 Smith Act trial of the Communist Party leaders would show.[129]

The logic that Schweinhaut advanced to justify the admission of *The Communist Manifesto* into evidence—that any materials in the defendants' possession that promoted revolution were integral to the conspiracy to advocate the overthrow of the government—was used to bring the articles, speeches, issues of the SWP *Bulletin*, and other SWP writings into the courtroom. On November 12, for example, he read to the jury an excerpt from the *Appeal* in which the growing strength of the Fourth International was celebrated, quoting how "'it took only two and one-half years of the last war to give rise to the first revolution. The next war will work more swiftly.'"[130] On November 14, among the things he read from were a SWP resolution that called for the continued agitation of class struggle even during war and a pamphlet by Dunne (*Revolutionary Tasks and Work in the Trade Union Movement*) that advocated the party's influence among workers and called for labor's "unifying [of] its armies" to defend itself.[131] On the last day of the prosecution's case, Anderson quoted from a number of exhibits, including Carlson's November 1940 radio speech in which she advocated workers' taking up arms and the SWP pamphlet *Trotsky's Military Policy*, which declared "to fight fascism at home means to fight against the war."[132] With this final presentation and implicit denunciation of the defendants' political beliefs, the government rested its case.

No Fifth Column Too Small: Judge Joyce's Directed Verdict

The same day the prosecution rested its case, the defense filed a motion for directed verdicts of not guilty on both counts on the grounds that there was insufficient evidence presented at trial.[133] Attorney M. J. Myer argued the motions for the defense, insisting that "there is no proof in the record here of any conspiracy, other than the party itself," which the defense refused to see as a conspiracy. He argued that a conspiracy has to include an act in the present not something that *may* develop in the future.[134] The evidence entered by the government—especially the excerpts from certain writings—dealt only with analysis of historical events and predictions for the future, not expressions of immediate opposition to the government.[135] Calling the government's interpretation of the UDG as an imminent threat a "preposterous idea" given that it had been disbanded for some time,[136] he argued that there was no real evidence to sustain count one.[137]

Myers also called for the second count of the indictment to be withdrawn, arguing that the "conspiracy [charged] is one which advocates the overthrow by force and violence" and that there was a clear lack of evidence to sustain that charge. Appealing for a speech protective application of the test set forth in the Supreme Court's *Schenck* decision (and in Brandeis's concurrence in

Whitney), Myer argued that "the lack of proof in the record of a clear and present danger . . . [raises] the question that any conviction here on this record, as it now stands, would be a violation of the Constitutional rights of the defendants."[138] And even if that conspiracy was the party itself (which the defense was not conceding), then the government must prove that every defendant knew what the "program and the principles of the party were." Myers asserted that for several of the defendants the prosecution did not demonstrate that knowledge.[139]

In responding to Myer's statement, Schweinhaut addressed "the legal questions by counsel" and Anderson discussed "the evidence as to the defendants."[140] When it came to the question of the clear and present danger test, Schweinhaut argued that in terms of the "sections involved in this proceeding—no court has ever held that as to such section the clear and present danger doctrine should be applied." Citing the 1925 *Gitlow* decision, which upheld the New York State anarchy law upon which portions of the Smith Act were modeled, he noted how the Court distinguished between "the type of case before the court" in 1925 and that in *Schenck*, where the clear and present danger test was formed. In demanding that this test be applied to protect free speech in a sedition case—and by extension to apply the test to the Smith Act itself—the defense was asking for something not yet accepted by the courts.[141] Although Holmes had used his test to limit federal restrictions on speech in the 1919 *Abrams* case, the application was in his dissent. And the Court's majority decision in the 1937 *Herndon* case relied on the clear and present danger test protectively, but against a state law, not a federal statute.[142] Driving home his point, Schweinhaut argued, "It seems to me an absurdity to say that the Federal Government could not punish, in order to prevent incipient rebellion, those who conspire to do anything about it, even though they may never be able to do anything."[143]

Even if the government was to concede the point (which it was not) and allow for a consideration of the clear and present danger that the defendants allegedly represented, Schweinhaut reminded the court that there was testimony about the nearing time of revolution—"that the party spoke of revolutionary situations as coming during the war or during the crisis which follows a war"—and that there were witnesses who testified that several of the defendants urged men who had already registered for the draft to "create unrest and dissatisfaction in the army." Taking the statements and the actions together, he argued, "It is not necessary either for the court or for counsel to say that a jury cannot find from that that there was not an imminent or reasonably imminent danger that the evil which the Congress sought to protect against was present."[144]

In his response to Myer, Anderson focused his comments on the evidence with respect to the defendants. He denied Myer's assertion that the prosecution failed to present evidence of a conspiracy, arguing that "we predicate the existence of a conspiracy on all the evidence before the Court," including all the "documentary evidence . . . all oral testimony . . . and all the inference that can be legitimately arrived at from both [the] oral and the written testimony or evidence before the Court." He also defended the legitimacy of count one, even if the events alleged had not yet taken place. In yet another stunning and sweeping definition of the kind of conspiracy the government had the power to criminalize—one in which the overt act had yet to occur— Anderson explained that the prosecution had proved a continuous conspiracy under which it "is a continuing crime until its object has been accomplished, or the defendants have been apprehended and incarcerated so that they are no longer able to carry out the conspiracy."[145] Finally, Anderson asserted, there was no evidence to show that "any member disassociated himself from the conspiracy." Thus, according to the prosecution, the defense had no grounds for its request.[146]

After reading the motion and hearing the interpretations of both the defense and the prosecution, Judge Joyce was ready to issue his finding. First, he told those assembled in language that echoed Holmes's decision in *Schenck*, "I might say that we should remember that the character of every act depends upon the circumstances in which it is done." But rather than invoke Holmes's test in the way that the defense had called for—as a defense of free speech—Joyce echoed its original meaning, as a justification for placing limits on that fundamental right: "The First Amendment, while prohibiting legislation against free speech, cannot have been and obviously was not intended to give immunity for every possible use of language." On those grounds the judge denied the constitutional rights of the defendants to preach revolution. He argued that in passing the Smith Act Congress acted so that "it need not wait until destruction is at the door before the door can be barred," and that ultimately "it had in mind the preservation of our liberties" through the implementation of such restrictions.[147]

Joyce then further revealed his take on the case and the motion at hand, expressing an opinion that was in line with that of the prosecution as well as with the original supporters of the Smith Act. He stated, in what became one of the most quoted portions of his findings that day:

> It may seem unreasonable to fear, when the size and power of the United States is considered, that this comparatively small group of individuals could accomplish successfully the objectives charged. But it is well to remember on this

point that Hitler went around in a greasy raincoat in his early days and was belittled for his efforts. The law is there. It binds all and any two or more who break its provisions are amenable to its penalties.[148]

Invoking the specter of Nazi Germany, Joyce echoed the logic that had been articulated by supporters (including Biddle) of the nation's strict new sedition law: that it was paramount for America to secure its national defense against all forms of fifth column threats—no matter how seemingly small or inept—lest democracy itself be lost to the cunning deeds of nefarious plotters. This was the central debate that supporters of the Smith Act and defenders of civil liberties had been engaged in for more than a year. The Faustian bargain that Roosevelt, Biddle, Anderson, Schweinhaut, and now Joyce seemed ready to make was clearly grounded in the contemporary wartime emergency context—the "circumstances in which it is done." The fifth column scare not only had enabled the passage of the Smith Act in June 1940 but now, it seemed, was also sustaining the first prosecutions under that law, all in the name of securing democracy.

The work of the FBI agents, like Perrin and Noonan, who had been involved with the case from the very beginning, also reinforced for Joyce the perceived need to prioritize national security over free speech. His reputation among agents as "'one of the friendliest of the judges to the FBI'" who had "'a high degree of confidence in the agents, often calling them to his chambers for information on a specific point,'" may help explain his near total support for the prosecution's case during the trial and his "greasy raincoat" comment. Joyce, deemed an "'eminently qualified and eminently satisfactory'" judge by the bureau, had come to share much of its and the government's understanding of the case.[149]

Further demonstrating his agreement with the prosecution's interpretation of the law, Joyce insisted that "the unlawful agreement [in question] need not have been in any particular form. It is sufficient that the minds of the parties met understandingly. A mutual, implied understanding is sufficient so far as the combination or confederacy is concerned." Thus the question of guilt or innocence hinged on the weak test of "implied understanding" of the alleged conspiracy.[150] Such an interpretation had grave implications for freedom of speech and assembly.

The implications for the defense's motion were equally significant and negative. Joyce refused to withdraw the indictment in toto and, instead, issued a much narrower finding. Joyce told those assembled in the courtroom that "as to the defendants Hagstrom, Schultz, Seiler, Frosig and Wagner there is not sufficient evidence to go to the jury, and not sufficient evidence of knowledge of the party by such defendants or that they participated in the activities to overthrow the Government by force and violence, and the motion as to such defendants will be sustained." As a result, "their bonds will be exonerated and they will be discharged from further attendance at this trial." But, Joyce declared, "As to the remaining defendants, the motion is denied."[151] The indictments against the remaining twenty-three defendants stood. Their fate still rested with the jury.

Goldman and the defense team had their work cut out for them as they readied themselves to present their side of the case. Outside the courtroom, the Trotskyists also confronted difficulties. They continued to face opposition from their Communist rivals who, tasting blood in the water, circled back for a new round of attacks. Speaking before the Communist Party faithful in Minneapolis, Robert Minor did not address the trial directly but launched a diatribe against Trotskyist fifth columnists, arguing that the United States could learn a great deal from Moscow when it came to dealing with such domestic traitors.[152]

Beyond the confines of this internecine fight, the public atmosphere within which the Trotskyists found themselves fighting for their freedom against sedition charges was also grim. The sense of the national emergency had deepened that fall. German submarine attacks on American vessels in the North Atlantic, begun in September, continued. And tensions increased between the United States and Japan when diplomatic communications broke down over the China question. In this context, and in the wake of the prosecution's lengthy and intense case, the Trotskyists prepared to defend their opposition to war, their call for socialist revolution, and their trade union work. It would be a tall order.

4

"If That Is Treason, You Can Make the Most of It"

November 18–December 8, 1941

When the time came for the defense team to present its case, it faced a difficult, but not impossible, challenge. As they had since the grand jury handed down the indictments, the defendants insisted on the applicability of the clear and present danger test to their situation, arguing that it rendered them innocent and made the Smith Act unconstitutional.[1] Even though their motion to have this test applied to the second count of the indictment was denied by the court at the outset,[2] Goldman and his team remained committed to this argument. During the trial, they invoked not only Justice Oliver Wendell Holmes's test as applied in a speech protective fashion in his *Abrams* dissent but also his call for tolerance in his *Schwimmer* dissent. The defense insisted that the SWP was a small organization that did not pose imminent or grave danger to the nation and argued that in robust democracies it was necessary to preserve "freedom for the thought that we hate," including the SWP's socialist teachings.[3]

This argument drew from a relatively new interpretation of free speech theory that had been embraced by many civil libertarians in response to the First Red Scare. But it was also based on a set of ideas that some Americans were coming to abandon, or at least alter, in the face of the new wartime crisis, and, it rested on a legal interpretation that the Supreme Court had not yet invoked to restrict federal limitations on free speech.[4] Drawing on such a theory for their defense was a strategy that ultimately proved only partially successful for the Trotskyists. But escaping the charges was not their prime concern; rather, it was remaining true to their revolutionary principles, using the courtroom to herald those beliefs, and defending their right to hold them.

"If That Is Treason, You Can Make the Most of It": The Defense's Case

The defense opened its case on the afternoon of November 18. Goldman led the legal team as he had during the presentation of the prosecution's case, playing the roles of both lead attorney and one of the defendants. Unlike the prosecution, which had taken eleven days and called more than three dozen witnesses, the defense took five days and called only sixteen people to the stand. Among its key witnesses were James Cannon, Vincent Dunne, Grace Carlson, and Farrell Dobbs. Having heard so much being said about them by the prosecution's witnesses in the preceding days, these defendants would now have the opportunity to tell their side of the story.

But in addition to presenting their defense in court, the Trotskyists planned to turn themselves, the accused, into the accusers by drawing out during their testimony all that they deemed wrong with capitalist society.[5] The witness stand became their soapbox for publicizing their beliefs and building public support for an acquittal, as well as the venue for proving their innocence to the jury. And they extended their proselytizing beyond the courthouse doors to the pages of both the *Militant* and the *Industrial Organizer*. The coverage of the trial that was meant to educate the public cast Goldman and the defendants as labor heroes in an epic battle against the "bosses" within the tradition of the 1934 strikes and the great political trials of Haymarket, the IWW leadership, and Sacco and Vanzetti.[6] Inside the courtroom, the defendants hoped that if they could at least win the sympathy and understanding of the jury— and perhaps even convert a few members to socialism—then they could secure a verdict of not guilty.[7] But given what the jury had just heard over the previous eleven days, this was a bold, and perhaps somewhat naive, strategy.

First called to the stand was James Cannon, who provided the lengthiest testimony for the defense. Over the course of three days he answered Goldman's questions, which were aimed at both properly explaining the principles of the party to the jury and refuting the prosecution's claim that the SWP was a threat to the nation. Throughout his testimony Cannon returned to his central assertion that he and his comrades were members of a militant and revolutionary party, but not necessarily a violent one. Parsing that identity would require several days and much verbal acumen.

After reviewing the institutional history of the party, Cannon clarified controversial aspects of its Declaration of Principles, which had already been entered into evidence by the prosecution. He argued that these passages had been either alluded to incorrectly by some of the government's witnesses or read out of context by Anderson. In particular, Cannon clarified the socialist vision of a new order as one without class conflict and one where government would "wither away" because it would not be needed. How society got there, Cannon explained, was not something he or his party could foment, for that process was inherent in the internal contradictions of capitalism itself, as Marx taught them. Rather, he told the jury:

> All that our agitation can do is to try to foresee theoretically what is possible and what is probable in the line of social revolution, to prepare people's minds

Figure 4.1 James Cannon and Albert Goldman at the time of the trial (fall 1941). Courtesy Hennepin County Library Special Collections.

for it, to convince them of the desirability of it, to try to organize them to accelerate it and to bring it about in the most economical and effective way. That is all agitation can do.[8]

In this way Cannon presented the SWP as a militant party that sought to advance the move to socialism, but he explained that it was limited in its actions by the restraints of what would be capitalism's own, internal transformation. Leading an inevitable movement, he argued, was not the same as advocating the overthrow of the existing system. He and Goldman hoped that the jury would recognize the difference and agree with this interpretation, which would, they believed, render the advocacy charge moot.

The same limits on the party's actions held true, Cannon explained, for its influence over the nature of the revolution. The SWP did not advocate a violent revolution but rather, given its members' adherence to Marxist theory, believed it understood how and why the social and political revolution against capitalism would come. The "conditions" for revolution included capitalism's exhausting all its possibilities, the ruling class's losing confidence, the eruption of war, the rise of fascism, the immiseration of the masses, and the creation of a workers party to lead and organize "the workers in a resolute fashion for a revolutionary solution of the crisis." The SWP saw itself as constituting that last condition—the workers party that would guide the revolutionary response to the crisis of capitalism. Because the prosecution had alleged that the SWP planned to exploit the current war (World War II) as a moment ripe for such an uprising, Goldman pushed Cannon to clarify when the revolution would come. But the question of when was something Cannon could not answer except to say that the conditions were "lacking" in America at that time.

This response—along with his explanation that the party only predicted that violence would erupt from the capitalist reaction to revolution—served the defense's argument that the SWP could not, and therefore did not, constitute an illegal conspiracy to advocate the overthrow of the government by force.[9] In a clear reference to the prosecution witnesses who said they heard SWP officials promote violent revolution, Cannon insisted, "I do not recall any discussion that has taken place in the party since its formation about violence in connection with the overthrow of the government." He admitted, however, that sometimes, because of the "great variation in the degree of knowledge of the party program and doctrines among the various members of the party," "the principles of the party" can be "misinterpreted by an individual."[10] Part of the reason he was on the stand was to clarify those principles, which, he argued, had been so poorly represented by the prosecution. Determined to defend the revolutionary integrity of the party, Goldman also hoped that the jury would find Cannon's word, as leader of that party, more convincing than that of the U.S. attorney and the prosecution's witnesses.

He held out the same hope for Cannon's clarification of the party's relationship with trade unions. Responding to this line of Goldman's questions, Cannon explained that the SWP supported the trade union movement "as the basic organization of the workers" and was "seriously interested in anything that benefits the workers," but that it did not seek to control those unions in the tyrannical ways portrayed by the prosecution. Admitting that the unions as mass organizations "offer the most productive fields for us to work in popularizing the ideas of the party," Cannon insisted that the party supported union democracy and secured its own "leading members in the union" only through fair elections or appointments.[11] Bartlett and the other members of the Committee of 99 would vehemently disagree with Cannon's characterizations of the SWP's trade union work, pointing specifically to the June 9 "bolt" and the deal that Local 544's executive board had made with Denny Lewis.

But Cannon voiced the view of the defendants. To them the decision to leave the IBT on June 9 was a democratic one, made to escape the "tyrannical" demands of Tobin. The jury was now getting a fuller picture of the Trotskyists' side of the story.

When it came to the party's antiwar stance, Cannon also refuted the prosecution's interpretation. In laying out the SWP's views, however, Cannon had to clarify a set of beliefs alien to most Americans. In addition, the global and domestic context in which Cannon spoke made his explanation of the Trotskyists' opposition to the war then being waged against fascism even less popular. In November 1941, the Nazi invasion of the Soviet Union had progressed to the point where the Germans had come within a few miles of Moscow. In Asia, the Japanese condemned American sanctions and defied U.S. calls to leave China. At home, John Lewis had led 250,000 United Mine Workers out on strike in the steel industry's "captive" coal mines, at a time when steel production was in high demand to meet Roosevelt's war preparedness plan. Explaining why the Trotskyists were opposed to the war would be a hard line for Cannon to sell to the jurors even if national and world events had not ratcheted up the tensions and emotions surrounding that fight.[12] Yet he stuck to his guns, explaining how the SWP was opposed to all wars, which it believed were the result of capitalist and imperialist exploitation. Drawing out the distinction between political beliefs and overt acts, Cannon also insisted that despite this opposition to war, "Our party has never at any time taken a position in favor of obstruction or sabotage of the military forces in time of war."[13]

He also agued that the party's opposition to war did not support the prosecution's charge that it had attempted to foment insubordination in the military. "So far as we are concerned," Cannon said of the Selective Service requirement, "if the young generation of American workers goes to war, our party members go with them, and share in all their dangers and hardships and experience."[14] Although the Trotskyists were opposed to the war, they had taken this unusual position of supporting the draft once it was put in place. Unlike pacifists, they were willing to fight. The SWP supported workers' military training and did not seek to disrupt it through protests or sabotage.

But Cannon did not explain on the stand that the SWP's ultimate goal was to have workers use that training when the revolution came. The position—as Trotsky himself clarified for Cannon and Dobbs when they spoke with him about the war in June 1940—was one not simply of protesting (as pacifists like Debs had done in the past) but ultimately of "taking power and launching the socialist society."[15] In his testimony, Cannon spoke about the party's desire for workers to control their own military training and to elect their officers.[16] But he did not bring up the discussions within the party about "taking power," for to do so would be admitting a technical violation of the Smith Act. Instead, he and the other defendants continued to voice the position Trotsky had counseled them to take if they were ever to be placed under suspicion. Trotsky's advice to Cannon and Dobbs revealed a larger revolutionary agenda, in which "naturally in principle we would overthrow so-called bourgeois democracy given the opportunity," but also a suggestion for a more narrowly framed defense in court, in which they would argue that all they asked for "was the right to give [their] opinions" if drafted in the army.[17]

Now that he found himself on trial for conspiring to overthrow the government by force, Cannon seemed to follow this advice. He remained focused in court on defending his right to discuss what his party stood for in principle— its hopes for a peaceful transition to socialism—and refrained from revealing what Trotskyists had discussed in June 1940 about the possibilities the war presented for the coming of the revolution. Since the summer of 1940, the party had focused on enforcing its "transitional program"—"the bridge between the present situation and the proletarian revolution"—and considered the war part of that program insofar as it "accelerated the development." Socialist Workers, the party had resolved, were to "participate in the military machine for socialist ends."[18] But Cannon did not reveal this on the stand. Limiting his explanation to the party's basic support for the draft, opposition to sabotage, and desire to see workers in control of their own military training, Cannon technically did not perjure himself, but neither did he implicate himself in any illegal deeds.

During Cannon's third and last day on the stand, Goldman pursued three additional interrelated issues that also dealt with the revolutionary nature of the party. He asked about the SWP's stance on the Russian Revolution, on Stalin and Trotsky, and on the Union Defense Guard. In asking Cannon about the first two topics, Goldman tried to demonstrate once again how the SWP's beliefs were revolutionary but stopped short of actually inciting violence. Cannon admitted that the party supported the 1917 revolution because it "embodies the doctrines and the theories of Marxism which we uphold," but he also argued that any violence in that revolution was instigated by the reaction of the czarists and the bourgeoisie, not the workers.[19] In an attempt to establish grounds for why the clear and present danger test—if applied—would reveal the SWP to be neither an evident nor an impending threat, Goldman attempted to have Cannon draw out the distinctions between the conditions in 1917 Russia and the present-day United States, but he was stymied by Anderson's objection, which was upheld by Joyce.[20]

Goldman did not give up. Instead, he tried a new set of questions to get at the same point about revolutionary conditions. This time Judge Joyce overruled Schweinhaut's objections and allowed Goldman to proceed. In response to this line of questions, Cannon clarified the party's stance on Stalin and on Trotsky. Cannon not only contrasted the bureaucracy that had corrupted Stalin's regime in Russia with the democracy touted by the SWP's founder but also contrasted the very different conditions in the United States that followers of Trotsky there faced as compared with the conditions in Russia that had developed since 1917. With democracy in the United States, Cannon insisted, violent revolution would most likely not be necessary. And any attempt to cast the Trotskyists as defenders of the Stalinist regime—another misrepresentation of the prosecution—was, he argued, gravely misplaced.[21]

Cannon further drew out the distinction between the SWP and the Communists when he explained one of the reasons for Local 544's Union Defense Guard. Denying that the guard had been the brainchild of Trotsky, Cannon claimed that it had been formed to defend laborers against attacks from Local 544's enemies. Those enemies included not only the fascist Silver Shirts but also the Communists who, during the late 1920s, had launched assaults on Trotskyists in Minneapolis. He cited an incident in 1929 when Oscar Coover had been beaten "with blackjacks while he stood at the door taking tickets" during one party event. Cannon defined the UDG as defensive in nature, with roots in the indigenous struggles of workers in Minneapolis, thereby implying that it was not an internationally hatched plot to overthrow the government by force, as Anderson contended.[22]

Cannon was correct about the indigenous and limited nature of the UDG as it was founded and as it had functioned in Minneapolis during the late 1930s. It was also true, however, that Trotsky supported such efforts at workers' self-defense and that party leaders discussed the relationship of those efforts to more formal training found in the army. Trotsky and SWP leaders in the United States considered both useful ways for workers to learn how to protect themselves from capitalist violence and reaction.[23] Although such closed-door discussions show an interest in armed workers' self-defense, they did not equal the overt act of violently overthrowing the government.

The government, however, believed that the party's position on workers' self-defense constituted a conspiracy to do just that. On cross-examination Schweinhaut pushed Cannon to explain how the SWP would respond to the capitalist resistance it predicted when workers struggled to gain power. Despite Schweinhaut's repeated attempts to catch Cannon in admitting the party's intent to incite violence, the SWP leader was careful to remain true to the party position: the party could not make the workers do anything they did not want to do or did not see as in their own interest, and therefore it could neither summarily incite revolution nor sustain it through the UDG or by any other means.[24]

But Schweinhaut persisted in his line of questioning and pushed the defendant on the real purpose of the party's support for workers' military training. While Cannon had explained that the SWP believed such training was necessary for laborers to defend themselves against the possible violent reaction of capitalists and fascists to revolution, Schweinhaut continued to portray it as support for a workers' army that would be central to the overthrow of the government by force. But Cannon would have none of that and stated defiantly: "I think that workers have a right to defend themselves. If that is treason, you can make the most of it."[25] As he had planned to do before the trial opened, Cannon did not back down from defending the revolutionary principles of his party. Nor did he accede to the prosecution's argument about what constituted sabotage, sedition, and treason, carefully positioning himself and the SWP just inside the boundaries of legal acts and speech.

On November 21, shortly after his tense exchange with Schweinhaut on the third day of the defense's case, Cannon finished his testimony and stepped down from the stand. An additional six witnesses were then called in quick succession. Each testified to much the same thing as the other: that they had been members of Local 544 but not the SWP, and that most had not been asked (let alone pressured) to join the party; that they had joined the UDG in 1938 because they understood the union to be threatened by the local Silver Shirts; and that none of them had ever heard any of the defendants call for the violent overthrow of the government.[26] The earnestness and consistency of their testimony, especially with respect to the nature of the Union Defense Guard, bolstered the defense's case.

Vincent Dunne, the defense's second key witness after Cannon, would attempt to reinforce that case. He was called to the stand and sworn in on Friday, November 21, and was recalled on Monday, November 24, to continue his testimony. Just as Goldman asked Cannon to lay out the history of the SWP at the beginning of his questioning, so too did he ask Dunne to explain the origins of Local 544. Dunne obliged and recounted the union's past,[27] but he spoke most passionately about its more recent tussle with the IBT. He detailed the origins and nature of Local 544's June 9 vote to leave the IBT-AFL for the CIO, emphasizing how a majority of the members present at the meeting voted freely in favor of this move. Claiming he could not see the materiality of this line of questioning, Schweinhaut objected, but the court agreed with Goldman's argument that the jury needed to understand that the majority of Local 544's membership favored secession from the AFL. Because the prosecution tried to argue that the SWP controlled Local 544 as part of its conspiracy, Goldman wanted "to show the jury that all of the officers in the union were elected, and that all the things done there were done by vote of the men."[28] Allowed to respond to this line of questioning, Dunne was able to testify to the democratic process within Local 544. The court did not allow Goldman much free rein, however, when it came to his attempt to question Dunne about Tobin's interference with the union after the June 9 split. Just as during his cross-examination of the prosecution's witnesses, whenever Goldman approached the question of Tobin's actions that summer, Joyce upheld the prosecution's objection.[29]

To aid the defense's case, much of Dunne's direct examination was focused on his refuting the accusations made about him by Bartlett. Goldman led Dunne into a discussion of his relationship with Bartlett to discredit the government's star witness by attempting to demonstrate that Bartlett held a long-standing, politically motivated grudge against Dunne. According to Dunne, in their early public encounters, Bartlett had spoken "very viciously over a period of time" about him. He cited an example from 1934, during an unemployment demonstration at the Minneapolis Court House, when Bartlett had "denounced me as a stool pigeon and a police spy, and as a traitor and a faker, and so forth for a considerable time" and even "advised the workers not to pay any attention to what I said, and to run me out of the demonstration, and so forth." Since Bartlett was a member of the Communist Party at the time, Dunne explained, "That was his line." The first time Dunne spoke directly with Bartlett was in 1936, he recalled for the jury, when Bartlett came to him to ask for Local 544's help in organizing the warehouse workers union. Bartlett said he was breaking with the CP's position on trade unions, and Dunne claimed that he told Bartlett he would help him if he were sincere in his political conversion. Dunne insisted that he did not ask Bartlett to join the Trotskyists and did not make that a requirement for his help organizing the workers in 1936, despite what Bartlett may have said during his testimony.[30] The implication of Dunne's testimony about Bartlett was that he was an opportunist with an ax to grind who could not be trusted.

Having attempted to undermine Bartlett's credibility in this way, Dunne then refuted all the serious accusations Bartlett had made against him on the stand. He denied ever having called for the violent overthrow of the government, charging Bartlett with having misunderstood the teachings of the party and his comments.[31] Dunne also denied ever calling for a general strike as the first step in perpetrating such a violent revolution and insisted that he never called for the disruption of the armed forces, as Bartlett claimed he did. In an attempt to explain why the prosecution's witness would have lied, Dunne insisted that Bartlett was unhappy at having lost the support of the union's executive board for his role as an organizer and in his run for president of Local

359. The reason for the board's disapproval of Bartlett was not his politics, Dunne explained, but "all of his bad work in the union, lack of work for the union, going into the bowling alley business as a private enterprise, generally conducting himself not for the union but for his own personal interests."[32] According to Dunne, if anyone allowed outside influences to interfere with trade union work, it was Bartlett with his selfish entrepreneurial gambits, not the Trotskyists. With Dunne's testimony, the defense team hoped to discredit the prosecution's star witness and give the jury pause to reconsider the motives for the prosecution. By offering an alternative explanation for Bartlett's opposition to Dunne and the other Trotskyists in Local 544, the defense tried to cast doubt on the government's entire case.

The defense team brought additional witnesses to the stand to construct a counternarrative to that which had been advanced by the prosecution. Of particular concern to the defense was clarifying the relationship between the SWP and Local 544. Roy Orgon explained how most of the drivers were in sympathy with the leadership of 544-CIO because they were honest union men. And both Ray Rainbolt and Miles Dunne stated that there was no SWP literature sold on the premises of the union's headquarters in Minneapolis.[33] The testimony of these men shored up the other main contention of the defense—that the SWP did not control, or seek to control, Local 544 for its own revolutionary ends.

When it came to demonstrating that the SWP was a legitimate political party that ran candidates for office and sought to effect change through the ballot, Grace Carlson was the defense team's key witness. She was sworn in on November 25. As the most prominent woman in the party, and the only female defendant left standing trial, Carlson stood out among her male colleagues. She later noted that her gender partly dictated why she testified, recalling how "Goldman said the jurors would just be outraged if they didn't hear a woman report."[34] But it was also because of her position in the party—and the need to refute serious charges that had been leveled directly against her—that she took the stand.

Carlson explained her past experiences with the party's electoral work going back to 1936 when Trotskyists had temporarily entered the Socialist Party, up through her most recent campaign for senator on the SWP ticket in 1940. Rejecting the prosecution's claim that the SWP was nothing but an illegal conspiracy to overthrow the government violently, Carlson demonstrated how the legitimate political workings of the party functioned. She cited the leaflets, newspaper articles, and speeches that SWP members used to educate the voters in the principles of socialism and win their support at the polls. Although they were not successful in their electoral attempts—Carlson was not elected to the Senate, and Cannon failed in his bid for the mayoralty of New York—she insisted that the Trotskyists sustained a genuine political party in the SWP.[35]

The legal functioning of that party was something Carlson discussed in her speech "The Road to Socialism," which she had delivered at the University of Minnesota in 1940. In that speech she argued that there needed to be nationwide electoral action to make socialism a reality in the United States, and she called on the students to join the party in that work.[36] Although she had been accused of calling for revolutionary violence in her speech by some of the prosecution's witnesses, she clarified its message as delineating the party's desire for peace but its prediction of violence. Far from being an illegal conspiracy whose purpose was to overthrow the government by force, the SWP was, according to Carlson's testimony, a functioning political party that advocated a peaceful transition to socialism but that also cautioned against what it believed was an inevitable reaction against that transition.[37] Like Cannon, Carlson portrayed the SWP as a militant party committed to the transformation to socialism, but not to the advocacy of violence. She too carefully positioned the Trotskyists just inside the boundaries of legal political action as they had been curtailed by the Smith Act.

Following this line of argument, Carlson explained that, even though it was opposed to the war, the party also did not advocate interference with the armed forces, as the prosecution charged. Carlson emphasized that the party supported its members' serving in the military if called, but that it also supported their right of free speech within the military. She explained to Schweinhaut when he pressed her on this issue that party members must, of course, do their duty as soldiers first and not interfere with the duty of others, but

> soldiers, as all other people, talk about the questions of the day, and if the socialists are in there, and someone asks them what they think about certain questions, of poverty and so on, existing in the country, we feel that socialists should be free to give their interpretation of the causes of those things, just as another soldier can give the Republican interpretation or the Democratic interpretation, or whatever party might exist.[38]

Although she had not been in Mexico when Trotsky discussed this very defense with SWP leaders (a soldier's asking merely for the "right to give his opinion"), Carlson presented a very similar argument in court to that offered by Cannon. She thus made the issue of Trotskyist advocacy of socialism in the armed forces a simple one of free speech and did not overtly engage in what, if any, the revolutionary implications of that speech might be.

Figure 4.2 Farrell Dobbs, James Cannon, and Felix Morrow (left to right) around the time of the trial. Courtesy Hennepin County Library Special Collections.

Farrell Dobbs followed Carlson to the stand on what would be the final day of the defense's presentation of its case. As a former Teamster, key supporter of the 1934 strikes in Minneapolis, chief organizer of the drivers' over-the-road contracts, and labor secretary of the SWP, Dobbs spoke specifically to the issue of the party's labor policy. He defined it as one of helping workers achieve the best conditions they could via their unions, helping them maintain democracy within their unions, urging party members to be the best union men "to win the confidence of the workers," and educating the workers in the party's principles.[39] As to the last policy goal, he noted, the party's work within the unions depended on persuasion, not force. Dobbs explained, "We can only recruit members in trade unions, into the party, insofar as we are successful in convincing men of our ideas, in whatever situation we may find such an individual."[40] He admitted that "if a party member is in an official or key position, within the union, his ability to recruit members would be greater than one in a lower position" but emphasized that the party's work was to support the best interests of the workers. And that, he explained, was to be achieved only through their democratic consent.

Dobbs thus shared Dunne's view of the relationship between the SWP and trade unions like Local 544. But that perspective was also one that had been contested by the opposition movement within the Minneapolis local; Bartlett and other Teamsters believed that the Trotskyists abused the power of their union offices and made Local 544 an arm of the SWP. The different experiences of the SWP's place in the union's business remained a point of deep and bitter division among its many members, and during the trial that division was laid bare before the jury with the prosecution and defense witnesses' contrasting testimony. Because Anderson and Schweinhaut claimed that the SWP's influence in Local 544 was evidence of its conspiracy to advocate the violent overthrow of the government, it was essential for the defense to clarify the party's relationship to the union. But in so doing, the defense witnesses found themselves walking a fine line: as they knew, as the SWP records showed, and as they even admitted on the stand, the party sought to use the trade union as a base through which to reach and organize workers with its socialist message. But as the lived experiences of Dunne and Dobbs had also shown (and as many of the members of Local 544 felt firsthand), the Trotskyists' efforts on behalf of the workers and in building up a strong union often came first: it was "number one," as Dunne had asserted in his testimony.[41] There were thus elements of truth in both the prosecution's and the defense's version of events, rendering this component of the case a challenging one for the jury.

The key for the defense, however, was to refute the most damning element of the prosecution's version of the SWP's ties to Local 544 and other unions: that the relationship was connected to a plan to overthrow the government violently through sabotage in the nation's industrial sector. To counter the related charges that the party was only interested in fomenting strikes, Dobbs explained how he had participated in arbitration many times as a labor organizer. When Schweinhaut tried to trip him up on this point, pushing him to admit that as a Marxist he believed there could be "no such thing as impartial arbitration in disputes between the contending forces in the class struggle," Dobbs agreed only in the most general sense. As he had experienced in his many years on the job and in the ranks of the union, Dobbs explained, there were hard-and-fast positions of the party, but then there was the reality on the ground; as a result, one deals with those hard-and-fast positions as best as one can but often finds oneself needing to be more flexible, embracing arbitration in the short term, for example. For while Dobbs was a committed party member, he was also, like Dunne, very much a union man who had learned on the street the real-life meaning of labor conflict. He thus refuted Schweinhaut's claim that the party supported strikes to foment revolution. Strikes were used by workers to advance their causes in terms of wages, hours, and union recognition. As such, he declared, strikes "are not a toy to play with at will, and we advocate in all instances that all reasonable efforts be made to avoid a strike before a strike is called, because strikes present real hardships to the workers." Advocating a strike to create a revolutionary situation, Dobbs asserted, "would be ridiculous in the extreme."[42] In this assertion, Dobbs was correct, but what he did not say—and what Schweinhaut failed to draw out—was that the party would not shy away from helping direct an independent strike to greater revolutionary ends if the opportunity arose.[43]

After Dobbs stepped down from the stand, Goldman entered one more exhibit into evidence (an article from the *Militant* that detailed the party's positions on several of the issues central to the case, including its position on the war). The defense then rested its case, and the court was adjourned for the day.[44] Although it did not bring as many witnesses to the stand as the prosecution, the defense team managed to cast doubt on the veracity of some of the government witnesses' statements and motives, especially James Bartlett's, and on the relevance of some of the prosecution's key exhibits, including certain passages from the party's Declaration of Principles. With Cannon's, Dunne's, Carlson's, and Dobbs's testimony in particular, Goldman and the other defense lawyers were able to build a counternarrative for the jury about the Trotskyists' beliefs and actions, especially with reference to the trade union movement and, specifically, to Local 544. They presented those beliefs and actions as militant, radical, and unconventional, but ultimately legal, making the case that the central question of the trial was one of free speech.

Illegal Revolutionary Advocacy or Protected Free Speech? The Closing Arguments

On November 26 the court reconvened for the closing arguments. Victor Anderson began with an opening statement for the prosecution that lasted the entire day. One of the first things Anderson did was to remind the jury of the charges in question and of the prosecution's interpretation of those charges. The two counts of conspiracy—to overthrow the government by force and to advocate the violent overthrow of the government—were presented to the jurors again, as they had been during his argument at the start of the trial. With respect to the alleged conspiracies, Anderson clarified just what the government had to prove, noting, "Whether anyone did one thing, took one step, said one word, wrote one letter, published one magazine or not would be of no concern except as that goes to show, was there a conspiracy."[45] His task, Anderson explained, was to highlight for the jury how the evidence presented at trial showed that such a broad conspiracy existed and how each of the defendants was a part of it.

Aware that the case had been criticized since the time of the indictments by civil libertarians and the labor left, Anderson spoke in his closing of the need for all involved in the case to steer clear of exciting the jurors' emotions. There was not to be a reprise of the red scare hysteria that had followed the First World War but instead "calm, deliberate and considerate judgment."[46] Yet almost as soon as he had taken this principled stand, Anderson violated it by launching repeatedly into highly emotionally charged rhetoric that invoked the specter of an insidious fifth column out to destroy American democracy through its blind loyalty to a foreign communist power. He argued that although it was difficult for simple rural folk like the jurors to believe that some people in Minneapolis and "the congested population of New York could or would confederate and join together and say, 'Not your stars and stripes, but give me the red flag; not a democracy of the people, but this proletariat dictatorship,'"[47] he insisted that is what the defendants had done. Far from avoiding a reprise of the emotions of the First Red Scare, Anderson trafficked quite freely in them.

And he did not stop there. Throughout his closing remarks, he came back again and again to the theme of the danger the defendants posed as members of an inherently un-American, communist fifth column. While technically granting the defendants the right to use any flag or symbol they chose for their movement, he drew the jurors' attention to their choice as suspect, arguing that "by that emblem . . . they are going to be judged, and anything that cannot be done within the folds of the Stars and Stripes, and what it stands for, is not what we want in the United States."[48] With reference to the defendants' extensive discussions about Russia in the party's literature and speeches, he claimed such speech was also unwelcome, serving only to "poison the mind" of other Americans. In rhetoric that harkened back to the supporters of the deportation of radicals on the "Russian ark" in 1919 he said of the defendants, "Let them go to Russia and leave the good people here alone."[49] And rejecting the Trotskyists' critique of Stalinism as irrelevant hairsplitting when it came to the question of the political system they were allegedly conspiring to impose on the good people of America, he thundered, "I don't know if it would be any better in the United States, if James P. Cannon, the head of this party, was the dictator for the United States than what they now claim is being meted out to the Russians under the regime of Stalin."[50] Through such comments

Anderson stirred the emotions of the jurors, abandoning his earlier call for calm and deliberate judgment.

Anderson's rhetorical flourishes also contributed to the vivid way in which he characterized the treacherous nature of the SWP conspiracy as something hatched out of Trotsky's mind in Mexico, communicated through top party operatives, spread through SWP literature that was disseminated by party members, and imposed on some of the more feebleminded followers who were pulled into the pernicious plot. The concept of the SWP as a legitimate political party was totally rejected, as it had been since the start of the trial and throughout the prosecution's making its case. Some of what Anderson described was true and supported by the documentary evidence: the SWP did look to Trotsky for guidance when he was alive; top party operatives did travel to Mexico to meet with him to discuss party strategy; and those ideas were disseminated through internal party communications. Because of these realities it may have been a challenge for the jury, especially in the heated wartime emergency context, to dismiss Anderson's conclusion that the party was an illegal conspiracy.

Anderson expanded his explanation of the effects of this alleged conspiracy for the jurors, looking at the twenty-three remaining defendants in turn and driving home how each expressed in one way or another the same shared ideas. Those ideas, he argued, coming from the "master head" Trotsky, had "saturated," "poisoned," and "distorted" the minds of the party's followers.[51] The arguments about class struggle, the opposition to war, the need to turn the imperialist war into a civil war, the expectation of violence when the revolution came, and the need for military training for workers and an armed union defense guard were repeated by each of the defendants to one degree or another in their speech or writings. Those ideas—because they were echoed over and over—were not of each defendant's own making, Anderson argued, but were in and of themselves evidence of the "whole program," the conspiracy of the party of which each was a member.[52] Not acknowledging that such a characterization of shared ideas could be applied to the committed membership of any given political party, Anderson insisted that the ability to "formulate in each state a separate proposition that was identical" came from the defendants' having "met in council." He argued that they "had confederated together. They had planned activities, and their very actions and their very words show that there was this conspiracy—and that is what we challenge them here because of, and for which we ask an accounting of their activities."[53]

Anderson believed that that accounting had to take place now. He insisted that any hesitancy could prove devastating to the nation. The SWP's own declarations—about turning the imperialist war into a civil war and about arming the workers for revolt—were expressions of "defiance and a challenge to the naval, the marine, the military and the aerial forces of the United States."[54] Its call for the overthrow of the capitalist state, he argued, was a clear "challenge to the very existence of our Government."[55] And its advocacy of armed workers guards as a first step in the creation of a proletarian front was "only a step" but a "short step" from which it "wouldn't take long having gone that far" to finish the deed. If the government did not act then, if it had "been duped into inactivity or failed to seize the opportunity to put a stop before that, it would no doubt be altogether too late."[56] Justifying the prosecution itself, as well as the Smith Act upon which the second count of the indictment was based, he summarized the perspective of those like himself, Berge, Biddle, and Roosevelt, who had come to believe it was necessary during times of national crisis to sacrifice absolute free speech rights for national security:

> The Government of the United States has a right to protect its existence regardless of any constitutional free speech, free press, free assembly, or anything else. No man and no woman has the power, the constitutional right, to use the Constitution to destroy the Government. That is our position in a nutshell. . . . Whether late or early we are here at the appointed time, and if I judge the situation correctly, if I can see beyond tomorrow's rising sun this thing isn't going to be the order for tomorrow, or the tomorrow after tomorrow. This is going to be called to a halt here and now. A strict, a full, a complete accounting is due, and here is the tribunal that will do the accounting.[57]

In his final summation, voicing an emotional plea for the protection of the nation-state and its loyal citizens, Anderson dismissed the notion of absolute freedom of speech, arguing that it was a luxury no longer affordable for a country facing foreign and domestic threats. Expressing his hope that this would be the first and last lawsuit of its kind to defend the nation against the internal threats of "sabotage, insurrection, revolt, challenge of authority, appeal to prejudice, urging civil war, destruction," he asked the jury to return a "true and just verdict" of guilty.[58]

Albeit perhaps an emotionally charged and rhetorically crude one, Anderson's closing statement was an expression of the position many Americans had come to take on the proper balance between First Amendment rights and national security in wartime. Although America was not yet at war, it had been thrust into a wartime emergency climate since Roosevelt's proclamation that May. And its continued support for Britain and its own wartime preparations contributed weight to the argument that civil liberties could be neither absolute nor absolutely protected in the face of the fascist menace abroad. Berge and Roosevelt had embraced this perspective early on, and Biddle and Schweinhaut came to accept it in the case of the Trotskyists. By the fall of 1941, legal scholars had joined them in making the case that the only way to safeguard civil liberties was by sacrificing the notion that they were absolute and by placing certain limitations on them for the sake and safety of the nation and the state.[59] Here in the courtroom in Minneapolis this great debate, which had been percolating among civil libertarians and legal thinkers since Holmes's speech protective use of the clear and present danger test in the 1919 *Abrams* dissent, was finally being tested in the real-life case of the Trotskyists and their prosecution under the federal Smith Act.

The court reconvened the next morning to hear Goldman present the closing argument for the defense. Over the next two days he spent ten hours before the jury.[60] One of the first issues Goldman addressed was the prosecution's theory that the SWP was itself a conspiracy. Such an idea was "monstrous," Goldman asserted, for it undermined the right of political parties to exist in a democracy. If the SWP was condemned as an illegal conspiracy, Goldman argued, "the possibility of any opposition to the powers that are in office" was destroyed "because if today you say the Socialist Workers Party is a conspiracy, then tomorrow you can say the Republican Party or the Socialist Party or any other party that strives to achieve power, of itself, is a conspiracy."[61] Furthermore, Goldman stated, the U.S. attorney's attempts during the trial to present the SWP as a secret conspiracy—his display of the party's office floor plan and his questioning witnesses about membership cards and member numbers—was "nonsense." It was a constructed "rigmarole," evoking "secret chambers" and "maybe some secret button," that was intended to communicate a "conspiratorial atmosphere" that did not exist. The SWP was a legitimate political party that did not hide its ideas, Goldman argued. Even if those ideas were "explosive"—indeed, they were the only "weapons" found and presented at trial—they were not kept secret. As a result, Goldman explained to the jurors, they would have to find a conspiracy outside of the party, and specifically (given the indictments) a conspiracy to overthrow the government by force or violence.[62] By thus rejecting the prosecution's definition of conspiracy, the defense asked the jury to consider a scenario in which the burden of proof would be much greater than just the existence of the party.

Goldman then advised the jurors that in looking for this broader conspiracy external to the SWP, they should distinguish between the types of evidence that had been presented to them during the trial. He argued that documentary evidence, properly contextualized and coming from official party sources, should be given more weight than what he insisted was the highly questionable testimony offered by the government's witnesses. "Memory is a very treacherous thing," Goldman argued, and even if the jury was convinced that the witnesses were telling the truth, "that they thought they heard a statement, it would really be monstrous to deprive the defendants of their liberty on the strength of statements alleged to have been made a year or two or three years ago, because the possibility of error is tremendous."[63] But in giving the documentary evidence more weight, the jurors had to take care as well, he argued. More than 200 exhibits had been entered into evidence by the prosecution. Many of those articles and speeches were not authored by any of the defendants, nor were they written by party leaders, and therefore they did not have party sanction. As a "proposition of fairness and justice," Goldman implored the jurors not to hold the defendants accountable for such unofficial works. Then, he asked them to go further and to judge each defendant only by his or her own writings, taking from the end of the day on Wednesday and into Thursday morning to argue this point.[64]

Goldman next turned his attention to one of the central questions in the case: Conceding that the defendants wanted to establish a socialist society in America, how exactly did they hope to achieve this? The indictments alleged that they had conspired to do this by a violent overthrow of the government. Such a charge was "absurd," Goldman insisted, because it completely misinterpreted the defendants' political beliefs. Delving into those beliefs for several hours, the defense attorney ranged from bold assertions of the SWP's revolutionary agenda to humble expressions of the party's simple desire to affect change peacefully and legally. Aware that he had to present a defense of his comrades and his party against the charges of their intent to overthrow the government violently, but also aware that the court in which he spoke was a public forum for advocating the SWP's core ideas, Goldman walked a fine line. He did not deny that the party's goal was to "change the social system upon which the government is based" from a capitalist to a socialist society. But he ultimately explained how, given the current conditions in the United States (which was a democracy, not a world of kings like that in which Marx wrote *The Communist Manifesto* in 1848), the SWP wanted to achieve that goal at the ballot box.[65]

The party's intention to effect change through peaceful political means, however, did not preclude others engaging in violence. Goldman clarified how any references to violence in the party's literature almost always dealt with the predictions of violence to come in the wake of the socialist change— violence carried out by the ruling classes in resisting the revolution. In bringing about that revolution, he argued, the defendants could not force anyone to join their movement but could only use verbal persuasion. In that persuasion, predicting the possibility of violence was not the same as inciting it or advocating the violent overthrow of the government. Such speech, Goldman argued, was "not against the law," even under the sweeping reach of the Smith Act.[66] To convict the defendants based on "a dozen expressions that might indicate" to the jury that they advocated violence would be "fantastic" and "a complete destruction of civil liberties, of every constitutional guarantee."[67] On such grounds, Goldman provocatively noted, one could convict Abraham Lincoln, Thomas Jefferson, and the authors of certain passages in the Bible.[68]

Having attempted to refute the charge that the defendants had conspired to advocate the violent overthrow of the government, Goldman addressed three additional, related issues: the Union Defense Guard, the defendants' antiwar views, and the party's trade union work. Although the prosecution pointed to these things as evidence of the wider conspiracy, the defense attorney insisted that none of them were relevant to the case. He pointed out that the UDG never advocated the violent overthrow of the government.[69] And Goldman noted that despite the Socialist Workers' best efforts, the party's antiwar views never influenced anyone outside of its small ranks. The only way the defendants' opposition to the war was relevant to the case was how it made them a target for a prosecution partly intended, Goldman asserted, to silence the president's war critics. It had nothing to do with the advocacy of revolution, which, he noted in another deprecation of the party's influence, was beside the point: "the class struggle goes on" regardless of those who can divine it because it is based on material conditions beyond the control of individuals or parties.[70] In arguing for the Trotskyists' innocence, Goldman had to insist on their impotence.

He deployed the same tactic when discussing the defendants' trade union work. By November 1941, the Trotskyists had very little influence in Minneapolis since the attacks against them that were launched by "the Federal Government, the State Government, Tobin, everybody else." But before the prosecution, SWP members dominated the leadership of Local 544. Dunne, Dobbs, DeBoer, Hansen, and the others gained the drivers' support not "by some devious method, not by force," but by open elections because they were good union men who took care of the drivers' interests. Although he admitted that the SWP sought to elect its members to union office "to benefit the interests of socialism," Goldman insisted that the methods never included force or threats about job security. And while this was true (Dunne and the other Trotskyists in Local 544 did not force anyone to join their party), the presence of so many SWP members in union offices and their talk of socialism in the union headquarters may have created what would now be considered a hostile work environment for those who did not share those politics. But, unable or unwilling to acknowledge this more sticky reality of the lived experience within the union, Goldman insisted that the defendants had done nothing wrong in their work as union leaders. And he argued that regardless of the nature of the internal union fight, none of it should have risen to the level of a federal criminal case.[71]

Goldman and the defendants believed that it was this factional divide that led to the prosecution. Asserting that the government had taken sides in the internal union fight against the defendants, Goldman cited the list of prosecution witnesses as proof. Almost all were among the disgruntled forces within the local, members either of the original Committee of 99 or of the new Local 544-AFL.[72] Chief among these witnesses was James Bartlett, whom Goldman asserted had perjured himself on the stand. Attempting to cast doubt on Bartlett's claim to have left the SWP in 1940 once he became aware of its revolutionary agenda, Goldman noted how other members (including Violet Williams) had testified that they caught wind of the radical nature of the party after attending only a few meetings. The discrepancy in their experiences within the party needed an explanation, as did the inconsistency in Bartlett's claim to have read two pamphlets when he was a member of the party that were not published until after he had left its ranks. Finally, Goldman insisted, Bartlett's comments about his conversation with Vincent Dunne in December 1940 also contained enough irregularities to throw them into question.[73]

Goldman argued that such inconsistencies indicated that Bartlett was lying. The other government witnesses, he claimed, had perjured themselves as well. How else to explain the almost identical accounts of comments allegedly made by certain defendants one, two, even three years prior? The attacks on Dunne in particular, Goldman insisted, seemed scripted and rehearsed. And how else to explain why these same witnesses could recall the defendants', especially Dunne's, speaking about violence and revolution, but they could not recall any other comments or discussions at the meetings when such statements were allegedly made? "In a parade of perjury," Goldman concluded, "a parade of perjury representing the Government witnesses, Bartlett rose to the ceiling and way above."[74] Mocking the odd turn of phrase that Anderson had used to praise Bartlett, Goldman now derided them both. Moving beyond his earlier attempts to discredit the government's witnesses, Goldman now asserted that they had all lied on the stand.

To explain why he believed that Bartlett and the other witnesses had committed perjury, Goldman came back to the argument he had tried to make several times during the interrogation of the witnesses: that the Committee of 99 had "invited the F.B.I. to participate" in its work, that the FBI "became a faction of the Committee of 99," and that "men higher up" set the prosecution in motion. While it was true that the presence of federal agents in Minneapolis had raised the stakes of the internal union fight and brought it to the attention of the Justice Department, Goldman's presentation of this history dismissed the autonomy and grievances of the opposition movement within Local 544. His conflation of the Committee of 99 with the FBI was understandable given that the cooperation between the two groups was what ultimately contributed to the federal indictments. But that cooperation, and the move to the indictments, came from the Justice Department's perception that there was a real national security threat in Minneapolis, not because of the "political debt" Roosevelt owed Tobin, as Goldman tried to argue. As he attempted to present that argument again, he was interrupted by the prosecution's objection, and so Goldman continued his attack by carefully staying within the bounds of what had been introduced as fact at trial. Drawing the jurors' attention to the timing of the indictments, which came just after the June 9 "bolt," he asked them if they believed this was "a coincidence."[75] Given that the SWP had been functioning openly for three and half years before this legal assault, Goldman insisted that the internal union fight and Tobin's intervention in that fight were central to the reason for the case: "It is a frame-up and nothing else. It is a faction of local 544, of the Committee of 99, and the unmentionable one [Tobin]. . . . That is the heart of the case."[76]

From this, Goldman argued, came the prosecution's attempt to define the entire SWP as a conspiracy to overthrow the government by force. If that interpretation were to stand, he explained, Socialist Workers would not be free to oppose the war, to join a trade union, to advise people to read Marx or Trotsky or Lenin, to attend social functions with others in the party, or to travel to Mexico, lest these actions be taken as evidence of their participation in the conspiracy. Employing emotional rhetoric of his own, Goldman argued that if the prosecution was successful, "a member of the Socialist Workers Party [would have] only one right, and that is to sit in jail."[77] If the jury were to find them not guilty, however, Goldman explained that they would be striking a blow in support of civil rights and for the eventual transformation of the world to socialism. In his final plea he faced the jury and said:

> We do not ask you to agree with us; we have not asked you to throughout the trial. We ask you only to permit us a chance to go on and teach our doctrines and our ideas, and a verdict of not guilty, will mean not only that you recognize the Bill of Rights and the Constitution, not only that you recognize the evidence, not only that you take into consideration our contention that we do not

advocate but predict, but it will mean on your part that you have struck a blow, a blow for the opportunity to transform the chaotic world in a peaceful way.

The greater the democracy, the greater the chances for a peaceful transformation. Give us that chance, for you cannot stop our voices by putting us behind bars. The conditions demand those voices and the voices will be heard.[78]

In what on its face seemed like an eminently reasonable final plea, Goldman not only cited the need to protect basic civil liberties but also defiantly expressed the Trotskyists' commitment to advocating socialist revolution, which they believed was an unstoppable force. Goldman and his fellow defendants would have to wait for the verdict to see if the jury believed that the advocacy he defended was inherently peaceful, and thus not subject to the Smith Act limitations, or essentially violent, and therefore illegal.

Schweinhaut certainly did not agree with the defense's presentation and made this clear in his closing statement issued the next day. Mainly engaging with specific points raised by Goldman in his summation, Schweinhaut's comments were brief but sharp. He staunchly refuted the defense attorney's allegation that the prosecution was directed by "men higher up" with ties to the federal government. Such tactics were diversionary and unconvincing, he asserted. Lawyers who blame conspiracies in Washington, Schweinhaut argued, "throw as much dust in the eyes of sworn jurors as possible" and depend on such "tricks" when they do not have a good defense.[79] Engaging in a few rhetorical tricks himself, Schweinhaut thus mocked Goldman's abilities as lead defense attorney.

Continuing his attack on Goldman's final statement, Schweinhaut rejected his dismissal of the prosecution's eyewitness testimony. The witnesses all testified to hearing the same thing, Schweinhaut explained, because that is what they heard; they recalled statements dealing with the violent overthrow of the government because such utterances were more shocking and memorable than other, quotidian conversations. And most of those who testified came from the ranks of Local 544 not because of a vendetta among those opposed to the Trotskyist leadership of the union but because, as Schweinhaut asked, "Who else would they be, but members of 544? They are the men that these defendants consorted with day after day. Who would hear the talk that came from these people, but the men that worked with them?"[80] Through such simple explanations, Schweinhaut tried to restore the credibility of the government's witnesses, whom Goldman had accused of perjury.

When it came to the documentary evidence that Goldman wanted the jury to dismiss, so that it would focus only on official party resolutions and writings, Schweinhaut argued that all of the exhibits must be considered. He told the jurors that Goldman did not want them to see the other materials, which had been entered into evidence, because those things betrayed the evil conspiracy in question. In his attempt at distinguishing among the written materials, Schweinhaut claimed, Goldman tried to "seduce you into believing they said something they did not say." Schweinhaut defended the ability of the excerpts that the prosecution entered into evidence to stand alone but implored the jury to "read it all" if it wished, insisting that the materials would show the defendants' program of violence.[81]

And that program of violence was very real, he insisted, despite the defendants' attempts to deny it now at trial. What else, Schweinhaut implored, was the jury to make of passages found in Goldman's own writings like "We can't wait. We will not wait. We will take it by force"? No matter what the defendants now say they meant, he argued, "the beans were spilled, because the Coopers, the Dobbs [sic] . . . the Skoglunds and the Hansons [sic] . . . were not so subtle." Again refuting the defense's contention that the reason for the prosecution was tied to the internal union fight, he offered the government's justification for what it deemed an independent investigation. Witnesses heard these things, and the government took that testimony and then laid it alongside the writings (which the witnesses had not read) and saw the pattern, Schweinhaut explained: "The mosaics and the patterns all complete. That is why the defendants are here."[82]

Driving home his point about the clear and present danger posed by the defendants, Schweinhaut told the jury that even though Goldman also tried to portray the SWP as "a futile, a puny, a weak and a kindly little minority," so too were the Bolsheviks just before they took power.[83] He summed up the central issue for the prosecution as "the right of the Federal Government to prevent, and to punish, if necessary, people who seek its destruction, not by constitutional means but by force; and I agree also that there is present here the question of the right of free speech; and also the question of its abuse."[84] For Schweinhaut and the attorney general's office he represented, the Constitution was not a suicide pact: free speech protections did not extend to the use of such speech to destroy the very government that guaranteed them.

With that position clearly and passionately expressed, the closing statements came to an end. In his instructions to the jury that followed, Judge Joyce recapped the arguments that had been set forth by each side. Although he reminded the jurors that the indictment was an accusation and not evidence of guilt, he also explained to them that in order to prove the intent in question under the Smith Act, "direct evidence is not necessary." Rather, the intent that needed to be proved for a conspiracy was "a state of mind which must be determined by reasonable inferences from the facts proved," which included "circumstantial evidence." Joyce acknowledged that the government and the defense team had presented two different interpretations of these facts during the trial, but that it was up to the jury to decide "which inferences you will draw," including a determination of the credibility of the witnesses.[85]

Perhaps reflecting some of the influence Biddle may have wielded by sending Schweinhaut to handle the case, Joyce at first seemed to instruct the jurors to interpret the Smith Act violation narrowly, speaking of the need to protect certain basic civil rights. He explained to the jury how "mere membership in the Socialist Workers' Party, without knowing the purposes thereof, does not impute guilt to any defendant." Joyce argued, "These defendants may not be found guilty because of their beliefs in or their exposition or defense of socialism. We have no law which says a man may not be a socialist if he so desires"; he may even "seek to enlist others to a like belief." And the judge specified other protected activities, which included "the right to be active in trade unions, of which they were members, participate in strikes, contribute 10 percent of their salary or any other sum, or solicit others to do, for the benefit of the Socialist Workers' Party." But Joyce then reminded the jury that while such acts were not in and of themselves crimes, they could be considered criminal if "you believe that they are evidence when taken together of activities in furtherance of the alleged conspiracy." He thus presented to the jurors both the defense's contention of the innocence of the Trotskyists' constitutionally protected political actions and the prosecution's interpretation that such actions combined to form an illegal conspiracy: it was now up to the jury to assess and decide between the two.[86]

Joyce offered similar instructions when it came to the specific illegal end of the alleged conspiracy: the violent overthrow of the government. He noted how "it is not the abstract doctrine of overthrowing organized government by unlawful means which is denounced by the law, but the advocacy of action for the accomplishment of that purpose." Echoing Schweinhaut's closing, however, Joyce also noted that the "government has the right to survive and one may not, under the law, knowingly conspire with others to indulge in or resort to methods, oral or written, which advocate its overthrow by force and violence." He called on the jurors to "keep their heads clear and cool" as they deliberated and urged that there be "no hysteria, no uncontrolled emotionalism, no approaches to our problems by consideration of hatred or prejudice, and no decision reached upon factors that result in injustice" on the part of the jury or the public following the trial.[87] With that, and after Joyce responded to some exceptions posed by the defense to his instructions, the jury was asked to file out and begin its deliberations.

In the Shadow of War: The First Smith Act Trial Verdict
and Sentencing

The jury remained out for several days, during which the defense team filed
a motion requesting a new trial on the grounds of insufficient evidence. Its
efforts were unsuccessful.[88] After fifty-six hours of deliberation, the jury
returned on December 1 with a verdict. The courtroom was packed that
morning with an "audience of 100," yet was so quiet "you could hear the
clock tick." The jurors entered the room at 8:20 a.m. and passed the verdict
to the clerk, who passed it to Judge Joyce. After reviewing the verdict, Joyce
passed it back to the clerk, who then read it out to those assembled.[89] Five
of the defendants—Miles Dunne, Ray Rainbolt, Roy Orgon, Harold Swanson, and Kelly Postal—were acquitted of all charges. The remaining eighteen
defendants were acquitted on count one but were found guilty on count two.
Perhaps because the Smith Act allowed for up to ten years in jail and a maximum fine of $10,000, the jury recommended leniency in sentencing.[90]

Satisfied that his work in Minneapolis was done, Henry Schweinhaut returned to Washington to brief the attorney general.[91] The local press approved
of the verdict, describing it as having been "arrived at with careful discrimination and earnest study, and in no aura of hysteria" after the defendants received
a "full and fair trial." Echoing the government's position on the case, the *Minneapolis Star Journal* reminded readers that "in times when the nation fears for
its security, the laws which bear on our civil liberties are stricter, and are more
strictly construed, than when there are no such fears." Because the jury found
that "force was advocated," the balance of protections fell in favor of national
security over that of Americans' cherished liberty.[92] But the defendants and
their supporters in 544-CIO and the SWP disagreed with this assessment and
expressed their grave disappointment with the verdict. Following its announcement, Goldman issued a statement to the press in which he again pointed a finger at Daniel Tobin, President Roosevelt, and Attorney General Biddle, blaming
them for a "frame-up" that violated "the will of the truck drivers in Minneapolis" and stifled "the voice of the revolutionary opposition to the second world
war." Goldman also announced that the defendants planned to "exhaust every
step and every resource for appeal purposes," including going to the "American
people in an attempt to convince them that the rights of free speech, free press,
and free assembly are in real danger of suppression." In that fight they had the
support of the ACLU and the Civil Rights Defense Committee.[93]

Americans' appreciation of the importance of free speech even in times of
crisis may have already influenced the jurors in their deliberations and in the
decisions they handed down on December 1. Based on the mixed verdict and

Figure 4.3 George Frosig, Carl Skoglund, Kelly Postal, Miles Dunne, and Vincent Dunne (left to right) taking a break around the time of the trial. The personal friendships among the Trotskyists sustained them during this stressful time, even after Frosig was exonerated by Judge Joyce, and Postal and Miles Dunne were acquitted by the jury. Courtesy Hennepin County Library Special Collections.

its recommendation of leniency, it appeared that the jury did not fully adopt the prosecution's argument that the SWP itself was an illegal conspiracy, but rather made distinctions among the various defendants. The five whom they acquitted either were no longer very active in the SWP, were not directly accused by any of the government witnesses of advocating the overthrow of the government by force, or both. None of these five men had penned any revolutionary statements either. The same could not be said for the eighteen who were convicted. Although the jury made this distinction among the twenty-three defendants, the five who were acquitted quickly issued a statement in which they voiced their solidarity with the convicted eighteen. And they articulated their commitment to rebuilding the drivers' movement in Minneapolis "on the basis of industrial unionism, union democracy and militant policies."[94] These men had not been not cowed by the ordeal of the trial and vowed to continue their trade union work.

The remaining defendants awaited their sentencing, which was scheduled for Monday, December 8. They gathered each day until then at the party's headquarters in Minneapolis, where they sat around, sipping beer, playing cards, and listening to the radio to help pass the time. On Sunday, December 7, their diversions were interrupted by the announcement on the radio about the attack on Pearl Harbor. Like all Americans who heard the news that day, the Trotskyists were shocked and horrified. But they also had more immediate and personal reasons for being quite worried. As they headed into the courthouse the next morning to hear their fate, Farrell Dobbs later recalled with a nervous laugh, "We thought that judge would put us away so deep they wouldn't find us until some archeologists three-hundred years from now start looking to see what's under the dirt."[95] For a group still staunchly opposed to the war, and now convicted of sedition, entering the courtroom on December 8, 1941, for sentencing was a daunting experience.

The atmosphere in the court that Monday morning was tense and, at times, emotional. In his comments before handing down the sentences, Judge Joyce acknowledged the jury's request for leniency and, surprisingly for the defense, stated that he intended to abide by it.[96] His decision may have been influenced somewhat by Attorney General Biddle, whose opinion Joyce had solicited after the verdict had been handed down. Biddle, "who felt that it would be unfortunate if severe sentences were imposed," suggested that a "term of eighteen months for the principal defendants would be fitting."[97] Joyce ultimately heeded Biddle's advice about leniency, but before announcing the sentences, he decided to issue a verbal condemnation of the defendants.

Joyce believed the evidence presented at trial demonstrated that the defendants had "gone beyond the limits of freedom of speech, and of the press, guaranteed by the Constitution of the United States." Just as there have been laws passed to protect individuals from "malicious written words and speech of others," Joyce explained, so too did Congress pass a law to protect the "Government of the people against attempts at its overthrow by force and violence," and the defendants had been found guilty of violating that law. In a moment that betrayed his raw emotion over the defense of his nation that had just been attacked by the Japanese, Joyce also stated how

> throughout the five weeks of trial of this case I have no recollection of a single word uttered in behalf of any defendant, expressing loyalty, fealty or devotion to our Government, its flag or its institutions. I do have vivid memory of written and spoken words, used and adopted by the defendants, expressing the hope for its overthrow and destruction by force.[98]

Although any such positive test of devotion or loyalty to the United States was not relevant to whether the defendants had violated the Smith Act, in his explanation of his deliberations over the sentences to be handed down, Joyce admitted that he was struck by the absence of such patriotic displays. With the country now literally about to fight to defend itself abroad, it had become even more difficult for many to tolerate the kind of political dissent offered by the Trotskyists. Torn between his disdain for the defendants' beliefs and the recommendations for leniency issued by the jury and by Biddle, Joyce handed down the sentences.

Each defendant then appeared before Joyce, one by one, to hear his or her sentence: Vincent Ray Dunne: sixteen months; Carl Skoglund: sixteen months; James Cannon: sixteen months; Farrell Dobbs: sixteen months; Felix Morrow: sixteen months; Grace Carlson: sixteen months; Oscar Coover: sixteen months; Max Geldman: sixteen months; Jake Cooper: sixteen months; Albert Goldman: sixteen months; Carlos Hudson: sixteen months; Emil Hansen: sixteen months; Ed Palmquist: one year and one day; Karl Kuehn: one year and one day; Oscar Schoenfeld: one year and one day; Clarence Hamel: one year and one day; Alfred Russell: one year and one day; Harry DeBoer: one year and one day.

The trial was over. The sentences had been handed down. But the fight for the Trotskyists had just begun. Immediately Goldman acknowledged that the defense planned to appeal. Joyce, recognizing that there was a "substantial question as to justify granting of bail on these appeals," issued a stay of execution of the sentences.[99] That same day, SWP leaders sent a telegram out to all party branches, communicating Cannon's message to "tolerate no jitteriness," "view the international situation," and ensure that "work goes on."[100] Now the "18," as the convicted defendants became known, began their struggle against the Smith Act outside the confines of the courthouse in the new and challenging context of a nation at war.

5

Battling the "Gag" Act in Wartime

December 1941–December 1943

In the two years following their conviction in December 1941, the Trotskyists appealed their case and challenged the constitutionality of the Smith Act.
First appealing to the Eighth Circuit Court in St. Louis and then to the U.S.
Supreme Court, the Trotskyists and their allies on the labor and liberal left
argued for the protection of civil liberties even in wartime. Through nationwide speaking tours and the Civil Rights Defense Committee's fund-raising
and advocacy efforts, the "18" won the support of the ACLU, National Association for the Advancement of Colored People (NAACP) branches, and
more than a hundred labor unions and trade councils. The fight against the
first Smith Act convictions became part of a larger conversation, which only
intensified once the United States entered the war, about how to balance free
speech protections and national security. The debate over the meaning and
applicability of the clear and present danger test in sedition cases that had
accompanied the Trotskyists' indictment and trial was carried on through
the appeals process that began in December 1941 and continued until the
end of 1943. While they fought to overturn their convictions and have what
they called the "Gag" Act declared unconstitutional, the Trotskyists also
confronted a number of related obstacles that included internal party factionalism, the difficult decision to dissolve Local 544-CIO, and continued FBI
surveillance. These were challenging years for the Trotskyists and, given the
Supreme Court's stand on the appeal, significant ones for Americans concerned about the fate of free speech in wartime.

"The Bill of Rights in Danger!": Taking the Case for the Appeal
to the Public

Leading the fight against the Smith Act convictions were George Novack
and the CRDC. Novack, the son of Jewish immigrants from Poland and the
Ukraine, grew up in Somerville, Massachusetts, attended Harvard, and in 1928
moved to New York, where, with a job in publicity, he joined the liberal-left
intellectual scene and was drawn into the Trotskyist orbit. As a well-educated

and financially well-off young man, Novack could have pursued any career but made "a very deliberate choice" to become a socialist revolutionary.[1] He became particularly interested in labor defense; he and Felix Morrow created the Non-Partisan Labor Defense, which merged with the Workers Defense League in 1936. As an intellectual, Novack served the SWP by using his talent for publicity to fight for civil rights, involving himself in the Scottsboro cases, for example, before being called upon to help the Trotskyists when they were caught in the crosshairs of the Smith Act.[2]

Novack and his soon-to-be second wife, Evelyn Reed, were in Minneapolis when the government indicted the twenty-nine in June 1941. Because of their experience with defense campaigns, they were asked to assist. Novack "immediately came east and took the first steps" by meeting with Margaret DeSilver and Carlo Tresca. DeSilver's late husband had been one of the founders of the ACLU, and Tresca was a well-known Italian anarchist who had worked with Novack previously. DeSilver and Tresca arranged to have Novack speak with the writer and activist John Dos Passos, and shortly thereafter "all three agreed to be initiating sponsors of the Civil Rights Defense Committee."[3] Novack then also met with Roger Baldwin, "with whom [he] had cooperated in a number of cases" and hoped he could count on now to help him with his new cause. Baldwin was receptive to Novack and took him to meet with Arthur Garfield Hays, chief attorney for the ACLU. The three men discussed the situation in Minneapolis at some length, whereupon Baldwin and Hays "said they were certain that the ACLU would back" the Trotskyists. Novack's close friend, the novelist James T. Farrell, agreed to become chairman of the CRDC.[4]

The group quickly went to work. Novack later recalled how "one of the chores we had was to explain to people what the substance of this gag law, the Smith Act, was and how alien it was to any constitutional provisions."[5] The CRDC engaged in a letter campaign to raise funds for and awareness of the case. Some individuals, like Bruce Bliven and Albert Hamilton, were moved enough by this campaign to write to Attorney General Biddle protesting the July indictments.[6] Once the trial began in October, the CRDC also published a pamphlet entitled *Witch Hunt in Minnesota: The Federal Prosecution of the Socialist Workers Party and Local 544-CIO*. In the foreword Farrell reminded readers that "it is our highest duty to remain free in a world of the most brutal oppression and tyranny" and made the CRDC's case that "we remain free men by defending the liberty of others, as well as ourselves, whether or not we agree with them."[7] Novack concurred and argued that the 1941 Smith Act case, as a politically motivated prosecution based on a dangerous peacetime sedition law, had to be challenged for the sake of the "democratic and constitutional rights" that all Americans cherished.[8]

Those cherished rights were guaranteed in the Bill of Rights. When President Roosevelt proclaimed December 15, 1941, a special "Bill of Rights Day" to mark its 150th anniversary, Novack and the CRDC held a mass meeting at the Hotel Diplomat in New York. As the *Militant* reported, 700 people gathered "to support the freedom of the 18" and to condemn the convictions "as a violation of the free speech and free press provisions of the Bill of Rights." Novack, Baldwin, Cannon, Goldman, and Farrell each addressed the crowd; they argued for the importance of defending civil liberties, especially in wartime, and decried the danger to civil liberties that the Minneapolis case presented.[9] Max Shachtman, national secretary of the Workers Party, warned that while today it was the "18" whose civil rights had been violated, tomorrow it could be "the entire working class" if a strong protest were not immediately launched.[10] Each of the speakers seized the moment of Roosevelt's Bill of Rights Day to call upon the public to take action against what they believed was an assault on free speech.

In addition to the political protest, there was also a practical side to the December 15 gathering. Dorothy Schultz, Grace Carlson's sister and one of the acquitted Trotskyists, spoke at the event and thanked the CRDC for the financial aid it provided to the defendants, many of whom had lost their jobs because of the trial. By coordinating the rally in New York, Novack's organization added $344 to its coffers from audience donations.[11] And through the sale of a pamphlet inspired by the night's events, entitled *The Bill of Rights in Danger! The Meaning of the Minneapolis Convictions*, the CRDC raised additional funds in subsequent months.[12] Over the next two years the organization would take in a total of $39,010.16 and would disburse $38,086.10 for the Trotskyists' defense and appeals.[13]

The CRDC worked hard to get the word out about the case and to raise funds to support the defendants. It was helped by others who responded spontaneously to the news of the verdict. The *Militant* and the *Industrial Organizer* reported on the case from the time of the June raids through the December sentencing and beyond. But other labor and radical publications also joined in the outcry against the verdict, including the IWW's *Industrial Worker* and the Social Democratic Federation's *New Leader*. The Socialist Party's paper, the *Call*, argued that the case was "a reflection of the hysteria of our time and a rank case of stupid and unjust persecution by the government."[14] The left-liberal media was also deeply concerned. The *New Republic* observed that "for the first time in peace since 1789, Americans have been convicted of sedition on the basis of their opinions." Because the jury "found no proof of overt acts," the editors found the verdict to be "a most disturbing and unfortunate" precedent.[15] And the *Nation*'s editors argued that the convictions were "challenges to every believer in civil liberties" because they were an example of just what the first ten amendments sought to prevent: "the imprisonment of men not for what they did but for what they thought and said." They too called on "all progressives of whatever political orientation" to "join the defense of the Minneapolis defendants" lest they "permit the establishment of a precedent that may some day be used against them."[16]

For the time being, however, members of the Communist Party did not share this concern. Rather than condemning the Smith Act as a violation of civil liberties, the Communists applauded the convictions, feeling secure enough in their own support for the war not to worry about the law's application against them. And although they celebrated the verdict, they insisted that the Trotskyists were really fascist fifth column supporters of Hitler (because of their opposition to the war) and therefore should have been convicted as "the servants of reaction" that they allegedly were, rather than as "a militant working class organization." It was the same critique they had launched in the *Daily Worker* in August, only now intensified in America's wartime context.[17] Once again the CPUSA used the moment to strike a blow against one of its most detested partisan rivals.

In taking this position the Communists were the exception. Most of those on the labor-liberal left criticized the Trotskyists' conviction by rejecting the validity of the Smith Act and warning of the dangers to civil liberties its first application portended. That certainly was the position of the CRDC, the ACLU, and most of the left-liberal, labor, and radical press reactions to the verdict. It was also the position of Adam Clayton Powell Jr., the Manhattan councilman who wrote to Novack in January 1942 endorsing the work of the CRDC. Although he may not have been sympathetic to the Trotskyists' political views, he argued that "whether we agree or disagree on basic philosophies of life . . . we are Americans all," and that "whenever the Civil Liberties of any one American or any one American group are threatened, then the Civil Liberties of all are in danger, and this is the issue in Minneapolis."[18] Powell's argument was exactly what Novack, Baldwin, and the other supporters of the "18" wanted to communicate to the American public. The CRDC, the ACLU, and the defendants hoped that through such public appeals they could secure financial support for the defense and direct popular pressure on the courts to reverse the convictions.

The defendants also used the SWP to aid them in this work. Cannon and Dobbs communicated with the locals and branches around the country, encouraging them to sell the pamphlet penned by Novack and those produced by Cannon and Goldman (*Socialism on Trial* and *In Defense of Socialism*).[19] SWP branches around the country, from Boston, to Detroit, to Los Angeles, to Seattle, held special meetings to publicize the case to its members soon after the verdict and to provide financial support for the defendants during the appeal campaign in 1942 and 1943.[20] And Vincent Dunne launched a national speaking tour in Milwaukee on February 2, 1942.[21] "We are fighting not only for ourselves," he explained, "but for the freedoms and democratic rights of the entire labor movement and the American people."[22] On his tour Dunne built support for local CRDC branches and the appeal campaign, but he also tried to expand the ranks of the party.[23] Rather than throw their hands up in despair, Dunne and the others took to the road and used the Smith Act convictions to rejuvenate the SWP.[24]

Trotskyists around the country and their supporters (some of whom were drawn into the party's ranks) were energized by Dunne's tour and by the CRDC's message about the danger to civil liberties inherent in the Minneapolis case.[25] The "18" had secured the backing of the ACLU in its appeal campaign, along with the sympathy of most of the radical and left-liberal press. Appealing to Americans' shared respect for the Bill of Rights, they made their case to the public with the aid of the CRDC, while at the same time using that case to grow the ranks of the party.

The Convicted Trotskyists on the Defensive

Although the Smith Act convictions energized the ranks, they also seriously challenged the integrity of the party. Almost all the top SWP leadership in the United States had been convicted of sedition and faced lengthy prison sentences. And the legality of the party had been challenged in federal court. Although Cannon quickly communicated to the rank and file that the work of the party was to continue despite the verdict,[26] he, Carlson, and Goldman soon faced criticism from within the wider Trotskyist movement that temporarily took their attention away from that work.

The critique was voiced by two of their comrades from Mexico, Natalia Sedova and Grandizo Munis. Sedova and Munis charged Cannon, Carlson, and Goldman in particular with undermining the revolutionary spirit of Trotskyism and deviating from the defense strategy outlined in the SWP's 1941 plenum conference, in which the accused were to enter the courtroom not as defendants but as "accusers of the war-mongers and the dying system which they were upholding."[27] According to Sedova, the "Cannon-Goldman dialogue" at the center of the defense "only served to pacify the jury and make the sentences lighter," when the party's task in the trial was to convince the "world proletariat" of the need for "revolution by violent means."[28] Munis, who had been general secretary of the Spanish Trotskyist movement during the time of the Spanish Civil War and later fled to Mexico, where he established a section of the Fourth International among Spanish exiles, also criticized Cannon and the others.[29] Munis voiced many of the same concerns raised by Sedova but did so in a lengthier and more forceful manner. He wanted the defendants to accuse the government and the bourgeoisie of being the real perpetrators of violence and argued that, instead, when these moments arose in the courtroom, "our comrades shrink themselves, minimize the revolutionary significance of their ideas, [and] try to make an honorable impression on the jury."[30]

Cannon moved quickly to defend himself and his allies against what he termed the ultraleftist tendency in the movement, seeing Munis's critique as an embodiment of this and Sedova's comments as evidence of its influence over her.[31] Cannon first wrote to Sedova on February 14, telling her that her criticism "must be due to misunderstanding or inadequate information,"[32] reproaching her gently while leaving her an opening to retract her criticisms. But when it came to Munis and his leftist allies, Cannon did not shy from launching a strong attack.[33] His argument, "Political Principles and Propaganda Methods," appeared in print with Munis's denunciation in the June 1942 *International Bulletin*. Cannon's response took on Munis point by point and demonstrated the defendants' commitment to Trotskyist orthodoxy.

Cannon explained, for example, how the trial provided "our first real opportunity to make the party and its principles known to wide circles of workers." He insisted that maintaining the legality of the party, remaining true to its principles, and reaching out to workers were vital concerns that were not mutually exclusive.[34] But because the consciousness of the American worker in 1941 was "far from revolutionary," Cannon argued that for the defendants "the task was *to get a hearing* for our ideas from the forum of the trial. These ideas had to be simplified as much as possible, *made plausible* to the workers and illustrated whenever possible by familiar examples from American history." That was why the tone of the defendants' testimony—especially the exchange between Cannon and Goldman—was one of "patient, school-room *explanations* of our doctrines and ourselves." The Trotskyists never wavered on their principles, but like their Marxist teachers, Cannon explained, they "changed their manner and tone and points of emphasis to suit the occasion" in which they defended them.[35] Therefore, when it came to their explanation that the party neither engaged in violence nor advocated it but rather predicted a violent response to the coming revolution, Cannon fiercely defended this stance as "100 per cent correct."[36] While detractors like Munis would remain, Cannon and his supporters stood by the approach he and the other defendants had taken in court.

By October 1942, when the *Militant* published a review of the Munis-Cannon exchange, Cannon and other defendants were busy moving on and "building the revolutionary party under the present conditions."[37] Carlson ran for mayor of St. Paul in the spring of 1942. Not cowed by her conviction for revolutionary advocacy in federal court just a few months prior, Carlson proclaimed: "I believe only a socialist government can bring a lasting peace, and freedom and plenty for all."[38] Ultimately defeated at the polls in April as a write-in candidate, she did not give up and announced her plans to run for the U.S. Senate that fall.[39] And although that campaign ended in failure too, Carlson remained committed to the SWP. Dunne ran for mayor of Minneapolis in the spring of 1943, positioned by the *Militant* as the "only candidate standing for independent working class political action."[40] But like Carlson, Dunne was unable to secure enough votes in the primary to be a viable candidate (winning only 793). It was difficult for the SWP to vie effectively with the other parties' political machines in the Twin Cities. When the Trotskyists did secure votes in Carlson's Senate campaign, for example, it was alleged that not all the counties reported them to the state canvassing board.[41] Even when the votes were counted properly, Dunne and Carlson faced the added difficulty of their opposition to the war and their sedition convictions when they tried to win the support of average Americans in these campaigns.

One constituency that was responsive to the Trotskyists, at least in terms of expressing solidarity with their struggle against the Smith Act, consisted of laborers. After recovering in Los Angeles from an illness that overtook him shortly after the trial, Dobbs began a speaking tour in May 1942 to expand the party's footprint in the labor movement.[42] From Los Angeles he traveled up the West Coast, then through the Midwest and the mid-Atlantic states, ending up in New York in August. There, before an audience of "150 members and friends of the Socialist Workers Party," he spoke about the growing labor movement in America and the Trotskyists' plans for a "mass labor party." By the end of the night he had helped raise $500 in donations for the SWP's campaign.[43]

Although the SWP's labor campaign was a program independent from the Smith Act case appeal, the Trotskyists' struggle won them sympathy from workers in these years. Some of that sympathy took the shape of financial aid to the labor campaign, and some took the form of workers joining the ranks of the party.[44] But the solidarity that most workers and their unions expressed was their public support for the appeal of the verdict and protest of the "Gag" Act; it was not necessarily an endorsement of the SWP or its politics. Public support took the form of resolutions, like that passed by the New Jersey State Industrial Union Council of the CIO in January 1942, which condemned "the convictions in the Minneapolis case" and protested "the use of the FBI to interfere in the democratic procedure of the labor movement."[45] And it was expressed when leaders from a variety of trade unions and state CIO councils turned out in force around the country at the CRDC meetings coordinated with Dunne's tour.[46] Among those unions expressing solidarity were more than three dozen United Auto Workers locals, more than a dozen United Steelworkers locals, seven United Rubber Workers locals, six United Textile Workers locals, four Industrial Union of Marine and Shipbuilding Workers locals, four Amalgamated Clothing Workers locals, four United Construction Workers Organizing Committee locals, three International Longshoremen and Warehousemen Union locals, and three United Electrical, Radio, and Machine Workers locals. AFL-affiliated unions were also represented, but in smaller numbers, most notably four International Ladies Garment Workers Union locals from New York and Brooklyn. In total, the *Militant* boasted, unions representing approximately 1 million workers supported the "18."[47]

Mostly these were members of the more progressive CIO unions and AFL affiliates. Because Communists were strongly represented throughout the CIO, Cannon dissuaded Novack from setting up a "national CIO committee to receive funds for the Minneapolis defense" because he feared "the Stalinists might well utilize such a Committee to set on top of the whole affair doing nothing."[48] Instead, the Trotskyists and their allies in the CRDC went directly to individual locals, explaining why workers needed to support the Smith Act case appeal.

Workers who were convinced expressed their concern with the federal government's interference in the internal union business of Local 544 and, in particular, with the disturbing role of the FBI in the case. These workers also vocalized wariness toward the Smith Act's powers and its sponsor, Representative Howard Smith, who in early 1942 introduced the antistrike legislation (the War Labor Disputes Act) that they referred to as the Slave Labor Bill.[49] These progressive elements within the labor movement rallying around the cause of the "18" came together to protest what they saw as a broader government attack on labor rights. Some of their energy fueled the SWP's labor campaign too, but most of it remained focused on the broader issue of the preservation of labor rights and civil liberties. On those issues, the CRDC, ACLU, and now left labor unions could agree; all three groups became part of this larger national conversation, coming together in the two years after the trial to demand that the Minneapolis verdict be overturned and the Smith Act be declared unconstitutional.

"Unnecessary Victimizations": Trotskyists under Fire from "Tobin's Men" and the FBI

Although the Trotskyists found supporters among unionized workers around the country, they remained estranged from many of their brothers in Minneapolis. Drivers there remained divided; most joined the ranks of 544-AFL, but some stayed loyal to the Dunnes and 544-CIO. The Smith Act convictions made this acrimonious situation worse by embittering the 544-CIO supporters, who believed Tobin was behind the prosecution. Those in 544-AFL, especially a core group from the Committee of 99, wanted to break their rival union and drive its Trotskyist leaders out of the labor movement. Working with IBT leaders and employers, they fought against 544-CIO's appeal of labor conciliator Alfred Blair's decision and blacklisted the Trotskyists. Very much aware of the opposition they continued to face from 544-AFL and the IBT, Dunne, Dobbs, and the others kept up the fight in Minneapolis for as long as they could, altering their trade union strategy only when it became clear that 544-CIO could no longer survive.

The ultimate defeat of 544-CIO was not inevitable, not even after its Trotskyist leaders were convicted of conspiring to advocate the violent overthrow of the government. There was still the possibility that those leaders could be vindicated on appeal. And there was also the trouble brewing within 544-AFL that threatened to undermine its campaign against the Trotskyists. In the center of the controversy were James Bartlett and a group of his supporters who, discontented with the IBT's trusteeship over 544-AFL, violently challenged it.

Concerns about Bartlett and his clique emerged even before the Smith Act trial came to a close. In November 1941, I. E. Goldberg wrote to Joseph Padway about the situation. Goldberg was a lawyer retained by the IBT to oversee its business in Minneapolis, and Padway was his legal partner and also one of the AFL's chief lawyers then stationed in Washington. According to Goldberg, Bartlett "seemingly is behaving," but a group of men with whom he had been meeting on a regular basis were seen congregating outside the union headquarters in parked cars where they talked about terminating the trusteeship. Although "there have been no open rump meetings," there was a rumor that Bartlett's clique was planning "a concerted movement at the general meeting of December 9 to demand the right to hold an election." In addition to these rumors, Goldberg reported, was the assault on Stephen Nehotte, 544-AFL's recording secretary and one of its organizers. Nehotte had been approached by some of Bartlett's followers to join their push for new elections; shortly after turning them down, "while riding home in his automobile [he] was cut off by another automobile and two shots were fired over his car." Worried about these disruptions, Goldberg suggested that the union gently push Bartlett and his clique out of their positions as organizers by holding "a little banquet" for them "with a few speeches and flowery remarks" praising their work. In this way, they could be "weeded out and no bad taste is left, nor antagonisms created" that might drive them to the CIO.[50]

The motives for this group's agitation against the trusteeship are unclear, but they continued to push for Bartlett's election to the union presidency in December. They could have felt constrained by the trusteeship and may have wanted a more locally based leadership put in place by democratic means. Or they may have just wanted to secure the spoils that would come from having their friend in control of the local union. The way these men waged their campaign for Bartlett's election, however, was disruptive and violent. In addition to the attack on Nehotte, some members of the Bartlett clique intimidated the trustees and officers of the local at gunpoint in the union office, placed menacing phone calls to those officers in their homes, and threatened to kill one of them (Fritz Snyder) by thrusting a gun in his ribs while he was having lunch at a diner near the union hall. After the general membership meeting was held in early December, and the group failed to secure the open election, Bartlett "went on an extended vacation" without permission from the IBT. When he returned and "refused to do any work" for the local, he was fired.[51]

But Bartlett would not go without a fight. Writing to executive assistant of the IBT Thomas Flynn twice in February, he insisted that he remained loyal to the Teamsters and offered to keep Flynn informed of the goings-on in the local, but to no avail.[52] By May, Bartlett became markedly desperate. Claiming "hundreds of members are going to refuse to pay dues" if something was not done to end the continuing trusteeship, Bartlett argued that he "could be of great use to the International Union on their payroll." If given the chance, Bartlett insisted, he "could prove my worth in short order." And "the fact that I gave leadership to a movement that finally resulted in the elimination of the Dunnes," he argued, "should mean something to my credit."[53]

But unfortunately for Bartlett, that was not the case. His efforts at eliminating the Trotskyists from the IBT were not to be rewarded because of his association with the disruptive rump movement in 544-AFL. Despite his many protestations to the contrary, Bartlett was pegged as the leader of this group. Flynn could not overlook that, especially when he continued to receive communications from Sidney Brennan, secretary-treasurer of the local, and other officers from 544-AFL alleging the connection.[54] Bartlett's heady desire to reap the spoils of his work against the Dunnes was foiled by the IBT's stronger will to maintain the trusteeship. Until they could be sure that the threat from 544-CIO and the Trotskyists had been fully eliminated, Flynn and Tobin (supported by Goldberg and Padway) were not going to allow open elections or any criticism from the ranks.

The threat from 544-CIO was lessened in May 1942, when Judge Carleton F. McNally upheld labor conciliator Alfred Blair's decision, certifying Local 544-AFL as bargaining agent of the drivers' citywide unit. Local 544-CIO had filed a writ of certiorari seeking the review in December 1941 but now suffered this defeat with McNally's finding in favor of 544-AFL.[55] Through its legal channels, 544-AFL was able to secure its bargaining rights in the city and undermine its loathed rival, winning "another victory in the Dunne fight."[56]

For the Trotskyists in 544-CIO, the McNally decision signaled the need to change tactics. Since Blair's original certification decision went against their local in September it had become increasingly difficult to organize in the city. And the December Smith Act convictions of the union's leading organizers and executive committee members further undermined the integrity of 544-CIO. By the late spring 1942 its funds were so depleted that it had to suspend publication of its newspaper, the *Industrial Organizer*, had trouble paying rent for its headquarters and largely relied on the work of dedicated volunteers. Kelly Postal, 544-CIO's president, also became the target of embezzlement charges leveled by the IBT.[57] As Dobbs later recalled, the Trotskyists realized they could not continue to lead militant workers down a losing road of "unnecessary victimizations." Later that year they called a meeting of the membership of 544-CIO and "sadly but resentfully" consented to dissolve the local. The members "agreed that they would go and apply for admission to the Tobin set up with the understanding that this was the best way in this losing situation, where we didn't have a chance, to be able to fight another day." For the Trotskyists there was the cold realization that there was "no longer any realistic basis on which to continue the trade union struggle" through 544-CIO.[58]

The consequences of this decision in terms of bread-and-butter gains were significant for the drivers. Local 544-CIO's Trotskyist leaders had secured a contract with one company (Waterman-Waterbury) in early 1942 that included a 14-cent wage increase, for example, even as the union struggled to survive.[59] Those negotiating for 544-AFL in a contract deal with a different company had settled for a 6-cent increase in late 1941, despite the workers' original demand of 17.5 cents, in sweetheart deals brokered with the employers and Blair that promised to block 544-CIO from the bargaining table.[60] This deal made by 544-AFL was yet another part of the process through which the IBT undermined the Trotskyist leadership of 544-CIO during the 1941–1943 period of intra-union warfare. In this case the IBT worked in tandem with employers who saw an opening to advance their own agenda of limiting wage increases for drivers. At least in the short term, during this period of internal union factionalism, 544-AFL's fight against 544-CIO limited workers' gains.

For the Trotskyists, the final dissolution of 544-CIO did not mean giving up on trade union work altogether; it just meant going about it a different way. As individual workers connected with other unions, they continued to agitate, educate, and organize, much to the chagrin of Brennan, Flynn, and others in 544-AFL and the IBT. In October 1942, for example, Harry DeBoer, Emil Hansen, and Clarence Hamel met with striking workers in the market district who were demanding higher pay. Stephen Nehotte, who was then president of 544-AFL, blamed DeBoer for the walkout among workers in companies with which the IBT was trying to negotiate.[61] The Trotskyists were still a thorn in 544-AFL's side.[62]

Sidney Brennan did not hesitate to draw this reality to the attention of Flynn. As one of the leaders of the Committee of 99, Brennan had long been opposed to the Trotskyists in the Teamsters movement. He shared with many of those in that rank-and-file opposition a concern about what he saw as the disruptive and destructive presence of the radicals in their midst, but he also used his crusade against them to build his union career. From the Committee of 99, Brennan was appointed recording secretary under 544-AFL's trusteeship. By August 1942, after demonstrating his loyalty to the IBT through his service to the local, and after securing a glowing recommendation from the mayor of Minneapolis, Brennan replaced T. T. Neal as trustee.[63] Unlike Bartlett, whose associates turned to heavy-handed tactics to try to help their friend, Brennan worked quietly to advance in the union. From that position he would lead the fight to blacklist the Dunnes and their associates and to purge the Trotskyists from the ranks of organized labor.

Brennan found support for his crusade among the Communists. The CPUSA continued to assert that the real reason the "18" were convicted was their alleged Nazi ties. Individual Communist Party members "in various unions" were "opposing the voting of union donations to the Civil Rights Defense Committee."[64] And Communists in the Minneapolis labor movement, specifically those associated with the CIO's United Electrical, Radio and Machine Workers Union, cooperated with 544-AFL to create a joint AFL-CIO council in order to "avoid trouble during these troublesome times and to further 'wash' the Dunns [sic] out of the picture." L. Clair Johnson, secretary-treasurer of Teamsters Joint Council 32, which was also involved in this deal, explained the process in a letter to Thomas Flynn in May 1942. He noted how "the CIO leaders with whom we were getting together were as anti-Dunn [sic] as we are, as well as anti–John Lewis."[65] These otherwise strange bedfellows came together and "laid out a program" creating what they called the Minnesota AFL-CIO Joint Council with the express purpose of "freezing jurisdiction where union agreements exist" and uniting "in joint action on problems of common interest" to settle them "amicably at the conference table."

On its face the deal was an attempt to smooth out relations between the two groups that would otherwise spar over jurisdiction and to cooperate for the "successful prosecution of the war effort."[66] But, as Johnson's letter revealed, there was more to this agreement than just patriotic jurisdictional cooperation. The Trotskyists quickly recognized that the new body was aimed at them.[67] And ultimately the Joint Council's plan to "wash out the Dunnes" was successful; the unusual cooperation between the AFL and CIO contributed to the eventual dissolution of 544-CIO.

But that was not enough for many of the Trotskyists' rivals, especially Sidney Brennan. In the two years after their Smith Act convictions, Brennan doggedly worked to see that none of the defendants would find employment as drivers in the city and even tried to undermine their attempts to secure jobs in other fields and in other cities. Harry DeBoer and Clarence Hamel's attempt to get work in Madison, Wisconsin, under assumed names in the fall of 1942, for example, was foiled when union leaders there placed a phone call to 544-AFL.[68] And Miles Dunne's job searches were almost always blocked by Brennan (often with Gillespie's help).[69] Brennan's concern that there were unions "whose members still are in sympathy with these people" and his fear that the Dunnes and their followers would influence more workers if they were not stopped fueled his use of the blacklist.[70] "Tobin's men in Minneapolis still fear our people," Carlson wrote Sedova; as a result, she explained, "They are trying to have our people fired from every job that they can find." Recognizing the unease many companies expressed at having to deal with the CIO, and with the convicted Trotskyists in particular, Carlson explained, "Usually they [Brennan et al.] meet with success because of the cooperation received from the employer."[71]

Brennan's efforts to run the Trotskyists out of the labor movement met with success, too, largely because of the cooperation of IBT and AFL officials. He and other 544-AFL officers used this network to blacklist the Dunnes and their allies from jobs and union offices. They even used it to question the chartering of locals led by suspected Trotskyists, as was the case with John Janosco and AFL Furniture Workers Local 1859. In these efforts Brennan, Nehotte, and others received support and cooperation from Daniel Tobin and even William Green, president of the AFL.[72] But Brennan was less effective when it came to his desire to expel Communists from 544-AFL in these years. Despite the formation of the joint council with the Communists in the CIO, Brennan was convinced that they could not be trusted,[73] believing that "whatever label they use," such radicals "are doing the same disruptive work in our Union" as the Dunnes had done.[74] But Tobin and Flynn, referencing America's wartime alliance with the Soviets, argued, "It is more than danger-ous to try and expel a man because he is a Communist, even though our Con-stitution permits us to do so." The purge Brennan sought was postponed until after the war, when the "friendly feeling created towards Russia as a result of the war" waned.[75] The Trotskyists' assertion that their persecution was due, in part, to their opposition to the war was confirmed by this correspondence, at least when it came to the IBT's readiness to target them and to its hesitancy to go after the Communists in its midst as long as the United States was allied with the Soviet Union.

Dissuaded from purging members of the CPUSA from the Teamsters, Brennan and his IBT and AFL colleagues maintained their focus on the Trotskyists who continued to work and organize in the city. Brennan and Flynn communicated frequently about the goings-on of the "Dunne set-up," tracing the Trotskyists' personal and professional connections in the city (and especially their ties to other AFL unions) that enabled them to keep work-ing and to fund their trade union organizing.[76] Even though they struggled under their sedition convictions, the blacklist, and the erosion of 544-CIO, the Trotskyists, many of whom had been active trade unionists since the 1934 strikes, still had friends in Minneapolis. By early summer 1943, Brennan ex-pressed a sense of exasperation, telling Flynn, "I do not see why we cannot do something to prevail upon the Supreme Court to push this case, and see that these people are taken care of."[77] For him, the only sure way to eliminate the influence of the Trotskyists was to see them put behind bars. The Smith Act conviction was not enough as long as the appeal process continued. Brennan wanted the full punitive power of the state to come to bear on his political enemies.

What Brennan did not know was that the developing national security state was already putting pressure on the convicted Trotskyists and the SWP. The "18" were unaware of most of the FBI's activities, conducted by un-dercover agents and informants, but they knew about some of the bureau's probes. Over the course of the two years when they pursued their appeal, the "18" and the SWP were placed under intense surveillance, despite the defen-dants' protestations of innocence and insistence on the legality of their party. In conjunction with the IBT's attempts to blacklist them and crush 544-CIO, the FBI's investigations made the Trotskyists' trade union work and political activism difficult. Despite these challenges, the Trotskyists, under Cannon's and Dobbs's leadership of a tactical reorientation, maintained their party's dissenting voice even during the wartime years. The Trotskyists' ability to sustain the party while they appealed their case was all the more remarkable given the extent of the surveillance they were under.

What the "18" most likely did not know at the time was that many of them had been flagged as candidates for internment by both the FBI and the Department of Justice. The latter agency created the Special Defense Unit (SDU) in April 1940 to "provide department oversight of federal prosecutions of internal security-related crimes." As Richard Steele described it, "The unit would review cases brought to its attention by the FBI, survey the statutes, and recommend to the attorney general the appropriate course of action." The idea was to increase Washington's oversight of the U.S. attorneys and the bureau at the district level especially when it came to cases of internal subversion, which had been the source of so much abuse during the First Red Scare.[78] Once war erupted, the SDU identified individuals for prosecution according to their alleged level of dangerousness. The FBI also used its own Custodial Detention list, created by Hoover in 1939 to keep track of individuals with communist or Nazi "tendencies" who, if war broke out, were thought to "constitute a menace to the public peace and safety of the United States Government." Those on the list were divided into "immediate internment and close surveillance categories." In addition, Hoover maintained an index card file of those on the list, classified according to their level of "dangerousness." As Frank Donner explains, the criteria for being placed on the list "were broadly interpreted to include distributors of propaganda favorable to foreign interests and hostile to 'the American way of life,' as well as agitators of 'internal strife' and 'hatreds.'"[79] In June 1940, then attorney general Robert Jackson approved the existence of the bureau's list (which Hoover had belatedly made known to him) "to be implemented following a declaration of war."[80]

The Trotskyists found themselves targets of both the SDU's recommendations and the FBI's Custodial Detention list.[81] A few of the "18" had already been categorized by Hoover in the most dangerous grouping—"A1"—before their prosecution.[82] Others were added after the trial. In addition to these watch lists, there were the individual files that the bureau maintained on several of the defendants. Those files grew in size and detail in the years after their Smith Act convictions, eventually running to more than a thousand pages each for Dunne and Dobbs over the course of their lifetimes. Dunne, for example, was tracked as he traveled around the country on his 1942 CRDC tour. From Chicago, to Newark, to Youngstown, to Philadelphia, to Seattle, reports were complied from agents and informants who infiltrated the meetings and detailed the content of Dunne's speeches, the groups of individuals assembled, and the nature of the petitions circulated. Dunne's smaller gatherings with workers in some of these cities—gatherings where he assisted them in their union organizing but also encouraged them to join the party—were described as "secret meetings." And those present who were not affiliated directly with the party but were in sympathy with the CRDC's cause were sometimes mentioned by name in these dispatches.[83]

Similarly detailed reports were compiled from the surveillance of other Trotskyists, including Farrell Dobbs (who conducted his speaking tour in 1943) and Edward Palmquist (who had become active in the party's Seattle branch after the trial).[84] Although some of the names of individuals referred to in these reports (and all of the confidential informants' names) were redacted in the files released by the FBI, the fact that such records exist of citizens' exercising their First Amendment rights remains troubling. The wartime emergency climate and the Smith Act convictions supported the argument that national security interests outweighed the Trotskyists' exercise of their First Amendment rights, which were intruded upon by these investigations. And the bureau did this even as the "18" defendants pursued an appeal of their convictions and insisted that the law under which they had been found guilty was unconstitutional.

In addition to tracking individual Trotskyists, the FBI also maintained surveillance on the SWP. Agents infiltrated branch meetings and CRDC gatherings around the country. A snapshot of the size and influence of the SWP emerges from these reports, showing the party between late 1941 and late 1943 to be quite strong in New York, Detroit, Seattle, and Philadelphia but struggling in Cleveland and Houston and "not active" in New Orleans and Memphis. The agents' reports from cities where the party was active detailed members' antiwar speech, their meetings in support of the "18," and their attempts to make inroads with various unions.[85] The FBI watched the SWP's national headquarters in New York in particular very closely.[86]

At the party's central branch meeting in New York in November 1942, Cannon spoke about the challenge the SWP faced conducting its business in a state of "semi-legality." Given the Minneapolis convictions, Cannon explained, one could make the case that the government considered the party illegal. Under those circumstances the SWP could either cease to exist or liquidate by becoming a mainstream party. But Cannon advocated a third way: "utilizing the partial legality that was open to us, without abandoning the communist program." Cannon urged his fellow Trotskyists to "keep out in the open and carry out work as best we can" rather than to go underground. Yet, reflecting the reality of the wartime context in which the Espionage Act and the Smith Act were in effect, Cannon also counseled caution in presenting the party's beliefs: "The speeches would not contain lies, but neither would they contain the full communist program—just small doses." With this strategy, he explained, there was at least the "possibility of a few hundred workers who never heard anything about the class struggle or socialism or its implications" doing so.[87]

Maintaining the ability to communicate its political message in the uneasy wartime context was the chief concern behind the party's restructuring of its newspaper, the *Militant*. After the conviction of the "18," the SWP turned over publication of the *Militant* to the Militant Publishing Association, so that it was technically no longer the party's official organ.[88] This thinly veiled attempt to distance the party from the paper was accompanied by an agreement among SWP leaders to alter the *Militant*'s tone and content to avoid its being legally suppressed.[89] Yet the paper still came under attack by the attorney general, who condemned the newspaper's opposition to the war as placing it in violation of the Espionage Act. Although Goldman and Osmond Fraenkel did their best to defend the publication at the hearing held in January 1943, the postmaster general signed the order revoking its second-class mailing rights.[90] The *Militant* immediately announced plans to challenge the order in court, but in the meantime it carried on using the third-class mail for its distribution.[91] The SWP, which ran the paper in all but name, launched a campaign to fight the order and to sustain the newspaper.[92]

Although the Trotskyists met this latest challenge to their ability to function openly as a revolutionary political party in wartime America by distributing the *Militant* through the third-class mail system and the SWP network, they still felt the pinch of the various forms of public and private persecution aimed at them in these years. While the party managed to carry on its work, running candidates for office and sponsoring nationwide speaking tours of its top leaders, it had to refrain from presenting its full message in most public forums in order to survive. In several of its electoral contests it could not even muster enough votes to get on the ballot, and when it did, there was suspicion of vote suppression. Although the appeal campaign and the work of the CRDC exposed the party to more supporters and party membership grew in these years, the gains were small (just over 100 nationwide in one year).[93] And its two most active branches remained under heavy FBI surveillance, riddled with well-placed informants.[94]

Other leading Trotskyists also suffered persecution and harassment. Because of his conviction under the Smith Act, Albert Goldman was disbarred in January 1943. The Chicago Bar Association was not convinced by his argument that he "had been guilty of no conduct involving moral turpitude" and upheld its decision that May.[95] Ray Rainbolt, who had moved to Seattle after the trial to start his life over, ended up returning with his family to Minneapolis in March 1943 a broken man. Rainbolt allegedly told an FBI informant who had befriended him that he had found the "world very difficult since he had been acquitted" and had little hope of its getting better.[96] Carl Skoglund also struggled in the years immediately after the trial, albeit with difficulties related to his immigration status. In February 1942, his lawyers defended him in a deportation hearing, securing his release on bond. But in July, the Immigration and Naturalization Service (INS) brought him before Judge Matthew Joyce, who denied his application for citizenship and "ordered him deported to Sweden." Because the war blocked communications with Skoglund's home country, "the order could not be carried out," and he remained under the strain of the impending deportation that would, as Dobbs later recalled, "plague him until the day of his death."[97] Grace Carlson, possibly due to the stress of the trial, suffered permanent damage to her heart and was told by her doctors in the spring of 1943 that she would have to slow down.[98] In these different ways, individual Trotskyists struggled in the two years after the trial.

Dunne, Palmquist, and Dobbs (and perhaps other members of the "18" whose FBI files have not been released) also remained on the FBI's Custodial Detention list after the trial. Even after the attorney general ordered its dissolution in 1943, these men continued to be tracked under an alternate (and secret) system devised by Hoover. With America's entry into the war in December 1941, Biddle used the Custodial Detention list in as limited a fashion as possible, authorizing the detention of "the listed dangerous German and Italian aliens" but not "communist aliens and not any of the listed American citizens."[99] By July 1943, Biddle officially suspended the bureau's program. Noting that the detention of alien enemies "is being dealt with under the procedure established by the Alien Enemy Control Unit," he argued that the bureau's list "has been found to be valueless." Biddle insisted that "there is no statutory authorization or other present justification for keeping a 'custodial detention' list of citizens." In addition, he believed the classification systems were "inherently unreliable." He took the bold step of asserting that "the adoption of this classification system was a mistake" and, by way of rectifying that, insisted that the classifications already made must not be considered as measures of the dangerousness of individuals or "as a determination of fact in any sense."[100] It would seem that in this instance, the Trotskyists who had been subjected to this form of government surveillance were now relieved of such pressure.

But that was not to be the case. Although Hoover officially suspended the Custodial Detention list, he continued to maintain a record of both aliens and citizens deemed dangerous by the bureau. In a confidential memo "sent to senior FBI officials in August 1943," Hoover stated, "'Henceforth, the cards known as Custodial Detention Cards will be known as Security Index.'" Having accumulated his list over the past four years, Hoover was not about to dispose of it; he just changed its name and ordered that it remain secret within the bureau, so as technically to comply with Biddle's order to dismantle the original project. Agents were not to mention the new Security Index (SI) in their reports, nor were they to discuss it with anyone outside the FBI, "with the exception of MID and MNI officials, and 'then only on a strictly confidential basis.'"[101] Those Trotskyists who had been classified as dangerous under the old system remained as such under the new. They remained subjects of intense surveillance whose files (and SI cards) grew in size with each passing year.[102] Even though they insisted that their convictions under the Smith Act were a miscarriage of justice, the Trotskyists continued to be hounded by the FBI and harassed by their trade union rivals. Neither those adversaries nor the bureau cared whether the "18" might be vindicated on appeal.

The Smith Act Upheld: *Dunne, et al. v. U.S.* at the Eighth Circuit and Supreme Court

Almost immediately after Judge Matthew Joyce sentenced the "18" to prison, the defendants announced that they would appeal the verdict.[103] They were aided by the ACLU, which remained a loyal champion of their cause. Osmond Fraenkel worked with Albert Goldman, Gilbert Carlson, and the other defense attorneys to produce the appellants' brief, which they filed with the circuit court on July 30, 1942. In making the case for why the verdict should be overturned, Fraenkel, Goldman, and the other attorneys took issue both with the Smith Act and with the case made by the government against the Trotskyists at trial. The first point in their argument had the broadest implications. They asserted that "the statute upon which this indictment is based, by its very nature and terms, operates as an unwarranted censorial threat to freedom of speech, press and assembly and is therefore in violation of Article I of the Amendments to the Constitution of the United States." Citing *Schenck v. U.S.* (in which the Espionage Act was upheld in a time of war) and *Herndon v. Lowry* (in which a state insurrection statute was struck down because it imperiled "the fullest freedom of discussion" in peacetime), the attorneys argued for the importance of context in defining the criminal status of speech and written expression. Since the Smith Act discounted that consideration, they argued that it posed an unconstitutional restraint on First Amendment rights.

Shifting to the details of the Minneapolis case, Fraenkel, Goldman, and the others asserted that the indictment was "insufficient in law" because it "merely repeats the words of the statute, fails to allege facts showing a commission of a crime, and is vague and uncertain." They then argued that the indictment did not "allege a conspiracy" even though that was what the government went on to pursue at trial. And, building on their first point, the attorneys asserted that the "statute as applied" was unconstitutional because the defendants did not pose a clear and present danger. In their remaining four points, the attorneys focused more narrowly still. They denied that the appellants had conspired to overthrow the government by force. They asserted that if there had been a conspiracy there was "not sufficient knowledge of the nature of the conspiracy" among the various defendants. They insisted that there was "not sufficient evidence that the alleged conspiracy existed after the enactment of the statute" in June 1940. Finally, they argued that for "certain appellants, there is no evidence that they were members of the alleged conspiracy after the date of the enactment of the statute."[104] Presenting this range of issues, from the larger constitutional questions down to the precise nature of the government's evidence against specific defendants, the appellants' attorneys hoped to persuade the judges on the Eighth Circuit to overturn the guilty verdict.

The government rejected the appellants' arguments and countered with its own brief penned by Wendell Berge, Victor Anderson, and four other Justice Department attorneys. As Anderson and Schweinhaut had done at trial, they argued for the constitutionality of the Smith Act and against the applicability of the clear and present danger test in this case. Shifting to the specifics of the Minneapolis prosecution, the attorneys insisted that the "verdict is fully supported by the evidence," arguing that the SWP clearly advocated the violent overthrow of the government and that any attempts by the defense to claim otherwise, or to try to distinguish between advocacy and prediction, was "untenable" and "based on an inexact resort to semantics." Building on the government's argument at trial that the SWP was an illegal conspiracy, Berge and Anderson submitted that "the appellants' leadership of the party, their acceptance, as members, of the party's Declaration of Principles, and their submission to the decisions of governing bodies, and to a party discipline that required 100 per cent loyalty" as well as "their duty assiduously to propagate the party program . . . *alone* constitute sufficient evidence of knowledge, mutual understanding and conspiracy." If this was not enough to convince the circuit court, the government attorneys argued that the appellants' guilt (and their awareness of the conspiracy in question) was also apparent in their "statements" and by their "presence" when statements were made about the overthrow of the government by force. Pointing to specific references in the testimony of prosecution witnesses and to selected party literature, the attorneys detailed examples of such statements and participation for each of the eighteen defendants. In so doing, they made a sweeping argument for the limitation of free speech and for guilt by association.[105] They filed their brief with the circuit court at the end of September.

It would be another full year before the circuit court handed down its decision. In large part this delay was due to the Supreme Court's decision to rehear the *Schneiderman* case in January 1943. Justice Murphy's forty-two-page opinion was handed down on June 21, 1943. Because this case dealt with an individual's association with a radical political party that was alleged to have advocated the violent overthrow of the government and addressed the question of whether that individual could be held to account for the alleged position of the party with which he or she was associated, it promised to speak to the issues at the core of the Minneapolis case.[106] And so, the circuit court delayed its findings until after the Supreme Court ruled on *Schneiderman*.

The *Schneiderman* case dealt with the first challenge to the country's wartime denaturalization program. Under that program the government could revoke the naturalization of a citizen whom it believed had procured it fraudulently or illegally or who had not demonstrated that he or she was "attached to the principles of the Constitution" for five years prior to his or her naturalization. William Schneiderman, born in Russia and raised in California, became a member of the Young Workers League in the early 1920s and later joined the Workers Party (what would become the Communist Party of the United States). Schneiderman was naturalized in 1927 and remained active in the party into the 1930s. It was in 1939 when the government began denaturalization proceedings against him, charging that at the time of his becoming a citizen he belonged to an organization that advocated the violent overthrow of the government and therefore could not have been truly "attached to the principles of the Constitution."[107]

When the case reached the Supreme Court, the justices were faced with the question of whether the government had provided enough evidence to sustain its revocation of Schneiderman's citizenship. As Jeffrey Liss has observed, Murphy refuted the government's argument that being "*an active and knowing member* of the League and Party" was sufficient evidence.[108] Murphy, writing for the majority, asserted that "'the constitutional fathers, fresh from a revolution, did not forge a political straight jacket for generations to come.'" Disagreeing with the government or believing in the need for sweeping change was not a demonstration of lack of attachment to the Constitution.[109] Schneiderman's membership in the league and the party did not necessarily indicate his belief in illegal doctrines, Murphy insisted. As Liss explains, "It might be difficult to impute to Schneiderman the precepts of those organizations," but even if one could, one would have to look at the league and the party at the time of his membership to ascertain whether they really did advocate the violent overthrow of the government. The Court looked to the party's literature, "including works written by Marx, Lenin and Stalin," and, as Liss notes, "concluded that it was at least possible to interpret the Party's rhetoric concerning the overthrow as merely a theoretical justification for the use of force and violence should all else fail." Because this left two interpretations open—a situation in which Schneiderman believed in the present need for violent action and one in which he held only to a theoretical commitment—the government would need "clear, unequivocal and convincing evidence" of the reprehensible interpretation to proceed with the denaturalization and have that procedure upheld by the Court. Because it found that the government did not provide that proof, the Court overturned Schneiderman's denaturalization.[110]

Betraying a deep divide when it came to questions of subversive advocacy and the clear and present danger test, the Court's ruling was not unanimous. Although Murphy wrote for the majority (of five), there was strong dissent among the remaining three justices (Felix Frankfurter, Owen Roberts, and Harlan Fiske Stone), who believed the government had "more than sustained its burden" of proof.[111] As the majority and dissenting opinions in *Schneiderman* showed, the Court was "sharply divided both on the merits of the clear and present danger test and on the issue of subversive advocacy."[112] There remained strong disagreements among the justices, particularly between Hugo Black and Felix Frankfurter, when it came to balancing the interests of free speech and national security in wartime.[113] Even after it ruled on *Schneiderman*, there was no guarantee that the Court would apply the clear and present danger test in subversive advocacy cases or that it would do so to protect free speech.[114]

The implications of the Court's decision for the Minneapolis case were clear to the Trotskyists. Because so much of the government's case against them hinged on the interpretation of the SWP's motives, inferred from party literature (including works of Marx and Lenin taken out of context), the defendants hoped that the *Schneiderman* decision would support their argument that the reprehensible interpretation of socialist doctrine imputed to them and their party was not supported by the evidence at trial. In particular, they hoped the decision would help them undermine the government's claim that each of the "18" shared in the intent to overthrow the government by force and violence, a claim for which the Trotskyists insisted there also was not enough evidence. Given that lack of evidence—and now with the Supreme Court's *Schneiderman* decision—they believed that the circuit court

would have to overturn the verdict by accepting the more innocuous interpretation of the SWP's agenda (the prediction, not advocacy, of violence).[115]
Victor Anderson, who also read the Court's decision that summer, neverthe-
less remained confident in the case he had built. Writing to Berge in July, he
admitted that "it is difficult to prognosticate what its effect will be on the
decision" in the *Dunne* case but also noted that there was no more that his
office could do to make its case any stronger than it already had.[116]

The Eighth Circuit Court ended the speculation when it handed down its
ruling in the *Dunne* case on September 20, 1943. Judges Kimbrough Stone,
Harvey M. Johnsen, and Walter G. Riddick had heard the case and read the
briefs submitted to them the year before. Stone delivered the opinion of the
court, organizing it under the three main categories in question: the validity
of the Smith Act, the sufficiency of the indictment, and the sufficiency of the
evidence.

When it came to the validity of the Smith Act, Stone argued that it was
"grounded upon specific Constitutional grants of power" that extended to
Congress the authority to guarantee protection "against domestic violence."
Dismissing the appellants' complaint that the peacetime nature of the Smith
Act rendered it unconstitutional, Stone argued that "there was a situation in
1940 which impressed Congress with the need for this Act." That situation, he
reminded his readers, "was the existence of war in Europe; the apprehension
that the country might be drawn into war; the knowledge of the effective use
of 'fifth column' activities by countries which might be our enemies; and the
apprehension that such activities were being or might be used in this country." Stone concluded that the Smith Act was "applicable in peace as well as
war conditions" because "it was enacted on the brink of war and to correct existing dangers."[117] And he noted that even with this law in place, "criticisms of
the government or of its polices (civil or military)" were still possible, as long
as those expressions "are not made with the intent to bring about the unlawful
things and situations covered by the section" in question and "as long as they
do not have a natural tendency and a reasonable probability of effecting these
forbidden results." Drawing on Supreme Court justice Sanford's discussion
of "intent" from *Gitlow* and on Holmes's use of the "natural tendency" test
from *Debs*, Stone interpreted as constitutional the restrictions placed on free
speech under the Smith Act.[118]

In addition, Stone rejected the appellants' claim that the subversive advocacy sections of the Smith Act were sweeping and vague and had a tendency to impose guilt by association. He insisted instead that "the guilt is
entirely individual and personal,"[119] and that it was up to the jury to "ascertain whether the organization has forbidden purposes and whether such req-

uisite knowledge exists" among all the members.[120] Claiming that although some of the appellants had used "words which may or may not mean the forbidden thing," intending "just one thing and that is to squirm through the statute leaving a haze which they hope will make it impossible or difficult to find any fracture by their passage," Stone insisted that "the sinister significance must [still] appear beyond a reasonable doubt." He also argued that the "difficulty of determining a fact is no argument against the validity of the statute."[121] With this logic he affirmed the integrity of subversive advocacy sections of the law.[122]

Stone also rejected the appellants' challenge to the validity of the Smith Act as applied. He dismissed their argument for the protective application of the clear and present danger test and instead argued that the Supreme Court's *Gitlow* decision was controlling. Whereas with the question of individual guilt he deferred to the jury's interpretation, with the question of the criminalization of certain kinds of utterances to protect public peace and safety he deferred to the authority of Congress to proscribe them. In doing so, Stone drew directly from the *Gitlow* opinion. He thus rejected the appellants' claim for the relevance of the *Herndon* and *Stromberg* decisions and the *Whitney* concurring decision, each of which applied the clear and present danger test protectively to limit legislative restrictions on speech.[123] He asserted, "The problem here is whether this Act falls within the rule of the Schenck case or the rule of the Gitlow case. We think it is within the Gitlow case." As such Holmes's test was not relevant. Stone concluded that the Smith Act was valid on application.[124]

Stone then turned his attention to the two remaining questions at hand: the sufficiency of the indictment and the sufficiency of the evidence. Closely following the logic in the government's brief, he supported the sufficiency of the indictment, arguing that the statutory language on which it was based was "fully descriptive" and therefore was not "vague and uncertain."[125] With respect to the questions of when and how the defendants advocated the overthrow of the government by violence—and how the individual defendants were connected to the conspiracy—Stone also drew from the trial record and did not find grounds to overturn the guilty verdicts.[126]

But what about the Supreme Court's *Schneiderman* decision: Was the circuit court bound to consider whether there was a benign interpretation of the SWP's agenda in the evidence before it? Given that the party leaders and members themselves (most notably Cannon and Goldman) advanced this legal formulation of the party at trial, did not the court of appeals now need to defer to that rather than accept the "reprehensible" interpretation put forth by the government? Stone essentially said "no" in a note at the end of the opinion, where he stated that although the circuit court held back its own decision in anticipation of the *Schneiderman* ruling, it now found that because "it is based upon a situation so different—legally and factually—from this case, that it has no application in the matter before us." Writing for the circuit court, Stone concluded that after a "thorough examination of the record" (more than 1,300 pages of it), there was "no doubt as to the sufficiency of the evidence and as to the justice of the verdict." As a result, "The judgment as to each appellant is affirmed."[127]

Responses to the circuit court's opinion were swift and varied. Victor Anderson wrote to Assistant Attorney General Tom Clark on September 22 expressing his pleasure that the verdicts remained in place. Characterizing the Court's opinion as "outstanding" for its attention to detail, Anderson noted that it was a "personal gratification to know that the Circuit Court of Appeals gave this important case such keen analysis" and found the appellants' contentions "wanting in merit and unfounded." Assuming, however, that the "18" were prepared to appeal the decision to the Supreme Court, Anderson told Clark that his office was "naturally . . . interested in having the convictions sustained . . . and will be glad to render all possible assistance to that end."[128] He was ready and willing to continue the fight.

The "18" were ready and willing to continue the fight too. Carlson, writing to Sedova on the day after the circuit court affirmed the convictions, explained how "immediate plans are being made for an appeal of the case to the United States Supreme Court."[129] Her allies in the CRDC and the ACLU pushed for a quick appeal, arguing that the case "strikes at the very heart of civil liberties in the United States." In a press release issued on the day the circuit court handed down its decision, James Farrell of the CRDC argued that "the upholding of their conviction sets an extremely dangerous precedent which can be used in witch-hunts against other trade-unionists and minority political groups." As a result, Farrell insisted that the *Dunne* case was now "recognized as test case of civil liberties in World War II."[130] In that fight the CRDC and the ACLU planned to lead the way.

The national office of the CRDC in New York quickly sent out word to its thirty local branches around the country. The goal was to raise $2,500 "to finance the preliminary legal and other expenses involved in the appeal."[131] Goldman and Fraenkel applied for a thirty-day stay of mandate of the circuit court's decision so that the defendants could "remain out of prison on the present bail arrangements until the Supreme Court decision is announced."[132] Neither Victor Anderson nor Tom Clark opposed the stay, recognizing that given the thirty-day window in which to submit an application for a writ to the Supreme Court, the process of this final appeal would move quickly.[133]

Fraenkel and Goldman wrote the petition for the writ in which they delineated several reasons why they believed the Supreme Court needed to review the case.[134] First, there were "important questions of Federal law" that needed to be addressed. The Eighth Circuit Court's decision in the *Dunne* case stood in conflict with other Supreme Court findings and the findings of two circuit courts on questions surrounding the sufficiency of indictments under federal statutes; the petitioners argued that such inconsistency had to be clarified.[135] Second, the *Dunne* case afforded the Court the chance to "pass upon the validity of a peacetime sedition statute," something that it never had the opportunity to do. Third, the attorneys argued for the importance of the Supreme Court's ruling on the "applicability of the clear and present danger rule to a statute of this character," noting again how the circuit court's ruling in the *Dunne* case left this answer unclear. Did *Gitlow* apply in all cases now, or should Justice Brandeis's concurring opinion in *Whitney v. California* hold, whereby "regardless of a legislative declaration that certain words are dangerous, a defendant in a particular case always has the right to a determination by the Court or by the jury that under circumstances of his case no clear and present danger existed"? Fraenkel and Goldman, who also cited the *Schneiderman* case to support their point, argued that the Court needed to clarify the discrepancy. And they concluded that they believed the Court should, given its own previous rulings, favor the Brandeis formula in *Whitney* over *Gitlow* in the *Dunne* case and reverse the verdict.

Fraenkel and Goldman filed their petition in the Supreme Court on October 16. The following month, Solicitor General Charles Fahy and Assistant Attorney General Tom Clark filed the government's brief in opposition. Whereas Fraenkel and Goldman argued against Stone's opinion in their petition, Fahy and Clark built their case on his findings. In a nutshell, the government's position was that the Smith Act did not violate the First Amendment, either inherently or on its application in the *Dunne* case, and that the evidence as to each of the petitioners was sufficient to sustain their convictions.[136] Summarizing the prosecution's evidence presented at trial, Fahy and Clark presented the SWP as an organization whose purpose was the "destruction of the existing constitutional government in the United States . . . and the substitution of a Party dictatorship resting on the armed force of mass militia having its basis in workers' councils or soviets" that was created in consultation with Trotsky.[137] According to Fahy and Clark, the danger the defendants presented was evident, imminent, and deadly serious.

In terms of the constitutional issues raised by the petitioners, Fahy and Clark, like Judge Stone, rejected their attempts to distinguish between wartime and peacetime sedition statutes. Instead, the government's lawyers insisted that "the power of Congress to 'raise and support armies' and to 'provide and maintain a navy' exists during peace as well as war; and a law whose plain object is to maintain loyalty, obedience, and integrity in the armed forces by protecting them from planned subversion, whether the nation be at peace or war, is we submit, 'necessary and proper for carrying into execution the foregoing powers.'"[138] When it came to the question of whether *Gitlow* or *Whitney* should control questions relating to free speech restrictions and sedition law, Fahy and Clark argued in favor of *Gitlow* just as Stone did. In *Gitlow* the Court deferred to the legislative judgment in criminalizing subversive advocacy. And in *Herndon* it clarified that the clear and present danger test only applies in such cases, as Harry Kalven Jr. explains, "where the statute does not reflect a legislative judgment as to the danger from a specific class of utterances."[139] The Smith Act was the product of such a legislative judgment, Fahy and Clark argued, and so the defendants' call for the protective use of the clear and present danger test was misplaced.[140] As the Court found in *Gitlow*, the legislature has the authority to impose such restrictions. Allowing that decision to control, Fahy and Clark explained, supported the constitutionality of the Smith Act and the validity of the guilty verdict in the *Dunne* case by voiding the petitioners' claim that the clear and present danger test applied.

In response to the petitioners' claim that the statute was invalid on application, Fahy and Clark rebutted with a litany of evidence against the various defendants, and they rejected the petitioners' attempt to use *Schneiderman* to exonerate themselves.[141] In the conclusion to their brief, Fahy and Clark argued that the "petitioners had a fair trial, the jury was properly instructed, and the verdict is supported by the evidence." They insisted that the "review by the court below was thoroughgoing" and that "in the context of the case, the constitutional issue is limited in scope and was properly decided."[142] They argued that if the Supreme Court took the case, it should sustain the findings of both the district court and the circuit court.

Neither the Justice Department nor the Trotskyists would have to wait long to find out the Supreme Court's position. On November 22 the Court announced that it had denied the writ.[143] Anderson wrote to Clark four days later noting that, according to *United States Law Week*, "the Court based its denial upon the fact that the law was not invalid as abridging freedom of speech or for indefiniteness." Although nothing more was made public about the Court's reasons for refusing review, since all such conferences are kept secret, the brief explanation in *Law Week* revealed that a majority of the justices believed the Smith Act was sound and validly applied in this case.[144] There were three who dissented from this position—Frank Murphy, Wiley Rutledge, and William O. Douglas—but they were fewer than the minimum number of four needed to accept the writ. These three justices were all struck by the appellants' argument about the constitutionally questionable nature of the Smith Act's application in times of peace, deeming that issue alone to be of sufficient public importance to warrant the Court's review.[145] But even though Murphy and Rutledge also expressed some interest in exploring the applicability of *Gitlow* to the *Dunne* case, the Court as a body, in denying the writ, decided to pass up the opportunity to support the protective application of the clear and present danger test. One law review article at the time commented in particular on Chief Justice Harlan Fiske Stone's "silence" on this issue during the 1943 and 1944 terms.[146] Even in cases, like *Hartzel v. U.S.* (1944), where the Court considered a conviction under the Espionage Act, it divided 5 to 4. And the majority in that case reversed the verdict on the grounds that there was insufficient evidence to prove intent; it did not believe it needed to consider whether or not the speech in question constituted a clear and present danger. Those justices who dissented (Reed, Frankfurter, and Jackson) revived the test but used it to validate the restriction of speech.[147] It is thus not all that surprising that the writ was denied in the *Dunne* case. In a time of war, the majority of the Court deferred to the legislative power of Congress to defend national security, allowing the restrictions on civil liberties inherent in the Smith Act to stand.[148]

This was a relief for Anderson and a vindication of his work. "It is very comforting to know the disposition made by the Supreme Court," he told Clark, "and suggest you tell Mr. Schweinhaut of your staff that the question of infringement on free speech or other questions involving the constitutionality of the so-called Smith Act did not make a very definite imprint upon any member of the Supreme Court." Aware that the constitutionality issue had been a major bone of contention between the government and the defense since the time of the indictments—and that it contributed to the ACLU's, the left-liberal press's, and the labor left's condemnation of the prosecution— Anderson wanted it made clear that the highest court in the land found no merit in the complaint. He also singled out Schweinhaut for this particular notification, perhaps knowing of the former Civil Rights Division attorney's initial discomfort with using the peacetime sedition statute for the first time in the 1941 case.[149] Although Anderson noted that "the Department is to be congratulated on the results obtained," his pride in his dogged pursuit of the Trotskyists was also boosted in the Court's refusal of the writ.[150]

The reaction among the Trotskyists was one of shock and dismay. Writing to Grace Carlson a few days after the Court announced its position, Bea Janosco, an active SWP member in the St. Paul branch, commented on how

she was "startled by the decision—or rather, the lack of one—and the afternoon that I saw it in the paper, I almost literally fell off my chair." She also
communicated the reaction of many of her comrades in the St. Paul and Minneapolis community. Despite their being caught off guard by the refusal, Janosco claimed that "everyone has reacted well to it, with the exception of
Max" Geldman, who "demanded to know 'why didn't someone prepare us
for this eventuality.'" Expressing his frustration with the situation through
anger, Geldman apparently was "looking for someone to blame" and "made
quite a harangue about it" in the executive committee meeting "but got no
sympathy from anyone." The majority of the defendants and their supporters
in the party's ranks, while surprised and upset at the turn of events, steeled
themselves to accept the defeat.[151]

As they had done through all the challenges they had faced previously, be
they attacks from the fascist Silver Shirts, criticism from the Communists, or
opposition from employers when they organized workers into trade unions,
the Trotskyists in Minneapolis and St. Paul were ready to confront the problem together. Janosco explained how "locally most of us feel that the problem
will not be too big, that is, in adjusting ourselves to the losses." With many of
their party leaders out of commission for the near future as they served their
time in prison, the remaining SWP members had to find a way to sustain the
movement. Many of those members were women, who had already begun
to pick up this work since the time of the trial. Janosco hoped to build on
that momentum to sustain the forums over the next few years when Carlson
and the others were behind bars.[152] Carlson shared her friend's hopes and
actively began to make plans along the same lines with her sister Dorothy
and brother-in-law Henry. Carlson was also concerned about maintaining the
party's press and suggested the names of comrades who could be approached
to write for the *Militant* and the *Fourth International*.[153]

As they pulled together to keep the SWP functioning, the Trotskyists remained dismayed over the Court's refusal to hear their case. But Fraenkel and
Goldman did not give up and submitted a petition for rehearing to the Court
on December 1. By refusing to rule on the case at bar, Fraenkel and Goldman
argued, the Court left it unclear whether it supported the circuit court's finding that in such cases the rule of *Gitlow* applied or whether it supported the
argument of the government in its brief that the legislative determination was
not rebuttable because it included the criminalization of intent. Unless the
Court reviewed the *Dunne* case, Fraenkel and Goldman concluded, "neither
the bench nor the bar nor the public can know what is the proper rule in such
cases."[154] The ACLU agreed and submitted an amicus curiae brief in support
of the petitioners' application for a rehearing.[155]

The Supreme Court justices remained unconvinced and denied the petition for a rehearing of the case.[156] Clifford Forster, staff counsel of the ACLU, requested permission from Charles Fahy "to file another petition for a rehearing,"[157] but this time Fahy refused.[158] For the ACLU, it was the end of the road in its journey to defend the rights of the "18" and challenge the constitutionality of the Smith Act with the *Dunne* case. Fraenkel and Goldman wrote a second petition for rehearing, urging the Court to appreciate their belief that "the petitioners' constitutional rights are being disposed of without adequate consideration of the same by this Court and without any such statement of the results as will enable the lower Federal courts properly to apply the law." If the justices were not convinced of the petitioners' claims about their innocence, the attorneys pushed them to consider the case for the constitutional questions it exposed.[159]

The justices did not accept the argument. The Court refused the third petition, and after almost two years pursuing their appeal, the "18" ran out of options.[160] The tasks before them now were to prepare themselves for prison and ready the party to weather their absence. At this crucial juncture, Trotskyists and their allies rallied around each other in solidarity. The CRDC announced the launch of its national campaign "to bring to the attention of the American people the vital issues involved in this case and to raise funds for the relief of the prisoners and their families." SWP branches from around the country sent supportive messages to the "18," calling for "redoubled and more effective effort wherever revolutionary hearts beat" and announcing that the "comrades are carrying on."[161]

In St. Paul, where Grace Carlson had worked extensively with the local NAACP chapter for many years, a number of African Americans came out in support of the "18," including the Reverend Clarence Nelson and his wife, Winnie, who were Carlson's close friends.[162] Such personal connections were not the only reason for their support. The Smith Act's restraints on First Amendment rights were also worrisome to these African Americans given what they might portend for free speech in the fight for civil rights. Such broader implications of the case had long concerned the ACLU; they now engaged the attention of the NAACP, some of whose members came out in support of the "18," including Milton Konvitz. Arguing that "any minority group in this country that has grievances must insist in keeping intact the First Amendment as interpreted by the Supreme Court in cases upholding the clear and present danger rule," Konvitz recommended to the NAACP that it endorse the Trotskyists' appeal.[163]

The constitutional and political implications of the Trotskyists' case had been a concern of the left-liberal press since the time of the indictments in July 1941. Now that the Supreme Court refused to review the case, those media outlets once more expressed their disappointment. Writing an opinion piece in the popular newspaper *PM*, I. F. Stone insisted that "to permit such convictions to stand is to establish a new and dangerous precedent. To refuse a hearing after the lower courts have set aside the 'clear and present danger' rule, is to invite the disregard in war and peace of one of the principal constitutional doctrines safeguarding freedom of speech and press."[164] The editors of the *Nation* also lamented "the injury done the Bill of Rights by [the Trotskyists'] prosecution and by the dangerous precedents established, from which the court has averted its face."[165]

The Trotskyists' case thus remained at the center of the larger public debate over balancing the protection of civil liberties with the pressures of national security concerns. The Supreme Court's refusal to review the case in 1943 placed the highest court on the side of security over liberty. The long-term implications of that decision, and of the Smith Act which was inherently upheld, were to be felt by many Americans in the years to come. Chafee's proverbial pistol had been taken out of the attorney general's desk drawer and fired once. Now the Supreme Court essentially gave license to the Department of Justice to aim it at others and pull the trigger in the name of national security.

6

"A Test of Fire"

December 1943–November 1948

When the Supreme Court denied the writ, it became clear that the "18" were headed to jail. Surrendering in late December 1943, they served their time but never stopped fighting to restore their civil rights. The Trotskyists, backed by the CRDC and the ACLU, conducted a national campaign to pardon the "18" and to repeal the Smith Act. The SWP survived this trying time, mostly because of the work of women like Rose Karsner and Dorothy Schultz, who temporarily took up the reins while Cannon, Dobbs, and the others were incarcerated. When all of the "18" were released from jail by January 1945, they stepped back into a thriving party. Dobbs later described these years as having constituted "a test of fire for the cadre and a test of fire for the party" through which it "as a whole came through with flying colors."[1] The struggle against the Smith Act energized the SWP and increased its ranks to almost 3,000 members during the last year of the war. Instead of breaking the spirit of the Trotskyists, the conviction, for the most part, unintentionally reinvigorated it; that renewed spirit helped fuel their continued denunciation of the Smith Act during the early Cold War years.

Serving Time and Serving the Party

Upon word of the Supreme Court's refusal to accept their case in November 1943, the Trotskyists were shocked and disappointed but also defiant. They and their allies in the CRDC coordinated a mass meeting in New York on December 16 at the Manhattan Center. Several hundred sympathizers supported the Trotskyists as "victims of political persecution, placed behind bars solely because of their ideas and union activities," and backed a resolution demanding their "immediate and unconditional pardon."[2] A smaller group gathered ten days later at the Irving Plaza Hotel for a farewell banquet in honor of the "18" that was sponsored by the New York Local of the SWP. Drawing mostly from the ranks of the party's faithful, the invitation list included as guests of honor six of the defendants who were in New York: Cannon, Dobbs, Morrow, Schoenfeld, Russell, and Kuehn. The other defendants, "addressing meetings in Minneapolis and Chicago," sent "messages of complete solidarity."[3] The dinner was a final opportunity for the defendants to speak in public about what the prosecution meant to them and for them, for the party, and for the American working class.

Controlled defiance, confidence, and optimism characterized the sentiments of those who spoke at the banquet. Celebrating the SWP's consistent opposition to the war, Cannon argued that the "Trotskyists told the truth" and "that is the reason, and the only reason, we are on our way to prison." Unlike other political groups, he explained, "the Trotskyists set no limit on what they will do for their ideas"; while "the others play for pennies . . . the Trotskyist stakes his head." Their imprisonment, he argued, ultimately was a temporary obstacle in a much longer fight: "We go to the next stage of the struggle with a sure self-confidence and a self-assurance," entering prison "not as criminals but because our duty takes us there."[4] When Dobbs, Russell, and Kuehn spoke, they each echoed Cannon's pride, defiance, and commitment to the cause.[5] Far from lamenting their victimization or admitting defeat, the Trotskyists interpreted their fate within the Marxist narrative familiar to them as proof of their place in the vanguard of the struggle against capitalism.

Staunch commitment to the party and its mission was also expressed in the speeches delivered at the special farewell banquet held in Minneapolis on December 28. Vincent Dunne, Grace Carlson, Jake Cooper, Oscar Coover, Harry DeBoer, Clarence Hamel, Emil Hansen, Max Geldman, and Carl Skoglund were joined by Miles Dunne at the speakers' table in the front hall of SWP headquarters.[6] Seated under a "huge Honor Roll, bearing the names of the 18 class-war victims," they opened the evening by singing "Solidarity" with the 250 people who gathered to bid them farewell.[7] A good number of these supporters came from Local 544-AFL, demonstrating to Carlson how many of those drivers "still respect and admire" their old union leaders.[8] Yet the majority of the night's speeches were more narrowly focused on the Trotskyists' concerns. Echoing his comrades who had gathered in New York two nights earlier, Coover insisted, "We shall come back as stronger individuals to a bigger and better party, ready once again to take our place on the firing line."[9] The Trotskyists had made one thing very clear in their final public pronouncements before heading to jail: their imprisonment would not break them but would facilitate a rededication to the beliefs that the government had found so dangerous.

They confirmed this position in private as well. On the eve of surrendering to authorities, Carlson wrote to Sedova, proudly noting how because "the comrades are rallying around in this emergency," there "has been no drop in morale or in the party activity, quite the contrary."[10] In the final days be-

Figure 6.1 Socialist Workers Party members, back row, left to right: Farrell Dobbs, Harry DeBoer, Edward Palmquist, Clarence Hamel, Emil Hansen, Oscar Coover, Jake Cooper; front row, left to right: Max Geldman, Felix Morrow, Albert Goldman, James Cannon, Vincent Dunne, Carl Skoglund, Grace Carlson. Fourteen of the convicted "18" Trotskyists gathered at the SWP headquarters in Minneapolis in December 1943 for a farewell banquet before beginning their prison sentences. Photos J1.6r13, negative number 4347, Minnesota Historical Society. Courtesy Minnesota Historical Society.

fore turning themselves in, the "18" were surrounded by the party faithful, who promised to keep their work alive. On December 30, all but three of the defendants gathered in the party's headquarters in Minneapolis, and "from morning until evening friends and well-wishers milled in and out to give their last greetings and expressions of solidarity." Karl Kuehn, Al Russell, and Oscar Schoenfeld had remained in New York and surrendered there the next day to a U.S. marshal before being transported to the federal correctional facility in Danbury, Connecticut.[11] In the final moments in Minneapolis, the Trotskyists reaffirmed their commitment to each other as they continued to discuss the ways of revolutionary political action, finding comfort and solace, but also renewed hope and energy, in their extended family of comrades.[12]

That family extended into the ranks of the party in Minneapolis and New York, but it was also particularly strong—and in some cases made up of literal family ties—among the "18" defendants. Their experience as the "18" during and since the time of the trial contributed to this closeness. So too did the long-standing friendships held among many of them going back to the days of the 1934 drivers strikes, like those among Dunne, Cannon, Skoglund, DeBoer, and Dobbs. Although Carlson was somewhat of a latecomer to the group, becoming a professional organizer only in 1940, she had forged close and extensive ties in the movement through her sister Dorothy and brother-in-law Henry Schultz; her husband, Gilbert Carlson; and those who became her close friends and confidants, like Dunne, Cannon, and Sedova. Max Geldman married Jake Cooper's sister Goldie, and Oscar Schoenfeld married Karl Kuehn's daughter Margaret (who had been convicted in the 1939 WPA strike).[13] And, of course, there were the Dunne brothers, Vincent and Miles. The tangle of personal connections strengthened the bonds of political comradeship and shared sense of mission in what the defendants perceived as an oftentimes cold and hostile capitalist world.

It was fitting, then, that the fifteen defendants who gathered in Minneapolis decided to surrender to the authorities together. Meeting once again at party headquarters on December 31, they "formed ranks at 2:30" and then, lined up two by two, "marched as a body through the crowded streets of the city to the Federal Court House," where they were "received by the United States Marshal." Joe Hansen, Cannon's close friend and comrade in the party, witnessed the day's events. Describing what he called the "historic march" of the fifteen, he noted the many friends and well-wishers who lined the streets to say good-bye and good luck, as well as the many photographers who crouched to get the best shot of the event for the "capitalist press." Waxing poetic, Hansen launched into his interpretation of the larger portent of the procession:

> They crossed the street to walk in the sun. As they strode past a bank they made a remarkable picture. That imposing structure, representing all the accumulated wealth and power of the capitalist society they have challenged, stood coldly and forbiddingly over them. But they did not look at all like trapped slaves. The sun high-lighted their hats, their shoulders, touched their swinging hands. In dark overcoats they seemed in uniform. They looked like a contingent of a powerful conquering army. In truth that is precisely what they were, coming down the streets of Minneapolis, the advance contingent of the army that will eventually destroy all the evil power represented by the bank in the background. [14]

Even in this moment of defeat, the Trotskyists remained defiant, at least in Hansen's melodramatic rendering of events. He did not describe a ragtag

Figure 6.2 Trotskyist defendants marching in formation as they surrendered to the courthouse to begin their prison sentences, December 1943. Courtesy Hennepin County Library Special Collections.

group of victims resigned to their fate but a disciplined phalanx of socialism's army ready to begin a new stage in the fight against capitalism. As they "marched into the gloomy maw" of the federal courthouse, Hansen commented that he could not help but think to himself that "if Trotsky could be here now to see how the leadership of our party conducted itself under persecution, he would have said: 'Good, very good.'"[15] For Hansen the final march of the Trotskyists represented a dignified culmination of their struggle against capitalism and the government's war policy. For Victor Anderson the march represented a very different kind of finale. Sending a photo of the surrender to Attorney General Biddle, he commented, "It might be well for you to pass this on to Mr. Henry Schweinhaut, to the end that he may refresh his recollection in the fact that his efforts in the matter have led to a successful conclusion."[16] Having waited for more than a year while the defendants appealed their case, Anderson was pleased to see them finally go to jail.

The fourteen men were processed and sent to Sandstone, the federal correctional facility about 100 miles outside of Minneapolis. Carlson, the only female convict, was held for a week in the Hennepin County Jail and then transferred to the women's correctional facility in Alderson, West Virginia. While she was held locally, her sister Dorothy and her friend Elaine Roseland (secretary at the Minneapolis party headquarters) were able to visit her regularly and bring her books, clean clothes, and candy. But after a four-day trip by car accompanied by a U.S. marshal, whom she described unflatteringly as a "big, beefy, flatfoot," Carlson arrived at Alderson, where she was truly separated from her friends and family. With her characteristic combination of sincerity, dry wit, and optimism, she commented, "Believe me, I really miss the comrades, the meetings and the fun. I used to mix with a much better class of people than I am now dealing with! These god-damn capitalists! But 16 months isn't forever."[17] Settling into her daily routine at Alderson fairly quickly, Carlson made the best of a difficult situation. Writing to Dorothy, she admitted, "I am not excessively happy, but neither am I terribly uncomfortable. People often must put up with more for less reason."[18]

Cannon and the men at Sandstone also adjusted to their new lives behind bars. They, too, missed their loved ones. Cannon wrote to Rose lamenting their having to endure the sixteen-month separation but noting that "the time will pass and we will be together again. Meantime we can live on memories of the past and hopes for the future." He implored her to "write, darling, especially about yourself," insisting that "every detail of your life is of vital interest to me." And he asked her to send photos of their grandchildren and to make sure she took care of herself while he was gone.[19] He maintained a running joke with Rose, sending her items to add to a "menu list" for them to enjoy upon his return home. "Put porterhouse steak, french-fried potatoes and a salad on the first page," he told her. "A long list will follow." On his birthday he requested "chicken stew with dumplings," dreaming of the day he would be able to share it with her.[20] Dobbs also tried to live on dreams and memories, recalling in a letter to his wife, Marvel, "those wonderful Wednesdays when we had a shish-ka-bob dinner (how good it would taste now!), then a movie or a Beethoven concert and the joy of companionship."[21] Like Carlson, the men quickly distracted themselves from the loneliness of separation from their loved ones by adapting to their new routines in prison, which also revolved around mealtimes, cleaning their small rooms, and reading. Their tedious days were peppered with breaks for visits to the doctor for inoculations at first, or with opportunities to visit the library or play checkers with some of the other inmates once they were out of quarantine.[22]

Not content to pass their time in jail aimlessly, however, the defendants used it to educate themselves and "to make themselves more effective agents of the revolutionary movement when they are free."[23] For the "18," the prison libraries became vital to improving themselves, as did the books they received from the CRDC. After one of his visits, Novack explained in a letter to Sedova how "all are studying some specialized subjects as well as doing generalized reading." He noted that "Ray Dunne is reading Browning's poetry," while "Harry DeBoer is deep in the History of the Russian Revolution," and Dobbs was mastering American history. Some of the other men also decided to learn a new language: "Jim is studying French and Spanish . . . Al G. is also studying French and Spanish . . . Carlos, German & Spanish. Felix is taking advanced courses in French and Spanish," and Dobbs "was learning French." Goldman also began teaching "a small class of 7 or 8 prisoners on current events." As Cannon explained to Novack, "Since Czarist days and long before, prisons have been the universities of the revolutionary movement. We are doing our best here at Sandstone to continue the tradition."[24] As one of the original founders of the Communist International Labor Defense in the 1920s, Cannon understood the political significance of "class-war prisoners"; rather than organizing the masses outside the prison gates in defense work, this time Cannon, along with the other Trotskyists, honed their revolutionary skills behind bars.[25]

Cannon, in particular, found another way to serve the party while he was still in prison: through his correspondence with his partner, Rose, he gave advice on SWP activities. Rose kept him informed of what was happening while he and the others were incarcerated, commenting early on how well the transition was made to the new leadership of Morris Stein in New York. Over the next year, Cannon offered suggestions to that leadership through Rose, recommending, for example, that the farewell speeches of the "18" be published in a pamphlet "to complete the record of the case" and that the *Militant* address the hundred-year history of Marxism by treating key events, like the Paris Commune, with detailed reports. He also laid out precise plans for an SWP-sponsored school that would service both new and older members. While he educated himself in the Sandstone library, Cannon also encouraged party members outside the prison walls to reach out to the American working class through teachable moments and effective propaganda.[26]

Carlson also engaged in educational work to benefit both herself and the other women in prison. As a college-educated and professionally trained psychologist, she was a valued resource in the prison. Filing case records in the medical office at first, Carlson soon was given more significant duties, including administering special IQ tests to the mostly illiterate prison population. Through this work Carlson found some professional satisfaction. But her contact with the other imprisoned women, many of whom were from the South and had been incarcerated for prostitution, also educated Carlson in the kinds of injustices that poverty, racism, and illiteracy sustained. It taught her about the failures of the American public education system and reinforced her understanding of what she believed were, at root, the injustices of the capitalist system.[27] "I am not in a position to do much educational work," she explained to Dorothy in one of her letters, "but I do the best I can."[28] Rose Karsner criticized her for that work, arguing that she should apply herself more to her studies to develop as an "outstanding leader" of the party. But Carlson defended her choice. For her, the prison hospital work was "a unique opportunity to gain a better knowledge of people and the effect which their impoverished environments have had on them." She believed that she would "be a much more valuable person in the movement as a result."[29]

Carlson's prison correspondence details her experiences with the other women prisoners, but it also reveals an important component of the Trotskyist movement during her time in jail. Writing mostly to her female comrades, Carlson kept in touch with the extended network of women who kept the SWP functioning when its most senior leaders were incarcerated. Among her regular correspondents were her sister Dorothy (from the St. Paul branch), Evelyn Anderson (assistant secretary of the CRDC in New York), Bea Janosco and Elaine Roseland (from the Minneapolis branch), Rose Karsner (organizer in New York and Cannon's life partner), and Miriam Carter (from the New York branch). The central role that women played in party activities—from planning meetings, to fund-raising, to speaking at forums, to selling subscriptions to the *Militant*, to cooperating with the CRDC's work—was made clear in these exchanges.[30] At times, the letters also reveal that this expanded party work was something these women had to balance with the continued demands of their lives as wives and mothers, cooking dinner for their families, packing lunches for their husbands, and caring for sick children.[31] Dorothy, in particular, took on added responsibilities in the party's St. Paul office and continued to juggle a busy home schedule with her two children, Ann and Jimmy. In June 1944, her husband, Henry, suffered a serious complication from appendicitis and required months of follow-up care. Without the support of her extended network of friends who picked up the slack in the party office and aided her at home, Dorothy admitted that she might not have made it through.[32] Responding to both the revolutionary and the domestic call, these women led busy and intense lives.

An important part of these women's lives was their friendship that was intertwined with, but also went beyond, their party work. In times of personal crisis, like when Henry was ill, they came to each other's aid. But they also enjoyed each other's company at the many social events that were central to the broader movement culture of the SWP and that shaped their lives outside of their homes in St. Paul and Minneapolis. There were the annual May Day picnics, June strawberry festivals, and July raspberry festivals, where Dorothy, Bea, Elaine, and their friends met and relaxed, shared recipes, talked about books, and shared stories about their children. They recounted these personal moments to Carlson in their letters too, teasing her with descriptions of the things she was missing out on, including the good food and especially the strong coffee that she so loved. Theirs was a rich professional and personal sisterhood.[33]

Their letters to Carlson not only shed light on their complex and intertwined lives but also reveal how much the CRDC and its women members, like Evelyn Anderson, were doing to build support for the pardon campaign. The organization's local branches gathered signatures on the pardon petition and urged "trade unions, fraternal, negro and other progressive organizations to pass resolutions urging the President to pardon the 18." By April 1944, the CRDC had secured the support of NAACP branches and the March on Washington Movement (MOWM), as well as the Michigan State CIO Council, which represented 750,000 workers, along with myriad smaller organizations. By May the newspapers of several large unions, including the ILGWU and the ACWA, began to express their support for the "18." And by July the CRDC reached and exceeded its goal of obtaining 10,000 signatures on the pardon petition.[34]

In these same months (from March through the summer of 1944), Novack toured the country to increase support from labor and progressive groups. His tour helped raise funds for the prisoners and their dependent families, as did the sale of the CRDC's pamphlets about the case. These included the new publication, *Who Are the 18 Prisoners in the Minneapolis Labor Case?*[35] Novack also spoke at an impressive mass meeting in New York on June 8, where he was joined by Roger Baldwin, Norman Thomas, Daniel Bell, and several local labor leaders. More than 800 people were in attendance, and a collection of $800 was made at the end of the night.[36]

The purpose of the mass meetings that Novack and the CRDC organized was not just to gain the support of unions and progressive groups for the pardon petition but also to build support for the repeal of the Smith Act. As it had done before the trial and when the "18" appealed their conviction, the CRDC emphasized the broader implications of the case for First Amendment rights, thereby securing its alliance with the ACLU and aiding its outreach efforts to groups like the NAACP and the MOWM. The CRDC's work was, however, also closely tied to that of the party; the "organizational forms and lines" between the SWP and the CRDC were quite blurred. Given that most of the people working on a day-to-day basis for the latter group in New York and in the local branches around the country were also party members, and that the goal of the CRDC with respect to winning a pardon for the "18" was the same as that of the SWP, it was sometimes unclear where the work of one organization ended and the other began. Novack's group was created as an independent defense committee, to be able to win support for the "18" from the widest range of people outside the party as possible; but to party members it was clear that the SWP was essentially managing the group with its own personnel.[37] Although the CRDC included non–party members in its ranks and among its leadership and tried to expand its base within progressive groups and unions, it was closely intertwined with the work of the SWP.[38] That link also made it the subject of FBI surveillance.

FBI, CPUSA, and IBT Opposition to the Pardon Campaign

The CRDC's efforts on behalf of the "18," its protest of the Smith Act, and its ties to the SWP concerned Hoover, who authorized his agents to continue their surveillance of Novack's group. The FBI gathered copies of the CRDC's fundraising letters, the model resolutions calling for the pardon of the "18" that had been distributed to unions to forward to President Roosevelt, and other items it deemed relevant to its ongoing investigation. Agents also intercepted Novack's mail and infiltrated the audiences of his national tour, reporting on who was there, what was said, how much money was raised, and what petitions or resolutions were supported.[39] Agents looked for evidence of the Trotskyists' advocacy of violence or of their infiltration of unions and progressive groups, like the NAACP, during these gatherings. Hoover approved the operations and sent copies of the more detailed reports to Assistant Attorney General Tom Clark. As he had done with Berge prior to the indictment of the twenty-nine, Hoover kept the activities of Trotskyists and their allies on the Justice Department's radar screen, creating around them an aura of suspicion and guilt so that if the attorney general decided to launch a prosecution under the Smith Act or other relevant law, he would have the bureau's reports to support it.

While the FBI surveilled the CRDC's work secretly, the Communists openly criticized it. As Novack's organization grew in influence among trade unions and progressive groups, the *Daily Worker* accused it of building up a "sucker list" of supporters. The Communists' attack against those who allied with the Trotskyists demonstrated that they were concerned to some degree about "the increasing trade union support for the Minneapolis case." Miriam

Carter viewed this partisan rivalry as evidence of a good thing: the Trotsky-ists, via the CRDC, were making new allies in the labor movement around the country.[40]

Those ties were something that the IBT was increasingly worried about and tried to undermine. Partly this opposition was just a continuation of the Team-sters' efforts to keep the Dunnes and their allies out of the labor movement, efforts that it had engaged in since the June 9, 1941, "bolt" of the Trotskyist-led group from Local 544-IBT. But during the spring and summer of 1944, it was also a reaction to the CRDC's aggressive pardon campaign that claimed the "18" had been railroaded to jail merely for trying to "organize workers in the Teamsters' Union."[41] Because of this claim, Tobin received letters from trade union leaders in New York and Chicago asking for an explanation of what had happened inside his union.[42] Tobin was happy to oblige, enclosing a letter prepared by Victor Anderson that laid out the government's version of events along with a copy of the record of the case (all 1,313 pages of it). In his letter, Anderson directed the union leaders' attention to the indictment and the jury's verdict to make it clear that the "18" were convicted of advocating the vio-lent overthrow of the government, not because of their trade union activity as the CRDC argued.[43] Tobin reiterated this interpretation in his response to the union leaders, advising that "if I were in your place I would pay no attention to the so called Civil Rights Defense Committee," and that it was best to "keep away from them."[44] His argument may have convinced some union leaders. But as the CRDC's records show, the organization had managed to win sup-port from locals and councils around the country for the Trotskyists' pardon, support that irritated the Communists and worried Tobin.[45]

The IBT's opposition to the CRDC's work, along with the Communists' criticism, were just two obstacles that Novack's organization confronted in 1944. Even among erstwhile allies in the pardon campaign there were divi-sions that emerged as the prison year wore on. Max Shachtman, who had left the SWP in 1940 to form the Workers Party, supported the "18" since the time of the trial, but his followers were not all necessarily as devoted to the cause. Miriam Carter recounted to Grace Carlson how at the June 8 meeting in New York the Shachtmanites arrived late and then milled about talking at the back of the hall, "creating such a disturbance that it was almost impos-sible to hear Novack." There may have been a host of innocuous reasons for this juvenile display, but for Carter, it was evidence of the Shachtmanites' in-ability "to demonstrate elementary labor solidarity with victims of capitalist persecution."[46]

Carter's comments on the episode reveal some of the tensions between the Trotskyists and their supporters that existed behind closed doors. Such details did not appear in the official reports on the CRDC's gatherings found in press releases or the *Militant*. For the most part, the Trotskyists maintained their solidarity among themselves and with their allies outside of the party during what was a very difficult year for the SWP; the prisoners found ways to improve themselves so as to better serve the party upon their release, and those on the outside, especially the women, kept the ranks active. But, as Carter's correspondence demonstrates, disagreements with their supporters in the fight against the Smith Act occasionally distracted them. And in one case those disagreements extended into the ranks of the "18" as they debated how and when to apply for a pardon.

The Pardon Fight and the Return Home

One dispute surrounding the pardon focused on Joe Hansen's description of the surrender of the "18" that was used as a publicity tool in the pardon campaign. Hansen's piece first appeared in the January 1944 *Fourth International* and in the *Militant* and later was published as part of a pamphlet entitled *Why We Are in Prison* that included the farewell banquet speeches of the defendants. Lydia Bennett and other leading members in the Chicago branch launched an extensive criticism of the article. She cited its melodramatic style, its "sentimental drooling," and its hero-worshipping quality as things that outraged her. "For us to handle the subject with any sentiment other than class indignation at a political act," Bennett explained, "is impermissible."[47] Morris Stein, as acting secretary of the SWP, defended the publication, arguing that it was "perfectly legitimate to pull at the heart-strings in your popular agitation, while in your cadre literature your emphasis is almost entirely on political analysis."[48] Yet objections to the piece continued to be registered, indicating in their detail that more was at stake than mere "literary criticism."[49] Goldman also condemned Hansen's article; he argued that Lenin would not approve of its "fawning and sentimental hero-worship." Claiming that his criticism was intended only to "prevent Stalinist germs from contaminating our party," Goldman pledged to work with anyone in the party, including "Cassidy" (Felix Morrow's pseudonym), to make sure that "contamination" did not happen.[50] As Cannon noted in a letter to Rose, the fuss over "Joe's artistry" was "only a pretext" for deeper differences within the party: he sensed correctly that there was opposition brewing to his leadership and the majority coalition he headed in the party.[51]

But in the meantime, there were other disagreements related to the pardon that distracted the Trotskyists. Although the SWP demonstrated a united front in public, not all members were in complete agreement on how best to respond to the case. At one of the spring meetings of the party's weekly discussion group in Minneapolis, the Saturday Lunch Club, a lengthy debate followed the introduction of a resolution that called for both a repeal of the Smith Act and the pardon of the "18." Certain members voiced support for the repeal of the legislation but not for the pardon. At a subsequent meeting when the item was brought up again, those who did not want to support the pardon convinced the others "one by one" to table the resolution in its entirety, including the language condemning the Smith Act. It is unclear from the account of these events (in a letter from Elaine Roseland to Grace Carlson) why certain members opposed the pardon, but it does hint that some may have been concerned about speaking out against the government. Having just witnessed their top leaders go to prison, these Trotskyists may have been worried about walking into the crosshairs of the Smith Act by condemning it in a resolution. They referred the matter to a committee that included a lawyer. "If and when they do pass a resolution," Roseland commented to Carlson, "you can be sure it will be a far cry from the original presented."[52] Some, like Roseland, were ready to man the barricades. Members in the San Diego branch were willing to picket the White House.[53] But others in the party wanted to be more cautious.

Even among the "18" there were disagreements surrounding the issue of the pardon. By early June the defendants had decided to make a formal pardon application to the Presidential Pardon Board in Washington. Roger Baldwin encouraged them to prepare applications that were "of brief and principled character to wit, that they should receive pardon because they have been unjustly deprived of their democratic and constitutional rights."[54] Cannon accepted this advice.[55] But Goldman disagreed vehemently, explaining that he favored "the idea of a political petition" that allowed them "to recapitulate the ideas which we presented during the trial." He saw the pardon petition "as a continuation of the trial" and "another opportunity to publish our views."[56] Cannon and Goldman were thus at an impasse. Cannon believed that the "18" had made their position "clear enough in the trial pamphlets and the pamphlet of farewell speeches" and that "silence now on our part while our friends conduct our campaign is a way of speaking that is most effective under the circumstances." He insisted that the "most effective way to proceed" was to allow the popular campaign to move forward so that "at the time of the formal presentation of these petitions to the President all publicity should be devoted to the new and essentially important fact that trade unions representing one and half million workers and many prominent individuals have formally demanded our liberation."[57] Cannon believed in the need to silence all other ideas for now so that he and the other leaders could be released from prison to fight another day.

The fourteen men at Sandstone met and debated the issue. Cannon won support for his position from eight of his fellow Trotskyists: Dunne, Dobbs, Coover, Skoglund, DeBoer, Geldman, Palmquist, and Hansen. Morrow, Hudson, Cooper, and Hamel backed Goldman's approach. In order to accommodate the split, Cannon suggested that the simple, constitutionally focused application be the template for all the defendants, but that "each individual may put any statement he wishes on his own application."[58] Word was sent to the three defendants in Danbury and to Carlson in West Virginia, and the "18" quickly drew up their documents. On August 2, 1944, Novack delivered their formal applications, along with the petitions and resolutions supporting the pardon by unions representing more than 2 million workers to Daniel Lyons, U.S. pardons attorney, in Washington, DC.[59] It was not until early October that they received word from Lyons, and then he merely reported that the decision was being held up because it was "still under consideration," offering no explanation for the delay.[60]

What the Trotskyists did not know was that what had been going on behind closed doors at the Justice Department that summer may have contributed to this delay. In late July 1944, as the "18" were contemplating the nature of their formal pardon application, Biddle was confronted with the Supreme Court's recent decision in the *Hartzel* case in which Justice Murphy, writing for the 5-to-4 majority, "construe[d] the statutory requirement of 'willfulness' [in the Espionage Act] so as to require specific intent."[61] One ACLU lawyer wrote to Biddle, arguing that as a result it was "impossible to justify the Trotskyists' conviction on the facts established at their trial."[62] Largely unconvinced by this point of view, Biddle offered to "consider the matter" to appease his liberal critics.[63] He requested input from his solicitor general, Charles Fahy.

In his memo to Biddle, Fahy concluded, "The *Hartzel* case has no bearing in the Minneapolis case except as indicating a reluctance on the part of the Supreme Court to sustain convictions which cut across the views of some of the Justices where freedom of speech is involved." Putting his finger on a division within the Court over the limits of subversive speech that had not abated since the time of the *Schneiderman* case, Fahy distinguished any trends in its findings on such questions from the facts in the Minneapolis case. He told Biddle that his "own judgment is the pardons should not be requested."[64] Fahy's conclusion was sustained by a memo from one of his staff, Philip Elman, that was also sent to Biddle.[65] When the "18" filed their formal applications for a pardon that same day, Biddle had Fahy's and Elman's recommendations in hand and presumably shared them with Lyons, making the case that the Trotskyists did not deserve clemency.

Lyons had to weigh this advice alongside the applications from the "18" and the CRDC petitions and resolutions that Novack had hand delivered to him. Those documents made the case for why the Trotskyists should be pardoned. That case was also made by the more than 100 letters that had been sent directly to President Roosevelt since the Supreme Court refused the writ in December 1943. Some of these letters were clearly inspired by the January 1944 article in the *Nation* condemning the Court's inaction. And some echoed the CRDC's talking points circulated in its pardon campaign. But others appear to be more independent reactions to what their authors perceived to be a gross injustice. All share the common themes of seeing the case as a miscarriage of justice and a violation of the nation's "fundamental civil liberties."[66] Many also cite the implications of the case as a dangerous precedent for trade union rights.[67] And several took Roosevelt to task for violating his promise to defend democracy in the fight against fascism. As Samuel Grakovic expressed in reference to the Smith Act, "It is a poor thing indeed, when our soldiers are dying on the battlefields in a war for the Four Freedoms, that those very freedoms should be outlawed here at home."[68] Along with these letters were resolutions passed by trade unions and progressive groups that similarly protested the criminal conviction of the "18" "because of their beliefs and their activities on behalf of labor."[69] It is unclear if Lyons had access to these documents, which had been sent directly to the White House, but whether he would find the petitions and resolutions Novack gave him on August 2 more convincing than the advice coming from the attorney general's office remained to be seen. He took two months to sift through everything in his possession before making a decision.

On October 10, Evelyn Anderson wrote to Grace Carlson with the news from Washington. Lyons had not even submitted the applications from the "18" to Roosevelt, citing as justification "the absence of a favorable recommendation from the United States Attorney or the trial judge." In an attempt to mitigate the disappointing news for the Trotskyists, Lyons emphasized that "in view of the character of the offence it does not appear that the sentences imposed are unduly severe" and that some of the defendants were due to be released that same month anyway. Lyons also noted that he and his board were "unable to agree" that the *Hartzel* case "or any other of the cited decisions of the Supreme Court controls the situation here presented so as to require clemency." As a result, he explained, "the Attorney General feels . . . he could not properly present this case to the President with a recommendation favorable to the exercise of clemency."[70] There would be no pardon.

The SWP quickly responded. The *Militant* lashed out with the screaming headline: "Roosevelt Attempts to Evade Responsibility for Decision. Administration Offers Flimsy Pretexts for Its Refusal to Free Railroaded Trotskyists."

Invoking the political debt theory once again, it argued that, like the Supreme Court, the president was "hiding behind a technicality to avoid direct responsibility for a case involving violation of labor and civil rights during this war, a case growing out of a deliberate frame-up prosecution directly initiated by Roosevelt himself."[71] Novack also prepared an official statement condemning the Pardon Board's decision. Taking offense at Lyons's assertion that it did not appear that the sentences imposed were unduly severe, Novack retorted, "Any punishment inflicted upon innocent people is totally unwarranted."[72] Reading Novack's words in the *Militant* from Alderson prison, Carlson wrote to Evelyn Anderson, "I can say an hearty Amen to that!"[73]

Although it was a crushing disappointment, Lyons's rejection was not the end of the road for the "18" or their supporters. They vowed to continue to "press our demand for Presidential pardon,"[74] starting with a mass meeting coordinated by the CRDC at the Manhattan Center on October 27. The meeting combined protest with a welcome home gathering for three of the six defendants who were released seven days earlier "after serving almost 10 months of a one year and one day sentence, with time off for good behavior."[75] As the guests of honor, Al Russell, Karl Kuehn, and Oscar Schoenfeld received "a tremendous ovation" from the several hundred people gathered that night. The former prisoners mostly thanked the CRDC for all its support and spoke of their joy at being reunited with their families, especially Russell, whose wife had a baby while he was incarcerated. But they also vowed to continue the struggle for the twelve who remained behind bars. The sharp attack on the pardon denial was left to George Novack, who called Lyons's explanation a "shameful and deceitful evasive denial of justice" that ignored "the basic questions of civil liberties." He committed the CRDC to continuing the fight for the pardon and the repeal of the Smith Act.[76]

Their comrades in Minneapolis shared these sentiments. Harry DeBoer, Clarence Hamel, and Edward Palmquist, who had been sent to Sandstone, were also released on October 20. DeBoer and Hamel were met at the train station by their families and friends from the SWP. There they spoke about their joy at being reunited with their loved ones, including Palmquist's young daughter and baby son, but they also spoke about their continued commitment to the Trotskyist beliefs for which they had been imprisoned. Palmquist, whose sister-in-law had recently died from a brain tumor, had left with his wife and children directly from Sandstone to assist his extended family in Seattle.[77] He did not attend the homecoming dinner arranged for the three men by the local branch of the SWP.[78]

Although the comrades were angry about the pardon denial, they were also happy to have some of their friends back with them. The homecoming dinner signaled this relief and the beginnings of the movement's process of reconstituting itself after the prison year.⁷⁹ As they waited for the remaining twelve comrades to be released from jail, the Trotskyists in Minneapolis, New York, and other cities around the country demonstrated the strength of their fellowship. They supported the CRDC's Christmas fund drive for the families of the imprisoned by holding special holiday bazaars and dances that raised more than $5,000 for the cause. And in Minneapolis the Trotskyists gathered for a Christmas party with the children of the "Labor Case Prisoners." These included Dobbs's three school-age children, Geldman's seven-year-old daughter and baby boy, and Hudson's six-year-old son and three-year-old daughter. Clarence Hamel, one of the "fondly termed . . . 600 twins" (along with Emil Hansen because of their size), dressed as Santa Claus as he and the other members of the SWP clan tried to make the holiday a happy one for the little ones separated from their parents who were still behind bars.⁸⁰

Those children did not have to wait much longer to see their parents. The remaining twelve defendants were released from prison on January 24. Greeted by their families and friends at the Great Northern Railway station in Minneapolis, the eleven male prisoners gave brief public statements in which each reaffirmed his readiness and desire to continue the "great work" of the party. As Coover announced, they "were ready to take our place in the ranks again and carry on the fight."⁸¹ The group walked together to the SWP headquarters for lunch, where they were able to greet more comrades and renew their connections. As the *Militant* reported, once they were back at the party office, "they were really home." Relaxing and enjoying the companionship of their friends, they talked about the future of the SWP and awaited the arrival of Carlson, who was on her way from Alderson by car. It was a "joyous occasion" and a symbolic one: after more than a year in jail, the "18" were "back home with their comrades" ready to "march more firmly forward to the Socialist future" by continuing to advocate the beliefs for which they had been imprisoned.⁸²

One of the first steps they took in this direction was gathering again in public to speak out against the Smith Act. Mass meetings were organized in Minneapolis, Chicago, and New York to welcome home all "the released Trotskyist fighters for workers' rights" and to "rally labor and progressive forces for the next steps in the campaign to repeal the infamous Smith 'Gag' Act."⁸³ On January 25, the Chicago branch of the CRDC sponsored a meeting at which Goldman denounced the peacetime sedition law that had sent him to jail.⁸⁴ On January 28, Carlson, Dunne, Geldman, Hudson, Hansen, Skoglund, Coover, and Cooper were the guests of honor at a welcome home banquet held at the Labor Lyceum in Minneapolis. There they helped raise

$350 for the CRDC's campaign against the "Gag" Act.[85] On February 2, Goldman joined with Dobbs and Morrow to speak at a mass meeting of more than 800 "unionists and other progressive fighters for civil liberties" in New York at the Hotel Diplomat. Cannon, who was ill, sent his greetings in which he thanked those who had supported the "18," especially Roger Baldwin and the CRDC.[86] Schoenfeld, Kuehn, and Russell were welcomed home again at this event and sat on the platform alongside Goldman, Dobbs, and Morrow. The newly released prisoners, joined by their long-standing allies Baldwin and Farrell, condemned the dangers of the Smith Act and demanded its repeal.[87] Freed from prison, the "18" renewed their battle against the criminalization of subversive speech and resumed their fight against the capitalist government that had instituted it.

Continuing the Struggle for Civil Rights and Socialism

Reconnecting to the work of their local SWP branch was central to these struggles. But the "18" soon found that work had become the target of renewed FBI investigations. After returning home from prison, Max Geldman, along with his wife, Goldie, and brother-in-law Jake Cooper, moved in with Jake's father and worked in his grocery store in the small town of Chaska outside of Minneapolis where Jake grew up. Geldman attended party meetings in Minneapolis regularly during these months but otherwise kept to himself. It was only after his probation ended that he and Goldie moved to Philadelphia, where they both became very active in the local SWP branch.[88] They joined Karl Kuehn, who had found a job there soon after his release from prison. All of them remained under FBI surveillance.[89] The same was true for the other released prisoners: agents and informants provided plentiful information on their whereabouts and actions as they began to rebuild their lives and reconnect with the SWP. Ed Palmquist, who had moved to Seattle with his wife, Rose, immediately after leaving Sandstone, found a home in the party branch there by the end of 1945. Ed and Rose became active in the SWP's efforts to form a labor party and were watched by informants who fed details of their activities to the FBI.[90]

The same was true for Vincent Dunne. At the time of his release, the Special Agent in Charge in St. Paul informed Hoover that his "office intends to maintain close contact with all types of informants in connection with the SWP, should Dunne again become active in the movement, his individual case file will be reopened."[91] It did not take long for this to happen; by March it was clear to the bureau that Dunne was back in action at SWP headquarters in Minneapolis, where he had become "the directing force of the local group."⁹² Anxious to move to New York to work for the party there as requested to by Cannon, Dunne had to wait until May, when his probation ended, to take up his new job as a national organizer for the SWP. There he joined Carlson, who, after spending about a month in St. Paul visiting with her family after her release from jail, had left for New York in mid-February to resume her work as a party organizer.⁹³

Both Carlson and Dunne were under intense surveillance, which included the use of an informant who had access to their personal correspondence and private conversations. According to this individual, the two Trotskyists were more than just comrades; it was alleged that they were carrying on "a clandestine affair." Carlson had been estranged from her husband, Gilbert, since the time of the trial; the two had separated in 1940. And Dunne seems to have drifted from his wife, Jennie, too. But there is no explicit evidence to corroborate whether the two may have entered into a romance in these years. There are some hints that such a relationship, known only to a certain few, may have blossomed in the aftermath of the trial. In letters from her sister Dorothy and her friend Bea, for example, Carlson was often asked about "Ray" (Dunne's nickname), and the two were referenced as a couple in conversations about other couples in the movement.⁹⁴ But, given the often-questionable reliability of informant testimony in FBI reports, it is difficult to determine if there was anything more than a close, platonic friendship between Carlson and Dunne.⁹⁵ In the spring of 1945, the two allegedly made plans to spend a few days alone together in New York before making Dunne's presence there known to their party comrades. They rendezvoused at the train station on Friday, May 4, and sequestered themselves in Carlson's apartment until May 6, when she left for Boston "to make a May day address" and he reported to SWP headquarters.⁹⁶ For the next seven years the two would work closely together as comrades, but whether their relationship ever became more than a friendship is hard to determine with any certainty.⁹⁷

Dunne and Carlson shared a passion for the SWP and for the Trotskyist vision of the socialist future. They worked hard to bring about that future. Beginning in late June 1945, Carlson toured the country speaking about her time in prison and the relationship she discovered there between poverty, illiteracy, and crime. Drawing from her unorthodox educational work at Alderson, she talked to audiences about "women of the working class who have been robbed by the capitalist system of a chance for a decent and hopeful life."⁹⁸ In 1946, she served the SWP in a more conventional way by running for Senate in Minnesota. Dunne also served the party by running as its candidate for mayor of Minneapolis in 1947. Neither Carlson nor Dunne was successful in their bids for office, but that did not stop them from try-

Figure 6.3 A Socialist Workers Party meeting. Vincent Ray Dunne and Grace Carlson in center. Dorothy Schultz, Carlson's sister, sits to her left. Photos J1.6p2, negative number 82998, Minnesota Historical Society. Courtesy Minnesota Historical Society.

ing again. In 1948, when Dobbs ran for president, Carlson stood as his vice president. Although they may not have captured a significant number of votes at the polls, the campaigns kept the party energized and focused on the fight for civil liberties. The purchase of that issue may have contributed to the growth in SWP membership in the closing years of the war. In 1944, the SWP's ranks increased by 300 and in 1945 by 1,005, so that by 1946 they stood at almost 3,000.[99]

Despite this growth, there were those in the party who believed a change of direction was needed. Goldman and Morrow led this faction, which called for unification of the SWP with Max Shachtman's Workers Party, ostensibly to strengthen the movement. Arguing that the question of "unconditional defense of the Soviet union" was "no longer acute and topical as it was" when the split occurred that led to the WP's creation in 1940, Shachtman was willing to consider unification.[100] But the Goldman-Morrow proposal, at least as far as Cannon was concerned, was based on more than a concern for the strength of the SWP. Rooted in the deterioration of the personal relationship between Cannon and Goldman that took place while the two were imprisoned at Sandstone—a break that was expressed, in part, in the disagreement over the nature of the pardon petition and Hansen's pamphlet—Goldman and Morrow's stand was also just as much about their opposition to Cannon.[101] Goldman and Morrow had drifted from the others during their time in prison. After their release the tension between Goldman and Cannon in particular was evident in the way each kept his distance from the other: Goldman did not gather with the others at SWP headquarters for lunch on the day they returned to Minneapolis but instead left immediately for Chicago. There he spoke at the CRDC meeting rather than attend the SWP's welcome home banquet in Minneapolis with the others.[102]

But, for Goldman, the personal was also political. As he hinted in his criticism of Hansen's pamphlet, Goldman believed there was a hero-worshipping tendency in the party that had been built up around Cannon that was dangerous to its work as a revolutionary movement. Arguing that the "hero cult" forced the rank and file to "accept without question all the policies handed down by the leadership," Goldman supported a minority within the party that he defined as standing for "an educated, alert, critical and disciplined membership." Feeling unable to launch his minority critique successfully from within the SWP after Cannon charged him with being a "'stooge for Shachtman,'"[103] Goldman called for the creation of "a closed faction to 'struggle' for unification with the Shachtmanites" in July 1945.[104] He was joined by Morrow, Coover, and others in the ranks who supported him, especially many of the comrades in Chicago, who shared Goldman's concerns about and dislike of Cannon.

Cannon had been worried about Goldman and Morrow since the "18" were released from prison. He was aware of the minority group they were gathering around them by early April 1945, and that was why, in part, he called Dunne to New York from Minneapolis to aid him. Carlson also stood by Cannon during the faction fight, which was most pronounced in New York, but which took shape in branches around the country too, including those in Minneapolis and Chicago. In Minneapolis, Dorothy and Henry Schultz stood firmly in the majority camp, while Coover worked to win supporters to the Goldman-Morrow group.[105] Initially Cannon hoped that his majority coalition could "put the factional struggle under control, regulate its tempo and, if possible, prevent a premature, abnormal and unprofitable development."[106] But he quickly launched an all-out attack when Goldman and his supporters—angry at the failure of their minority resolution before the political committee in July 1945—formed their closed faction in support of the WP.[107] Over the next year and a half, Cannon and his allies managed to stave off unification with the Workers Party.[108] Frustrated by this turn of events, Goldman left the SWP in May 1946 and joined with Shachtman. Left holding the bag, as Cannon later described it, Morrow was expelled for his "unauthorized collaboration" with the WP by a vote of 101 to 4 at the SWP's convention in November.[109] Thus while most of the Trotskyists reaffirmed their commitment to the SWP and to each other as an extended family of comrades after the "18" were freed, some dissented bitterly, leading to a painful and disruptive rift in the ranks and among the leadership.

Despite this difficulty, Cannon and the others in the majority of the SWP carried on their fight for the restoration of their civil rights and for the repeal of the Smith Act. In 1948, they launched a significant effort along these lines. The time seemed ripe to file for a pardon again because it was a presidential election year and one in which the question of civil rights had become an openly debated issue. President Truman's proposal for the first major civil rights bill of the twentieth century in February 1948 pushed the question onto the national political stage, as did the Democratic Party's approval of a civil rights plank in its platform later that year. Dobbs and Carlson, who were running for president and vice president on the SWP ticket, placed the issue of civil rights at the forefront of their campaign. The SWP's political committee, which approved this agenda, linked the focus on civil rights to three things: the demand for the pardon of the "18," the repeal of the Smith Act, and the removal of the SWP from the attorney general's "subversive list."[110] The Trotskyists hoped that the atmosphere of the 1948 presidential election—which also saw the creation of Henry Wallace's Progressive Party—would aid them in their fight. Not all Americans supported the civil rights agenda of those on the left of the Democratic Party or in the Progressive Party. Truman lost the support of the "Dixiecrats" by proposing the civil rights law. But the campaign year brought national attention to the issue, and the SWP tried to take advantage of it for its own benefit.

The SWP's engagement with questions of civil liberties also resonated with those (also mostly on the political left) who were becoming increasingly concerned with the federal government's creation and use of the mechanisms of the Second Red Scare. As the Cold War heated up abroad, the Truman administration became concerned with the threat of communist infiltration at home, in part because of Hoover's continued public insistence on the breadth and immediacy of that danger.[111] Also under political pressure from conservatives to crack down on the "red menace," the president issued Executive Order 9835, establishing the Federal Employee Loyalty Program. Under this program "every federal civilian employee and every applicant for federal civilian employment would henceforth undergo a loyalty investigation, without regard to whether the job in question had anything to do with national security." The president's order also authorized the attorney general "to list those organizations that he considered 'totalitarian, fascist, communist, or subversive.'" Individuals with ties to groups on the list could be deemed disloyal. The first list issued by the Department of Justice came out in late 1947, followed by a longer one in early 1948.[112] The SWP found itself on the attorney general's list that summer. Protesting this designation became part of the Trotskyists' fight for their civil rights. This struggle, along with the continued call for the repeal of the Smith Act and the renewed attempt for a presidential pardon, became the focus of the party's and the CRDC's work in 1948.

Novack had kept the CRDC going to fight for the repeal of the Smith Act even after the "18" were released from prison. In 1948 he shifted the organization into full gear for the new presidential pardon campaign. Already secure in the ACLU's support for this cause, Novack wanted to get the backing of both Henry Wallace and the Progressive Party. Put on the spot at his party's convention in Philadelphia that July by Norman Thomas, Wallace said he would support a pardon for the "18."[113] As far as getting the Progressives to include a plank in their platform "demanding a repeal of the Smith Act and restoration of civil rights to all those victimized by this discriminatory legislation," Novack and Karl Kuehn (who assisted him in this endeavor) were not successful. They had mistimed bringing the item to the floor, but the main reason they failed was the opposition of Communists within Wallace's party. Despite this setback, Novack had secured both Thomas's and Wallace's endorsements for the pardon and used them, along with the ACLU's support, in the CRDC's publicity campaign.[114]

Central to the fight for the pardon was getting the support of the "18." Dobbs, Carlson, and Dunne agreed with the idea early on, but Novack was unsure where the others stood. He was particularly worried about "how Goldman and his friends will react" and was not sure "whether we can easily reach a number of the others, like Ed Palmquist."[115] Nonetheless, he wrote to each of the former prisoners in July explaining the CRDC's work on their behalf and asking for their consent to proceed. Although several of them responded positively to Novack, not all did. As he had feared, the Goldman-Morrow split still resonated. Oscar Schoenfeld, writing to Goldman about Novack's proposition, explained that he had "no intention of going through with any common activity with those people and will so write them." Aside from the old factional divide that kept him from cooperating with Novack's plan, Schoenfeld cited another concern: "Publicity would be very damaging to me, personally." Wary of dredging up the past and eager to move on with his life (having "no inclination whatsoever to become involved in any so-called political activity"), he refused to join his former comrades in the pardon application.[116] These fears and hesitations were some of the less visible, but no less significant, legacies of the 1941 prosecution and of the Goldman-Morrow split.

Those Trotskyists who wanted to sign the pardon application quickly found themselves confronted with another obstacle. Unlike the forms they had filled out in 1944 when they had last applied for a presidential pardon, the paperwork required of them in 1948 included a loyalty oath. Geldman questioned "whether it would be correct in principle for the 18 to sign the loyalty oath attached to the pardon petition," leading the CRDC by mid-August to "reconsider our procedure in this matter." In the context of the Cold War and the early days of the Second Red Scare, the Trotskyists were confronted with this new challenge to their attempt to restore their full civil rights. Aware that refusing to file the complete paperwork might "create some complications" with their application to the pardon board, they considered sending a letter directly to President Truman instead in order to bypass the loyalty oath.[117] Given all the obstacles they faced, they were ultimately unsuccessful in their attempt to secure a pardon in 1948.

They were also unsuccessful in their attempt to have the SWP removed from the attorney general's subversive list, despite Dobb's vociferous condemnation of the procedure in late July and his request to the Justice Department for a public hearing at which the party's representatives could formally protest.[118] In early August the SWP retained the attorney M. J. Myer, who also wrote to Clark repeating the "request for [a] hearing open to the public and press" and for a bill of particulars.[119] But neither Dobbs's nor Myer's efforts bore fruit: on August 16 the attorney general's office denied their requests.[120]

Unsatisfied with the answer he received from the Department of Justice, Dobbs wrote directly to President Truman. In decrying the "blacklisting" of the SWP, Dobbs spoke of the many "members and friends of my party" who were "being victimized by federal officials and departments and deprived of their employment and means of livelihood." Dobbs characterized the list and its use as akin to "the methods of a police state which you have vehemently condemned as President of the United States." It allowed for "guilt by association," thereby sweeping aside the "constitutional safeguards and traditional democratic procedures which have maintained the innocence of a person until proved guilty," including a "trial by jury of one's peers, the examination of charges and the introduction of evidence, the presentation of and cross-examination of witnesses." Dobbs argued that "all of these, despite manifold assurances to the contrary, are being ground to bits by your executive orders and their administration by your Department of Justice."

As a result, Dobbs demanded that Truman "take steps to quash the Department of Justice 'subversive' blacklisting as it is clearly unconstitutional and in violation of the Bill of Rights" and that he remove "immediately" the SWP from that list. Referring to the context of the 1948 presidential election year, Dobbs told Truman, "This is the least you can do, Mr. President, in the interest of upholding and protecting the civil rights you so often refer to." Throwing down the gauntlet, he concluded, "Anything less will prove that the principles of fascism are gaining a foothold in the highest circles of U.S. government."[121] Carlson, Dobbs's running mate in the upcoming election, sent a similar letter to Truman, charging that if his "vehement and repeated professions of devotion to democracy and civil rights [were to] have any meaning," he would "declare the 'subversive' blacklist null and void and tear up root and branch the hideous procedures which produced this blacklist."[122] Convinced of the soundness of their arguments, Dobbs and Carlson awaited a reply from the president.

The president's secretary forwarded their letters to the attorney general's office where, it was promised, they would be given "appropriate attention."[123] As H. L. Mencken said of Clarence Darrow's speech during the *Scopes* trial, the effect of Dobbs's and Carlson's passionate protests "seems to be precisely the same as if [they] had bawled it up a rainspout in the interior of Afghanistan." No matter how significant they believed their arguments against the subversive list to be, the president's staff bounced them back to the attorney general, who had already asserted that the list would remain in place. The same thing happened again in October when Dobbs appealed directly to Truman for a second time.[124] Although Truman talked about the importance of civil rights, his administration's support was defined almost exclusively in racial terms, in part because of the pressures of the Cold War. The persistence of racial discrimination in America was proving damaging to the nation's posture as the self-professed leader of the free world. At the time Secretary of State Dean Acheson warned that America "might not be able to win the Cold War until it cleaned up its own act." Protecting the civil liberties of communists was not considered in the same light; indeed, tracking and restricting the actions of those associated with the communist menace was seen as part of the same Cold War fight to defend democracy and freedom.[125]

The Trotskyists were beginning to learn this lesson during their struggles in 1948. They had tried to leverage the attention being paid to questions of civil rights and civil liberties in that presidential election year to benefit their fight for a pardon, for the repeal of the Smith Act, and for the removal of the SWP from the attorney general's subversive list, but they instead found themselves on the losing end of the liberal bargain that helped sustain the emerging Second Red Scare. So although they had passed the test of fire of the prison year, the Trotskyists now faced a new round of challenges in their continued fight against the Smith Act in the inhospitable climate of the deepening Cold War.

7

The Ongoing Struggle for Civil Liberties

June 1951–August 1986

The FBI followed the Trotskyists for more than four decades after their conviction in 1941. Agents surveilled the "18," the SWP, its youth group (the Young Socialist Alliance [YSA]), and the CRDC, compiling thousands of reports; by 1986 the bureau "admitted to having gathered at least ten million pages of files on the SWP and YSA."[1] Hoover's belief that the Trotskyists constituted a fifth column thus did not wane with the imprisonment of the "18." The bureau's investigations cast a pall of suspicion over the group that marginalized it from prospective members. During the height of the Second Red Scare, this suspicion weighed particularly heavily on the party, leading even some of the "18" to leave the SWP. By the late 1950s, those who remained were still investigated by the FBI, but as the Second Red Scare waned, the voices of those who had been calling for the preservation of civil liberties, even in times of national emergency, grew louder both on and off of the Supreme Court, as the 1957 *Yates* decision demonstrates.

It would not be until 1986, however, when the SWP achieved vindication for the decades of harassment it endured by the nation's growing security state, including the invasive surveillance techniques to which it was subjected through the FBI's COINTELPRO from 1961 until 1976. With Judge Thomas Griesa's ruling on the unconstitutionality of that program and its use against the SWP, the Trotskyists achieved a significant victory in the struggle for civil liberties that it had waged for decades. The story of their struggle demonstrates the promises and limitations of both free speech law and radical political activism during the latter half of the twentieth century.

The Smith Act Upheld: *Dennis v. U.S.*

During the height of the Second Red Scare, the Justice Department was not receptive to the SWP's protests against its subversive list and the Smith Act partly because it was then actively implementing both in a campaign against the Communist Party. The nation's U.S. attorneys, who were supported and, some have argued, encouraged by Hoover,[2] used the list and the sedition

7

197

law to ferret out Communists who, they alleged, posed a threat to national security because of their ties to the CPUSA. Although they considered the Communists on trial their political enemies, the Trotskyists rallied to their defense as a part of their ongoing battle against the Smith Act. The *Dennis* case became their fight too because they appreciated its implications for the fate of civil liberties for all Americans, particularly for radical dissenters like themselves.

On July 28, 1949, a federal grand jury in New York indicted eleven Communist Party leaders under the Smith Act. As with the case of the Trotskyists, the judge dealing with the CPUSA defendants denied all the motions filed by the defense before the trial. As Michal Belknap has noted, in his deliberations Judge Murray Hilbert looked to "Judge Stone's opinion in the Trotskyist case" and "ruled in favor of the constitutionality of the Smith Act, upheld the indictment, . . . and turned down . . . a defense motion for a bill of particulars."[3] Hilbert was not the only one at the time to look back at the 1941 case for guidance. In May, after Attorney General Tom Clark authorized the prosecution, he asked Victor Anderson to provide his office with a copy of the record in the Dunne case, which was then forwarded to the U.S. attorney in New York.[4]

It was therefore not coincidental that the prosecution's strategy in the 1949 case was so similar to Anderson's. Both prosecution teams focused on the "'historic mission'" of each political party: that is, that its "adherence to the doctrines of Marxism-Leninism automatically obligated it to seek the overthrow of the government by force and violence." Both teams explored the foreign ties of the political party in question: for the SWP it was the link to Trotsky in Mexico and the Fourth International; for the CPUSA it was the tie to Moscow that contributed to its "'illegal aims and purposes.'" Both teams also emphasized the secret nature of each party as evidence of its conspiratorial composition. Both the prosecution in 1941 and that in 1949 presented the relationships between the party in question and the labor movement as evidence of "'infiltration'" that was a "prelude to sabotage." Anderson cited the influence of the Trotskyists within Local 544 in Minneapolis and the central role of the trucking industry in wartime preparedness; the prosecutors in the CPUSA case pointed to the Allis-Chalmers strike as their "Exhibit A." Finally, both teams also pored over the literature found in the respective party's offices, bookstores, and schools to prove the advocacy charge. They introduced at trial "the most incendiary passages in the works of Marx, Lenin, Stalin, and other communist heavies, excerpted . . . to show that the 'basic doctrines of Marxism-Leninism' required revolutionary violence."[5]

The trial itself lasted from January 17 to October 14, 1949, and resulted in a conviction of each of the eleven leaders and a confirmation of the Smith Act's legitimacy. After explaining that the Smith Act "did not prohibit advocacy of 'the abstract doctrine' that it was moral or principled to overthrow 'organized government by unlawful means,' but it did prohibit the 'advocacy of *action* for the accomplishment of that purpose,'" Judge Harold Medina told the jury that "'there is sufficient danger . . . to justify the application of the statute under the First Amendment.'" The jury found the defendants guilty, and "a week later, Judge Medina sentenced them to the maximum penalty of five years in prison."[6]

In his Second Circuit Court opinion upholding the convictions in 1950, Judge Learned Hand made a bargain similar to Medina's. Looking back over almost thirty years of Supreme Court decisions dealing with the First Amendment, Hand offered a modified version of the clear and present danger test in arriving at his conclusion. He argued that the courts "in each case . . . must ask whether the gravity of the 'evil,' discounted by its improbability, justifies such invasion of free speech as is necessary to avoid the danger."[7] Hand's emphasis on "the gravity of the evil" came closer to Holmes's version of the test in *Schenck* but took a step back from Brandeis's insistence on the significance of imminence in *Whitney*. As Belknap argues, with this new formulation of the test, "Hand . . . rather largely wrote the time element out of the formula."[8]

Hand's opinion influenced Chief Justice Fred Vinson's plurality opinion in *Dennis v. U.S.*, handed down on June 4, 1951. The Supreme Court, which had granted a writ of certiorari only on the question of the constitutionality of the Smith Act, upheld the convictions in a 6-to-2 decision.[9] Like Hand, Vinson emphasized gravity over imminence, arguing that "the words [of the clear-and-present danger test] cannot mean that before the Government may act, it must wait until the putsch is about to be executed, the plans have been laid and the signal is awaited."[10] Sherman Minton and Harold Burton joined Vinson in the plurality opinion in which he expressed accord with the circuit court in its having "affirmed the trial court's finding that the requisite danger existed" in the CPUSA to justify the conviction under the Smith Act.[11] Justices Jackson and Frankfurter concurred with the majority in two separate opinions. Jackson, seeing the clear and present danger test as applicable only to imminent threats, argued that "if applied as it is proposed here, it means that the Communist plotting is protected during its period of incubation" and that "its preliminary stages of organization and preparation are immune from the law." If that were to be the case, Jackson argued, then "the Government can move only after imminent action is manifest, when it would, of course, be too late." For Frankfurter it was a matter of deferring to the judgment of Congress that had already "determined that the danger created by advocacy of overthrow justifies the ensuing restriction on freedom of speech."[12] As Kalven notes, "The combined effect of the majority's uncritical acceptance of the conspiracy framework" and Vinson's "reformulation of the clear and present danger test is to enlarge the censor's domain so that it once again includes general advocacy of violent overthrow."[13]

Justices Douglas and Black each filed separate dissenting opinions. For Douglas, the communist conspiracy was neither significant nor grave, and certainly was not serious enough to warrant the restrictions imposed by the Smith Act. Communists were the "miserable merchants of unwanted ideas," he argued, whose "wares remained unsold" in America, where "free speech has destroyed" their beliefs. "The fact that their ideas are abhorrent does not make them powerful," Douglas asserted. And, given their subjection to FBI surveillance, congressional committee investigations, trade union purges, and deportation, Douglas argued that the "invisible army of petitioners is the best known, the most beset, and the least thriving of any fifth column in history." He insisted that "only those held by fear and panic could think otherwise." Douglas thus refuted Vinson's and Hand's application of the reformulated clear and present danger test as a justification for the restriction of such speech in this case.[14] His words echoed the sentiments of many liberal anticommunists who wanted "the [Communist] Party to be fought through the democratic process, to let the public make up its own mind" in the marketplace of ideas.[15] But his ideas formed one of the dissenting opinions and could not prevent the majority of the Court from making communism a crime.

Black also dissented from the majority and from Vinson's use of the clear and present danger test. Quoting from the Court's decision in *Bridges v. California*, Black insisted that the test did "not mark 'the furthermost constitutional boundaries of protected expression,' but does 'no more than recognize a minimum compulsion of the Bill of Rights.'" He argued that Section 3 of the Smith Act was "a virulent form of prior censorship of speech and press" and held that such restraint was "unconstitutional on its face and as applied." But Black recognized that he too was in a minority in taking this position, both on the Court and in American society, because of the emotions surrounding the Cold War and Red Scare. He noted, "Public opinion being what it now is, few will protest the conviction of these Communist petitioners. There is hope, however, that in calmer times, when present pressures, passions and fears subside, this or some later Court will restore the First Amendment liberties to the high preferred place where they belong in a free society."[16]

But at the time, in 1951, that was not to be. Too much had happened since the case was first brought in New York to allow those passions to subside. The "fall" of China, the Soviet acquisition of the bomb, Joseph McCarthy's accusations, continued investigations by the House Un-American Activities

Committee (HUAC), the outbreak of the Korean War, the arrests of Julius and Ethel Rosenberg and the start of their trial for atomic espionage all fanned the flames of anticommunism.[17] By being unable to resist these pressures—or, for some, by being convinced of the legitimacy of the threat that the Communist Party posed to America—the majority of the justices did not act as a counterbalance to them. Their decision opened the floodgates to new Smith Act prosecutions. Two weeks later, on June 20, 1951, the FBI arrested seventeen "second-tier" Communist Party leaders in New York, followed by twenty-four more around the country in the subsequent three months. Over the next six years, "the government arrested and prosecuted under the Smith Act 145 members and leaders of the Communist Party."[18]

The Trotskyists, who were the Smith Act's first targets, had tried to alert Americans about the law's implications for civil liberties for almost a decade at this point. When the trial of the CPUSA leaders began in January 1949, Dobbs, covering the case for the *Militant*, observed the proceedings from the press box. He expressed the Trotskyists' opposition to the prosecution on the grounds of the "democratic principles involved" and pointed out how, in so doing, he and his comrades were taking the high road of solidarity with those who had "sabotaged our defense" in 1941.[19] The Trotskyists' condemnation of the 1949 prosecution was expressed in Dobbs's articles about the case in the *Militant* and during a SWP mass meeting held at the Beethoven Hotel in New York on February 6. More than 200 people turned out that night to hear Dobbs and Cannon "protest against the trial of the Communist leaders" and express the SWP's willingness to "support the Stalinists in their attack on the Smith Act at this time."[20]

But no matter how much the SWP was temporarily willing to side with the CPUSA in the fight against the Smith Act, the Communists showed no sign of cooperation. Their hostility manifested itself openly on June 25, 1949, at the Conference for Civil and Human Rights in New York sponsored by the CP-dominated Civil Rights Congress. Dobbs attended as national chairman of the SWP but soon discovered that he had not been placed on the speakers' list for the main session. After he requested and was denied the floor twice, Dobbs waited for a chance to speak at a separate panel discussion "dealing with the suppression of civil rights." There he "called upon the Conference to join in the fight for a Presidential pardon and restoration of the civil liberties of the SWP leaders and he pleaded for a united front among liberal groups to defend democratic rights." Dobbs and the SWP delegation managed to get a "resolution introduced calling for full pardon of the eighteen Trotskyites and restoration of their civil rights and for the cessation of the trial of the [eleven] Communists," but the Communists at the conference voted it down.[21]

That rejection did not stop the Trotskyists from using the publicity that the CPUSA's case attracted to promote their pardon campaign and expand the SWP. Vincent Dunne took the lead, launching a nationwide speaking tour in November 1949 centered on the theme "Labor and Civil Rights." Subjects he addressed included "The 'Cold War' and the Witch-Hunt," "The Smith Act and the Conviction of the 11 Leaders of the Communist Party," "The Min-neapolis Trial of 1941—Precedent for the New York Trial of 1949," and "The Witch-Hunt in the Unions." The main focus of each of Dunne's stops was his public lecture, but he also made himself available for "internal meetings of party members and sympathizers, and for conferences with party commit-tees and trade union fractions." The tour was thus intended not just to aid the fight for democracy and civil rights but also to contribute "to our Party Building Program."[22] From late November 1949 through early February 1950, Dunne visited SWP strongholds throughout the West, Midwest, and North-east.[23] But while he drew audiences and created a buzz among the SWP's membership, Dunne's tour did not succeed in securing a pardon for the "18," nor did it significantly increase the ranks of the party.

The overall takeaway for the Trotskyists from the *Dennis* case was therefore negative. Despite its drawing attention to their experience as a precedent, it did not help them restore their full civil rights. And with the Supreme Court's decision upholding the Smith Act, it made that goal all the more difficult.

The Second Red Scare Tests the Trotskyists' Resolve

Even before the Court handed down its decision in the *Dennis* case in 1951, the Trotskyists' hopes for change were dashed. The civil rights debate that had been reignited during the presidential election season of 1948 was essentially doused by the cold water of anticommunism. During the Second Red Scare, the Trotskyists' resolve was tested once again, as it had been during the first Smith Act trial and the year the "18" spent in prison. But in the face of it all, and with their waning trade union influence, several of the "18" remained true to the cause. They not only continued to advocate their Trotskyist beliefs but also carried on the struggle to defend their civil liberties and the rights of all Americans to speak about their political beliefs freely.

Carl Skoglund remained true to his belief in socialism and to the SWP in the years after his release from prison. But he suffered for it, especially during the Second Red Scare. At first Skoglund found work in a washing machine repair business, but after a serious car accident, he was laid up for more than a year. When he was well enough to work again, he took a job at the Henne-pin County Highway Department. But that only lasted about a year too, this time because he was fired for his political associations and criminal record.[24] By the spring of 1949, he was working in New Jersey. At the end of March, he "was found subject to deportation" because of his membership in the SWP. He had been free on bond since the last time deportation proceedings were filed against him just after his release from Sandstone prison in 1945. But, as Novack noted, in March 1949 his "case has suddenly been reopened" by immigration officials who denied "the application of Skoglund's attorney to set aside the deportation order pending against him since 1941."[25]

The government's infamous attempt to deport Harry Bridges followed a similar course of starts and stops over the same decades.[26] Novack believed that the government had reopened Skoglund's case as part of a broader attack on "foreign-born leaders in the labor movement," especially those with radical political ties, like Skoglund. Indeed, as Ellen Schrecker has found, the INS "worked closely with the FBI" on these deportation cases that were instigated (or reopened) within a year after the end of World War II. They became "an early, but important, feature" of the Justice Department's anticommunist campaign during the Cold War years.[27] Seeing Skoglund's situation as a "clear case of political persecution," Novack sent a letter to the national committee members of the CRDC requesting help setting up a fund-raising campaign for Skoglund's defense.[28] About a dozen committee members quickly signed on.

By September Novack was able to share some good news with Skoglund's friends Carlson and Dunne: the Board of Immigration Appeals had set aside his deportation and ordered a new hearing. In the meantime, Skoglund's comrades in the SWP and CRDC held a series of smaller gatherings and a mass meeting to raise money for his defense.[29] Despite these efforts, immigration officials ordered Skoglund deported at the hearing on December 15, 1950. He had been "found liable to deportation under the terms of the recently enacted McCarran Law," which dramatically restricted the rights of individuals who were members of communist or "communist front" organizations.[30] Skoglund appealed the decision. But over the next four years he endured stressful encounters with immigration officials, as one order for deportation was withdrawn only to have another put in place a few months later. During the summer of 1954, he was held for several weeks at Ellis Island while he awaited another appeal. The use of such "indefinite detention" without bail on Ellis Island was not uncommon in these INS cases. In one case, Skoglund was saved from deportation only by the quick action of his lawyer, who secured his release a few minutes before the outward-bound ship's departure.[31] As Dunne later explained, the persistent threat of banishment "halted his regular party work," which for Skoglund was "the hardest blow of all."[32]

Skoglund was not the only Trotskyist to be harassed by the government during the Second Red Scare. The other members of the "18" and the party as a whole remained an object of concern for Hoover. In February 1945, shortly after the release of the "18" from jail, then assistant attorney general for the Criminal Division Tom Clark told him that "no further specific investigation" of the SWP was "required at this time." But within a few months Hoover asked for authorization to initiate inquiries again "to determine the degree to which this group has infiltrated labor organizations."[33] Granted that authority by the new head of the Criminal Division, James McInerney, in July 1945,[34] the FBI director went after the SWP with a vengeance. He continued to gather reports on the party from agents stationed around the country, who worked closely with well-placed informants. And he sought expanded powers for the bureau in its surveillance of the SWP by asking for, and receiving, authorization from the Justice Department to wiretap party offices in cities throughout the United States. In his request he invoked the alleged threat of sabotage from Trotskyist intervention in unions and cited a possible violation of the Foreign Agents Registration Act of 1938 resulting from the SWP's failure to disclose its revived association with the Fourth International. With these allegations, Hoover persuaded the attorney general's office to grant him continued authority to investigate the SWP (including the use of electronic surveillance) through 1948 and beyond. He also maintained the steady flow of memos to the attorney general highlighting the possible dangers and alleged criminal activity of the party and of individual members, like Cannon and Carlson, found in the agents' reports that he also forwarded to the Justice Department on a regular basis.[35]

As the Cold War heated up, Hoover's pursuit of the SWP took on added intensity. The investigation of the party expanded with the growth of anticommunist sentiment and the new mechanisms created to facilitate such sentiment during the early 1950s that became hallmarks of the Second Red Scare. In addition to the HUAC hearings, McCarthy's accusations in the Senate, and the many state-level imitators of those committees around the country that constituted those mechanisms, there was the McCarran Act (1950). This law had a direct effect on the Trotskyists in ways distinct from, but related to, the ongoing FBI investigation of the SWP. The McCarran Act, in addition to requiring the registration of communist and communist front organizations with the attorney general, "finally authorized the custodial detention plan the FBI had been unofficially implementing for years."[36] Now the president was authorized, "in the event of war or insurrection, to detain all persons he reasonably believed might participate in 'acts of espionage or sabotage,'" with "no provision for judicial review and no right to confront adverse witnesses."[37] By

July 1950 "there were nearly 12,000 people on the Security Index; by the end of 1954 there were over 26,000, most of them Communist Party functionaries and other activists." Some of the Trotskyist "18" were listed among this group, including Dobbs and Dunne. Their expansive FBI files show their having been categorized based on their level of activity in the party and on their other associations throughout the next decade as either DETCOM (detain as communist) or COMSAB (having a job in a company with government contracts that could be sabotaged).[38] Marked in this way, it was only the president's discretion that stood between their freedom and their being summarily arrested and imprisoned if the nation declared war.

In these same years the Trotskyists also faced the hostility of fellow workers when they tried to revive the SWP's presence in labor unions. The desire to keep radicals of all stripes out of the Teamsters union was something that resonated with Tobin, Flynn, and Brennan. By 1946, these men sought to remove from the IBT not only Trotskyists but also members of the CPUSA. With the end of the war and the collapse of the Big Three alliance, any reservations Tobin and Flynn had about purging Communists disappeared. The radicals that Brennan had long wanted to oust soon found themselves shown the door.[39] By the late 1940s, the IBT leadership had no larger political concerns to hold them back from cleaning house, and they targeted for expulsion Communists and Trotskyists alike. Most other unions were doing the same thing at this time; the IBT was thus also a part of the more familiar story of late-1940s and early-1950s labor anticommunism. By 1949, even the CIO purged its ranks of individuals and chartered unions as a result of not just the Red Scare political climate but also the pressures of the Taft-Hartley Act. Under its infamous Section 9h, this law threatened access to NLRB elections to unions whose leaders refused to sign affidavits swearing they were not Communists.[40]

The combined pressures of the blacklistings, the FBI's investigations, and the other mechanisms of the Second Red Scare directed at them made life difficult for the "18." But not all of them responded in the same way. Ed Palmquist, who had moved from Seattle to Anchorage, found it increasingly difficult to find and hold down a job. Several times his past came back to haunt him, and his 1941 Smith Act conviction cost him employment. Although he initially remained active in the SWP after his release from prison in 1945—working with his wife, Rose Seiler, in the Seattle branch—by 1947 he showed signs of wanting to leave his radical political associations behind. Not only was he no longer seen working for the party once he arrived in Alaska, but he also was found to have lied about his criminal record on a job application. His attempts to distance himself from his past, in conjunction with FBI reports indicating his lack of participation in local Trotskyist affairs, seem to indicate a growing separation from the SWP.[41] By 1950, after being fired from his job as a janitor because of his political past, Palmquist sought a fresh start in life as a landlord of some rental properties.[42] By 1954, a new circle of friends told FBI agents that they "had no reason to question his loyalty towards the U.S. government."[43] And by 1956, other friends noted that Palmquist had "'cooled off' since his separation and divorce from Rose."[44] In 1957, when Palmquist was interviewed by agents, he "denied having ever knowingly been a member of the SWP" and attributed his having attended a few meetings to his ex-wife's associations with the party. He insisted that he was "no longer interested in any functions or activities of the SWP and that he would be happy to inform the FBI in the event he is ever contacted by any of his former associates."[45]

For a complex combination of reasons, Palmquist essentially rewrote the story of his past in an attempt to create a different future for himself. His change of heart may have come from the breakdown of his marriage; Seiler had been a committed member of the party for many years, and their personal separation may have also formalized a political break for Palmquist. But his about-face also seems to have come from either anger or fear or some combination of both after struggling for several years against the consequences of his 1941 conviction that included the blacklist and the various forms of FBI harassment to which he was subjected in these years. These included the use of informants against him, attempts to have him prosecuted for perjury for lying on his job application in 1947, and the open interviewing of his friends and associates in the late 1940s and early 1950s. By 1957, his break with the party was complete.

Albert Goldman took a path similar to that of Palmquist, although his disaffection with the SWP emerged much earlier in the form of the factional split with Cannon in 1945 and 1946. Having joined Shachtman's Workers Party in 1946, Goldman still considered himself a socialist in the political sense, but he soon began to drift from that commitment too. As a disbarred lawyer with a criminal record, he struggled to support himself. By February 1948, things had gotten so bad that Goldman took a position as a taxi dispatcher in Chicago.[46] Following the advice of Roger Baldwin and other old friends outside the SWP, Goldman applied for readmission to the Illinois bar and sought a presidential pardon for his 1941 conviction. In the process, he indicated his desire to distance himself from his former comrades in the party so as to improve his chances.[47] But Goldman was neither reinstated to the bar nor pardoned in 1948; by March 1949, he was bankrupt and had to start over again.[48] At this point he had abandoned his political commitment to socialism too.

Goldman explained this transformation in 1951 when he was questioned by the Personnel Security Board of the Atomic Energy Commission. The board was conducting an inquiry into the "associations and loyalty" of his sister-in-law Betty June Jacobsen, whose "eligibility for security clearance and for employment on Atomic Energy Commission work" was in question, partly because of Goldman's past political ties. In his interview, Goldman explained to the agents how "in 1948, after many years of questioning, I came to the conclusion that my whole life was based on the wrong premise." He clarified that he still considered himself a socialist, but that his "socialism is based purely on ethical grounds. It has nothing to do with Marxism or the class struggle." Instead, it was based on "the ethical concepts of Christ and the prophets," the latter of which he learned about during his early training as a reformed rabbi, training that he found himself "more and more . . . going back" to as he reassessed his life. Expressing his frustration over his recent difficulty finding work because of his Trotskyist past, he claimed that all he wanted now was to "lead a retired life." He did not even take up the FBI's offer to work as a full-time informant, Goldman explained, preferring instead to "help them out in so far as I can" as a consultant "not only with reference to particular individuals, but . . . for me to explain to them what the differences are between groups." Insisting that he refused to testify against "these poor individuals who are deported," he presented himself as someone still deeply conflicted. No longer a member of either the SWP or the WP, but a Jew who confessed a Christian socialism, Goldman was willing to give information on former communist associates to the FBI but not on potential deportees.[49] Desperate to restore his professional identity, Goldman was willing to work with the FBI, but, holding on to some sense of ethical boundaries, he set out self-defined limits to that new role.

Goldman maintained these distinctions as he navigated his new life of very different and complicated Cold War political commitments. Although Goldman's testimony may have been weighted toward demonstrating that he was no longer a Trotskyist or political socialist of any stripe to aid his sister-in-law's employment application, his break with radical political parties and his finding God were not contrived for the hearing. His former comrades knew about his defection. Cannon later chalked Goldman's transformation up to a "personal sickness" for which he could hold him no malice.[50] But such an interpretation was fraught with its own assumptions about a very different kind of loyalty, about solidarity, and about what constituted a worthwhile political commitment. For Cannon, it had long been and always would be commitment to Trotskyism as advanced through the SWP. For Goldman, beginning with the factional split during his time at Sandstone and developing with his personal and professional struggles during the Second Red Scare, it became more and more about political disillusionment, individual survival, and the restoration of his career.

Considered from this perspective, Goldman's denunciation of the movement eventually paid off. In 1956 he was finally reinstated to the Illinois bar. Henry Schweinhaut, then a U.S. district judge for the District of Columbia, expressed his pleasure at the news with a backhanded reprimand. Referring to Goldman's years of disbarment that resulted from the 1941 conviction, Schweinhaut said, "I am sure that the whole business was rather rough on you but possibly you are the author of your own misfortune." But because Goldman had served his time and had walked away from organized socialism, Schweinhaut was willing to extend his "very best wishes for success and happiness in the future."[51] Goldman's transformation was complete; he not only had turned his back on his former comrades but now also had reconciled with his one-time courtroom nemesis.[52]

Grace Carlson also eventually defected from the SWP, but she made a very different kind of reconciliation in the process, returning both to her estranged husband, Gilbert, and to the Catholic Church. Unlike Goldman, Carlson had maintained an active and visible presence in the SWP in the years following her release from prison. She conducted a nationwide speaking tour in late 1945, ran for Senate in Minnesota in 1946, and stood with Dobbs as vice president in his bid for the White House in 1948. She had become a party luminary whose singular devotion to the cause inspired Trotskyists around the country.[53] She and Vincent Dunne, who had moved back to Minneapolis in 1946, dominated the workings of the party there.[54] But while they worked well together in public, behind closed doors their relationship was increasingly fraught with tension. That tension may have contributed to Carlson's decision to leave the party.

Carlson and Dunne's relationship was a complex one. They were comrades in the movement, friends, and, possibly for a time, lovers. Each was also intensely committed to the cause of socialism but in quite different ways. Carlson came from a professional background and, with the relationships she built in New York, considered herself more in tune with the intellectual wing of the party. Dunne, who came up through the rough-and-tumble world of the IWW and the Teamsters, identified first with the trade union struggle and the party's role in leading that fight. This tension was not insurmountable. Their shared embrace of Trotskyism presumably was one of the things that first brought them together.

But their different priorities and respective aspirations within the SWP eventually drove them apart. During the late 1940s, when Carlson worked with Dunne in Minneapolis, the two crossed swords more than once over questions bound up in personal and professional jealousies. In August 1946, for example, Carlson allegedly told Dunne that she "could have gone to New York and could have been an intellectual there," but that she had decided to "place my lot to the workers in the party" and return to Minneapolis with him. Upset at Dunne for not listening to her and for criticizing her work in the party, she angrily asserted that she did not "have to have [his] approval on every word." Although the confidential informant who passed on the details of this argument to the FBI claimed that Carlson was drunk at the time it took place, the account made clear Carlson's frustrations at having set aside her larger aspirations to work with Dunne, only to find him critical of her. Those frustrations gradually eroded both their working relationship and their personal relationship.[55]

Over the next few years the heated arguments allegedly continued. FBI reports detail several "violent quarrel[s]" between Carlson and Dunne. Arguing over "some technical aspect of Leninism" in 1947, for example, Carlson told Dunne that she resented his "speaking to her in 'accusing tones.'" During another argument that year, she "severely reprimanded him for creating an embarrassing situation at a dinner which was attended by a group of Trotskyists."[56] Things intensified on November 23, 1948, when Dunne "rebuked her for her arrogance and 'too much talk attitude,'" pointing out "that he did not like the way she was running the meetings." According to the informant who related the incident to the FBI, "the quarrel became so violent that [Carlson] in a rage cried that she would ask to be transferred from the Twin Cities leadership before taking any more insults from Dunne."[57] In December, they fought over who should go to the plenum in New York.[58] By the spring of 1949, the disputes heated up even more. Carlson accused Dunne of "not 'doing a solitary thing'" and of "having no organizational ability." Dunne "criticized her for her superior attitude."[59] Theirs had become quite a contentious and unhappy personal and working relationship.

That unhappiness may have contributed to Carlson's decision to leave the party a few years later. She explained at the time, and elaborated later in an interview, however, that the main reason for her departure was her decision to return to the Catholic Church. When she wrote to James Cannon informing him of this choice on June 18, 1952, it was, as Elizabeth Raasch-Gilman later described it, "a complete bombshell." She had not told anyone of her plans; "even her sister [Dorothy] did not know she was contemplating this step." In fact, right before Carlson sent her letter to Cannon, she had been in the early stages of planning her "second-run for vice-president of the U.S." on the SWP ticket.[60]

Scrambling to respond to press inquiries about Carlson's defection, Dunne initially denied it and refused to comment, but the party quickly prepared a press release acknowledging the loss of one of its leading figures. In early July the *Militant* ran an article by James Cannon in which he characterized Carlson as a "victim" against whom the "powers of reaction hammered and pounded . . . until they finally beat her down, broke her spirit of resistance and *compelled* her to leave the party." Unable and unwilling to acknowledge Carlson's choice as one she freely made (if with difficulty), Cannon cast it as the result of years of her victimization at the hands of the capitalist system and, without missing a beat, proudly proclaimed that while "individuals, broken by many blows, may fall by the wayside," the "great socialist movement for emancipation of mankind will march on."[61] At the SWP national convention in New York that month, Dunne echoed Cannon's final assessment of Carlson's defection, stating that "the best thing for the party was to forget it" and move on.[62] The intensity and depth of Dunne's connection to her—their ties within the extended family of the SWP and within their private friendship—were thus severed in this ultimate dismissal.

Carlson's choice to leave the SWP seems to have been an intensely personal one. Unlike Goldman, she did not attribute any political motivation to her leaving, but she must have been disenchanted enough with the party and with Trotskyism to turn her back on the movement to which she had devoted most of her adulthood. In an interview later in her life, Carlson criticized the Trotskyists' failure "to appreciate the fact that a worker had a rounded life" that included the concerns of his wife and children, and she also condemned what she saw as the movement's intense polemical nature.[63] When she spoke directly about her decision to leave the party, however, she addressed the trauma of her father's death in 1951 and the spiritual crisis it triggered within her. She explained that for her, "the whole philosophical question came up: Who would make up to him everything that he had missed in his life? All the problems that he'd had (and I certainly had been one of them.) That's when I went back to the church." Although Cannon dismissed this choice as the result of Carlson's desire to "escape" from the pressures of her work in the party, saying that she "just got tired," it seems to have resulted from a genuine change of heart when Carlson found herself at a crossroads in her personal and spiritual life.[64]

She testified to that change of heart when interviewed by the FBI in 1954, repeating, as the agent recorded, that "she left the SWP solely for one reason, and that was the absence of God in their program." Apparently initially hoping to be able to "serve God and the SWP" when she joined the movement, Carlson soon discovered she could not. By the early 1950s, she found the tension too great to bear any longer. That realization, along with the death of her father, instigated some soul-searching. Yet, even with her return to the church the agent noted how "she has a great fondness to this date for Socialism, and a greater fondness for the friends she met in the SWP."[65] She later admitted about her commitment to "the problems of human beings for over thirty years while I was in and out of the Church," that she "would still be out of the Church, if I had been able to find true spiritual satisfaction in human relationships alone."[66] Her "defection" from the party was thus not an easy one.

Carlson's choice not only ended her relationship with Dunne but also "led to a painful estrangement" between her and her sister Dorothy that lasted until "Dorothy herself dropped out of the SWP" in the late 1950s.[67] Carlson also "had a hard time getting a job," given her conviction and what had been her high profile in the SWP. Eventually she found work as a clerk "in the pediatrics department over at St. Mary's Hospital" and later, in 1955, transitioned to a teaching position at the hospital's school of nursing. She worked as a professor of psychology there until she retired in 1972. During the same years she restarted her professional life at St. Mary's in the mid-1950s, she also reunited with her husband, Gilbert.[68] Like Goldman, Carlson continued to identify herself as a socialist, "only as a religious, rather than an atheist" one. Unlike Goldman, Carlson never cooperated with the FBI. Although agents came calling once they heard of her defection, she later explained, "I never worked with the Justice Department or the Immigration [and Naturalization] Service. . . . I never testified."[69] Nonetheless, hers was a complete break with the movement that had been at the center of her life for more than a decade.

That movement carried on without her, sustained by the devotion of the members who remained true to the cause. Chief among them were Cannon, Dunne, and Dobbs. But others among the "18" also remained committed to the party, including Max Geldman. He and his wife, Goldie, were prominent members of the SWP's Philadelphia branch. When she died in 1952, Max continued to be an active Trotskyist, moving first to Chicago, then to Newark, and by 1960 to Los Angeles with his second wife, Shevi. There the two "tried to be active in the various organizations that are attempting to beat back reaction." In an interview in February 1988, Geldman admitted that as he aged, "I can't do much myself," but that he "remained connected with a political organization called Solidarity, and I will die with my boots on."[70] He had been expelled from the SWP in 1983, in one of many trials of members held during the early 1980s that, as Barry Sheppard argues, "strengthened the cult" around national secretary Jack Barnes. Yet Geldman found ways to "continue to uphold and participate in the building of a movement for Socialist America."[71] He remained true to the music of his youth until his death in December 1988.

Figure 7.1 Vincent Dunne and James P. Cannon with Arne Swabeck in Los Angeles. In 1953, after stepping down as national secretary of the SWP, Cannon moved to Los Angeles. Photos J1.6p12, negative number 43648, Minnesota Historical Society. Courtesy Minnesota Historical Society.

Despite the loyalty of members like Geldman, the SWP dwindled in the 1950s Cold War context. Cannon estimated that the ranks shrank to about 500 in that decade from a high of 3,000 in 1946.[72] At the age of sixty-three, Cannon stepped aside as national secretary in 1953, allowing Dobbs to take the reins in New York. Cannon moved to Los Angeles but remained very active in the party, sometimes to the annoyance of Dobbs and others who felt at times that Cannon was attempting to create "a dual center in Los Angeles that challenged the authority of the political committee in New York." Despite any tensions this may have created with Dobbs during the 1950s and 1960s, both men remained well-respected elder statesmen in the movement.[73] Cannon also took heart in the changed political climate of the 1960s, believing that with the rise of the African American civil rights movement, the feminist movement, and the antiwar movement, circumstances were finally shifting to the point where the revolution was "not far off."[74] A month before his death in 1974, Cannon told Sidney Lens, "I don't want to make any categorical statements, but I say we're living in a time when capitalism is plunging towards its climactic end."[75] Although Cannon was proved wrong, his faith, like Geldman's, remained true to the last.

So too did Dunne's. Weathering the shock of Carlson's departure, he continued to devote his life to Trotskyism. He moved temporarily to Los Angeles in 1956 to assist Cannon and launched another speaking tour in 1957. His goal on these trips around the country was once again to build the ranks of the party, but this time with the specific focus of drawing disgruntled members away from the CPUSA in the aftermath of the Khrushchev revelations.[76] By 1959, at the age of seventy, Dunne finally slowed down. The FBI registered the shift in his activities in its file, removing him from the list of "top functionaries" in the party and describing him as an "old man." Despite his efforts to promote the SWP up until then, it did not expand much in these years either. By 1960, the Minneapolis and St. Paul branches of the party merged because of declining membership. But that did not stop Dunne from continuing to work for organized labor and the SWP. Playing the part of the elder statesman, he gave speeches when he could, denouncing the Marshall Plan in 1962, for example, and condemning the Vietnam War in 1966. A rebel to the end, it was not until his death in 1970 that the FBI finally took his name off the Security Index.[77]

Dobbs, who was almost two decades younger than Cannon and Dunne, remained more centrally involved with the party through the 1950s and 1960s. He ran for president of the United States three more times (in 1952, 1956, and 1960), twice while acting as national secretary of the party. In those campaigns he advocated the "Socialist Road to World Peace and Security," criticizing America's Cold War foreign policy and condemning its capitalist economic system.[78] Although his bids for the White House failed, he continued to try to get the Trotskyist message out to the American people. He was more successful in recruiting young people into the party during the 1960s and educating them as the new generation that would "gradually take over the reins" by the 1970s, helping breathe new life into the movement.[79] After 1972, when he stepped down from the role of national secretary, Dobbs turned to speaking tours and writing to communicate the Trotskyist message. His series of books on the history of the Minneapolis Teamsters, *Teamster Rebellion, Teamster Power, Teamster Politics,* and *Teamster Bureaucracy,* interpreted that past—from the 1934 strikes through the 1941 trial—through a distinctly Trotskyist lens. When they were originally published during the 1970s, the books functioned as much as a history of those important events as a teaching tool for young radicals looking for inspiration. Dobbs not only weathered the storm of the Second Red Scare but also remained committed to the Trotskyist cause as he handed over the party and the history of the movement to the next generation.

The Next Generation of the SWP: Limited Trade Union Influence and the Civil Rights Fights of the 1960s and 1970s

This next generation of Trotskyists would take the SWP in a new direction in the closing decades of the twentieth century, particularly when it came to the party's relationship with trade unionism. Some of this shift began when Cannon and Dobbs were still at the helm. There were Trotskyists in cities around the United States who provided revolutionary trade union leadership after World War II, like Frank Lovell and George Breitman in the United Auto Workers in Detroit during the 1950s and early 1960s. But the SWP never again secured the kind of influence within a union as it had done with Local 544 in Minneapolis during the 1930s. In part this was the result of the hostile climate, epitomized in the purges, experienced by all political radicals who were interested in working in trade unions during the era of Taft-Hartley and the Second Red Scare.[80] But it was also due to a general shift in the SWP's focus toward supporting the new mass movements of the 1960s and 1970s. Trade union work remained important for those who sustained the Lenin-Cannon tradition of the party and could find a home in more progressive unions, but increasingly (and especially for newer, younger members), energy was channeled during the 1960s and 1970s toward the African American civil rights movement, the antiwar movement, the Cuban Revolution, and the antinuclear/peace movement.[81] For some Trotskyists, like Dobbs, there was the hope that the revolutionary spirit of these movements would "serve as a catalyst for a new labor upsurge." He understood this influence not just in terms of the numbers of unionized workers who might support an independent labor party to advance the transition from capitalism to socialism but also in terms of the redemption of the union movement itself. Dobbs decried what he saw as the corrupt and bankrupt leadership of organized labor in the Cold War era, but he remained hopeful that the mass movements that the SWP supported could infuse unions with a more progressive spirit.[82]

Others, especially those from the younger generation entering the party during the 1960s and 1970s, saw their efforts within the New Left mass movements as a means of democratic revolutionary action through which to achieve socialism. Adapting their tactics to the changing times, these Trotskyists carried on the struggle against capitalism during the late twentieth century through these other forums. But disagreements in the party over such tactics contributed to the movement's decline by the late 1980s. Membership dropped to "less than half its size from its high point in 1976–1978" of 3,000, a trend that "has continued in the decades since." Even with the turn back to industry in 1978, the party was unable to form close ties to the "wider class struggle" because, in seeking connections in auto and steel, the Trotskyists undermined their existing strength in the professional and pink-collar sectors that had organized in the American Federation of Teachers and the American Federation of State, County and Municipal Employees. That "abstentionism," as Barry Sheppard calls it (in conjunction with the party trials of the early 1980s and the pressure for members to remain unquestionably loyal to the national secretary, Jack Barnes), undermined the strength and potential of the SWP as a revolutionary workers party by the end of the twentieth century.[83] Partly because of these internecine fights, it was neither able successfully to challenge capitalism nor to revitalize organized labor in the latter half of the twentieth century as Dobbs had hoped it might.

External obstacles also contributed to the SWP's limitations with respect to its trade union mission, as well as to its survival as a party. Exploring some of the challenges the SWP confronted on the national political stage illuminates a larger historical reality: the possibilities and limitations that radical activists faced within the realm of free speech law and under the shadow of the nation's expanding security state as they tried to influence the labor movement (and indeed the various mass political movements of these decades) to support a more social democratic (or, in the case of the Trotskyists and other Marxist groups, a socialist) agenda for America during the late twentieth century. Several historians have explored how "Big Labor" failed to serve as a vehicle for social democratic change after World War II because of the impact of the postwar labor-management accord, the context of the Cold War, and the role of corruption in unions.[84] And some have traced how even democratically motivated "insurgencies" within unions during the early 1970s (like the Miners for Democracy movement within the United Mine Workers) ultimately "achieved little institutional presence in the labor movement."[85] But there has not been much exploration of how the FBI's interference with groups like the SWP influenced the shape of trade unionism *after* the Second Red Scare and foreclosed the possibility of the "labor upsurge" for which Dobbs and others hoped. The Supreme Court increased legal protections for free speech and for subversive speech in these decades, partly as a result of the mass political movements of the 1950s, 1960s, and 1970s. But the FBI dramatically violated citizen's civil liberties at the same time, especially the liberties of those supporting the progressive causes of many of those mass movements. The combined effect was the existence of various protest campaigns that were ultimately hampered in achieving their fullest possible manifestation because of the domestic political spying conducted by the nation's growing security state.[86] Here too the Trotskyists found themselves at the center of the story.

In order to engage in revolutionary democratic action, the Trotskyists first found themselves having to continue to fight for their right to free speech. During the remainder of their lives, Cannon, Dunne, Dobbs, and the other members of the "18" who stayed with the party also remained committed to the campaign to repeal the Smith Act. But like the socialist revolution, this too was an aspiration never realized. Until the Supreme Court restricted the application of the Smith Act in its 1957 *Yates* decision, that peacetime sedition law remained a powerful tool for suppressing dissent.

The winds of political change first began to shift in favor of civil liberties more broadly and of the constitutional protection of subversive speech specifically by the late 1950s, when events around the world and in the United States harkened a turn away from the virulent anticommunism that had marked the height of the Second Red Scare. As Geoffrey Stone summarizes: "Stalin died in 1953; an armistice was declared in Korea; the Senate condemned Joseph McCarthy; and the public attitude toward the Red menace began to relax." In those same years, between 1951 and 1957, there also were "four changes in the makeup of the Court." Earl Warren replaced Fred Vinson as chief justice, and Justices Brennan, Whittaker, and Harlan replaced Justices Reed, Minton, and Jackson.[87] The Eisenhower appointments in particular made it a "Court that was more interested in protecting political freedom than curbing the Communist menace."[88] The changes both on and outside of the Court, therefore, contributed to its new interpretation of the Smith Act and the constitutionality of subversive speech.

In its 1957 decision in *Yates v. United States*, the Supreme Court "reversed the convictions under the Smith Act of the leaders of the California branch of the Communist Party." Writing for the majority, Justice Harlan articulated what has been termed the "incitement-to-future-action" standard, distinguishing between advocacy that urges others to take action and that which only urges others to believe something. His opinion marked a new direction in the Court's interpretation of subversive advocacy law because it required the demonstration of an overt act to assign guilt. It also marked a new direction in the Court's assessment of the constitutionality of the Smith Act. Focused on the question of the law's application, Harlan insisted that the conspiracy charges filed under it must be based on sufficient evidence of advocacy that results in action. His ruling limited the future use of the Smith Act.[89] With this narrowing of the "definitions of acceptable evidence," many of the "prior convictions [were] reversed immediately" and others sent back for retrial. The Justice Department responded by virtually abandoning the use of the Smith Act "because of the burden of meeting the more stringent evidentiary requirements."[90]

The Justice Department's decision to stop seeking convictions under the now ineffectual Smith Act was a significant turning point in the history of free speech. But it would not be until 1969, with its decision in *Brandenburg v. Ohio*, that the Court significantly widened protections for subversive speech. By then currents on the Court and in American society had been pulsing toward greater tolerance for dissent. In its 1964 decision in *New York Times v. Sullivan*, for example, the Court upheld the principle that "in America seditious libel cannot be made a crime."[91] On the streets, Americans in the civil rights movement, the growing antiwar movement, and the feminist movement boldly challenged the political, economic, and social status quo. The Cold War still raged, indeed burned hot in several areas around the globe, but it also had been mobilized by many Americans to make a claim on the democracy that their nation professed to defend against communism abroad.[92] While their struggles were by no means easy or without resistance, they helped legitimize the role of criticism in democracy.

That shift resonated with the Court, which also looked to its own tradition of free speech law to decide a challenging case involving the First Amendment rights of members of the Ku Klux Klan. In its 1969 *Brandenburg* decision the Court overturned *Whitney v. California*, specifying that the illegal actions resulting from speech also had to be imminent, thus protecting expression up until that ultimate moment and establishing "this distinction as the constitutional boundary."[93] As Harry Kalven Jr. explains, the decision "placed beyond censorship the 'mere advocacy' of violence" and "reset the boundary line of permissible censorship" to where such speech "'is directed to inciting or producing imminent lawless action.'"[94] As Geoffrey Stone notes, the Court not only invalidated the Ohio law used to prosecute Klansmen for threatening racial violence but also, "exactly fifty years after *Schenck*, finally and unambiguously embraced the Holmes-Brandeis version of clear and present danger!"[95] The argument that the "18," the CRDC, and the ACLU had made for years with respect to the 1941 case was essentially now accepted by the Court, albeit under very different circumstances.

This more broadly protective understanding of speech and dissent has held sway in the courts ever since,[96] holding out the possibility of more radical activism within and outside of the labor movement. But it did not stop the FBI from expanding its domestic political investigations, which remained a challenge to that activism for the remainder of the century. Rather than only investigating groups on suspicion of wrongdoing in order to compile evidence for a criminal prosecution under statutes like the Smith Act, the bureau also intensified its "undercover infiltration, disruption, and monitoring [of groups] in order to undermine wartime dissent." Many of the same mass movements that engaged in dissent technically protected by the Court (including the antiwar movement and the civil rights movement) were marked by Hoover's agents for aggressive investigation. Some, like the Black Power movement, became targets of its COINTELPRO operations. Formed in 1956, the Counterintelligence Programs was the formal name given to the new grouping of many of the FBI's domestic spying operations whose "express goal was to 'disrupt,' 'discredit,' and 'neutralize' domestic protest groups." As the history of the FBI's investigation of the SWP dating back to 1940 demonstrates, the disruption of radical groups was not a new technique for Hoover's agency. What was new about COINTELPRO, Athan Theoharis explains, was that the bureau "initiated a formal program based on written directives and responsive to the direct supervisory control of the FBI director." Frustrated with the limits of the criminal justice system, Hoover decided explicitly to condone and encourage "more aggressive and extralegal techniques" against communists and other groups defined as enemies of the state.[97]

The SWP, which had long been under FBI surveillance as a threat to national security, became a target of COINTELPRO in 1961. David Cole and James Dempsey explain how from 1961 to 1976, "the FBI used 1,300 informants in the investigation, who supplied the Bureau with detailed reports on SWP debates and activities, as well as at least 12,600 pilfered SWP documents." Bureau agents "conducted 204 illegal break-ins" during which they gathered "an additional 9,864 documents." And, in addition to extensive telephone wiretapping and the bugging of party offices, the FBI "conducted aggressive interviews of SWP members and their relatives, neighbors and employers, which an FBI memorandum at the time said were intended to 'enhance the paranoia' of members." As Cole and Dempsey explain, "The explicit purpose of the investigation was the disruption of the SWP. The FBI sought to create hostility and racial discord within the organization, to frustrate its efforts to form alliances with other groups, and to cause certain members to lose their jobs." They note how "the investigation was doggedly pursued even though none of the 1,300 informants ever reported a single instance of planned or actual espionage, violence, terrorism, or other illegal activities, and even though the investigation did not result in a single arrest for any federal violation."[98] The SWP was only one of many organizations thus targeted during the years that COINTELPRO was in force. The New Left and white supremacist groups were also investigated.[99]

The bureau's actions remained hidden from public view until 1975, when the Church Committee launched an inquiry. The special committee chaired by Senator Frank Church of Idaho, officially named the Select Committee to Study Governmental Operations with Respect to Intelligence Activities, was formed in the wake of the Watergate scandal and President Richard Nixon's resignation "to determine the extent 'if any' of 'illegal, improper, or unethical activities' engaged in by *any* federal agency or persons acting 'on or behalf of the Federal Government.'"[100] As Theoharis explains, it was only because of the public reaction to the recent Watergate scandal and the revelation of intelligence abuses that accompanied its investigation that the Ford administration and FBI officials agreed to cooperate with Church's committee. And, even then, that cooperation was limited to providing the Senate with "a tightly controlled and selected examination of what had been the closed records of the intelligence agencies, the National Security Council, and the White House's 'national security' documents." But what Church uncovered was, as Theoharis describes, "eye-opening" in terms of the "scope of the intelligence community's past abuses of power."[101]

For the Trotskyists, the Senate investigations reassured them that their decision (made in 1973) to file suit against the FBI was a good one. Complaining that the bureau had "engaged in massive violations of the constitutional rights of the SWP, [its youth organization, the] YSA, and their members," the Trotskyists sought justice through the courts. It took thirteen years, five decisions in district court, three major decisions in the court of appeals, and three applications to the Supreme Court, but the SWP eventually forced the FBI to release "tens of thousands of pages of files" that "contained evidence of thousands of unlawful acts committed by the FBI and its informers."[102] In 1978, at the age of seventy-one and with the power of the 1966 Freedom of Information Act, Dobbs succeeded in gaining access to his FBI file. Revealing how the FBI followed him for more than three decades with the use of informants, agents, and "black bag" break-ins to the SWP offices, it confirmed for him and his wife, Marvel Scholl Dobbs, what they had sensed all along: the FBI's harassment of them and the party had taken place for years and included illegal methods.[103]

The trial, which took place in the federal district court in Manhattan, finally opened in April 1981. Many of the files secured by the SWP in the eight years of pretrial proceedings were entered into evidence. Dobbs testified as a key witness, tracing the FBI's interventions and harassment of him and the party from the origins of the Minneapolis Teamsters faction fight in 1940 through the early 1970s, when he retired as national secretary. He argued that this harassment, along with the party's placement on the attorney general's list during the height of the Cold War, "had a disadvantageous effect on" it by scaring "people away from us." It thus undermined both the SWP's party and trade union work in these years. His testimony contributed to the SWP's case that it had been damaged by the bureau's actions and that its members' constitutional rights had been violated.[104] At the age of seventy-four, Dobbs thus kept up the fight for the party and for civil liberties, decades after his Smith Act conviction.

This time, he and the party were vindicated in the courtroom: in 1986, Judge Thomas Griesa "found the FBI guilty of violations of the constitutional rights of the SWP . . . and of [its] members," ruling that the government could not use any of the FBI's files on the party or its members that had been compiled through illegal methods.[105] Griesa also ruled "that the FBI's COIN-TELPRO operations against the SWP, including the FBI's use of informants to obtain private information about political meetings, demonstrations and other lawful SWP events, were 'patently unconstitutional and violated the SWP's First Amendment rights of free speech and assembly.'"[106] And with access to the FBI's files, he substantiated the SWP's contention that the bureau's investigations of its activities and members began in 1940. Griesa cited not only Hoover's requests for information about the party from the New York office but also Agent Perrin's inflammatory report that came out of St. Paul in April 1941 and was "given wide circulation within the FBI."[107] He then detailed "several of the fifty-seven disruption operations conducted by the FBI" during the COINTELPRO years, concluding that they were illegal. As a result, Griesa "ordered the government to pay the SWP and YSA $264,000 in damages." More significantly, as Margaret Jayko explains, "For the first time a federal court has ruled that the very presence of government informers in a political organization is a violation of the constitutional rights of free speech and association and the right to privacy."[108]

Griesa's ruling vindicated the SWP, which had been a target of such violations since 1940. Although the party had rallied to a high of 3,000 members in 1945, invigorated, in part, by the fight against the Smith Act, the long-term disruptions of the FBI's investigations, especially as experienced through the excessive and illegal practices of COINTELPRO, had a negative effect on the SWP's ability to function as a revolutionary workers party,[109] even after free speech law had been eased and the Smith Act essentially defanged. The 1986 ruling was, in some ways, an acknowledgment of this almost fifty-year fight. Dobbs, who died in 1983, did not live to see this vindication, but he most likely would have been pleased and proud of his contribution in securing it.

Coda and Conclusion

The SWP's 1986 victory against the FBI was a fleeting one. Although COIN-TELPRO was dismantled, the FBI continued to engage in domestic political spying. The bureau found sanction for such investigations by applying the secret "Foreign Intelligence/Terrorism" guidelines set out by the Ronald Reagan administration to domestic opponents of America's foreign policy, "including unions and church and political organizations, such as the SWP and YSA."[1] The bureau not only bypassed the guidelines on domestic security and terrorism set out by former attorney general Edward Levi in 1976, which "required suspicion of criminal conduct before a domestic security operation was opened," but also those set out by Reagan's attorney general, William French Smith, who rewrote the guidelines "to make it clear that the FBI could open an investigation based on mere advocacy of crime."[2] Griesa's ruling in 1986 found the bureau's aggressive investigative techniques to be violations of fundamental civil liberties. Yet the FBI outmaneuvered it in subsequent years by seeking authorization for its investigations of subjects with real or alleged overseas ties under foreign intelligence guidelines and of purely domestic subjects under Smith's loosened rules.[3]

And yet investigations of alleged spies, saboteurs, and seditionists diminished in number during the late 1980s and early 1990s, as the FBI's domestic intelligence division declined and as threats to America changed.[4] Although the Soviets remained a concern in these decades, as the espionage cases of the 1980s show (including Robert Hanssen's and Aldrich Ames's spying), communism and the CPUSA no longer were primary targets of the FBI as the Cold War ended. The variants of domestic terrorism that the bureau had learned to investigate in the late 1960s (including groups like the Weathermen and radical white supremacist groups) also had either largely faded or were kept in check by the bureau.[5] These changes dovetailed with and were used to justify the drastic reduction in the bureau's intelligence budget under its director William Sessions during the 1980s.[6] By the early 1990s, the FBI had very few analysts and no strategic plan for dealing with threats to national security.[7]

Partly because of those problems, the FBI was blindsided by the Oklahoma City bombing in 1995. In its wake, the Smith guidelines were "further relaxed" to give the bureau even more free rein to investigate domestic subversion. Expressed in a Justice Department memo, "the language of which was negotiated by FBI Director Louis Freeh," the new guidelines allowed domestic terrorism investigations in cases of "statements threatening or advocating the use of violence," the "'apparent' ability to carry out violence," and "potential federal crime."[8] This gave the bureau much more latitude in determining who and when to investigate, in essence reauthorizing the criminality of advocacy that the Court had rejected in its *Yates* decision. Whether the bureau needed such expansive authority to pursue those who actively planned to harm the United States went largely unquestioned at this juncture. And the impact of the budget cuts and the structural deficiencies of the bureau remained unaddressed.

The tragedy in Oklahoma, along with the 1993 bombing of the World Trade Center that also took the country by surprise, instigated a discussion in Congress about how the nation should best handle such new terror threats. Some of the proposals put forth eventually found a home in the Antiterrorism Act (1996), which provided new statutory cover for the bureau's political investigations. Those provisions included "the resurrection of association as grounds for exclusion and deportation of noncitizens; the ban on supporting lawful activities of groups labeled 'terrorist' by the executive branch; and the secret evidence provision." The notion of guilt by association—specifically that of making membership in a proscribed group grounds for deportation or exclusion—had been a hallmark of the Second Red Scare's McCarran Act. Congress repealed "most of the ideological grounds for exclusion and deportation in 1990," but it revived them again in 1996 in the wake of the Oklahoma City bombing.[9]

The first two provisions of the 1996 law—guilt by association and fundraising bans—allowed the FBI "to justify wide-ranging investigations into targeted communities." Although the government tried to use the secret evidence provision to deport "about two dozen immigrants, almost all of them Muslims," almost every case was overturned and the accused released when the evidence "was revealed to be worthless." As a result, the use of secret evidence waned by the start of the new millennium.[10] Although the federal courts had not yet weighed in on the constitutionality of the 1996 law, support was growing for a repeal of the secret evidence provision.[11]

That sentiment changed on the morning of September 11, 2001. After the horrific attacks on the World Trade Center and the Pentagon and the downing of United Airlines Flight 93 in Shanksville, Pennsylvania, Americans were in shock. Quickly, shock turned to sadness, fear, and anger. Six weeks later, very much in the heat of the moment and as Americans reeled from the frightening series of anthrax attacks then being unleashed on political offices and media outlets in Washington, DC, New York, and Florida,[12] Con-

gress passed the Uniting and Strengthening America by Providing Appropriate Tools Required to Intercept and Obstruct Terrorism Act (USA PATRIOT
Act). Almost entirely a representation of the Bush administration's proposals,
the bill was strongly pushed on the Hill by Attorney General John Ashcroft.
In those fearful weeks after the September 11 attacks, many in Congress came
to believe that deference to the action of the executive was necessary to ex-
pedite a defensive response during what was perceived as an unusually dangerous time.[13] Although there were some dissenters,[14] Congress as a whole
dispensed with its traditional deliberative process; the bill "was never the
subject of a committee debate or markup in the Senate," and there was only a
"truncated process in the House." Passing in the Senate by a vote of 98 to 1 on
October 11, the 342-page bill was introduced and passed in the House the next
day. President Bush signed it into law on October 26.[15]

In the anguished days after September 11, members of Congress supported
expanded surveillance powers, in part because they believed they were long
overdue. Most did not fully consider the implications of those powers or fret
over how they might be abused, choosing speedy action instead.[16] President
Bush had also already defined the parameters of the debate by describing
the attacks as having placed the nation in a "'new kind of war' [that as Mary
Dudziak explains] was against an enemy that would not warrant the honor or
protection that historically a warring nation accorded its foe." Instead, he and
his administration spoke of operating on "'the dark side'" and at the "'edges
of the law,'" as the nation entered "an exceptional state, a new time zone when
the usual rules would not apply."[17] By deploying this kind of wartime narrative, the Bush administration was able to secure the sweeping provisions
found in the PATRIOT Act.

In contrast, when the Smith Act was being considered during the summers
of 1939 and 1940, the United States had not been attacked and was not at war.
Although the fighting intensified in Europe and there was a deepening fear
of fifth column sabotage at home when the legislation was making its way
through Congress, the law's supporters opened it to debate. The hearings in
the House influenced the shape of bill, leading to the removal of its most radical provision: the detention camps for deportable aliens. Because there was no
similar institutional pushback against the PATRIOT Act, and because it was
being promoted so strongly by the attorney general, it passed without any of
its provisions being substantially challenged or with any mechanisms being
placed within it, such as reporting requirements, to ensure against its abuse.[18]
Very limited safeguards were put in place in March 2006 when Congress renewed the law's provisions. Despite attempts by some lawmakers to include
more stringent protections of civil liberties—including Russ Feingold's fili-

buster in the Senate in December 2005—fourteen of the sixteen measures were renewed in perpetuity. Although most libraries were exempt from secret government requests for information because of the popular pushback against this provision, no other significant protections were secured.[19]

As has happened in the past (with *Yates*, for example), the courts have weighed in to counterbalance the executive and legislative branches' attempts to increase the authority of the Justice Department and the FBI in pursuing threats to national security. After the Bush administration authorized the holding of several hundred foreign nationals for more than two and a half years with no trial, no charges, and no hearings in the prison hastily constructed at the American naval base at Guantánamo, the Supreme Court ruled against it. In June 2004, in *Rasul v. Bush*, the Court found that the Guantánamo detainees had a right to challenge the legality of their detention regardless of whether they were U.S. citizens. Because the prison was located in a territory "under U.S. jurisdiction and control," the inmates had a right "to seek court review."[20] On the same day it handed down this ruling, the Court also found against the government in *Hamdi v. Rumsfeld*. In an 8-to-1 decision, the Court ruled "that while the government had a right to hold U.S. citizens captured on a foreign battlefield fighting for the enemy, due process demanded that the individual be afforded notice of the charges against him and a meaningful opportunity to confront the charges before a neutral decision maker."[21] Justice Sandra Day O'Connor drove home the point, arguing that "a state of war is not a blank check for the President when it comes to the rights of the Nation's citizens."[22] Commenting on the *Rasul* and *Hamdi* decisions, Fred Korematsu, the plaintiff who unsuccessfully challenged the constitutionality of Japanese internment during World War II, told Geoffrey Stone:

> By recognizing the overriding importance of civil liberties even in wartime, the Supreme Court has taken a critical step away from some of its more regrettable decisions of the past. . . . Perhaps more importantly, it has learned the lesson of our own history—that especially in wartime, the nation depends on independent federal courts to guard the liberties of all and to be skeptical of claims of military necessity.[23]

Agreeing with this sentiment has been hard for some Americans after witnessing the streets of one of their great cities littered with the body parts of their fellow citizens. In the context of the post-9/11 world, the debate over how to balance civil liberties with national security has remained, at times, an emotionally fraught and difficult one. But it is an important debate and one that can be usefully informed by the past, as Korematsu indicates.

One of the lessons from the past is how war or a wartime emergency context influences many Americans to compromise civil liberties in the name of national security. While many civil libertarians have tried to expose the premise of this choice as a false dichotomy—good national security can be compatible with the safeguarding of rights—such compromises continue to happen. Franklin Roosevelt made them when empowering Hoover to conduct domestic political surveillance in the late 1930s. Francis Biddle made a similar bargain when authorizing the prosecution of the twenty-nine Trotskyists in 1941. And even the Supreme Court allowed the pressures and passions of the Cold War to influence its position on the Smith Act in 1951. More recently, and with consequences for human rights more broadly defined, John Woo's torture memo and the Bush administration's argument that waterboarding was necessary to diffuse ticking time bombs have trafficked in the assertion that in extraordinary times safety must come at the cost of liberty.[24] If in the past the wartime emergency context has justified such bargains, and if it has done so again more recently with the passage of the PATRIOT Act and the defense of torture, what becomes of those liberties and of the dissent made possible by them when the nation exists in a constant state of emergency?

As it faces continued terror threats today, America finds itself in a strange "twilight zone" somewhat akin to that which Biddle described in the months before the United States officially entered World War II, when "it may be necessary at any time to take steps which would not be considered in ordinary times."[25] Today there is a heightened state of emergency, and there are serious concerns about sabotage and attacks on the homeland, but even as the nation winds down the second of its two overseas ground wars and continues to wage undeclared war remotely with drones and other means, there also is not a sense of that fight among the American people on a daily basis. As Mary Dudziak describes, "It is not a time without war, but instead a time in which war does not bother everyday Americans."[26] Although the Smith Act was sustained and given new life in many ways by the outbreak of World War II and the subsequent Cold War, it was eventually reined in as the politics of emergency eased by the late 1950s.[27] A period of readjustment followed with the flowering of dissent during the 1960s and 1970s, the Church Committee revelations and reforms, and the SWP's court victory in the mid-1980s. But with the rise of new terror threats during the early 1990s and with the horrific attacks of September 11, the United States once again has found itself in a state of heightened anxiety.

America now is enmeshed in a new experience of perpetual war, but a war that is no longer fully defined as war and that is conducted on multiple fronts by various means, including the expanded powers and authority granted to the nation's domestic intelligence agencies. It might seem that a modification of the national security provisions that have tended to abuse civil liberties will never come if the threat of another attack always looms. But if the past is a guide, with the persistence of committed individuals and groups (like the "18," the CRDC, the ACLU, and the NAACP) in fighting to preserve those rights, and with the wisdom of the courts in upholding them (specifically through the application of the Holmes-Brandeis test), that rebalancing can take place. By considering both the gravity and the immediacy of possible threats to the United States, Americans can be vigilant and effective in preserving the life of the nation while they protect the freedoms that give life to their nation.

NOTES

INTRODUCTION

1 Philip A. Korth, *The Minneapolis Teamsters Strike of 1934* (East Lansing: Michigan State University Press, 1995); Bryan Palmer, "Minneapolis Militants," draft chapter from forthcoming volume 2 of *James P. Cannon and the Origins of the American Revolutionary Left*, in possession of the author. Members of Local 544 who were indicted included Jake Cooper, Harry DeBoer, Grant Dunne, Miles Dunne, Vincent Ray Dunne, George Frosig, Walter Hagstrom, Clarence Hamel, Emil Hansen, Carlos Hudson, Kelly Postal, Ray Rainbolt, Carl Skoglund, and Nick Wagner.

2 The others from the FWS included Karl Kuehn, Roy Orgon, Oscar Schoenfeld, and Harold Swanson. Note that in some of the primary sources I consulted (e.g., in the original district court stenographic records). Kuehn's first name is sometimes given as "Carl." I have used "Karl" throughout.

3 Felix Morrow was also included in the contingent indicted from the SWP in New York.

4 Oscar Coover, Rose Seiler, and Alfred Russell were the remaining defendants from Minnesota.

5 George Frosig, Walter Hagstrom, Dorothy Schultz, Rose Seiler, and Nick Wagner were found not guilty by Judge Joyce's directed verdict. Miles Dunne, Roy Orgon, Kelly Postal, Ray Rainbolt, and Harold Swanson were acquitted by the jury on both counts. See Farrell Dobbs, *Teamster Bureaucracy* (New York: Pathfinder, 1977), 196, 218, 280, 320; and *U.S. vs. Dunne, et al.*, Abstract of the Record (microfilm: 1 reel), 67, 72–74 (Tamiment Library and Robert F. Wagner Labor Archives, Elmer Holmes Bobst Library, New York, New York) (hereafter cited as *U.S. vs. Dunne, et al.*).

6 To date there is no book and only three articles on the Minneapolis case: Ralph C. James and Estelle James, "The Purge of the Trotskyites from the Teamsters," *Western Political Quarterly* 19, no. 1 (1966): 5–15; Thomas Pahl, "The G-String Conspiracy, Political Reprisal or Armed Revolt? The Minneapolis Trotskyite Trial," *Labor History* 8, no. 1 (1967): 30–51; and Joe Allen, "Free Speech in the Shadow of War," SocialistWorker.org (July 8, 2011), http://socialistworker. org/2011/07/08/free-speech-in-wars-shadow (accessed January 26, 2013). Limited in sources or to a partisan interpretive lens, these authors focused almost exclusively on the story of the arrests and prosecution and hewed closely to the defense team's arguments.

7 These include, for example, the Wisconsin Historical Society's acquisition of Daniel Tobin's unpublished memoirs in 2005 and Department of Justice and FBI

files released under Freedom of Information Act requests after 1975, with most declassified in the late 1980s.

8 U.S. Congress, Senate, Subcommittee of the Committee on the Judiciary, Hearing on H.R. 5138, *Crime to Promote Overthrow of Government*, 76th Cong., 3rd sess., May 17, 1940, 1–2.

9 Geoffrey R. Stone, *Perilous Times: Free Speech in Wartime, from the Sedition Act of 1798 to the War on Terrorism* (New York: Norton, 2004), 67.

10 U.S. Congress, House, Subcommittee of the Committee on the Judiciary, Hearings on H.R. 5982, *Crime to Promote the Overthrow of Government*, 76th Cong., 1st sess., April 12 and 13, 1939, 6–95; Senate, Committee on the Judiciary, *Crime to Promote Overthrow of Government*, 17–67.

11 Senate, Committee on the Judiciary, *Crime to Promote Overthrow of Government*, 6–11.

12 Nelson Lichtenstein, *The Most Dangerous Man in Detroit: Walter Reuther and the Face of American Labor* (New York: HarperCollins, 1995), 90–131, 154–158; Bert Cochran, *Labor and Communism: The Conflict That Shaped American Unions* (Princeton, NJ: Princeton University Press, 1977), 127–155; Joshua Freeman, *In Transit: The Transport Workers Union in New York City, 1933–1966* (Philadelphia: Temple University Press, 2001), 128–161.

13 On the "little red scare," see M. J. Heale, *Red Scare Politics in State and Nation, 1935–1965* (Athens: University of Georgia Press, 1998), 94–98. On respectability, see Nelson Lichtenstein, *Labor's War at Home: The CIO in World War II* (Philadelphia: Temple University Press, 2003), 6, 44–66; Lichtenstein, *Dangerous Man in Detroit*, 177.

14 Lichtenstein, *Labor's War at Home*, 63.

15 Cochran, *Labor and Communism*, 145–155; Lichtenstein, *Dangerous Man in Detroit*, 192–193; James R. Green, *The World of the Worker: Labor in Twentieth-Century America* (Urbana: University of Illinois Press, 1980; Illini edition, 1998), 177.

16 Richard W. Steele, *Free Speech in the Good War* (New York: St. Martin's, 1999), 72.

17 On left-right factionalism in the labor movement in the 1930s, see, for example, Cochran, *Labor and Communism*, 82–195; Lichtenstein, *Dangerous Man in Detroit*, 90–131; Freeman, *In Transit*, 128–161; Steve Rosswurm, ed., *The CIO's Left-Led Unions* (New Brunswick, NJ: Rutgers University Press, 1992); Harvey Levenstein, *Communism, Anti-Communism, and the CIO* (Westport, CT: Greenwood Press, 1981); Gerald Zahavi, "Passionate Commitments: Race, Sex, and Communism at Schenectady General Electric, 1932–1954," *Journal of American History* 83, no. 2 (1996): 514–548.

18 On ties between early labor anticommunists and the FBI, see, for example, Jennifer Luff, *Commonsense Anticommunism: Labor and Civil Liberties between the World Wars* (Chapel Hill: University of North Carolina Press, 2012).

19 On rank-and-file cooperation with the FBI during the postwar period, see, for example, Gerald Zahavi, "Uncivil War: An Oral History of Labor, Communism, and Community in Schenectady, New York, 1944–1954," in *American Labor and*

the Cold War: Grassroots Politics, ed. Robert Cherny, William Issel, and Kieran Walsh Taylor (New Brunswick, NJ: Rutgers University Press 2004), 25–57.

20 William W. Keller, *The Liberals and J. Edgar Hoover* (Princeton, NJ: Princeton University Press, 1989), 154–155; Athan Theoharis, *The FBI and American Democracy: A Brief Critical History* (Lawrence: University Press of Kansas, 2004), 46–52.

21 For Japanese internment, see, for example, Peter Irons, *Justice at War: The Story of the Japanese-American Internment Cases* (Berkeley: University of California Press, 1983); Greg Robinson, *By Order of the President: FDR and the Internment of Japanese Americans* (Cambridge, MA: Harvard University Press, 2001). On the prosecution of anti-interventionists, see, for example, Steele, *Free Speech in the Good War*, 53–233; and Douglas Charles, *J. Edgar Hoover and the Anti-Interventionists: FBI Political Surveillance and the Rise of the Domestic Security State, 1939–1945* (Columbus: Ohio State University Press, 2007).

22 Steele, *Free Speech in the Good War*; Charles, *J. Edgar Hoover*; Stone, *Perilous Times*. On the evolution of anticommunism, see also Richard Gid Powers, *Not without Honor: The History of American Anticommunism* (New York: Free Press, 1995).

23 Prichard to Biddle, July 14, 1941, f. 3, box 108, Socialist Workers Declassified Papers 146-1-10, General Records of the Department of Justice, RG 60, National Archives at College Park, Maryland (hereafter cited as SWP 146-1-10).

24 On Haymarket, see James Green, *Death in the Haymarket: A Story of Chicago, the First Labor Movement and the Bombing That Divided Gilded Age America* (New York: Pantheon, 2006), 214–230; and Chicago Anarchists on Trial: Evidence from the Haymarket Affair, People's Exhibits, http://memory.loc.gov/cgi-bin/query/S?ammem/haybib:@field(TITLE+@od1(People's+Exhibit))::SortBy=DOCID (accessed May 3, 2013). On the *Dennis* case, see Ellen Schrecker, *Many Are the Crimes: McCarthyism in America* (Princeton, NJ: Princeton University Press, 1998), 190–196.

25 *Yates v. United States*, 347 U.S. 298, June 17, 1957.

26 Michal Belknap, *Cold War Political Justice: The Smith Act, the Communist Party, and American Civil Liberties* (Westport, CT: Greenwood Press, 1977), 41; Vincent Dunne speaking tour press release, December 1, 1949, series II, Letters, Vincent Raymond Dunne Papers (microfilm edition, 1994), Wisconsin Historical Society (hereafter cited as Dunne Papers, WHS).

CHAPTER 1. MILITANCY AND FEAR

1 Interview with Max Geldman and Shevi Geldman by Steven Trimble, 1977 (?), Minnesota Historical Society (hereafter cited as MHS).

2 Dale Kramer, "The Dunne Boys of Minneapolis," *Harper's*, March 1942, 388.

3 Interview with Vincent Raymond Dunne by Lila Johnson Goff, April 27, 1969, MHS; Farrell Dobbs, *Teamster Rebellion* (New York: Pathfinder, 1972; repr., New York: Pathfinder, 2004), 38.

4 Kramer, "Dunne Boys," 390; Vincent Dunne's FBI file 100-18341, p. 4, FOIA, in the author's possession.

5 Interview with V. Dunne by Goff, April 27, 1969, MHS.

6 Interview with Carl Skoglund, 20th Century Radicalism in Minnesota Oral History Project, interviewer unidentified, n.d., MHS; Civil Rights Defense Committee, *Who Are the 18 Prisoners in the Minneapolis Labor Case? How the Smith "Gag" Act Has Endangered Workers Rights and Free Speech* (New York: Civil Rights Defense Committee, 1944), 27.

7 Interview with V. Dunne by Goff, April 27, 1969, MHS.

8 Bryan Palmer, *James P. Cannon and the Origins of the American Revolutionary Left, 1890–1928* (Chicago: University of Illinois Press, 2007), 39–135.

9 Civil Rights Defense Committee, *Who Are the 18 Prisoners in the Minneapolis Labor Case?*, 15–17.

10 Palmer, *James P. Cannon*, 316–349; Dunne's FBI file 100-18341, p. 43.

11 Civil Rights Defense Committee, *Who Are the 18 Prisoners in the Minneapolis Labor Case?*, 14.

12 Interview with V. Dunne by Goff, April 27, 1969, MHS.

13 Palmer, *James P. Cannon*, 334–349; Constance Ashton Myers, *The Prophet's Army: Trotskyists in America, 1928–1941* (Westport, CT: Greenwood Press, 1977), 32–41; Korth, *Minneapolis Teamsters Strike*, 8.

14 Palmer, *James P. Cannon*, 362–366.

15 Testimony of James Cannon in *Socialism on Trial: The Official Court Record of James P. Cannon's Testimony in the Famous Minneapolis Sedition Trial*, ed. James P. Cannon and Joseph Hansen (New York: Pioneer Publishers, 1944), 37.

16 Korth, *Minneapolis Teamsters Strike*, 24. On the Citizens Alliance, see ibid., 13–22; William Millikan, *Union against Unions: The Minneapolis Citizens Alliance and Its Fight against Organized Labor, 1903–1947* (St. Paul: Minnesota Historical Society Press, 2003); George Dimitri Tselos, "The Minneapolis Labor Movement in the 1930s" (PhD diss., University of Minnesota, 1970), 12–25; Dobbs, *Teamster Bureaucracy*, 98–99; Dobbs, *Teamster Rebellion*, 57.

17 In certain industries—like dairy and ice—the IBT supported industrial unionism. But this was not the case in all industries (as Local 574's original leadership demonstrated). David Witwer, *Corruption and Reform in the Teamsters Union* (Chicago: University of Illinois Press, 2003), 14, 18, 71.

18 Korth, *Minneapolis Teamsters Strike*, 23–32; interview with V. Dunne by Goff,, April 27, 1969, MHS; Kramer, "Dunne Boys," 389, 392.

19 Korth, *Minneapolis Teamsters Strike*, 58–63; interview with V. Dunne by Goff,, April 27, 1969, MHS.

20 Korth, *Minneapolis Teamsters Strike*, 63–64; Dobbs, *Teamster Rebellion*, 58–70.

21 Dobbs, *Teamster Rebellion*, 81.

22 Ibid., 70–86; Korth, *Minneapolis Teamsters Strike*, 80–81.

23 Dobbs, *Teamster Rebellion*, 94–126; Korth, *Minneapolis Teamsters Strike*, xii, 92–105; Green, *World of the Worker*, 143–146.

24 Dobbs, *Teamster Rebellion*, 127–145.

25 Dobbs, *Teamster Rebellion*, 146–172.

26 Korth, *Minneapolis Teamsters Strike*, 162–163; Thaddeus Russell, *Out of the Jungle: Jimmy Hoffa and the Remaking of the American Working Class* (Philadelphia: Temple University Press, 2001), 36–37.

27 Palmer, "Minneapolis Militants."

28 Dobbs, *Teamster Bureaucracy*, 101.

29 Civil Rights Defense Committee, *Who Are the 18 Prisoners in the Minneapolis Labor Case?*, 21.

30 Tselos, "Minneapolis Labor Movement," 269–290, 331, 341–351, 365–368.

31 Dobbs, *Teamster Bureaucracy*, 104.

32 Russell, *Out of the Jungle*, 35; Korth, *Minneapolis Teamsters Strike*, 142–145, 157.

33 Interview with Grace Holmes Carlson by Carl Ross, 20th Century Radicalism in Minnesota Project, July 9, 1987, MHS.

34 Tselos, "Minneapolis Labor Movement," 332, 516.

35 Thomas Hughes, General Secretary-Treasurer, IBT, to Farrell Dobbs, n.d., f. 1, box 5, Correspondence, Farrell Dobbs Papers, Wisconsin Historical Society, Madison, Wisconsin (hereafter cited as WHS); Farrell Dobbs to Thomas Hughes, April 20, 1935, and Daniel Tobin to Farrell Dobbs, April 22, 1935, f. 1, box 5, Correspondence, Dobbs Papers, WHS; Dobbs, *Teamster Bureaucracy*, 104–105.

36 Daniel Tobin, "Memoir," typescript, pp. 2–147, 226–227, 305, 319, WHS; Joy M. Copeland, *Daniel J. Tobin: A Teamster's Life* (Hyattsville, MD: Peake Delancey, 2007), 95, 99.

37 Daniel Tobin to Westbrook Pegler, June 25, 1941, f. Pegler, box 11, series V, International Brotherhood of Teamsters, Chauffeurs, Warehousemen, and Helpers of America, Records, 1904–1952, Wisconsin Historical Society (hereafter cited as IBT, WHS); Dobbs, *Teamster Bureaucracy*, 104–105.

38 Dobbs, *Teamster Bureaucracy*, 105.

39 Dobbs, *Teamster Bureaucracy*, 105.

40 Russell, *Out of the Jungle*, 37–40; Dobbs, *Teamster Bureaucracy*, 124–127.

41 Dobbs, *Teamster Bureaucracy*, 118.

42 Dobbs, *Teamster Rebellion*, 110–112, 124–125.

43 Farrell Dobbs to Locals and Branches, March 22, 1940, Circular Letters 1940–1944 (microfilm: reel 27), Administrative Records, Part 1: Original Collection, 1928–1993, Socialist Workers Party Records, 1928–2002, Wisconsin Historical Society (hereafter cited as SWP Records, WHS); Vincent Dunne to Farrell Dobbs, December 28, 1940; "The Union Ticket," n.d.; Vincent Dunne to Farrell Dobbs, February 20, 1941; Vincent Dunne to James P. Cannon, March 18, 1941 (microfilm: reel 47), Activities and Organizing Records, Part 1: Original Collection, 1928–1993, SWP Records, WHS; Vincent Dunne to James P. Cannon, March 11, 1941, f. 1941, box 5, Correspondence, James P. Cannon Papers, WHS (hereafter cited as JPC, WHS).

44 Myers, *Prophet's Army*, 83–145.

45 Ibid., 44–51; Declaration of Principles and Constitution of the Socialist Workers Party, Government's Exhibit 1, *U.S. vs. Dunne, et al.*, 1176–1219; Dunne's FBI file 100-18341, p. 54.

46 Interview with Carlson by Ross, July 9, 1987, MHS.

47 Ibid.; Elizabeth Raasch-Gilman, "Sisterhood in the Revolution: The Holmes Sisters and the Socialist Workers Party," *Minnesota History*, Fall 1999, 361.

48 Tselos, "Minneapolis Labor Movement," 412–415, 424–428.

49 Interview with Carlson by Ross, July 9, 1987, MHS.

50 Raasch-Gilman, "Sisterhood in the Revolution," 360–362.

51 Elizabeth Faue, *Community of Suffering and Struggle: Women, Men and the Labor Movement in Minneapolis, 1915–1945* (Chapel Hill: University of North Carolina Press, 1991), 12–13; Marjorie Penn Lasky, "'Where I Was a Person': The Ladies' Auxiliary in the 1934 Minneapolis Teamsters' Strikes," in *Women, Work and Protest: A Century of U.S. Women's Labor History*, ed. Ruth Milkman (Boston: Routledge and Kegan Paul, 1985), 181–205.

52 Raasch-Gilman, "Sisterhood in the Revolution," 362, 368–373.

53 Faue, *Community of Suffering*, 142–143.

54 Palmquist was married to Rose Seiler, who became a Trotskyist supporter. See Faue, *Community of Suffering*, 144.

55 Civil Rights Defense Committee, *Who Are the 18 Prisoners in the Minneapolis Labor Case?*, 18–19, 24.

56 Interview with Geldmans by Trimble, 1977 (?), MHS; Dobbs, *Teamster Bureaucracy*, 104.

57 Farrell Dobbs, *Teamster Politics* (New York: Monad Press, 1975), 197.

58 Herman Erickson, "WPA Strike and Trials of 1939," *Minnesota History*, Summer 1971, 203–204.

59 Ibid., 205.

60 Ibid., 206; Dobbs, *Teamster Politics*, 217–234; Faue, *Community of Suffering*, 156–161.

61 Erickson, "WPA," 207.

62 Ibid., 206, 207; Dobbs, *Teamster Politics*, 217; Faue, *Community of Suffering*, 161.

63 Dobbs, *Teamster Politics*, 219; Faue, *Community of Suffering*, 161.

64 Erickson, "WPA," 213. On the use of conspiracy prosecutions, see Ellen Schrecker, "Political Repression and the Rule of Law: The Cold War Case of William Sentner" (paper prepared for the Eighth Middelburg Conference of European Historians of the United States, April 2007), in the author's possession.

65 Dobbs, *Teamster Politics*, 234.

66 Ibid., 220; Erickson, "WPA," 209.

67 H. Roger Grant, ed., *Iowa Railroads: The Essays of Frank P. Donovan, Jr.* (Iowa City: University of Iowa Press, 2000), 46–47.

68 Dobbs, *Teamster Politics*, 228–229.

69 Ibid., 223–229; Erikson, "WPA," 212.

70 Interview with Geldmans by Trimble, 1977 (?), MHS.

71 Dobbs, *Teamster Politics*, 229, 232–233.

72 Erickson, "WPA," 213; Dobbs, *Teamster Politics*, 231.

73 Erickson, "WPA," 212.

74 Stone, *Perilous Times*, 259; Attorney General's Office, Memorandum re. Silver Shirts, May 17, 1938, for President Roosevelt, May 25, 1938, f. Justice: Hoover, J. Edgar, 1937–1940, box 57, PSF, Franklin D. Roosevelt Presidential Library, Hyde Park, New York (hereafter cited as FDRPL).

75 Dobbs, *Teamster Politics*, 140–141.

76 George K. Belden, the AI's president, sympathized with the Silver Shirts and attended the July 1938 Zachary meeting. Millikan, *Union against Unions*, 337, 432n51; Laura E. Weber, "'Gentiles Preferred': Minneapolis Jews and Employment, 1920–1950," *Minnesota History*, Spring 1991, 172–173.

77 Dobbs, *Teamster Politics*, 141.

78 Ibid.

79 Ibid., 143; Union Defense Guard armband, Exhibit 41, f. #7256 U.S. v. Dunne 41–60, box 195 Exhibits, Minnesota, Fourth Division, Minneapolis, 1890–1983, Records of the District Courts of the United States, RG 21, National Archives at Kansas City, Kansas City, Missouri (hereafter cited as RG 21 KC).

80 Dobbs, *Teamster Politics*, 143.

81 Interview with Vern F. Bennyhoff, October 16, 1941, in FBI report 100-1246, f. 1, box 108, SWP 146-1-10.

82 Dobbs, *Teamster Politics*, 142; *U.S. vs. Dunne, et al.*, 1102–1106.

83 Dobbs, *Teamster Politics*, 144.

84 Ibid., 145; cross-examination of John J. Novack, *U.S. vs. Dunne, et al.*, 522.

85 Jack Barnes, "Introduction to the Spanish Edition," in Dobbs, *Teamster Rebellion*, 17.

86 According to David Witwer, the Teamsters had a tradition of interracial unionism dating back to 1903; see Witwer, *Corruption and Reform*, 15. But Rainbolt's unique position as head of the UDG may also indicate the more progressive character of Local 544.

87 See, for example, J. Edgar Hoover to L. M. C. Smith, Special Defense Unit, March 31, 1941, and October 7, 1941, f. 1, box 108, SWP 146-1-10; Special Defense Unit file card on UDG classifying it as "A-1," f. 1, box 108, SWP 146-1-10; and Alfred Blair, "Storm over the Union," 40–43, box 7, Harold E. Stassen Papers, MHS.

88 Green, *Death in the Haymarket*, 65, 74, 86, 91, 156; William C. Blizzard, *When Miners March* (Oakland, CA: PM Press, 2010).

89 For the charge of an overt attempt to overthrow the government, the defendants were indicted (count one) under a Civil War era insurrection statute. *U.S. vs. Dunne, et al.*, 6–10.

90 On the details of the mobilization, see Dobbs, *Teamster Politics*, 145, and cross-examination of Karl Bath, *U.S. vs. Dunne, et al.*, 535. That masculine subculture included the patronage of prostitutes by some men: see Lasky, "'Where I Was a Person,'" 197. On hunting, fishing and drinking, see Kramer, "Dunne Boys," 389, 392.

91 I. F. Stone, "The G-String Conspiracy," *Nation*, July 26, 1941, 67.

92 President Roosevelt received almost daily communications from Hoover in these years on possible threats of sabotage and espionage, particularly against defense plants. See, for example, memo from Hoover to Roosevelt, June 17, 1940, OF 10b, box 12 #142; memo from Hoover to Roosevelt, June 17, 1940, OF 10b, box 12 #144; abstract of report from Hoover to Roosevelt, August 13, 1940, OF 10b box 12, #273; abstract of report from Hoover to Roosevelt, September 28, 1940, OF 10b, box 12 #331, FDRPL. Secretary of War, Henry Stimson, and Secretary of the Navy, Frank Knox, also expressed their concern over slow-downs and sabotage in defense plants in the spring of 1941: Stimson and Knox to Roosevelt, May 29, 1941, OF 10b, box 11, f. OF 10b Justice Dept., FBI Reports, 1941–1942, FDRPL.

93 Richard W. Steele, "Fear of the Mob and Faith in Government in Free Speech Discourse, 1919–1941," *American Journal of Legal History* 38, no. 1 (1994): 55–83.

94 Belknap, *Cold War Political Justice*, 16.

95 Ibid.

96 Ibid., 16, 17; Powers, *Not without Honor*, 124.

97 Belknap, *Cold War Political Justice*, 16–19.

98 Francis MacDonnell, *Insidious Foes: The Axis Fifth Column and the American Home Front* (New York: Oxford University Press, 1995), 42–47.

99 Charles, *J. Edgar Hoover*, 31.

100 Hoover recounting Roosevelt's order quoted in ibid., 33–34; Frank J. Donner, *The Age of Surveillance: The Aims and Methods of America's Political Intelligence System* (New York: Vintage, 1980), 53.

101 Charles, *J. Edgar Hoover*, 33–34.

102 Donner, *Age of Surveillance*, 54.

103 Charles, *J. Edgar Hoover*, 36; MacDonnell, *Insidious Foes*, 49–71.

104 MacDonnell, *Insidious Foes*, 49, 16, 50.

105 Powers, *Not without Honor*, 124–125; Belknap, *Cold War Political Justice*, 21.

106 Donna T. Haverty-Stacke, *America's Forgotten Holiday: May Day and Nationalism, 1867–1960* (New York: NYU Press, 2009), 111–112; Richard Polenberg, "Introduction," in *The Letters of Sacco and Vanzetti*, ed. Marion Denman Frankfurter and Gardner Jackson (New York: Penguin, 1997), ix–xvi.

107 Bruce J. Dierenfield, *Keeper of the Rules: Congressman Howard W. Smith of Virginia* (Charlottesville: University Press of Virginia, 1987), 76–79.

108 House, Committee on the Judiciary, *Crime to Promote the Overthrow of Government*, 1–4.

109 Ibid., 4–5.

110 Ibid., 25–26.

111 Ibid., 31.

112 Ibid., 29, 36, 37–38.

113 Ibid., 15–16.

114 Ibid., 42.

115 Ibid., 57.

116 In *Gitlow v. New York*, 268 U.S. 652 (1925) the Court upheld the New York law on the grounds that it outlawed the express advocacy of the overthrow of the government by "unlawful means." See Stone, *Perilous Times*, 237.

117 House, Committee on the Judiciary, *Crime to Promote the Overthrow of Government*, 83–85.

118 Ibid., 11.

119 Ibid., 12–15.

120 Ibid., 23–24.

121 Ibid., 40.

122 Ibid., 70–71.

123 Ibid., 78.

124 Ibid., 73.

125 Dierenfield, *Keeper of the Rules*, 80–81.

126 House, Committee on the Judiciary, *Crime to Promote the Overthrow of Government*, 71–76.

127 Belknap, *Cold War Political Justice*, 23. On the bill's being reported from the committee to the House, see *New York Times*, June 28, 1939, 4.

128 Charles, *J. Edgar Hoover*, 37–38; confidential memo for the Secretary of State, the Secretary of the Treasury, the Secretary of War, the Attorney General, the Postmaster General, the Secretary of the Navy and the Secretary of Commerce from President Roosevelt, June 26, 1939, OF 10b, box 10, FDRPL.

129 Steele, "Fear of the Mob," 55–83.

130 Charles, *J. Edgar Hoover*, 38. See also Donner, *Age of Surveillance*, 57–58.

131 On the details of the pact, see Gerhard L. Weinberg, *Hitler's Foreign Policy: The Road to World War II, 1933–1939* (New York: Enigma, 2005), 906–911. On its impact on the political left in America, see Haverty-Stacke, *America's Forgotten Holiday*, 170–172.

132 MacDonnell, *Insidious Foes*, 77.

133 Donner, *Age of Surveillance*, 162–163.

134 Keller, *The Liberals and J. Edgar Hoover*, 60. Attorney General Frank Murphy requested 150 additional agents and additional appropriations for the FBI to handle the domestic intelligence mission. See Frank Murphy to President Roosevelt, December 18, 1939, OF 10b, box 10, FDRPL.

135 Richard Gid Powers, *Secrecy and Power: The Life of J. Edgar Hoover* (New York: Free Press, 1987), 17–18, 33, 44–92, 96–118, 137–139, 161–167.

136 Senate, Committee on the Judiciary, *Crime to Promote Overthrow of Government*, 1–2.

137 Ibid., 2–5.

138 Mark Donnelly, *Britain in the Second World War* (New York: Routledge, 1999), 46–48.

139 Senate, Committee on the Judiciary, *Crime to Promote Overthrow of Government*, 6.

140 Ibid., 6, 8.

141 Raymond Aresenault, *The Sound of Freedom: Marian Anderson, the Lincoln Memorial and the Concert That Awakened America* (New York: Bloomsbury Press, 2009), 140.

142 Senate, Committee on the Judiciary, *Crime to Promote Overthrow of Government*, 17.

143 On *Schenck v. U.S.*, see Richard Polenberg, *Fighting Faiths: The* Abrams *Case, the Supreme Court, and Free Speech* (Ithaca, NY: Cornell University Press, 1987), 212–224.

144 Senate, Committee on the Judiciary, *Crime to Promote Overthrow of Government*, 18.

145 Steele, *Free Speech in the Good War*, 135.

146 Senate, Committee on the Judiciary, *Crime to Promote Overthrow of Government*, 19–20.

147 Ira Katznelson, *When Affirmative Action Was White: An Untold History of Racial Inequality in Twentieth-Century America* (New York: Norton, 2005), 17, 65–73; Dierenfield, *Keeper of the Rules*, 84–100.

148 Senate, Committee on the Judiciary, *Crime to Promote Overthrow of Government*, 52. According to Ellen Schrecker, "The Roosevelt administration initiated denaturalization proceedings against" him in December 1942 but dropped the case after it quickly "aroused considerable opposition." After he left the Senate, Nowak became the subject of denaturalization proceedings in 1952 in part because he refused to cooperate with HUAC. See Ellen Schrecker, "Immigration and Internal Security: Political Deportations during the McCarthy Era," *Science and Society* 60, no. 4 (1996/1997): 396, 412.

149 U.S. Congress, Senate, *Congressional Record* (June 22, 1940), 8952.

150 Ibid., 9033.

151 Ibid.

152 Ibid., 9034.

153 Vito Marcantonio, *I Vote My Conscience: Debates, Speeches and Writings of Vito Marcantonio, 1935–1950* (New York: Vito Marcantonio Memorial, 1956), 129–130.

154 U.S. Congress, Senate, *Congressional Record* (June 22, 1940), 9035.

155 Ibid., 9036.

156 Belknap, *Cold War Political Justice*, 26.

157 Franklin D. Roosevelt, "Statement by the President on Signing the Alien Registration Act, June 29, 1940," in *The Public Papers and Addresses of Franklin D. Roosevelt. 1940 Volume. War—and Aid to Democracies* (New York: Macmillan, 1941), 274–275.

158 MacDonnell, *Insidious Foes*, 28; Franklin D. Roosevelt, Confidential Press Conference #649-A, Held with Representatives of the American Youth Congress in the State Dining Room of the White House, June 5, 1940, 8:50 p.m., in *Complete Presidential Press Conference of Franklin D. Roosevelt*, vol. 15, introduction by Jonathan Daniels (New York: DaCapo Press, 1972), 484–498.

159 In addition to the intelligence reports the president received, there was growing public fear of the fifth column threat expressed (and partly cultivated) by media coverage of alleged subversive activities and the two dozen Hollywood movies that dealt with espionage, sabotage, and subversion between 1939 and 1941. See MacDonnell, *Insidious Foes*, 45, 70–77.

160 Steele, *Free Speech in the Good War*, 82.

161 Stone, *Perilous Times*, 284–285.

162 Ibid., 283–296.

CHAPTER 2. DISSENT BECOMES A FEDERAL CASE

1 "An Open Letter to the Membership of Local 544 from Tom Williams," February 28, 1941, Teamsters January–April 1941 (microfilm: reel 47), SWP Records, WHS; Vincent Dunne to Farrell Dobbs, December 28, 1940, Original Collection, 1928–1993 (microfilm: reel 47), SWP Records, WHS.

2 FBI report 100-1117, St. Paul, Minn., 5/2/41 by R. T. Noonan, f. 1, box 108, SWP 146-1-10; Blair, "Storm over the Union," 6–7, 63, 73–74, 78, box 7, Political and Gubernatorial Activities, 1933–1942, Harold E. Stassen Papers, MHS.

3 Korth, *Minneapolis Teamsters Strike*, 135–165, 187–196.

4 *Minneapolis Star Journal*, March 3, 1941, n.p., Teamsters January–April 1941 (microfilm: reel 47), SWP Records, WHS.

5 The SWP stepped up its activities in unions during the spring of 1940: see Farrell Dobbs to All Locals and Branches, March 22, 1940, Circular Letters 1940–1944 (microfilm: reel 27), SWP Records, WHS. It also pushed for monetary contributions later that summer to defend Trotsky and then fund a memorial after his death: see James P. Cannon and Farrell Dobbs to All Locals and Branches, July 11, 1940, Circular Letters 1940–1944 (microfilm: reel 27), SWP Records, WHS. See also testimony of James Bartlett, testimony of Arnold Johnson, and testimony of Helen Hanifan in *U.S. vs. Dunne, et al.*, 268–271, 60, and 697, respectively

6 Testimony of James Bartlett, *U.S. vs. Dunne, et al.*, 194–198, 378–380; Dobbs, *Teamster Bureaucracy*, 136–138; *Minneapolis Star Journal*, March 3, 1941, 1, 3.

7 Testimony of James Bartlett, *U.S. vs. Dunne, et al.*, 430–431; James Bartlett to Member and Friend, January 2, 1941, Exhibit 196, f. #7256 U.S. v. Dunne, box 195 Exhibits, Minnesota, Fourth Division, Minneapolis, 1890–1983, RG 21 KC.

8 Vincent Dunne to Farrell Dobbs, December 28, 1940, Original Collection, 1928–1993 (microfilm: reel 47), SWP Records, WHS; testimony of Vincent Dunne, *U.S. vs. Dunne, et al.*, 1035.

9 Testimony of James Bartlett, *U.S. vs. Dunne, et al.*, 410–414.

10 Ibid., 202, 414.

11 Victor Anderson to Wendell Berge, September 27, 1941, f. 5, box 108, SWP 146-1-10; I. E. Goldberg to Joseph Padway, November 29, 1941, f. Local 544, Minneapolis, Minn., 1939–1941, box 44, series II, IBT, WHS.

12 "An Open Letter," February 28, 1941 (microfilm: reel 47), SWP Records, WHS.

13 *Minneapolis Star Journal*, March 3, 1941, 1, 3; "An Open Letter," February 28, 1941 (microfilm: reel 47), SWP Records, WHS.

14 Testimony of James Bartlett, *U.S. vs. Dunne, et al.*, 452, and of Vincent Dunne, 1041.

15 Blacks, Latinos, and Asian Americans made up only 1 percent, while Swedes and Norwegians made up 60 percent of those of foreign birth or parentage. Faue, *Community of Suffering*, 29–32.

16 There is no hint in the language of the committee (or of its leadership) of any kind of racial or religious hatred: see Bartlett's letter re. his contested election and Williams's open letter of February 28 (microfilm: reel 47) SWP Records, WHS.

17 FBI report 100-1246, St. Paul, 7/26/41, by R. T. Noonan, f. 3, box 108, SWP 146-1-10; *U.S. vs. Dunne, et al.*, 259–273, 409, 492, 651, 697, 700, 1049.

18 The defendants asserted that those contributions were voluntary. See testimony of Vincent Dunne, *U.S. vs. Dunne, et al.*, 1049.

19 Testimony of James Bartlett, *U.S. vs. Dunne, et al.*, 452; International Brotherhood of Teamsters, Chauffeurs, Stablemen and Helpers of America, *Proceedings of the Fourteenth Convention*, Washington, D.C., Tuesday, September 10, 1940, p. 83, and Thursday, September 12, 1940, pp. 8, 28–30.

20 Blair, "Storm over the Union," 73–74. A job steward is a union representative on a job site who enforces the contract, handles grievances, and organizes workers.

21 FBI report 62-14, St. Paul, 10/14/40, by E. N. Notesteen, f. 2, box 108, SWP 146-1-10.

22 Dobbs, *Teamster Bureaucracy*, 137; cross-examination of Henry M. Harris, *U.S. vs. Dunne, et al.*, 569–570.

23 Dobbs, *Teamster Bureaucracy*, 137.

24 Thomas Williams to Ray Rainbolt, February 24, 1941, f. Local 544, Minneapolis, Minn., 1939–1941, box 44, series II, IBT, WHS.

25 *Minneapolis Tribune*, March 11, 1941, 7; Kelly Postal to Farrell Dobbs, March 3, 1941, Teamsters January–April 1941 (microfilm: reel 47), SWP Records, WHS; Dobbs, *Teamster Bureaucracy*, 137.

26 "An Open Letter," February 28, 1941 (microfilm: reel 47), SWP Records, WHS; *Minneapolis Tribune*, March 11, 1941, 7.

27 *Minneapolis Tribune*, March 11, 1941, 7.

28 Dobbs, *Teamster Bureaucracy*, 138; *Minneapolis Star Journal*, March 11, 1941, 4.

29 *Minneapolis Tribune*, March 11, 1941, 7; testimony of Elmer Buckingham, *U.S. vs. Dunne, et al.*, p. 764.

30 *Minneapolis Star Journal*, March 11, 1941, 1, 4; *Minneapolis Tribune*, March 11, 1941, 1, 7.

31 Dobbs, *Teamster Bureaucracy*, 108.

32 Such suspicions were never substantiated. Such explosive allegations became a part of what the Bartlett group communicated to the FBI. FBI report 100-499, 4/25/41, by L. J. McGee, f. 1, box 108, SWP 146-1-10. They also informed the state labor conciliator's understanding of events in Minneapolis. See Blair, "Storm over the Union," 42, 73.

33 *Minneapolis Tribune*, March 11, 1941, 7.

34 Vincent Dunne to James Cannon, March 11, 1941, f. 4, box 5, Correspondence, JPC, WHS. Rainbolt was then recording secretary of the local.

35 Ibid.; *Minneapolis Star Journal*, March 11, 1941, n.p.

36 John Geary to Daniel Tobin, March 14, 1941, f. Local 544, Minneapolis, Minn., 1939–1941, box 44, series II, IBT, WHS.

37 *Minneapolis Star Journal*, March 14, 1941, n.p.

38 "An Open Letter to the Members of Local 544 and Other Teamster's Unions," March 23, 1941, f. 4, box 15, Correspondence, JPC, WHS.

39 Ibid.

40 Dunne to Cannon, March 11, 1941, f. 4, box 5, Correspondence, JPC, WHS.

41 Dobbs to Cannon, March 14, 1941, f. 4, box 5, Correspondence, JPC, WHS.

42 Geary to Tobin, March 18, 1941, f. Local 544, Minneapolis, Minn., 1939–1941, box 44, series II, IBT, WHS.

43 Geary to Tobin, March 22, 1941, f. Local 544, Minneapolis, Minn., 1939–1941, box 44, series II, IBT, WHS.

44 Report dated September 15, 1936, "Communist Organizations Active in Minneapolis and Communist Leaders Occupying Strategic Positions of Leadership in the Minneapolis Local Labor Movement," f. 1, box 108, SWP 146-1-10; FBI report 100-1022, St. Paul, 4/5/41, by Perrin, f. 1, box 108, SWP 146-1-10; J. Edgar Hoover to SAC New York, December 7, 1940, and Farrell Dobbs's Custodial Detention Cards, July 24, 1940, in Farrell Dobbs's FBI file 65-12453, FOIA, in the author's possession; Edward Palmquist's Custodial Detention Card, May 16, 1941 (detailing FBI surveillance from October 1940) in Edward Palmquist's FBI file 146-7-1214, FOIA, in the author's possession.

45 Geary to Tobin, March 22, 1941, f. Local 544, Minneapolis, Minn., 1939–1941, box 44, series II, IBT, WHS.

46 Tobin to Geary, March 24, 1941, f. Local 544, Minneapolis, Minn., 1939–1941, box 44, series II, IBT, WHS.

47 Robert Hawn to Daniel J. Tobin, April 17, 1941, f. Local 544, Minneapolis, Minn., 1939–1941, box 44, series II, IBT, WHS.

48 FBI report 100-1117, St. Paul, 5/2/41, by R. T. Noonan, f. 1, box 108, SWP 146-1-10.

49 On the FBI's use of informants, see Frank J. Donner's discussion of planted infiltrators, in-place informants, and defectors in *Age of Surveillance*, 133–138. On the FBI's use of the "snitch jacket" scripts it wrote about loyal members it framed as turncoats in order to sow dissent in the organizations under investigation, see Donner, *Age of Surveillance*, 193. Hawn may have been an in-place informant, or he could have been the object of an FBI "snitch jacket."

50 Dobbs, *Teamster Politics*, 38–43; Korth, *Minneapolis Teamsters Strike*, 8–9, 23–33, 53–67, 79–105, 135–165; *New York Times*, May 22, 1934, 1; May 23, 1934, 1; May 25, 1934, 3; July 10, 1934, 4; July 16, 1934, 3; July 18, 1934, 5; July 21, 1934, 1; July 22, 1934, 1, 3; July 27, 1934, 1; August 5, 1934, N13, 20; August 12, 1934, N12.

51 On custodial detention, see Donner, *Age of Surveillance*, 162–163.

52 Dunne's FBI file 100-18341, p. 2 of 269-page overview report.

53 Hoover to SAC NY, January 14, 1941; Hoover to SAC NY, February 5, 1941; Hoover to SAC NY, March 25, 1941, in Dobbs's FBI file 65-12453.

54 Hoover to Special Defense Unit, March 28, 1941, in Dobbs's FBI file 65-12453.

55 FBI report 100-1117, 5/2/41, by R. T. Noonan, f. 1, box 108, SWP 146-1-10; FBI report 100-1051, Houston, 3/28/41, by C. W. Wall, f. 1, box 108, SWP 146-1-10; statement of Jurod W. Lee, St. Paul, to SA Perrin, May 1941, f. 3, box 108, SWP 146-1-10.

56 FBI report 100-1022, St. Paul, 4/5/41, Perrin, f. 1, box 108, SWP 146-1-10.

57 On Victor Anderson's having "referred the matter to the Attorney General," see final page of FBI report 100-1022, 4/5/41, by Perrin, f. 1, box 108, SWP 146-1-10. On Schweinhaut's request for information and Hoover's response, see Hoover to

Schweinhaut, April 21, 1941, f. 1, box 108, SWP 146-1-10. On the Department of Justice's belief that "there might have been a real fifth column in Minneapolis," see Berge to Hoover, April 29, 1941, and Berge to Anderson, April 29, 1941, f. 1, box 108, SWP 146-1-10.

58 Search warrant for 138 E. Sixth Street, St. Paul, Minnesota (SWP offices), for June 27, 1941 and search warrant for 919 Marquette Avenue, second floor, Minneapolis, Minnesota (SWP offices), for June 27, 1941, f. 8 of 10, #7256 US v. Dunne, Writs and Warrants, box 192, RG 21 KC. List of materials taken from the FBI during the June 27, 1941, raid (microfilm: reel 15), 1929–1945, SWP Records, WHS.

59 Vincent Dunne to James Cannon and Farrell Dobbs, March 22, 1941, f. 4, box 5, Correspondence, JPC, WHS.

60 Martin to Jones and Barr (James Cannon to Vincent Dunne and Farrell Dobbs), n.d., f. 4, box 5, Correspondence, JPC, WHS.

61 Vincent Dunne to James Cannon, April 4, 1941, f. 4, box 5, Correspondence, JPC, WHS.

62 James P. Cannon to Vincent Dunne, March 24, 1941, f. 4, box 5, Correspondence, JPC, WHS.

63 Sherman House statement, April 8, 1941, f. Gillespie 1941–1943, box 3, series I, IBT, WHS.

64 Dobbs, *Teamster Bureaucracy*, 142.

65 Vincent Dunne to Farrell Dobbs, April 11, 1941, Original Collection, 1928–1993 (microfilm: reel 47), SWP Records, WHS.

66 Wendell Berge to J. Edgar Hoover, April 29, 1941, f. 1, box 108, SWP 146-1-10.

67 Wendell Berge to Victor Anderson, April 29, 1941, f. 1, box 108, SWP 146-1-10.

68 J. Edgar Hoover to Wendell Berge, May 2, 1941, f. 1, box 108, SWP 146-1-10, includes FBI report 100-1117, St. Paul, May 2, 1941, Roy T. Noonan.

69 Daniel J. Tobin, editorial, *Minnesota Teamster*, May 1941, attachment to May 13, 1941, letter from James Cannon to locals and branches, Circular Letters, 1940–1944 (microfilm: reel 27), SWP Records, WHS.

70 James Cannon to All Locals and Branches, May 13, 1941, Circular Letters, 1940–1944 (microfilm: reel 27), SWP Records, WHS.

71 On May 13, 1941, for example, Hoover sent Berge extensive FBI reports detailing the activities of the UDG from 1940, f. 2, box 108, SWP 146-1-10. And on May 24, 1941, the FBI sent Anderson a lengthy report by Agent Noonan on the ties between the SWP and Local 544, f. 2, box 108, SWP 146-1-10.

72 David Kennedy, *Freedom from Fear: The American People in Depression and War, 1929–1945* (New York: Oxford University Press, 1999), 474.

73 Doris Kearns Goodwin, *No Ordinary Time: Franklin and Eleanor Roosevelt: The Home Front in World War II* (New York: Simon and Schuster, 1994), 238–239.

74 Andrew E. Kersten, *Labor's Home Front: The American Federation of Labor during World War II* (New York: NYU Press, 2006), 27.

75 Statement by the Executive Council of the American Federation of Labor, May 28, 1941, f. 1941 April–June, box 14, series IIIA, IBT, WHS.

76 Dobbs, *Teamster Bureaucracy*, 158; Daniel Tobin to Franklin Delano Roosevelt, June 5, 1941, PPF 6851, Franklin D. Roosevelt Papers, FDRPL.

77 Dobbs, *Teamster Bureaucracy*, 144; *Northwest Organizer*, May 29, 1941, 1, 4.

78 *Minneapolis Star Journal*, June 4, 1941, n.p.

79 *Northwest Organizer*, June 12, 1941, 4; Dobbs, *Teamster Bureaucracy*, 154–155.

80 Memo from J. Edgar Hoover to Attorney General Francis Biddle, forwarded to Assistant Attorney General Matthew McGuire, June 9, 1941, f. 2, box 108, SWP 146-1-10.

81 Witwer, *Corruption and Reform*, 115.

82 FBI report 100-1200, Indianapolis, 11/7/41, by Bliss Morton, f. 5, box 108, SWP 146-1-10; *Northwest Organizer*, June 12, 1941, 4.

83 Russell, *Out of the Jungle*, 62–72; Dobbs, *Teamster Bureaucracy*, 157–158; Kersten, *Labor's Home Front*, 20–22.

84 Dobbs, *Teamster Bureaucracy*, 160.

85 *Minneapolis Star Journal*, June 10, 1941, 1.

86 Farrell Dobbs, notes for "Speech to 544 Membership," June 9, 1941, f. 3, 1941, box 8, Speeches and Writings, Farrell Dobbs Papers, WHS.

87 Dobbs, *Teamster Bureaucracy*, 160; *Minneapolis Star Journal*, June 10, 1941, 4; *Minneapolis Morning Tribune*, June 10, 1941, 5.

88 *Minneapolis Star Journal*, June 10, 1941, 4.

89 *Northwest Organizer*, June 19, 1941, 1; *Minneapolis Star Journal*, June 10, 1941, 4; telegram from Geary to Tobin, June 10, 1941, f. Local 544, Minneapolis, Minn., 1939–1941, box 44, series II, IBT, WHS; *Minneapolis Star Journal*, June 10, 1941, 4.

90 *Minneapolis Star Journal*, June 10, 1941, 4; June 11, 1941, 1.

91 Copeland, *Daniel J. Tobin*, 110–114.

92 Blair, "Storm over the Union," 63, 78–80.

93 If the conversation between Green and FDR took place that week, it may have been by phone. There is no correspondence from Green to the president on this matter, and there is no record of a meeting. See f. "William Green," box 5, President's Alphabetical File, Franklin D. Roosevelt, Papers as President, FDRPL; and entries for June 9–13, 1941, in the Stenographer's Diary and Usher's Log, http://www.fdrlibrary.marist.edu/daybyday/search/?str=&start_date=1941-06-09&end_date=1941-06-13&type=daylog&search_submit=&submitted=t (accessed June 14, 2013).

94 Blair, "Storm over the Union," 63, 78–80.

95 Tobin, "Memoir," 340; Copeland, *Daniel J. Tobin*, 81–114.

96 This would have been after Tobin demanded that Local 544 accept the receivership on June 3, but before he heard its refusal on June 7. Entry for 11:45 a.m., June 5, 1941, Stenographer's Diary, and entry for 11:45 a.m. June 5, 1941, Usher's Log, http://www.fdrlibrary.marist.edu/daybyday/daylog/june-5th-1941/ (accessed June 14, 2013).

97 Witwer, *Corruption and Reform*, 137; Dobbs, *Teamster Bureaucracy*, 77; Dobbs, *Teamster Politics*, 32.

98 Tobin to Early, June 12, 1941, f. OF 2798, box OF Collection, FDRPL.

99 Albert Goldman, *The Truth about the Minneapolis Trial of the 28: Speech for the Defense by Albert Goldman* (New York: Pioneer Publishers, 1942), 6; George Novack, *Witch Hunt in Minnesota: The Federal Prosecution of the Socialist Workers Party and Local 544-CIO* (New York: Civil Rights Defense Committee, 1941), 7–13, 18; *Militant*, June 21, 1941, 6.

100 For scholarly accounts, see James and James, "The Purge of the Trotskyites from the Teamsters," 6; Belknap, *Cold War Political Justice*, 38–39; Leo P. Ribuffo, "*United States v. McWilliams*: The Roosevelt Administration and the Far Right," in *American Political Trials*, revised and expanded edition, ed. Michael R. Belknap (Westport, CT: Praeger, 1994), 179; and Allen, "Free Speech in the Shadow of War." Allen acknowledges the deeper infiltration of the FBI in Local 544 as early as 1940 but also argues that Tobin's telegram was the "immediate spark for the prosecution." For accounts that shaped the popular memory of the "political debt" theory in the party, see Civil Rights Defense Committee, *Who Are the 18 Prisoners in the Minneapolis Labor Case?*, 5–6; Dobbs, *Teamster Bureaucracy*, 185.

101 Wendell Berge to Victor Anderson, April 29, 1941, f. 1, box 108, SWP 146-1-10.

102 Memo from J. Edgar Hoover to Edwin M. Watson, June 9, 1941, OF 10, box 14 #809, FDRPL. Richard W. Steele discusses the implications of this memo for undermining the "political debt" theory. See Steele, *Free Speech in the Good War*, 132.

103 Because the pages in Tobin's unpublished memoir that correspond to the timing of these events are missing, it is difficult to substantiate his motives. Donated to the Wisconsin Historical Society in 2005, Tobin's unpublished memoir is missing pages 149–200 and 404–429. Vincent Tobin, Daniel's grandson and donor of the memoirs, explains that the pages were missing when he found the memoir in his father's house. For a fuller discussion of how Tobin's telegram may have provided political cover for the Roosevelt administration, see Donna T. Haverty-Stacke, "'Punishment of Mere Political Advocacy': The FBI, Teamsters Local 544, and the Origins of the 1941 Smith Act Case," *Journal of American History* 100, no. 1 (2013): 87.

104 Telegram from Victor Anderson to Wendell Berge, June 12, 1941, f. 2, box 108, SWP 146-1-10.

105 Hoover to SG and McGuire, June 19, 1941, f. 2, box 108, SWP 146-1-10; Hoover to Edwin Watson, June 19, 1941, OF 10b, box 14, #834, FDRPL.

106 AG to Stassen, June 19, 1941, f. 2, box 108, SWP 146-1-10.

107 Ibid.

108 Francis Biddle, *In Brief Authority* (Garden City, NY: Doubleday, 1962), 151.

109 The library's supervisory archivist confirmed that everything currently in the collection was all that it had received with the bequest from Mrs. Biddle's estate in 1981.

110 J. Edgar Hoover to Matthew McGuire, June 25, 1941, f. 2, box 108, SWP 146-1-10.

111 Wendell Berge to Henry Schweinhaut, June 25, 1941, f. 2, box 108, SWP 146-1-10.

112 J. Edgar Hoover to Matthew McGuire, June 25, 1941, f. 2, box 108, SWP 146-1-10. For Hoover's general caution in launching investigations of radicals without political cover, see Powers, *Secrecy and Power*, 159–169.

113 Telegram from David Beck to Joseph Casey, June 13, 1941, f. Casey, Joseph M. 1941, box 12, IBT, WHS.

114 *Minneapolis Star Journal*, June 13, 1941, 1, 12. On Padway's defense of the AFL's affiliates against CIO encroachment, see Kersten, *Labor's Home Front*, 42–49.

115 Local 221 had about 300 members, and Local 778 about 100. See *Minneapolis Star Journal*, June 14, 1941, 1; June 16, 1941, 1, 4; *Militant*, June 21, 1941, 1.

116 *Minneapolis Star Journal*, June 14, 1941, n.p.

117 *Minneapolis Star Journal*, June 16, 1941, 4.

118 Ibid., 3.

119 *Minneapolis Star Journal*, June 18, 1941, 4.

120 *Northwest Organizer*, June 19, 1941, 3.

121 *Minneapolis Star Journal*, June 19, 1941, 4.

122 Telegram from Joseph Casey to Daniel Tobin, June 19, 1941, f. Casey, Joseph M. 1941, box 12, series I, IBT, WHS.

123 *Minneapolis Star Journal*, June 17, 1941, 1, 4; *Minneapolis Star Journal*, June 14, 1941, 1.

124 *Minneapolis Morning Tribune*, June 20, 1941, 6.

125 Ibid.

126 Dobbs, *Teamster Bureaucracy*, 181.

127 *Minneapolis Morning Tribune*, June 20, 1941, 6; Dobbs, *Teamster Bureaucracy*, 182.

128 *Washington Post*, June 16, 1941, 4.

129 *Minneapolis Star Journal*, June 18, 1941, 1.

130 *Minneapolis Star Journal*, June 19, 1941, 1.

131 *Minneapolis Star Journal*, June 21, 1941, 1.

132 Ibid.

133 Blair, "Storm over the Union," 258–262. During the Blair hearing, dozens of CIO witnesses testified to being subjected to intimidation by AFL "organizers": see Blair, "Storm over the Union," 209–301.

134 *Minneapolis Star Journal*, June 24, 1941, 4.

135 *Northwest Organizer*, June 28, 1941, 2.

136 *Northwest Organizer*, June 26, 1941, 1, 3.

137 Daniel Tobin to Joseph Casey, June 23, 1941, f. Casey, 1941, box 12, series I, IBT, WHS.

138 Notes from telephone conversation of Joe Casey, June 24, 1941, f. Casey 1941, box 12, series I, IBT, WHS.

139 *Minneapolis Star Journal*, June 25, 1941, n.p.; Minneapolis Central Labor Union resolution, June 26, 1941, f. 1941 April–June, box 14, series III A, IBT, WHS; *Minneapolis Star Journal*, June 26, 1941, 2.

140 Dobbs, *Teamster Bureaucracy*, 206.

141 *Minneapolis Morning Tribune*, June 28, 1941, 1, 13.

142 Ibid., 1.

143 *Northwest Organizer*, July 3, 1941, 4.

144 Ibid.

145 James Cannon to All Locals and Branches, June 28, 1941, Circular Letters, 1940–1944 (microfilm: reel 27), SWP Records, WHS.

146 Telegram from James Cannon and Albert Goldman to Francis Biddle, June 30, 1941, f. 2, box 108, SWP 146-1-10.

147 Ibid.

148 *Minneapolis Morning Tribune*, July 2, 1941, 1, 7; *Minneapolis Star Journal*, July 1, 1941, 1; Dobbs, *Teamster Bureaucracy*, 191.

149 Telegram from John Haynes Holmes to Francis Biddle, June 30, 1941, f. 3, box 108, SWP 146-1-10.

150 Frances Biddle to John Haynes Holmes, July 10, 1941, f. 3, box 108, SWP 146-1-10.

151 On Biddle's hesitancy to indict the seditionists, see Patrick S. Washburn, "FDR versus His Own Attorney General: The Struggle over Sedition, 1941–42," *Journalism Quarterly* 62, no. 4 (1985): 717–724.

152 Edward F. Prichard to Francis Biddle, July 14, 1941, f. 3, box 108, SWP 146-1-10. On the clear and present danger test, see Polenberg, *Fighting Faiths*, 212–224, 236–242; Steele, *Free Speech in the Good War*, 135.

CHAPTER 3. "SOCIALISM ON TRIAL"

1 Hand quoted in Schrecker, "Political Repression and the Rule of Law."

2 FBI report 100-1246, St. Paul, 7/26/41, by R. T. Noonan, f. 3, box 108, SWP 146-1-10.

3 See summary of interviews with Harriet Karlin, Robert Willis, Stephen Nehotee, Emmanuel "Happy" Holstein, Donald Palm, Harry Penas, Price Amo, George Palmquist, and Hilma Palmquist in FBI report 100-1246, St. Paul, 7/26/41, by R. T. Noonan, f. 3, box 108, SWP 146-1-10.

4 See summary of interviews with Peter Bove and Franklin Page in FBI report 100-1246, St. Paul, 7/26/41, by R. T. Noonan, f. 3, box 108, SWP 146-1-10. For the accusations of revolutionary speech, see interview summaries of Ed Blixt and Jack Grant.

5 Summary of interviews with Jack Novack, Ed Blixt, Price Amo, J. J. Kenny, Emmanuel Holstein, and Chris Moe in FBI report 100-1246, St. Paul, 7/26/41, by R. T. Noonan, f. 3, box 108, SWP 146-1-10.

6 Summary of interviews with James Morris and Anthony Seinco in FBI report 100-1246, St. Paul, 7/26/41, by R. T. Noonan, f. 3, box 108, SWP 146-1-10.

7 Summary of interviews with Louis White, Louis Fondow, and George Viens in FBI report 100-1246, St. Paul, 7/26/41, by R. T. Noonan, f. 3, box 108, SWP 146-1-10.

8 See Noonan's notations regarding those who did not testify before the grand jury on pages 13–14 and 22 in FBI report 100-1246, St. Paul, 7/26/41, by R. T. Noonan, f. 3, box 108, SWP 146-1-10.

9 See Noonan's notation on page 8 in FBI report 100-1246, St. Paul, 7/26/41, by R. T. Noonan, f. 3, box 108, SWP 146-1-10; *Minneapolis Daily Times*, July 15, 1941, 1; *Minneapolis Star Journal*, July 15, 1941, 1.

10 FBI report 100-1246, St. Paul, 7/26/41, by R. T. Noonan, page 8, f. 3, box 108, SWP 146-1-10.

11 *U.S. vs. Dunne, et al.*, 5–10. Schweinhaut, former head of the Justice Department's Civil Liberties Unit, had originally asked Berge for the "authority to proceed under

Section 6 of Title 18, instead of under [the] Smith Act," betraying qualms about applying the peacetime sedition law. Berge deferred to his and Anderson's judgment. Possibly swayed by Anderson, Schweinhaut ultimately supported the two-count indictment. See entry for June 25, 1941, Daily Calendars, box 2, and Wendell Berge to Henry Schweinhaut, June 25, 1941, General Correspondence, box 24, Wendell Berge Papers, Manuscript Division, Library of Congress, Washington, DC; and FBI report 100-1246, St. Paul, 7/26/41 by R. T. Noonan, f. 3, box 108, SWP 146-1-10.

12 *U.S. vs. Dunne, et al.*, 10–12.

13 Raasch-Gilman, "Sisterhood in the Revolution," 365.

14 Bail reduction motion, July 19, 1941, f. 7, #7256 US v. Dunne, box 192, Affidavits, Minnesota, Fourth Division, Minneapolis, 1890–1983, RG 21 KC.

15 Dobbs, *Teamster Bureaucracy*, 197–198.

16 Bail reduction motion, July 19, 1941, f. 7, #7256 US v. Dunne, box 192, Affidavits, Minnesota, Fourth Division, Minneapolis, 1890–1983, RG 21 KC; *Minneapolis Star Journal*, July 16, 1941, 1; July 17, 1941, 15; July 21, 1941, 1; July 22, 1941, 1; *Minneapolis Morning Tribune*, July 16, 1941, 1; July 21, 1941, 5; July 22, 1941, 1, 5.

17 *Minneapolis Star Journal*, July 16, 1941, 4; July 22, 1941, 1. See also Albert Goldman's statement in the *Militant*, August 9, 1941, 6; July 19, 1941, 1; July 26, 1941, 1; July 26, 1941, 6; "The FBI-Gestapo Attack on the Socialist Workers Party," *Fourth International* 2, no. 6 (1941): 163–166; *Minneapolis Star Journal*, July 10, 1941, 1; *Industrial Organizer*, July 24, 1941, 1, 2.

18 Bryan Palmer, *Revolutionary Teamsters: The Minneapolis Truckers' Strikes of 1934* (Chicago: Haymarket, 2014), 245. *Minneapolis Morning Tribune*, July 3, 1941, 1.

19 *Minneapolis Morning Tribune*, July 3, 1941, 1; July 10, 1; July 11, 1941, 9; *Minneapolis Star Journal*, July 1, 1941, 1; July 2, 1941, 13; July 7, 1941, 2; July 8, 1941, 1; July 9, 1941, 20.

20 *Minneapolis Star Journal*, July 22, 1941, 12; July 23, 1941, 1.

21 *Militant*, July 19, 1941, 1, 3; July 26, 1941, 1, 5; *Industrial Organizer*, July 17, 1941; 4; July 24, 1941, 1, 2.

22 See Grace Carlson to Natalia Trotsky, August 18, 1941, f. SWP Correspondence 1, 1939–1942, box 1, Grace Carlson Papers, MHS.

23 Milton Howard, "The Prosecution of the Minneapolis Trotskyites," *Daily Worker*, August 16, 1941, 5.

24 *Industrial Organizer*, October 23, 1941, 2.

25 *Minneapolis Morning Tribune*, July 25, 1941, 20; *Militant*, August 2, 1941, 1.

26 *Minneapolis Star Journal*, July 17, 1941, 15.

27 "Civil Liberties in Minneapolis," *New Republic*, July 28, 1941, 103–104.

28 I. F. Stone, "The G-String Conspiracy," *Nation*, July 26, 1941, 66–67. In Local 544, a union of more than 5,000 members, only about 40 belonged to the SWP, and in a country of 132,122,446 citizens, only about 3,000 people belonged the party. Historical National Population Estimates: July 1, 1900, to July 1, 1999, Population Estimates Program, Population Division, U.S. Census Bureau Internet Release Date: April 11, 2000, revised date June 28, 2000, http://www.census.gov/popest/data/national/totals/pre-1980/tables/popclockest.txt (accessed April 1, 2015).

29 Albert Hamilton to Francis Biddle, July 16, 1941, f. 3, box 108, SWP 146-1-10.

30 Bruce Bliven to Francis Biddle, July 23, 1941, f. 3, box 108, SWP 146-1-10.

31 Francis Biddle to Bruce Bliven, July 30, 1941, f. 3, box 108, SWP 146-1-10.

32 Steele, *Free Speech in the Good War*, 115–128, 137–141.

33 Henry Schweinhaut to Ira Latimer, July 14, 1941, f. 3, box 108, SWP 146-1-10.

34 *Minneapolis Daily Times*, July 16, 1941, 1

35 Steele, *Free Speech in the Good War*, 23; Stone, *Perilous Times*, 239, 279.

36 Concern about the content of FBI reports can be seen in the synopsis Schweinhaut penned for Berge and Biddle that contained details of the defendants' alleged use of revolutionary speech, stockpiling of weapons, and plans to cause disruption in the armed services. Biddle underlined the most shocking passages in red. Wendell Berge to Francis Biddle, August 18, 1941, f. 4, box 108, SWP 146-1-10.

37 Biddle, *In Brief Authority*, 151. On Schweinhaut's eagerness to pursue the case, see Henry Schweinhaut to Wendell Berge, July 5, 1941, and memo from Matthew McGuire to J. Edgar Hoover, June 30, 1941, f. 3, box 108, SWP 146-1-10.

38 John Haynes Holmes, Arthur Garfield Hays, and Roger Baldwin to Francis Biddle, August 20, 1941, f. 4, box 108, SWP 146-1-10.

39 Wendell Berge to Victor Anderson, September 8, 1941, f. 5, box 108, SWP 146-1-10.

40 Victor Anderson to Wendell Berge, September 26, 1941, f. 5, box 108, SWP 146-1-10.

41 Wendell Berge to Victor Anderson, October 9, 1941, f. 5, box 108, SWP 146-1-10.

42 Reuben Oppenheimer, "The Constitutional Rights of Aliens," *Bill of Rights Review: A Quarterly* 2, no. 1 (1941): 100–111; Grenville Clark, "Civil Rights in Times of Crisis," *Bill of Rights Review: A Quarterly* 1, no. 3 (1941): 177–180; G. Gordon Post, "The Subversive Party," *Bill of Rights Review: A Quarterly* 2, no. 1 (1941): 23–30; John Mulder, "Changing Concepts of Civil Liberties," *Bill of Rights Review: A Quarterly* 1, no. 2 (1941): 95–97.

43 Francis Biddle, "Civil Rights in Times of Stress," *Bill of Rights Review: A Quarterly* 2, no. 1 (1941): 14–15, 20.

44 James Cannon to All Locals and Branches, July 29, 1941, re. "Civil Rights Defense Committee" (microfilm: reel 27), SWP Records, WHS.

45 Dick Gregg to Francis Biddle, September 18, 1941, f. 5, box 108, SWP 146-1-10. See also letters from Anne Paulson to Francis Biddle, October 8, 1941; J. George Butler to Francis Biddle, October 16, 1941; telegram from Albert Fowler to Biddle, October 21, 1941; Frank W. McCulloch to Biddle, October 21, 1941; Carl Raushenbush to Biddle, October 24, 1941; James Loeb to Biddle, November 12. 1941; Helen McMillian Meyers to Biddle, November 14, 1941; and Albert Fowler to Francis Biddle, October 4, 1941, f. 5, box 108, SWP 146-1-10.

46 Biddle, *In Brief Authority*, 110–116, 150–152.

47 Victor Anderson to Wendell Berge, August 11, 1941, f. 4, box 108, SWP 146-1-10.

48 *Industrial Organizer*, August 14, 1941, 4; *Militant*, August 16, 1941, 1.

49 James Cannon, "Why the Trotskyists Have Been Indicted," *Militant*, August 30, 1941, 3, 5.

50 *U.S. vs. Dunne, et al.*, 13–57; Victor Anderson to Wendell Berge, September 26, 1941, f. 5, box 108, SWP 146-1-10.

51 *Industrial Organizer*, September 18, 1941, 3; *Minneapolis Star Journal*, September 26, 1941, n.p.; *Militant*, October 4, 1941, 2; October 11, 1941, 3.

52 James Cannon to All Locals and Branches, September 27, 1941 (microfilm: reel 27), SWP Records, WHS; James Cannon to All Branches and Locals, September 30, 1941 (microfilm: reel 27), SWP Records, WHS.

53 "Certification of Bargaining Agent," September 18, 1941, f. Local 544, Minneapolis, Minn., 1939–1941, box 44, series II, IBT, WHS; *Minneapolis Star Journal*, September 19, 1941, 1; *Industrial Organizer*, September 25, 1941, pp. 1, 2; *Militant*, September 27, 1941, 1, 2.

54 I. E. Goldberg to J. A. (Padway), September 16, 1941, p. 2, Affiliated Bodies Series, Local Unions, #544, Minneapolis, Minn., 1939–1941, International Brotherhood of Teamsters Records: digital edition produced from microfilm, 1904–1952, George Washington University Library, Washington, DC. On the padding of the numbers, see D. J. Shama's cross-examination of Helen Hanifan Blair in Blair, "Storm over the Union," 167–174.

55 Blair, "Storm over the Union," 209–301, 425–451.

56 *Militant*, September 27, 2, 6. By September 1941, the AFL's lawyers claimed that Local 544-AFL could demonstrate that it had 4,215 drivers in its jurisdiction. See I. E. Goldberg to J. A. Padway, September 16, 1941, f. Local 544, Minneapolis, Minn., 1939–1941, box 44, series II, IBT, WHS.

57 *Militant*, October 11, 1941, 1, 4.

58 *Minneapolis Sunday Tribune*, October 5, 1941, 1.

59 *Militant*, October 11, 1941, 1, 4.

60 *Industrial Organizer*, October 9, 1941, 1.

61 Ibid. William Dunne (who had become a committed Communist) is not mentioned as having been at the funeral.

62 Farrell Dobbs, notes on "Funeral Address—for Grant John Dunne" October 7, 1941, Minneapolis, Minnesota, f. 3, 1941, box 8, Speeches and Writings, Farrell Dobbs Papers, WHS.

63 Ibid.

64 James Cannon, Speech at Chicago Mass Meeting, October 10, 1941, f. 8, box 30, Speeches and Writings, JPC, WHS. The FBI, which was conducting surveillance on the SWP's plenum, reported on Cannon's statements to the attorney general. See memo from Hoover to AG re. SWP Overthrow of Government, October 14, 1941, f. 5, box 108, SWP 146-1-10.

65 *Militant*, November 15, 1941, 3–4.

66 *Militant*, November 1, 1941, 1, 4.

67 Grace Carlson to Natalia Sedova, October 20, 1941, f. SWP Correspondence 1, 1939–1942, box 1, Grace Carlson Papers, MHS.

68 Novack, *Witch Hunt in Minnesota*.

69 American Civil Liberties Union, *Sedition! The First Federal Peacetime Prosecution for Utterances and Publications since the Alien and Sedition Act of 1798* (New York: ACLU, 1941).

70 *Militant*, November 1, 1941, 1–2; *Industrial Organizer*, November 1, 1941, 4.

71 Court proceedings, pp. 2–3, f. 4, #7256 US v. Dunne, box 192, Testimony Taken, RG 21 KC.

72 *Militant*, November 1, 1941, 2; *Industrial Organizer*, November 1, 1941, 1; *Minneapolis Star Journal*, October 28, 1941, 4.

73 *Industrial Organizer*, November 1, 1941, 1. Biddle rejected Hoover's suggestion (prompted by Schweinhaut) to investigate the prospective jurors. Memo from Hoover to Biddle, October 15, 1941, f. 5, box 108, SWP 146-1-10.

74 Victor Anderson's opening statement to the jury, October 28, 1941, pp. 9–16, f. 4, #7256 US v. Dunne, box 192, Testimony Taken, RG 21 KC.

75 Ibid., 18–20.

76 Ibid., 20–25.

77 Ibid., 34.

78 Ibid., 43.

79 Ibid., 44, 45.

80 Ibid., 53.

81 Albert Goldman's opening statement to the jury, October 28, 1941, pp. 54–55, f. 4, #7256 US v. Dunne, box 192, Testimony Taken, RG 21 KC.

82 Ibid., 55–57.

83 Ibid., 58–60.

84 Ibid., 60–61.

85 Ibid., 62–65.

86 Ibid., 66–69.

87 Albert Goldman's opening statement to the jury, October 29, 1941, pp. 73–77, f. 4, #7256 US v. Dunne, box 192, Testimony Taken, RG 21 KC.

88 Ibid., 78–85.

89 Ibid., 85.

90 *U.S. vs. Dunne, et al.*, 61, 193.

91 Testimony of James Bartlett, *U.S. vs. Dunne, et al.*, 194–209.

92 Ibid., 216–227.

93 Ibid., 240–242.

94 Testimony of Thomas Perrin, *U.S. vs. Dunne, et al.*, 224–227.

95 Goldman's cross-examination of Agents Perrin and Noonan, *U.S. vs. Dunne, et al.*, 246–248.

96 Testimony of James Bartlett, *U.S. vs. Dunne, et al.*, 255–258.

97 Ibid., 268–273.

98 Ibid., 261–267, 275.

99 Ibid., 283–289.

100 Ibid., 287–288.

101 Testimony of Thomas Smith and Malcolm Love, *U.S. vs. Dunne, et al.*, 334–342.

102 Testimony of James Bartlett and discussion of counsel, *U.S. vs. Dunne, et al.*, 348–351.

103 Testimony of James Bartlett, *U.S. vs. Dunne, et al.*, 363–377.

104 Ibid., 377.

105 Goldman's cross-examination of Bartlett, *U.S. vs. Dunne, et al.*, 380.

106 Testimony of James Bartlett, *U.S. vs. Dunne, et al.*, 429.

107 Goldman's cross-examination of Bartlett, *U.S. vs. Dunne, et al.*, 380–414.

108 Ibid., 394–395.

109 Testimony of James Bartlett, *U.S. vs. Dunne, et al.*, 431.

110 Ibid., 443–448.

111 Ibid., 472.

112 Testimony of Roy Noonan and Goldman's cross-examination of Noonan, *U.S. vs. Dunne, et al.*, 473–474.

113 Testimony of Walter Stultz, *U.S. vs. Dunne, et al.*, 474–483.

114 Testimony of Franklin Page, *U.S. vs. Dunne, et al.*, 488.

115 Testimony of Roy Wieneke, *U.S. vs. Dunne, et al.*, 491.

116 Ibid., 494.

117 Ibid., 490.

118 Ibid., 509, 513.

119 Testimony of John Novack, *U.S. vs. Dunne, et al.*, 514.

120 Ibid., 515.

121 Ibid., 516.

122 Ibid., 518–521.

123 Testimony of Elizabeth Humpfner, John Majersky, and Henry M. Harris, *U.S. vs. Dunne, et al.*, 522–537, 541–543.

124 Testimony of Henry M. Harris, *U.S. vs. Dunne, et al.*, 541–543.

125 See, for example, Goldman's cross-examination of Harris, *U.S. vs. Dunne, et al.*, 564–565.

126 *U.S. vs. Dunne, et al.*, 584–630, 653–688, 737–765, 784–792.

127 See, for example, Goldman's cross-examination of Harry Holstein, *U.S. vs. Dunne, et al.*, 666.

128 Testimony of Sidney Brennan, *U.S. vs. Dunne, et al.*, 684–685, 688.

129 Green, *Death in the Haymarket*, 213–230; Belknap, *Cold War Political Justice*, 82–83.

130 Anderson's presentation of exhibits, *U.S. vs. Dunne, et al.*, 636.

131 Ibid., 766, 778–780.

132 Ibid., 792–796, 799–800.

133 *U.S. v. Dunne, et al.*, 825–829.

134 M. J. Myer argues motion for defense, *U.S. vs. Dunne, et al.*, 830–831.

135 Ibid., 831–832.

136 Ibid., 832–834.

137 Ibid., 832–834, 836.

138 M. J. Myer argues motion for defense, *U.S. vs. Dunne, et al.*, 837; *Schenck v. U.S.*, 249 U.S. 47 (1919); *Whitney v. California*, 274 U.S. 357 (1927).

139 *U.S. vs. Dunne, et al.*, 835.

140 Schweinhaut's response to the defense motion, *U.S. vs. Dunne, et al.*, 839.

141 Ibid., 842.

142 Steele, *Free Speech in the Good War*, 135.

143 *U.S. vs. Dunne, et al.*, 842.

144 Ibid., 843.

145 Anderson's response to the defense motion, *U.S. vs. Dunne, et al.*, 845–846.

146 Ibid., 851.

147 Joyce's ruling on the defense motion, *U.S. vs. Dunne, et al.*, 854.

148 Ibid., 855.

149 FBI report on Joyce quoted in Alexander Charns, *Cloak and Gavel: FBI Wiretaps, Bugs, Informers, and the Supreme Court* (Urbana: University of Illinois Press, 1992), 15.

150 *U.S. vs. Dunne, et al.*, 855.

151 Ibid., 856–857.

152 *Militant*, November 22, 1941, 3.

CHAPTER 4. "IF THAT IS TREASON, YOU CAN MAKE THE MOST OF IT"

1 For the explanation of this argument, see the debate between defense attorney M. J. Myer and assistant to the U.S. attorney general, Henry Schweinhaut, during the trial discussed in chapter 3.

2 *U.S. vs. Dunne, et al.*, 32–36, 56.

3 Oliver Wendell Holmes's opinion in *Schenck v. U.S.*, 249 U.S. 47 (1919), and his dissent in *U.S. v. Schwimmer*, 279, U.S. 644 (1929).

4 Steele, *Free Speech in the Good War*, 135, 271n52.

5 Speech of James P. Cannon at New York Solidarity Banquet, October 3, 1941, and Speech of James P. Cannon at Chicago Mass Meeting, Friday, October 10, 1941, f. 8: Speech Notes and Manuscripts 1941, box 30, JPC, WHS; Grace Carlson to Natalia Sedova, October 20, 1941, f. SWP Correspondence 1, 1939–1942, box 1, Carlson Papers, MHS; "The Federal Prosecution and the Present Tasks of the Party," draft resolution, Minutes of the Plenum, 1941 (microfilm: reel 2), SWP Records, WHS.

6 See, for example, *Industrial Organizer*, October 16, 1941, 1–2; November 1, 1941, 4; November 8, 1941, 3; November 29, 1941, 4; *Militant*, November 22, 1941, 6; November 29, 1941, 1–2.

7 *Militant*, December 20, 1941, 3; Raasch-Gilman, "Sisterhood in the Revolution," 365; Dobbs, *Teamster Bureaucracy*, 282–283.

8 Testimony of James Cannon, *U.S. vs. Dunne, et al.*, 857–869, and quote on 868–869.

9 Ibid., 874–885.

10 Ibid., 890–893.

11 Ibid., 896, 899.

12 Melvyn Dubofsky and Foster Rhea Dulles, *Labor in America: A History* (Wheeling, IL: Harlan Davidson, 2004), 309. On popular hostility to the miners'

strike, see "NLRB Regional Director . . . Warns . . . 'Every Hour on the Picket Line Is Outright Gift to Hitler,'" *New York Times*, November 18, 1941, 30. On Japan, see *New York Times*, November 17, 1941, 1. On the German advance into Russia, see *New York Times*, November 18, 1941, 1.

13 Testimony of James Cannon, *U.S. vs. Dunne, et al.*, 907.

14 Ibid., 915–922.

15 Discussion with Lund (Trotsky), Confidential for N.C. Members and Alternates, June 12, 1940, p. 6, f.1 Trade Unions, box 14, Subject Files, Farrell Dobbs Papers, WHS.

16 *U.S. vs. Dunne, et al.*, 915–917, 971–975.

17 Discussion with Lund, Confidential for N.C. Members and Alternates, June 12, 1940, p. 6, f.1 Trade Unions, box 14, Subject Files, Dobbs Papers, WHS.

18 Lund (Leon Trotsky) to Al (Goldman), July 9, 1940; Albert Goldman to Lund (Leon Trotsky), July 6, 1940; and Political Committee for the Plenum Conference, SWP, Resolution on Proletarian Military Policy, Minutes of the Plenum, Chicago, September 1940 (microfilm: reel 1), SWP Records, WHS.

19 Testimony of James Cannon, *U.S. vs. Dunne, et al.*, 924–930.

20 Ibid., 930–931.

21 Ibid., 932–937.

22 Ibid., 947–950.

23 Lund to Goldman, July 9, 1940 (microfilm: reel 1), SWP Records, WHS.

24 Testimony of James Cannon, *U.S. vs. Dunne, et al.*, 967–969.

25 Ibid., 989.

26 Testimony of Kenneth McKenzie, Daniel Doyle, Ole Reirson, Harold Martin, Richard Atherton, and Gustave Reirson, *U.S. vs. Dunne, et al.*, 1004–1013.

27 Testimony of Vincent R. Dunne, *U.S. vs. Dunne, et al.*, 1016–1020.

28 Goldman's comments to Joyce, *U.S. vs. Dunne, et al.*, 1021–1022.

29 *U.S. vs. Dunne, et al.*, 1023.

30 Testimony of Vincent R. Dunne, *U.S. vs. Dunne, et al.*, 1026–1030.

31 Ibid., 1031–1033.

32 Ibid., 1033–1036.

33 Testimony of Roy Orgon, Ray Rainbolt, and Miles Dunne, *U.S. vs. Dunne, et al.*, 1098, 1100, 1106, 1108.

34 Interview with Grace Holmes Carlson by Carl Ross, 20th Century Radicalism in Minnesota Project, July 9, 1987, p. 35, MHS

35 On Cannon's failed run for the mayor of New York in 1941, see *Industrial Organizer*, November 8, 1941, 1; Testimony of Grace Carlson, *U.S. vs. Dunne, et al.*, 1110–1111.

36 Testimony of Grace Carlson, *U.S. vs. Dunne, et al.*, 1111.

37 Interview with Carlson by Ross, July 9, 1987, MHS.

38 Testimony of Grace Carlson, *U.S. vs. Dunne, et al.*, 1115.

39 Testimony of Farrell Dobbs, *U.S. vs. Dunne, et al.*, 1118–1119.

40 Ibid., 1123–1124.

41 Testimony of Vincent Dunne, *U.S. vs. Dunne, et al.*, 1024.

42 Testimony of Farrell Dobbs, *U.S. vs. Dunne, et al.*, 1121–1122, 1124.

43 Dobbs quoted in Jack Barnes, "Introduction" to Dobbs, *Teamster Rebellion*, 16–20.
44 *U.S. vs. Dunne, et al.*, 1128.
45 Anderson's closing argument, p. 2442, f. 7, #7256 US v. Dunne, box 194, RG 21 KC.
46 Ibid., 2447.
47 Ibid., 2451.
48 Ibid., 2451–2452.
49 Ibid., 2478.
50 Anderson's closing argument, p. 2536, f. 8, #7256 US v. Dunne, box 194, RG 21 KC.
51 Anderson's closing argument, pp. 2461, 2462, 2486, 2478, 2477, f. 7, #7256 US v. Dunne, box 194, RG 21 KC.
52 Anderson's closing argument, pp. 2499–2500, f. 8, #7256 US v. Dunne, box 194, RG 21 KC.
53 Ibid., 2518–2519.
54 Ibid., 2551.
55 Ibid., 2553.
56 Ibid., 2556–2557.
57 Ibid., 2557.
58 Ibid., 2559–2562.
59 See, for example, Francis Biddle, "Civil Rights in Times of Stress," *Bill of Rights Review: A Quarterly* 2, no. 1 (1941): 13–33; John E. Mulder, "Changing Concepts of Civil Liberties," *Bill of Rights Review: A Quarterly* 1, no. 2 (1941): 95–97; Grenville Clark, "Civil Rights in Times of Crisis," *Bill of Rights Review: A Quarterly* 1, no. 3 (1941): 177–180; and C. Gordon Post, *Bill of Rights Review: A Quarterly* 2, no. 1 (1941): 23–30.
60 Goldman's closing argument, pp. 2571–2572, f. 8, #7256 US v. Dunne, box 194, RG 21 KC.
61 Ibid., 2579.
62 Ibid., 2582–2592.
63 Ibid., 2596.
64 Goldman's closing argument, pp. 2598–2599, f. 8, #7256 US v. Dunne, box 194, RG 21 KC; Goldman's closing argument, pp. 2600–2610, f. 9 #7256 US v. Dunne, box 194, RG 21 KC.
65 Goldman's closing argument, pp. 2620–2652, f. 9, #7256 US v. Dunne, box 194, RG 21 KC.
66 Ibid., 2655–2661.
67 Ibid., 2672.
68 Ibid., 2673–2679.
69 Ibid., 2681, 2721–2722.
70 Ibid., 2680–2695, 2699–2700.
71 Goldman's closing argument, pp. 2699, f. 9, #7256 US v. Dunne, box 194, RG 21 KC; Goldman's closing argument, pp. 2749–2761, f. 1, #7256 US v. Dunne, box 194, RG 21 KC.
72 Goldman's closing argument, pp. 2749, 2772–2774, f. 1, #7256 US v. Dunne, box 194, RG 21 KC.

73 Ibid., 2775–2785.
74 Ibid., 2782.
75 Ibid., 2795–2796, 2801–2802.
76 Ibid., 2817.
77 Ibid., 2815.
78 Ibid., 2824.
79 Schweinhaut's closing argument, p. 3, f. 2, #7256 US v. Dunne, box 194, RG 21 KC.
80 Ibid., 3, 7, 16.
81 Ibid., 13.
82 Ibid., 17–19.
83 Ibid., 19.
84 Ibid., 23.
85 Judge Matthew Joyce's instructions to the jury, November 29, 1941, *U.S. vs. Dunne, et al.*, 1144–1162.
86 Ibid., 1163–1164.
87 Ibid., 1165–1169.
88 Motion for a new trial, f. 3, #7256 US v. Dunne, box 194, RG 21 KC.
89 *Minneapolis Morning Tribune*, December 2, 1941, n.p., clipping, Scrapbook Volume 3 July–December 1941, Sedition Trial, box 7, SWP MN Section Records, MHS.
90 *U.S. vs. Dunne, et al.*, 72–80; *Minneapolis Star Journal*, December 2, 1941, 1, 8.
91 *Minneapolis Star Journal*, December 2, 1941, 8.
92 Ibid., n.p.
93 *Militant*, December 6, 1941, 1, 2; *Minneapolis Morning Tribune*, December 8, 1941, n.p.; *New York Times*, December 2, 1941, 1.
94 *Industrial Organizer*, December 6, 1941, 1.
95 Farrell Dobbs, interviews from Chicago, "Lecture 4: 1941 Fight, the Indictment, the War Years (Part 1)," Holt Labor Library Collection, http://www.marxists.org/history/etol/audio/ (accessed December 13, 2011).
96 Ibid.
97 Henry Schweinhaut to the Solicitor General, August 1, 1944, f. 14, box 109, SWP 146-1-10.
98 Judge Joyce's sentencing, pp. 9–10, f. 3, #7256 US v. Dunne, box 194, RG 21 KC; Grace Carlson, Notes on the Trial, f. SWP, 1941 Treason Trial, box 2, Grace Carlson Papers, MHS.
99 Judge Joyce's sentencing, pp. 11–16, f. 3, #7256 US v. Dunne, box 194, RG 21 KC.
100 C. Charles, telegram, December 8, 1941 (microfilm: reel 27), SWP Records, WHS.

CHAPTER 5. BATTLING THE "GAG" ACT IN WARTIME

1 George Novack interview with Constance Myers, July 20, 1972, 1–26 (microfilm: reel 1), Biographical Material, George Novack Papers (1905–1992), WHS.
2 Ibid., 4–14.
3 Ibid.

4 Ibid., 4.

5 Ibid.

6 Albert Hamilton to Francis Biddle, July 16, 1941, f. 3, box 108, and Bruce Bliven to Francis Biddle, July 23, 1941, f. 3, box 108, SWP 146-1-10.

7 James T. Farrell, "Why This Case Is So Important," foreword to George Novack, *Witch Hunt in Minnesota: The Federal Prosecution of the Socialist Workers Party and Local 544-CIO* (New York: CRDC, 1941), 3–4.

8 Novack, *Witch Hunt in Minnesota*, 20.

9 *Militant*, December 20, 1941, 1–2.

10 Ibid.

11 Ibid., p. 2.

12 George Novack, *The Bill of Rights in Danger! The Meaning of the Minneapolis Convictions* (New York: CRDC, 1941).

13 Civil Rights Defense Committee, Statement of Receipts and Disbursements, July 18, 1941, to May 31, 1944, attached to Louis Lapides to CRDC, July 3, 1944, f. Financial Statements, box 2, Civil Rights Defense Committee Records, WHS.

14 See reprints of the *Industrial Worker*, the *New Leader*, and the *Call* in *Industrial Organizer*, December 13, 1941, 2.

15 "Opinion and Sedition," *New Republic*, December 8, 1941, 748.

16 "The Issue at Minneapolis," *Nation*, December 13, 1941, 602.

17 *Militant*, January 31, 1942, 3; *Daily Worker*, December 19, 1941, 5.

18 A. Clayton Powell Jr. to George Novack, January 21, 1942, f. SWP, Minneapolis, Minn. Papers, Civil Rights Defense Committee Correspondence and Misc. Papers, 1941–1944, box 1, SWP MN Section Papers, MHS.

19 Farrell Dobbs to Locals and Branches, March 6, 1942 and National Office Information Letter, August 11, 1942 (microfilm: reel 27), SWP Records, WHS.

20 FBI report 100-3476, LA, 12/31/41, and FBI report 100-442, Boston 1/9/42, f. 6a, box 108; FBI report 100-3864, Seattle, 8/27/42, and FBI report 100-4013, New York, 12/4/42, f. 7, box 108; FBI report 100-1334, Detroit, 1/19/43, f. 8, box 108; FBI report 100-2036, Philadelphia, 2/12/43, f. 9, box 108, SWP 146-1-10.

21 *Militant*, February 7, 1942, 3; February 14, 1942, 2.

22 *Militant*, March 21, 1942, 2; March 28, 1942, 1.

23 Vincent Dunne to Farrell Dobbs, April 4, 1942, Letters, Vincent Raymond Dunne Papers, WHS.

24 *Militant*, May 2, 1942, 2.

25 See, for example, his tour in Seattle: *Militant*, May 30, 1942, 2; Vincent Dunne to Farrell Dobbs, April 29, 1942, Letters, Dunne Papers, WHS.

26 James Cannon to All Branches, December 8, 1941, telegram, (microfilm: reel 27), SWP Records, WHS.

27 Grace Carlson to Natalia Sedova, October 20, 1941, f. SWP Correspondence 1, 1939–1942, box 1, Carlson Papers, MHS.

28 Natalia (Sedova) to Grace (Carlson), January 6, 1942, f. SWP Correspondence 1, 1939–1942, box 1, Carlson Papers, MHS.

29 *Militant*, January 31, 1942, 3.

30 Grandizo Munis, "A Criticism of the Minneapolis Trial," p. 1, January 7, 1942, f. 3, box 18, Correspondence Secretariat, JPC, WHS.

31 Martin (James Cannon) to Barr (Farrell Dobbs), February 12, 1942 (microfilm: reel 2), SWP Records, WHS.

32 James Cannon to Nancy (Natalia Sedova), February 14, 1942, f. 5, box 5, Correspondence, JPC, WHS. Carlson penned a similar response. See Grace Carlson to Natalia Sedova, February 17, 1942, f. SWP Correspondence, 1939–1942, box 1, Carlson Papers, MHS.

33 Martin (James Cannon) to Franklin (Albert Goldman), February 16, 1942 (microfilm: reel 2), SWP Records, WHS.

34 James Cannon, "Political Principles and Propaganda Methods," in *Defense Policy in the Minneapolis Trial* (New York: Pioneer Publishers, 1942), 16–17.

35 Ibid., 18–21 (emphases in original).

36 Ibid., 26–27.

37 *Militant*, October 3, 1942, 3.

38 *Militant*, February 21, 1942, 1.

39 *Militant*, October 3, 1942, 4.

40 *Militant*, April 24, 1943, 1–2.

41 *Militant*, May 22, 1943, 2; Rodney (Vincent Dunne) to Jim (Cannon), November 19, 1942 (microfilm: reel 15), and "Minnesota Vote," Minutes of the Club Executive No. 5, November 25, 1942 (microfilm: reel 2), SWP Records, WHS.

42 James Cannon to Farrell Dobbs, April 21, 1943, f. 2, box 5, Correspondence, Farrell Dobbs Papers, WHS; James Cannon to Locals and Branches, May 13, 1943 (microfilm: reel 27), SWP Records, WHS; *Militant*, May 22, 1943, 1.

43 *Militant*, August 7, 1943, 3.

44 Farrell Dobbs to Locals and Branches, November 23, 1942, December 8, 1942, and January 5, 1943 (microfilm: reel 27), SWP Records, WHS; FBI report 100-1334, Detroit, 1/19/43, f. 8, box 108, SWP 146-1-10.

45 *Militant*, January 3, 1942, 1.

46 *Militant*, March 7, 1942, 2; May 6, 1942, 3.

47 *Militant*, July 11, 1942, 2; *Industrial Organizer*, February 3, 1942, 2.

48 Jim (James Cannon) to George (Novack), February 13, 1942, f. 5, box 5, Correspondence, JPC, WHS; letter to Rodney (Vincent Dunne), February 10, 1942, Letters, Dunne Papers, WHS.

49 *Militant*, January 31, 1942, 1.

50 I. E. Goldberg to Joseph Padway, November 25, 1941, f. Local 544, Minneapolis, Minn., 1939–1941, box 44, series II, IBT Records, WHS.

51 Local #544-AFL to Thomas Flynn, January 15, 1942, f. Local 544, Minneapolis, Minn., 1942 January–September, box 44, series II, IBT, WHS; *Militant*, February 7, 1942, 3.

52 James Bartlett to Thomas Flynn, February 7, 1942, f. Local 544, Minneapolis, Minn., 1942 January–September, box 44, series II, IBT, WHS; Thomas Flynn to James Bartlett, February 16, 1942, f. Local 544, Minneapolis, Minn., 1942,

January–September, box 44, series II, IBT, WHS; James Bartlett to Thomas Flynn, February 24, 1942, f. Local 544, Minneapolis, Minn., 1942 January–September, box 44, series II, IBT, WHS.

53 James Bartlett to Thomas Flynn, May 2, 1942, f. Local 544, Minneapolis, Minn., 1942, January–September, box 44, series II, IBT, WHS.

54 Thomas Flynn to Sidney Brennan, May 19, 1942, f. Local 544, Minneapolis, Minn., 1942, January–September, box 44, series II, IBT, WHS.

55 *Militant*, February 28, 1942, 2; Goldberg to Padway, May 20, 1942 telegram, f. Local 544, Minneapolis, Minn., 1942, January–September, box 44, series II, IBT, WHS.

56 Goldberg to Padway, May 20, 1942 telegram, f. Local 544, Minneapolis, Minn., 1942, January–September, box 44, series II, IBT, WHS.

57 James Cannon to All Branches, June 24, 1942, "The Conviction of Kelly Postal," in James P. Cannon, *The Socialist Workers Party in World War II*, 3rd ed. (New York: Pathfinder, 2002), 254–255.

58 Dobbs, *Teamster Bureaucracy*, 346–351; Dobbs, interviews from Chicago, "Lecture 4 (Part 1)."

59 Dobbs, *Teamster Bureaucracy*, 345–346; *Militant*, March 28, 1942, 1; *Industrial Organizer*, May 16, 1942, 1.

60 *Militant*, August 9, 1941, 1; August 23, 1941, 1; Russell, *Out of the Jungle*, 83.

61 Stephen Nehotte to Thomas Flynn, October 15, 1942, f. Local 544, Minneapolis, Minn., 1942 October–1943 May, box 45, series II, IBT, WHS.

62 L. Claire Johnson, Joint Council 32, Jack J. Jorgensen, Local 359, Sid Brennan, Local 544, Joseph O'Hare, Local 289, and Harold Seavey, Joint Council 32, to Thomas Flynn, November 25, 1942, f. JC Minneapolis, 1941–1954, box 107, series II B, IBT, WHS.

63 Marvin L. Kline to Daniel Tobin, June 16, 1942, f. Local 544, Minneapolis, Minn., 1942, January–September, box 44, IBT, WHS; Thomas Flynn to John Gillespie, August 7, 1942, f. Local 544, Minneapolis, Minn., 1942, January–September, box 44, series II, IBT, WHS.

64 *Militant*, May 2, 1942, 4.

65 L. Clair Johnson to Thomas Flynn, May 8, 1942, f. Joint Council 32, box 107, series II B, IBT, WHS.

66 *Minnesota Teamster*, May 14, 1942, 1–2.

67 *Militant*, June 20, 1942, 2.

68 Stephen Nehotte to Thomas Flynn, October 15, 1942, f. Local 544, Minneapolis, Minn., 1942 October–1943 May, box 45, series II, IBT, WHS.

69 Sidney Brennan to Thomas Flynn, March 16, 1943; Thomas Flynn to Sidney Brennan, March 19, 1943; John Gillespie to Arnold Zander, April 5, 1943; Gordon Chapman to John Gillespie, April 8, 1943; Arnold Zander to John Gillespie, April 20, 1943; Thomas Flynn to Sidney Brennan, April 23, 1943, f. Local 544, Minneapolis, Minn., 1942 October–1943 May, box 45, series II, IBT, WHS.

70 Sidney Brennan to Thomas Flynn, March 16, 1943, f. Local 544, Minneapolis, Minn., 1942 October–1943 May, box 45, series II, IBT, WHS.

71 Grace Carlson to Natalia Sedova, January 29, 1942, f. SWP Correspondence 2, 1943, box 1, Carlson Papers, MHS.

72 Daniel Tobin to William Green, May 10, 1943, f. 1943 April–Dec. box 16, series III A, IBT, WHS; William Green to Daniel Tobin, May 17, 1943, f. 1947 April–Dec. box 16, series III A, IBT, WHS.

73 Sidney Brennan to Thomas Flynn, March 8, 1943, f. Local 544, Minneapolis, Minn., 1942 October–1943 May, box 45, series II, IBT, WHS.

74 Sidney Brennan to Thomas Flynn, April 2, 1943, f. 544, 1942 October–1943 May, box 45, series II, IBT, WHS.

75 Thomas Flynn acting for Daniel J. Tobin to Sidney Brennan, March 9, 1943, f. Local 544, Minneapolis, Minn., 1942 October–1943 May, box 45, series II, IBT, WHS.

76 See, for example, Sidney Brennan to Thomas Flynn, May 7, 1943, f. Local 544, Minneapolis, Minn., 1942 October–1943 May, box 45, series II, IBT, WHS.

77 Ibid.

78 Steele, *Free Speech in the Good War*, 60–61, 125.

79 Donner, *Age of Surveillance*, 162–163.

80 Theoharis, *The FBI and American Democracy*, 54.

81 J. Edgar Hoover to Special Agent in Charge, New York, June 16, 1942, re. Farrell Dobbs, Internal Security, in Farrell Dobbs's FBI file 100-21226, FOIA, in the author's possession; Joseph Prendergast, Acting Chief SDU, to Wendell Berge, January 31, 1942, and Wendell Berge to J. Edgar Hoover, April 25, 1942, in Farrell Dobbs's FBI file 146-7-1355, FOIA, in the author's possession; Chief of SDU to J. Edgar Hoover, February 26, 1942, in Dunne's FBI file 100-18341.

82 Edward Palmquist's Custodial Detention Card, in Palmquist's FBI file 146-7-1214; J. Edgar Hoover to Chief of SDU, March 31, 1941, in Dunne's FBI file 100-18341.

83 See Dunne's FBI file 100-18341, summary pp. 129, 132–134, 138–139, 141, 143, 145–147, 150–151, 154, 157, 165, 168, 170, 180–181, 183, 189, 197.

84 Dobbs's FBI file 100-21226, especially pp. 44–50 of summary; FBI report 100-11990, Seattle, 11/8/43, re. Edward Loring Palmquist, FOIA, in the author's possession.

85 See, for example, FBI reports in f. 6a, f. 7, and f. 8, box 108, and f. 9, f. 10, and f. 11, box 109, SWP 146-1-10.

86 Cannon protested FBI agents' harassment of him in a letter to Biddle. James P. Cannon to Francis Biddle, November 18, 1942, quoted in J. Edgar Hoover to Francis Biddle, memo, November 30, 1942, f. 7, box 108, SWP 146-1-10.

87 James P. Cannon, Speech at Central Branch Meeting, New York, November 19, 1942, f. Speech Notes and Manu., 1942, box 31, Speeches and Writings, JPC, WHS.

88 *Militant*, December 13, 1941, p. 6.

89 Statement on the war question and the *Militant*, 1942, f. 3, box 18, Correspondence Secretariat, JPC, WHS; "General Principles to Guide Editors of Militant in Dealing with War Question," 1942, f. 3, box 18, Correspondence Secretariat, JPC, WHS.

90 Francis Biddle to the Postmaster General, December 28, 1942, reprinted in *Militant*, January 30, 1943, 1; Grace Carlson to Natalia Sedova, January 29, 1943, f. SWP Correspondence 2, 1943, box 1, Carlson Papers, MHS; *Militant*, January 30, 1943, 1.

91 *Militant*, March 13, 1943, 1; James Cannon to All Locals and Branches, March 8, 1943 (microfilm: reel 27), SWP Records, WHS; Dunne's FBI file 100-18341 p. 187.

92 "Proposed Plan . . . around Suppression of Militant" (microfilm: reel 2), SWP Records, WHS.

93 Dobbs celebrated the addition of 101 new members in November 1942, and by January 1943 he claimed 110. Farrell Dobbs to All Locals and Branches, November 23, 1942, December 8, 1942, and January 5, 1943 (microfilm: reel 27), SWP Records, WHS.

94 For New York see, for example, FBI report 100-4013, NYC, 10/20/42 and 12/3/42, f. 7, box 108, SWP 146-1-10. For Seattle see, for example, FBI report 100-3864, Seattle, 8/27/42, f. 7, box 108, and FBI report 100-3864, Seattle, 2/10/43, f. 9, box 109, SWP 146-1-10. See also FBI report 100-11990, Seattle, 11/8/43, re. Edward Loring Palmquist, 146-7-1214, FOIA, in the author's possession.

95 Albert Goldman to Mike Myer, January 9, 1943, Mike Myer to Albert Goldman, January 12, 1943, and Goldman's Appeal of His Disbarment, 1943, Correspondence 1940–1959, box 1, Goldman Papers (microfilm edition), WHS; State of Illinois Supreme Court in the Matter of Albert Goldman, Complaint of the Committee on Inquiry of the Chicago Bar Association, "Report of the Commissioners," Briefs Concerning Disbarment, box 1, Goldman Papers (microfilm edition), WHS.

96 FBI report 100-12, 839 Seattle, 4/28/43, f. 9, box 109, SWP 146-1-10.

97 Dunne's FBI file 100-18341, p. 137; *Minneapolis Morning Tribune*, April 26, 1949, f. SWP, Minneapolis, Carl Skoglund Case, box 2, SWP Minneapolis Section, MHS; Dobbs, *Teamster Bureaucracy*, 78; Dobbs, interviews from Chicago, "Lecture 4 (Part 1)."

98 Grace Carlson to Natalia Sedova, April 17, 1943, f. SWP Correspondence 2, 1943, box 1, Carlson Papers, MHS.

99 Theoharis, *The FBI and American Democracy*, 54; Stone, *Perilous Times*, 290, 293–294.

100 Francis Biddle to Hugh B. Cox, Assistant Attorney General, and J. Edgar Hoover, Director Federal Bureau of Investigation, July 16, 1943, in Dobbs's FBI file, 100-21226.

101 Theoharis, *The FBI and American Democracy*, 55; Donner, *Age of Surveillance*, 163.

102 See, for example, the addition to Vincent Dunne's Security Index card sent by J. Edgar Hoover to the Special Agent in Charge in St. Paul, August 28, 1943, in Dunne's FBI file 100-18341.

103 *Militant*, December 13, 1941, 1.

104 Osmond K. Fraenkel, James Lipsig, Albert Goldman, et al., "Appellants' Brief," in the United States Circuit Court of Appeals, Eighth Circuit, no. 12195 criminal, Vincent Raymond Dunne, et al., vs. United States of America, 15–17.

105 Wendell Berge, Victor Anderson, et al., "Brief for Appellee," in the United States Circuit Court of Appeals, Eighth Circuit, no. 12195 criminal, Vincent Raymond Dunne, et al., vs. United States of America, I–III, 1–17, 46–49 (emphasis added).

106 Jeffrey F. Liss, "The *Schneiderman* Case: An Inside View of the Roosevelt Court," *Michigan Law Review* 74, no. 3 (1976): 501–503.

107 Ibid.

108 Ibid., 503 (emphasis added).

109 Ibid., 503–504.

110 Ibid., 504–505.

111 Ibid., 503, 505–506. Justice Robert Jackson recused himself "because he had been appointed Attorney General shortly after the case was instituted" in June 1939.

112 Harry Kalven Jr., *A Worthy Tradition: Freedom of Speech in America*, ed. Jamie Kalven (New York: Harper and Row, 1988), 185.

113 Ibid., 181; Joseph P. Lash, "A Brahmin of the Law: A Biographical Essay by Joseph P. Lash," in *From the Diary of Felix Frankfurter* (New York: Norton, 1975), 68–81.

114 This uncertainty undermines Kalven's assertion that the war years constituted the "heyday" of the clear and present danger test. See Kalven, *Worthy Tradition*, 179–189.

115 *Militant*, July 10, 1943, 3.

116 Victor Anderson to Wendell Berge, July 2, 1943, f. 10, box 109, SWP 146-1-10.

117 United States Circuit Court of Appeals, Eighth Circuit, Opinion, No. 12,195, Vincent Raymond Dunne, et al. vs. United States of America, 1317–1321, in Goldman Papers (microfilm edition: reel 1), WHS.

118 Kalven, *Worthy Tradition*, 136, 152; Court of Appeals, Eighth Circuit, Opinion, No. 12,195, 1323.

119 Court of Appeals, Eighth Circuit, Opinion, No. 12,195, 1324–1325.

120 Ibid., 1326.

121 Ibid., 1327.

122 Ibid., 1329.

123 On *Stromberg, Herndon*, and *Whitney*, see Kalven, *Worthy Tradition*, 174, 158.

124 Court of Appeals, Eighth Circuit, Opinion, No. 12,195, 1330.

125 Ibid., 1331.

126 Ibid., 1333–1338.

127 Ibid., 1344.

128 Victor Anderson to Tom C. Clark, September 22, 1943, f. 11, box 109, SWP 146-1-10.

129 Grace Carlson to Natalia Sedova, September 21, 1943, f. SWP Correspondence 2, 1943, box 1, Carlson Papers, MHS.

130 Civil Rights Defense Committee, Press Release, September 20, 1943, f. SWP, 1941 Sedition Trial Appeal, Newspaper Clippings, 1943, box 1, Carlson Papers, MHS.

131 *Militant*, October 2, 1943, 1.

132 *Militant*, September 25, 1943, 1.

133 Victor Anderson to Tom C. Clark, September 25, 1943, and Tom C. Clark to Victor Anderson, September 30, 1943, f. 11, box 109, SWP 146-1-10.

134 Osmond K. Fraenkel and Albert Goldman, Petition for Writ of Certiorari to the Circuit Court of Appeals for the Eighth Circuit and Brief in Support Thereof, in the Supreme Court of the United States, October 1943 term, Vincent Raymond Dunne, et al., petitioners against United States of America, respondent, 6–7, in Goldman Papers (microfilm: reel 1), WHS.

135 They cite *United States v. Hess*, 124 U.S. 483 (1888), and cases from the Ninth and Fourth Circuits. See Fraenkel and Goldman, Petition for Writ, 8.

136 Charles Fahy, Tom C. Clark, Edward G. Jennings, and Irving Shapiro, Brief for the United States in Opposition, on Petition for a Writ of Certiorari to the United States Circuit Court of Appeals for the Eighth Circuit, in the Supreme Court of the United States, October Term, 1943, Vincent Raymond Dunne et al. v. United States of America, 4 and 42, in Goldman Papers (microfilm: reel 1), WHS.

137 Ibid., 10, 12, 15.

138 Fahy et al., Brief for the United States in Opposition, Dunne, et al. v. U.S., 18–20, 37–41; Kalven, *Worthy Tradition*, 158.

139 Kalven, *Worthy Tradition*, 174.

140 Fahy et al., Brief for the United States in Opposition, Dunne, et al. v. U.S., 21–22.

141 Ibid., 23–40.

142 Ibid., 41.

143 Tom C. Clark to Victor Anderson, November 23, 1943, f. 12, box 109, SWP 146-1-10; *Dunne, et al. v. United States*, 320 U.S. 790.

144 Victor Anderson to Tom Clark, November 26, 1943, f. 12, box 109, SWP 146-1-10; *United States Law Week* 12, sec. 3 (November 23, 1943): 3149, n.p., 3187.

145 Frank Murphy, Note on Memo for No. 431, OT 1943, f. 1943 term, unpublished opinions and other cases, box 67 (microfilm edition: reel 129), Frank Murphy Papers, Bentley Historical Library, University of Michigan; Wiley Rutledge, Case Memoranda, *Dunne, et al. v. U.S.* No. 431, OT 1943, f. Case Memoranda, Nos. 401–450, box 108, Wiley Rutledge Papers, Library of Congress, Washington, DC; William O. Douglas, Office Memo OT 1943 No. 431 *Dunne, et al. v. U.S.*, f. 10, box 95, Office Memo, Cases Denied, Part I: Supreme Court File, 1938–1953, William O. Douglas Papers, Library of Congress, Washington, DC. Douglas initially voted to grant the writ on the appellants' first application, but he denied the second petition for a rehearing filed in early December 1943 because the "petitioners merely reiterate their claim that the statute in question is defective for failure to provide a clear and present danger." His interest in granting review was thus tied to the question of the *peacetime* nature of the Smith Act's sedition provision. See Douglas, Office Memo OT 1943 No. 431 *Dunne, et al. v. U.S.* Petition for Rehearing, f. 10, box 95, Office Memo, Cases Denied, Part I: Supreme Court File, 1938–1953; and Douglas, Office Memo OT 1943 No. 431 *Dunne, et al. v. U.S.* Second Petition for Rehearing, f. 10, box 95, Office Memo, Cases Denied, Part I: Supreme Court File, 1938–1953, William O. Douglas Papers, Library of Congress, Washington, DC.

146 John Raeburn Green, "Liberty under the Fourteenth Amendment: 1943–1944," *Michigan Law Review* 43, no. 3 (1944): 465.

147 Kalven, *Worthy Tradition*, 186–187.

148 In so doing, the Court was not acting atypically. See Eric A. Posner and Adrian Vermeule, *Terror in the Balance: Security, Liberty and the Courts* (New York: Oxford University Press, 2007), 16.

149 Wendell Berge, Daily Calendars, June 25, 1941, box 2, and Wendell Berge to Henry Schweinhaut, June 25, 1941, box 24, Wendell Berge Papers, Library of Congress.

150 Victor Anderson to Tom C. Clark, November 26, 1943, f. 12, box 109, SWP 146-1-10.

151 Bea Janosco to Grace Carlson, November 29, 1943, f. SWP Correspondence 2, 1943, box 1, Carlson Papers, MHS.

152 Ibid.; Raasch-Gilman, "Sisterhood in the Revolution," 370.

153 Grace Carlson to Dorothy and Henry Schultz, November 30, 1943, f. SWP Correspondence 2, 1943, box 1, Carlson Papers, MHS.

154 Osmond K. Fraenkel and Albert Goldman, Petition for Rehearing, Vincent Raymond Dunne et al. v. United States of America, Supreme Court of the United States, October 1943 Term, No. 431, December 1, 1943, 5, in Goldman Papers (microfilm: reel 1) WHS.

155 Clifford Forster to Charles Fahy, December 1, 1943, f. 12, box 109, SWP 146-1-10; American Civil Liberties Union, Arthur Garfield Hays, John F. Finerty, Carl Rachlin, and Clifford Forster, Brief of American Civil Liberties Union, *Amicus Curiae*, Vincent Raymond Dunne, et al. v. United States of America, Supreme Court of the United States, October Term 1943, in Goldman Papers (microfilm: reel 1), WHS.

156 "Rehearing Denied," No. 431 Dunne v. United States, *United States Law Week* 12, sec. 3, p. 3187. Justice Douglas denied the second petition (based solely on the clear and present danger issue) but granted the third, which engaged with the question of the Smith Act's peacetime implementation. See Douglas, Office Memo OT 1943 No. 431 *Dunne, et al. v. U.S.* Petition for Rehearing, f. 10, box 95, Office Memo, Cases Denied, Part I: Supreme Court File, 1938–1953; and Douglas, Office Memo OT 1943 No. 431 *Dunne, et al. v. U.S.* Second Petition for Rehearing, f. 10, box 95, Office Memo, Cases Denied, Part I: Supreme Court File, 1938–1953, William O. Douglas Papers, Library of Congress, Washington, DC.

157 Clifford Forster to Charles Fahy, December 14, 1943, f. 12, box 109, SWP 146-1-10.

158 Charles Fahy to Clifford Forster, December 17, 1943, f. 12, box 109, SWP 146-1-10.

159 Osmond K. Fraenkel and Albert Goldman, Second Petition for Rehearing, Vincent Raymond Dunne, et al. v. United States of America, Supreme Court of the United States, October Term 1943, 3, in Goldman Papers (microfilm: reel 1), WHS.

160 *New York Times*, December 7, 1943, 47; January 4, 1944, 37.

161 *Militant*, December 4, 1943, 1–2.

162 Dorothy Schultz to Grace Carlson, December 1, 1943, f. SWP Correspondence 2, 1943, box 1, Carlson Papers, MHS.

163 Milton Konvitz, Memo on Dunne, et al. v. United States (Trotskyist sedition case), [December 1943?], Papers of the NAACP, Part 18: Special Subjects, 1940–1955, Series A: Legal Department Files (microfilm: reel 3), Schomberg Center for Research in Black Culture, New York Public Library, New York, New York.

164 I. F. Stone, "The Case of the Trotskyites," *PM*, December 31, 1943, 2.

165 "Justice Denied," *Nation*, January 15, 1944, 1.

CHAPTER 6. "A TEST OF FIRE"

1 Dobbs, interviews from Chicago, "Lecture 4 (Part 1)."

2 *Militant*, December 11, 1943, 1, 4; December 25, 1943, 1, 4; J. Edgar Hoover to Tom Clark, December 28, 1943, with attached flyer announcing the meeting, f. 12, box 109, SWP 146-1-10.

3 *Militant*, January 1, 1944, 1, 5.

4 *Why We Are in Prison: Farewell Speeches of the 18 SWP and 544-CIO Minneapolis Prisoners* (New York: Pioneer Publishers, 1944), 10–15.

5 Ibid., 16–18, 27, 30–31.

6 Carlos Hudson planned to attend but was ill. See *Militant*, January 8, 1944, 5.

7 *Militant*, January 8, 1944, 1.

8 Grace Carlson to Natalia Sedova, December 30, 1943, f. SWP Correspondence 2, 1943, box 1, Carlson Papers, MHS.

9 See *Militant*, January 8, 1944, 5; *Why We Are in Prison*, 31.

10 Grace Carlson to Natalia Sedova, December 30, 1943, f. SWP Correspondence 2, 1943, box 1, Carlson Papers, MHS.

11 Because they had family in New York, these men may have chosen to surrender there so prison visitations would be easier. See Dobbs, *Teamster Bureaucracy*, 368. See also Grace Carlson to Dorothy and Henry Schultz, December 11, 1943, f. SWP Correspondence 2, 1943, box 1, Carlson Papers. MHS.

12 *Militant*, January 8, 1944, 5.

13 Civil Rights Defense Committee, *Who Are the 18 Prisoners in the Minneapolis Labor Case?*, 10–27.

14 *Militant*, January 8, 1944, 5.

15 Ibid.

16 Victor Anderson to the Attorney General and Tom Clark, January 7, 1944, f. 12, box 109, SWP 146-1-10.

17 Grace Carlson to Evelyn Anderson, January 7, 1944, f. SWP Correspondence 3, January–February 1944, box 1, Carlson Papers, MHS.

18 Grace Carlson to Dorothy Schultz, January 16, 1944, f. SWP Correspondence 3, January–February 1944, box 1, Carlson Papers, MHS.

19 James Cannon to Rose Karsner, January 6, 1944, in James Cannon, *Letters from Prison* (New York: Merit, 1968), 2.

20 Cannon to Karsner, January 20, 1944, in Cannon, *Letters*, 7; Cannon to Karsner, February 7, 1944, in Cannon, *Letters*, 14.

21 Farrell Dobbs quoted in Evelyn Anderson to Grace Carlson, March 6, 1944, f. SWP Correspondence 3, January–February 1944, box 1, Carlson Papers, MHS.

22 Cannon to Karsner, January 12, 1944, in Cannon, *Letters*, 4.

23 James Cannon quoted in George Novack to Natalia Sedova, May 1, 1944, copy attached to memo from J. Edgar Hoover to Tom Clark, May 17, 1944, f. 12, box 109, SWP 146-1-10.

24 George Novack to Natalia Sedova, May 1, 1944, copy attached to memo from J. Edgar Hoover to Tom Clark, May 17, 1944, f. 12, box 109, SWP 146-1-10.

25 Palmer, *James P. Cannon*, 260–280; Cannon to Karsner, April 17, 1944, in Cannon, *Letters*, 48.

26 Rose Karsner to James Cannon, February 1, 1944, f. January–March Letters from Prison, box 5, JPC, WHS; Cannon, *Letters*, 13, 21, 27, 53, 62, 68–70. Morris Stein was the pseudonym used by Morris Lewit when he served as national secretary of the party during the year Cannon was imprisoned.

27 Interview with Carlson by Ross, July 9, 1987, MHS.

28 Carlson to Dorothy, February 27, 1944, f. SWP Correspondence 3, January–February 1944, box 1, Carlson Papers, MHS.

29 Rose Karsner to Grace Carlson, August 3, 1944, f. SWP Correspondence 8, July–August 1944, box 1, Carlson Papers, MHS; Grace Carlson to Evelyn Anderson, July 24, 1944, f. SWP Correspondence 8, July–August 1944, box 1, Carlson Papers, MHS.

30 See, for example, Miriam Carter to Grace Carlson, February 22, 1944, and February 27, 1944, f. SWP Correspondence 3, January–February 1944, box 1; Carter to Carlson, March 26, 1944; Bea Janosco to Carlson, March 29, 1944; and Dorothy Schultz to Carlson, March 30, 1944, f. SWP Correspondence 4, March 1944, box 1; Janosco to Carlson, April 13, 1944; Elaine Roseland to Carlson, April 17, 1944; and Rose Karsner to Carlson, April 18, 1944, f. SWP Correspondence 5, April 1944, box 1; Elaine Roseland to Carlson, May 5, 1944, f. SWP Correspondence 6, May 1944, box 1; Carter to Carlson, June 9, 1944, and June 15, 1944, f. SWP Correspondence 7, June 1944, box 1, Carlson Papers, MHS. See also Raasch-Gilman, "Sisterhood in the Revolution," 368–371.

31 Miriam Carter to Grace Carlson, June 9, 1944, and June 15, 1944, f. SWP Correspondence 7, June 1944, box 1, Carlson Papers, MHS; Bea Janosco to Grace Carlson, October 23, 1944, f. SWP Correspondence 9, September–October 1944, box 1, Carlson Papers, MHS.

32 Raasch-Gilman, "Sisterhood in the Revolution," 370.

33 Ibid., 368–371.

34 *Militant*, January 15, 1944, 1, 3; January 22, 1944, 1; January 29, 1944, 1; February 5, 1944, 1; February 12, 1, 3; May 27, 1944, 3; July 15, 1944, 1, 4; John Green, President, Industrial Union Marine and Shipbuilding Workers of America, to George Novack, March 3, 1944; Herbert B. Moyer, Executive Secretary, Industrial Union of Marine and Shipbuilding Workers Local 42, to CRDC, March 3, 1944; J. Baskin, General Secretary, Workmen's Circle to WC Branches, March 7, 1944; Robert Parker, National CIO War Relief Committee, to James Farrell, March 8, 1944; John Gibson, President, Michigan CIO Council, to Franklin D. Roosevelt, March 16, 1944; August Scholle, Regional Director, CIO Political Region 6, to James Farrell, March 27, 1944; and Frank Boyd, Secretary-Treasurer, BSCP Twin Cities, to Dorothy Schultz, April 4, 1944, f. SWP, Mpls, CRDC Correspondence and Misc. Papers, 1941–1944, box 1, SWP MN Section Records, MHS.

35 *Militant*, March 11, 1944, 1, 3; Miriam Carter to Grace Carlson, March 26, 1944, f. SWP Correspondence 4, March 1944, box 1, Carlson Papers, MHS; Bea Janosco to Grace Carlson, April 13, 1944, and Elaine Roseland to Carlson, April 17, 1944, f. SWP Correspondence 5, April 1944, box 1, Carlson Papers, MHS.

36 *Militant*, June 17, 1944, 1, 4; CRDC to Grace Carlson, June 9, 1944; Miriam Carter to Grace Carlson, June 9, 1944, and June 15, 1944, f. SWP Correspondence 7, June 1944, box 1, Carlson Papers, MHS; Rose Karsner to James Cannon, June 9, 1944, f. 7, April–June 1944, Letters from Prison, box 5, JPC, WHS.

37 Henry Schultz to Morris Stein, January 19, 1944, f. 3, box 18, Correspondence Secretariat, JPC, WHS.

38 George Novack to Morris Stein, March 20, 1944; March 22, 1944; March 26, 1944; March 31, 1944; April 11, 1944; April 13, 1944; May 26, 1944, CRDC Tour 1944, Correspondence, Special Files, George Novack Papers (1905–1992) (microfilm: reel 2), George Novack and Evelyn Reed Papers, WHS.

39 J. Edgar Hoover to Tom Clark, April 21, 1944; May 17, 1944; May 22, 1944, f. 13, box 109; J. Edgar Hoover to Tom Clark, June 23, 1944, f. 14, box 109; FBI report 100-13811, New York, July 5, 1944, f. 14, box 109, SWP 146-1-10.

40 Miriam Carter to Grace Carlson, June 9, 1944, and June 14, 1944, f. SWP Correspondence 7, June 1944, box 1, Carlson Papers, MHS; *Militant*, June 17, 1944, 1, 4.

41 Louis Weinstock to Daniel Tobin, May 11, 1944, box 2, series V, IBT Records, WHS.

42 Ibid.; J. D. Spiegel to Daniel Tobin, June 20, 1944, box 21, series V, IBT Records, WHS.

43 Victor Anderson to Louis Weinstock, June 7, 1944, box 2, series V, IBT Records, WHS; Daniel Tobin to J. D. Spiegel, June 22, 1944 (forwarding Anderson's letter), box 21, series V, IBT Records, WHS.

44 Daniel Tobin to Louis Weinstock, June 2, 1944, box 2, series V, IBT Records, WHS.

45 These were mostly CIO affiliates. See correspondence in f. SWP, Mpls, CRDC Correspondence and Misc. Papers, 1941–1944, box 1, SWP MN Section Records, MHS.

46 Carter to Carlson, June 15, 1944, f. SWP Correspondence 7, June 1944, box 1, Carlson Papers, MHS.

47 Lydia Bennett to Morris Stein, February 20, 1944, f. 5, box 16, General Correspondence, JPC, WHS.

48 Morris Stein to Lydia Bennett, March 22, 1944, f. 5, box 16, General Correspondence, JPC, WHS.

49 Mike Bartell to Morris Stein, May 31, 1944, f. 5, box 16, General Correspondence, JPC, WHS.

50 From Albert Goldman, July 3, 1944, f. 3, box 18, Correspondence Secretariat, JPC, WHS.

51 James Cannon to Rose Karsner, March 6, 1944 in Cannon, *Letters*, 25.

52 Elaine Roseland to Grace Carlson, May 5, 1944, f. SWP Correspondence 6, May 1944, box 1, Carlson Papers, MHS.

53 The idea was squelched by the National Committee as something that would create the wrong kind of publicity for the pardon campaign. See Morris Stein to

Comrades, San Diego Branch, February 23, 1944, f. 3, box 18, Correspondence Secretariat, JPC, WHS.

54 Rose Karsner communicating Baldwin's sentiments to James Cannon, June 10, 1944, f. 7, box 5, Correspondence, JPC, WHS.

55 James Cannon to Rose Karsner, June 21, 1944, in Cannon, *Letters*, 99.

56 Letter from A. Goldman, n.d., f. 7 April–June 1944, Letters from Prison, box 5, Correspondence, JPC, WHS.

57 James Cannon to Rose Karsner, June 21, 1944, in Cannon, *Letters*, 99–101.

58 Ibid., 100.

59 *Militant*, August 12, 1944, 1, 2.

60 *Militant*, October 7, 1944, 1, 2.

61 Kalven, *Worthy Tradition*, 186.

62 Vincent Johnson to Francis Biddle, July 18, 1944, f. 14, box 109, SWP 146-1-10.

63 Francis Biddle to Vincent Johnson, July 25, 1944, f. 14, box 109, SWP 146-1-10.

64 Charles Fahy to Francis Biddle, August 2, 1944, f. 14, box 109, SWP 146-1-10.

65 Philip Elman to Charles Fahy, July 29, 1944, f. 14, box 109, SWP 146-1-10.

66 Quote from Alfred Blair Lewis to President Roosevelt, February 9, 1944, f. 12, box 109, SWP 146-1-10. See, for example, also, Constance Rose Zigman to the Department of Justice, January 27, 1944, f. 12, box 109, SWP 146-1-10. And, for example, Marion Weinstein to President Roosevelt, January 19, 1944; Frieda Charles to President Roosevelt, January 20, 1944; Milton Stern to President Roosevelt, January 25, 1944; Victor Davis to President Roosevelt, February 1, 1944; Gordon Adler to President Roosevelt, February 11, 1944; Gilbert Miller to President Roosevelt, February 11, 1944; Robert Shaw to President Roosevelt, February 14, 1944; Lydia Boring to President Roosevelt, February 12, 1944; Earl Hendler to President Roosevelt, February 14, 1944; and E. L. Ramsay to President Roosevelt, February 15, 1944, f. 12, box 109, SWP 146-1-10. See similar letters in f. 13 and 14, box 109, SWP 146-1-10.

67 See, for example, Janice Neuberger to President Roosevelt, January 16, 1944, and Arthur Calhoun to President Roosevelt, February 12, 1944, f. 12, box 109, SWP 146-1-10. And see George P. Masi to President Roosevelt, March 6, 1944; Petition from the Phoenix Brass Workers Union No. 462, March 8, 1944; Resolution from Local 7 Brewers and Malters, San Francisco; and Resolution from ACWA, Milwaukee Joint Board and Resolution from United Shoeworkers of America, CIO Local 56A, f. 13, box 109, SWP 146-1-10. See also Resolution from Minnesota State Federation of Labor, September 20, 1944, f. 14, box 109, SWP 146-1-10.

68 Samuel Grakovic to President Roosevelt, January 20, 1944, f. 12, box 109, SWP 146-1-10. Other letters that address this contradiction include Laura Sloke to President Roosevelt, January 20, 1944; Charles Geochario to President Roosevelt, January 21, 1944; R. Aonis to President Roosevelt, February 5, 1944; and Ethel Harrison to President Roosevelt, February 12, 1944, f. 12, box 109, SWP 146-1-10.

69 "Trade Union Resolution Asking Pardon for the 18," Local 9-213, IWA-CIO, March 17, 1944, f. 13, box 109, SWP 146-1-10.

70 Lyons quoted in Evelyn Anderson to Grace Carlson, October 10, 1944, f. SWP Correspondence 9, September–October 1944, box 1, Carlson Papers, MHS.

71 *Militant*, October 14, 1944, 1.

72 *Militant*, October 21, 1944, 1, 3.

73 Grace Carlson to Evelyn Anderson, October 21, 1944, f. SWP Correspondence 9, September–October 1944, box 1, Carlson Papers, MHS.

74 Evelyn Anderson to Grace Carlson, October 10, 1944, f. SWP Correspondence 9, September–October 1944, box 1, Carlson Papers, MHS.

75 *Militant*, October 21, 1944, 1, 3.

76 *Militant*, November 4, 1944, 1, 3. See also Rose Karsner to James Cannon, October 29, 1944, f. 8 July–October 1944, box 5, Correspondence, JPC, WHS.

77 *Militant*, October 28, 1944, 1, 3.

78 Dorothy Schultz to Grace Carlson, October 24, 1944, and Bea Janosco to Grace Carlson, October 23, 1944, f. SWP Correspondence 9, September–October 1944, box 1, Carlson Papers, MHS. See also *Militant*, November 4, 1944, 1, 3.

79 Evelyn spoke of her relief at the release of the six. See Evelyn Anderson to Grace Carlson, October 25, 1944, f. SWP Correspondence 9, September–October 1944, box 1, Carlson Papers, MHS.

80 *Militant*, November 25, 1944, 1; December 2, 1944, 1; December 9, 1944, 1; December 16, 1944, 1; December 23, 1944, 1; December 30, 1944, 1; January 6, 1945, 4; January 13, 1945, 1; Civil Rights Defense Committee, *Who Are the 18 Prisoners in the Minneapolis Labor Case?*, 17–26.

81 *Militant*, January 27, 1945, 1, 3.

82 *Militant*, February 3, 1945, 1, 4; Dorothy Schultz to Grace Carlson, January 1945, f. SWP Correspondence 11, January–June 1945, box 1, Carlson Papers, MHS.

83 *Militant*, January 13, 1945, 1.

84 *Militant*, February 3, 1945, 1.

85 FBI report 100-1246, St. Paul, 2/26/45, p. 10, f. 15, box 109, SWP 146-1-10.

86 James Cannon, "Dear Friends and Comrades," n.d., f. 9, box 31, Speeches, Speeches and Writings, JPC, WHS.

87 *Militant*, February 10, 1945, 1, 3.

88 Max Geldman's FBI file, 146-7-39-17, reports from 2/26/45—9/10/46, FOIA, in the author's possession.

89 Karl Kuehn's FBI file 146-7-62-1072, reports from 5/12/45 through 1/16/46, FOIA, in the author's possession.

90 Palmquist's FBI file 146-7-1214, report for 1/22/46.

91 SAC, St. Paul, to the Director, January 25, 1945, in Dunne's FBI file, 100-18341.

92 FBI report 10-932, St. Paul, 3/21/45, Vincent Dunne, f. 15, box 109, SWP 146-1-10.

93 Ibid.; FBI report 100-166, St. Paul, 3/17/45, Grace Carlson, f. 15, box 109, SWP 146-1-10.

94 See, for example, Bea Janosco to Grace Carlson, September 29, 1943; Grace Carlson to Dorothy and Henry Schultz, November 30, 1943; Dorothy Schultz to Grace Carlson, December 1, 1943; and Grace Carlson to Dorothy and Henry

Schultz, December 11, 1943, f. SWP Correspondence 2, 1943, box 1, Carlson Papers, MHS.

95 There is no evidence of the alleged affair in either Carlson's papers or Dunne's. Carlson's letters to and from her husband, Gilbert, written during her time in prison, while indexed in a notebook she kept of her correspondence, are not archived. See Grace Carlson, prison notebook, f. SWP, Carlson's Notebook Prison, 1943–1944, box 1, Carlson Papers, MHS. There may have been references to their marital problems in those exchanges, but they have not been preserved, perhaps because of the personal nature of such details. Neither Carlson nor Dunne spoke about any romantic affair when interviewed later in life, either because it never took place or perhaps because they each deemed the affair too personal and no longer relevant. Interview with Dunne by Goff, April 27, 1969, MHS; interviews with Carlson by Ross, July 9 and 14, 1987, MHS.

96 FBI report 100-932, St. Paul, 5/21/45, f. 15, box 109, SWP 146-1-10.

97 The informant alleged that, when in New York, the two lived together in Carlson's apartment. Dunne did not receive mail at Carlson's apartment, but the FBI confirmed Dunne's residence there through "a discreet contact with the elevator operator." See FBI report 100-59477, New York, Vincent Dunne, 12/20/45, p. 2, f. 19, box 110, SWP 146-1-10.

98 "Ms. Carlson Speaks on Women in Prison," *Minneapolis Times*, September 10, 1945; and Carlson's notes for her "Women in Prison" speech, f. SWP, "Women in Prison" Speech Tour, June–September 1945, box 1, Carlson Papers, MHS. Re. Carlson's tour, see also FBI report 100-1320, St. Louis, 8/14/45, and FBI report 100-17375, Los Angeles, SWP, 9/10/45, f. 17, box 109, SWP 146-1-10.

99 FBI report 100-4013, New York, 1/18/46, f. 19, box 110, and FBI report 100-1246, St. Paul, 6/6/45, f. 16, box 109, SWP 146-1-10. See also James Cannon, interview with Harry Ring, March 29, 1974, p. 17, f. 1, Interviews—Ring II, box 2, Biographical and Background Material, JPC, WHS; interview of James Cannon by Sidney Lens, July 16, 1974, in *James P. Cannon: A Political Tribute* (New York: Pathfinder, 1974; repr., New York: Pathfinder, 2007), 41.

100 Statement of the National Committee, Workers Party, enclosed with Max Shachtman to James Cannon, August 22, 1945, f. 1, 1945, box 6, Correspondence, JPC, WHS.

101 James Cannon, interview with Harry Ring, March 29, 1974, pp. 17–18, f. 1, Interviews—Ring II, box 2, Biographical and Background Material, JPC, WHS; James Cannon to Murray Weiss, April 4, 1945, f. 1, box 6, Correspondence, JPC, WHS.

102 *Militant*, February 3, 1945, 1, 4.

103 Oscar Williams, Felix Morrow, and Albert Goldman, "Call for the Formation of a Faction to Support the P.C. Minority Resolution on Unity with the Workers Party," f. 1, box 6, Correspondence, JPC, WHS.

104 James Cannon to Mike Bartell, July 26, 1945, f. 1, box 6, Correspondence, JPC, WHS.

105 FBI report 100-932, St. Paul, 3/21/45, p. 3, and 5/21/45, p. 3, f. 15, box 109, SWP 146-1-10; FBI report 100-1246, St. Paul, 4/17/45, p. 17, f. 15, box 109, SWP 146-1-10.

106 James Cannon to Murry Weiss, April 4, 1945, f. 1, 1945, box 6, Correspondence, JPC, WHS.

107 James Cannon to Mike Bartell, July 26, 1945, f. 1, 1945, box 6, Correspondence, JPC, WHS.

108 Albert Goldman to C (Cassidy, aka Morrow), October 30, 1945, Historical Files: Albert Goldman Correspondence (microfilm: reel 50), SWP Records, WHS.

109 James Cannon, interview with Harry Ring, March 29, 1974, p. 18, f. 1, Interviews—Ring II, box 2, Biographical and Background Material, JPC, WHS; glossary entries for Albert Goldman and Felix Morrow in *James P. Cannon, Writings and Speeches, 1940–43: The Socialist Workers Party in World War II*, ed. Les Evans (New York: Pathfinder, 1975; repr., New York: Pathfinder, 2002), 432, 438. Morrow was expelled by a vote of 101 to 4: see FBI report 65-645, Chicago, 1/22/47, SWP, f. 22, box 110, SWP 146-1-10.

110 George Clarke to Jean Blake, July 26, 1948, f. 4, 1948, box 6, Correspondence, JPC, WHS.

111 Tim Weiner, *Enemies: A History of the FBI* (New York: Random House, 2012), 148–159.

112 Stone, *Perilous Times*, 343–344.

113 *Militant*, September 1, 1948, 1; October 11, 1948, 1.

114 George Novack to Vincent Dunne (copy to James Cannon), July 26, 1948, f. 4, 1948, box 6, Correspondence, JPC, WHS.

115 Ibid.

116 Oscar Schoenfeld to Albert Goldman, August 10, 1948, box 1, Correspondence, Goldman Papers (microfilm edition: reel 1), WHS.

117 George Novack to Jim et al. (James Cannon and the other "NC members among the defendants"), August 18, 1948, f. 4, 1948, box 6, Correspondence, JPC, WHS.

118 Farrell Dobbs to Tom Clark, July 29, 1948, f. 27, box 110, SWP 146-1-10.

119 M. J. Myer to Tom Clark, August 11, 1948, f. 27, box 110, SWP 146-1-10.

120 Alexander M. Campbell to Farrell Dobbs, August 16, 1948; Campbell to M. J. Meyer, August 16, 1948, f. 27, box 110, SWP 146-1-10.

121 Farrell Dobbs to President Truman, August 26, 1948, f. 27, box 110, SWP 146-1-10.

122 Grace Carlson to President Truman, August 26, 1948, f. 27, box 110, SWP 146-1-10.

123 Attorney General's Office to Matthew J. Connelly, September 2, 1948, f. 27, box 110, SWP 146-1-10.

124 *Militant*, October 25, 1948, 2.

125 Schrecker, *Many Are the Crimes*, 394.

CHAPTER 7. THE ONGOING STRUGGLE FOR CIVIL LIBERTIES

1 Margaret Jayko, ed., *The FBI on Trial: The Victory in the Socialist Workers Party Suit against Government Spying* (New York: Pathfinder, 1988), 12.

2 Stone, *Perilous Times*, 396–397.

3 Belknap, *Cold War Political Justice*, 63.

4 Victor Anderson to the Attorney General, attn. T. Vincent Quinn, May 3, 1948, f. 26, box 110, and T. Vincent Quinn to Thomas J. Donegan, May 7, 1948, f. 27, box 110, SWP 146-1-10.

5 Schrecker, *Many Are the Crimes*, 192–195.

6 Stone, *Perilous Times*, 398 (emphasis in the original).

7 Belknap, *Cold War Political Justice*, 129.

8 Ibid., 129–130.

9 Tom Clark, who had joined the Court in the summer of 1949, recused himself because as attorney general he had brought the original case.

10 C. J. Vinson, Judgment of the Court, *Dennis v. United States*, 341 U.S. 494, p. 509.

11 Vinson, *Dennis v. United States*, 341 U.S. 494, p. 510; Belknap, *Cold War Political Justice*, 133; Kalven, *Worthy Tradition*, 205.

12 Jackson, Concurring Opinion, *Dennis v. United States*, 341 U.S. 494, p. 571; Frankfurter, Concurring Opinion, *Dennis v. United States*, 341 U.S. 494, pp. 551–552; Belknap, *Cold War Political Justice*, 138; Stone, *Perilous Times*, 405–406.

13 Kalven, *Worthy Tradition*, 210.

14 Douglas, Dissenting Opinion, *Dennis v. United States*, 341 U.S. 494, pp. 589–590.

15 Powers, *Not without Honor*, 227.

16 Black, Dissenting Opinion, *Dennis v. United States*, 341 U.S. 494, pp. 580–582.

17 Stone, *Perilous Times*, 410–411; Schrecker, *Many Are the Crimes*, 199–200.

18 Stone, *Perilous Times*, 411.

19 Frederick Woltman, "No. 1 Trotskyist Watches Red Trial," n.d., in Dobbs's FBI file 65-12453. See also Farrell Dobbs, "Unreported Precedent," letter to the editor, *Newsweek*, August 23, 1948, clipping, f. 2, 1940–1948, box 5, Correspondence, Farrell Dobbs Papers, WHS. For coverage of the trial in the *Militant* see, for example, January 24, 1949, 1, 4; February 14, 1949, 1, 2; April 4, 1949, 1, 2; and October 24, 1949, 1–3.

20 Farrell Dobbs's FBI file, NY 100-7388, p. 22, FOIA, in the author's possession. The SWP condemned the prosecution of the CPUSA leaders from the moment the indictment was handed down. See *Militant*, August 2, 1948, 1–3; August 9, 1948, 1.

21 Farrell Dobbs's FBI file, CG 100-21226, pp. 27. 60, and NY 100-7388, pp. 5–7, FOIA, in the author's possession; *Militant*, July 4, 1949, 1–2; July 11, 1949, 1, 3.

22 James Cannon to All Locals and Branches, November 10, 1949, Letters, Dunne Papers, WHS.

23 SAC, Minneapolis to Director, FBI, December 3, 1949, and SAC, Cleveland to Director, FBI, February 28, 1950, in Dunne's FBI file 100-18341; letter to Vincent Dunne, November 13, 1949, Letters, Vincent Dunne Papers, WHS; Seattle Confidential Informant report, in Dunne's FBI file 100-18341, summary p. 504.

24 Interview with Carl Skoglund, 20th Century Radicalism in Minnesota Oral History Project, OF30.64, interviewer unidentified, n.d., MHS.

25 George Novack to All National Committee Members, April 30, 1949, f. Skoglund, 1943–1951, box 2, CRDC Records, WHS.

26 On Bridges, see Ellen Schrecker, "Labor and the Cold War: The Legacy of McCarthyism," in *American Labor and the Cold War: Grassroots Politics and Postwar Political Culture*, ed. Robert W. Cherny, William Issel, and Kieran Walsh Taylor (New Brunswick, NJ: Rutgers University Press, 2004), 14; Schrecker, *Many Are the Crimes*, 93–103.

27 Schrecker, "Immigration and Internal Security," 399, 401.

28 George Novack to All National Committee Members, April 30, 1949, f. Skoglund, 1943–1951, box 2, CRDC Records, WHS. See also *Militant*, August 22, 1949, 3; September 12, 1949, 1.

29 See Ballots from CRDC members; George Novack to Grace and Vincent, September 6, 1949; Vincent Dunne to George Novack, September 26, 1949; October 10, 1949; October 15, 1949, f. Skoglund—Correspondence, 1943–1951, box 2, CRDC Records, WHS.

30 CRDC press release, December 15, f. Skoglund—Correspondence, 1943–1951, box 2, CRDC Records, WHS. Re. the McCarran Act, see Schrecker, "Immigration and Internal Security," 410–412.

31 George Novack to Friend (CRDC Members), July 15, 1954, and November 22, 1954, f. Skoglund Correspondence, 1952–1957, box 2, CRDC Records. On indefinite detention in these kinds of deportation cases, see Schrecker, "Immigration and Internal Security," 402.

32 Vincent Dunne quoted in FBI report MP 100-932, p. 6 in Dunne FBI file 100-18341.

33 Tom Clark to J. Edgar Hoover, February 13, 1945, f. 14, box 109; J. Edgar Hoover to James McInerney, July 11, 1945, f. 17, box 109, SWP 146-1-10.

34 James McInerney to J. Edgar Hoover, July 28, 1945, f. 17, box 109, SWP 146-1-10.

35 Hoover to Assistant Attorney General T. L. Caudle, August 4, 1945; Hoover to Attorney General, September 14, 1945, f. 17, box 109, SWP 146-1-10; Hoover to Caudle, November 20, 1945; Hoover to Caudle, November 28, 1945, f. 18, box 109, SWP 146-1-10; Hoover to Attorney General, March 26, 1945, f. 20, box 110, SWP 146-1-10; Hoover to Attorney General, August 6, 1946, and September 24, 1946, f. 21, box 110, SWP 146-1-10; Hoover to Attorney General, October 29, 1946, and November 7, 1946, f. 22, box 110, SWP 146-1-10; Hoover to Caudle, February 17, 1947, and February 20, 1947, and Hoover to Attorney General, March 13, 1947, f. 23, box 110, SWP 146-1-10; Hoover to Attorney General, November 15, 1947, and Hoover to Assistant Attorney General, December 20, 1947, and January 14, 1948, f. 25, box 110, SWP 146-1-10; Hoover to Attorney General, June 13, 1948, and July 7, 1948, f. 27, box 110, SWP 146-1-10.

36 Schrecker, *Many Are the Crimes*, 208.

37 Stone, *Perilous Times*, 335.

38 Schrecker, *Many Are the Crimes*, 208; SAC Minneapolis to Director, June 10, 1955, tabbing Dunne as DETCOM in his SI file, in Dunne's FBI file 100-18341; SAC New York to Director, January 30, 1950, and SAC Chicago to Director, January 30, 1953, tabbing Dobbs as DETCOM in his SI file, and SAC Chicago to Director, May 14,

1951, tabbing Dobbs as COMSAB (a designation that is then removed in June), Dobbs's FBI file 100-21226.

39 Helen Hanifan to Thomas Flynn, July 12, 1946; Flynn to Hanifan, July 12, 1946; and I. E. Goldberg to Flynn, November 2, 1946, f. Local 544, Minneapolis, Minn., 1945–1946, box 44, series II, IBT Records, WHS.

40 Levenstein, *Communism, Anticommunism, and the CIO*, 299; Nelson Lichtenstein, *State of the Union: A Century of American Labor* (Princeton, NJ: Princeton University Press, 2002), 98–177; Cochran, *Labor and Communism*, 297–331; Schrecker, "Labor and the Cold War," 7–24.

41 Ed Palmquist's FBI file AN 74-10, Anchorage, 11/7/47, FOIA, in the author's possession.

42 Ed Palmquist's FBI file AN 100-1381, Anchorage, 2/7/48, 5/7/48, 4/2/48, 12/4/48, and 8/22/50, FOIA, in the author's possession.

43 Ed Palmquist's FBI file AN 100-1381, Anchorage, 11/5/54, p. 1, FOIA, in the author's possession.

44 Ed Palmquist's FBI file AN 100-1381, Anchorage, 11/30/56, pp. 1–2, FOIA, in the author's possession.

45 Ed Palmquist's FBI file SU 100-9142, Salt Lake City, 5/6/57, pp. 1, 6–8, FOIA, in the author's possession.

46 James Farrell to Osmund Fraenkel, August 12, 1947; Fraenkel to Farrell, August 21, 1947; Farrell to Goldman, January 31, 1948; Farrell to Nat Weingerb, February 10, 1948, Correspondence 1940–1959, box 1, Albert Goldman Papers (microfilm: reel 1), WHS.

47 Goldman to Baldwin, May 6, 1948; Sidney Hook to Goldman, May 10, 1948; Baldwin to Goldman, May 10, 1948; Goldman to Baldwin, May 13, 1948; Baldwin to Goldman, May 18, 1948; Farrell to Goldman, July 23, 1948; (re. Wallace) Goldman to Norman Thomas, August 5, 1948, Correspondence 1940–1959, box 1, Albert Goldman Papers (microfilm: reel 1), WHS.

48 Goldman to Oscar Schoenfeld, March 27, 1949, Correspondence 1940–1959, box 1, Albert Goldman Papers (microfilm: reel 1), WHS.

49 U.S. Atomic Energy Commission Personnel Security Board, in the Matter of Betty June Jacobsen, Chicago, January 25, 1952, pp. 43, 46, Security Clearance Hearings, box 1, Goldman Papers (microfilm: reel 1), WHS.

50 James Cannon interview by Harry Ring, 3/29/74, pp. 18–19, f. 1 Interviews—Ring II, box 2, Biographical and Background Material, JPC, WHS.

51 Henry Schweinhaut to Albert Goldman, December 13, 1956, Correspondence 1940–1959, box 1, Goldman Papers (microfilm: reel 1), WHS.

52 FBI reports indicate that Felix Morrow also became an informer after he was expelled from the SWP. See Dunne's FBI file 100-18341, overview report p. 505.

53 See, for example, Max and Goldie Geldman's birthday greetings to Carlson on April 15, 1949, in Karl Kuehn's FBI file PH 100-30508, 11/30/49, p. 12, FOIA, in the author's possession.

54 FBI report 100-932, St. Paul, Vincent Dunne, 6/12/47, pp. 1–3, and FBI report 100-932, Minneapolis, Vincent Dunne, 1/15/51, p. 11, FOIA, in the author's possession.

55 FBI report 100-166, St. Paul, Grace Carlson, 9/20/46, p. 3, SWP 146-1-10; Dunne's FBI file 100-18341, overview p. 348.

56 Dunne's FBI file 100-18341, overview p. 399 .

57 FBI report 100-932, 3/1/49, St. Paul, Vincent Dunne, p. 2, FOIA, in the author's possession.

58 Dunne's FBI file 100-18341, overview p. 469.

59 FBI report 100-932, 5/12/49, St. Paul. Vincent Dunne, p. 2, FOIA, in the author's possession.

60 Raasch-Gilman, "Sisterhood in the Revolution," 373.

61 *Militant*, July 7, 1952, 4 (emphasis added).

62 Dunne's FBI file 100-18341 overview p. 41, and FBI report 100-932, 12/24/52, Minneapolis, Vincent Dunne, p. 5, FOIA, in the author's possession.

63 Interview with Grace Holmes Carlson by Carl Ross, 20th Century Radicalism in Minnesota Project, July 14, 1987, pp. 40–41, MHS.

64 Carlson and Cannon quoted in Raasch-Gilman, "Sisterhood in the Revolution," 373.

65 Grace Carlson's FBI file 900-50430, St. Paul, 4/13/54, f. SWP files, Misc. information, correspondence with party members and FBI reports, box 1 Grace Carlson Papers, MHS.

66 Grace Carlson to Reverend Timothy McCarthy, December 2, 1968, f. General Correspondence and Miscellany, 1929–1972, box 2, Carlson Papers, MHS.

67 They resumed a close correspondence again by the late 1960s. See the exchange of letters in f. General Correspondence and Miscellany, 1929–1972, box 2, Carlson Papers, MHS.

68 Interview with Grace Holmes Carlson by Carl Ross, 20th Century Radicalism in Minnesota Project, July 9, 1987, p. 11, MHS; Joanie Machart to Mr. and Mrs. Carlson, n.d., f. General Correspondence and Miscellany, 1929–1972, box 2, Carlson Papers, MHS.

69 Interview with Grace Holmes Carlson by Carl Ross, 20th Century Radicalism in Minnesota Project, July 14, 1987, p. 38, MHS. See also Grace Carlson's FBI file, 900-50430, St. Paul, 4/13/54, f. SWP files, Misc. information, correspondence with party members and FBI reports, Grace Carlson Papers, MHS.

70 Interview with Max Geldman by Carl Ross, 20th Century Radicalism in Minnesota Project, February 18, 1988, p. 13, MHS.

71 Geldman was expelled on the grounds of leaving a Dobbs memorial meeting with his wife when she refused to pay the three-dollar admission charge. See Statement of Max Geldman at His Expulsion Trial, December 1983, http://www.marxists.org/history/etol/document/fit/rpiioverview.htm (accessed June 12, 2012). On the crisis that gripped the party during the early 1980s, see Barry Sheppard, *The Party: The Socialist Workers Party, 1960–1988*, vol. 2, *Interregnum, Decline and Collapse, 1973–1988: A Political Memoir* (London: Resistance Books, 2012), 21–211, 287–288.

72 Interview with James Cannon by Sidney Lens, July 16, 1974, in *James P. Cannon: A Political Tribute* (New York: Pathfinder, 1974; repr., New York: Pathfinder, 2007), 41.

73 SAC New York to Director, 6/2/57, in Dunne's FBI file 100-18341; Barry Sheppard, *The Party: The Socialist Workers Party, 1960–1988*, vol. 1, *The Sixties: A Political Memoir* (London: Resistance Books, 2005), 217–224.

74 Joseph Hansen, "Jim Forged the Nucleus of the Revolutionary Party in the U.S.," in *James P. Cannon: A Political Tribute* (New York: Pathfinder, 1974; repr., New York: Pathfinder, 2007), 8.

75 Interview with James Cannon by Sidney Lens, July 16, 1974, in *James P. Cannon: A Political Tribute* (New York: Pathfinder, 1974; repr., New York: Pathfinder, 2007), 42.

76 Tom Kerry to Vincent Dunne, March 6, 1957, and Farrell Dobbs to Larry Trainor, II Letters, Dunne Papers, WHS; interview with James Cannon by Sidney Lens, July 16, 1974, in *James P. Cannon: A Political Tribute* (New York: Pathfinder, 1974; repr., New York: Pathfinder, 2007), 41.

77 SAC Minneapolis to Director, 2/19/70, in Dunne's FBI file 100-18341.

78 Dobbs's FBI file 146-7-1355 (for quote, see FBI report SU 100-9480, 10/20/60, p. 1, in FBI file 146-7-1355).

79 Sheppard, *The Party*, 1:222, 336. Sheppard estimated the numerical high point of the movement in these decades to be in 1977 with 3,000 members. See *The Party*, 2:123.

80 Haverty-Stacke, *America's Forgotten Holiday*, 206–218; Levenstein, *Communism, Anticommunism, and the CIO*, 299; Lichtenstein, *State of the Union*, 98–177; Schrecker, "Labor and the Cold War," 7–24.

81 Sheppard, *The Party*, vol. 1. On Cuba, see especially pp. 50, 83–85, 146. On the African American civil rights movement, see especially pp. 57, 76–77, 94–100, 119–123, 249. On the antiwar movement, see especially pp. 129–138, 156–160, 168–170, 183–187, 252–260, 266–273, 293.

82 Farrell Dobbs, interviews from Chicago, "Lecture 4: After the War: Forces Operating in and upon the Labor Movement for Change (Part 2)," Holt Labor Library Collection, http://www.marxists.org/history/etol/audio/ (accessed December 12, 2011).

83 Sheppard, *The Party*, 2:6–7, 123–142, 207–211, 287–288, 267–277, 299, 322, 328–329.

84 See, for example, Lichtenstein, *State of the Union*, 98–177.

85 Jefferson Cowie, *Stayin' Alive: The 1970s and the Last Days of the Working Class* (New York: New Press, 2010), 23–74, quote on 70.

86 On the negative effects of COINTELPRO and other surveillance programs on these various mass political movements, see, for example, Donner, *Age of Surveillance*, 178–240; James Kirkpatrick Davis, *Spying on America: The FBI's Domestic Counterintelligence Program* (Westport, CT: Greenwood Press, 1992).

87 Stone, *Perilous Times*, 413.

88 Susan J. Siggelakis, "Advocacy on Trial," *American Journal of Legal History* 36, no. 4 (1992): 503.

89 Kalven, *Worthy Tradition*, 211–221.

90 Siggelakis, "Advocacy on Trial," 504, 505.

91 Kalven, *Worthy Tradition*, 228.

92 For the relationship between the Cold War and the advancement of the modern civil rights movement, see, for example, Jonathan Rosenberg, *How Far the Promised Land? World Affairs and the American Civil Rights Movement from the First World War to Vietnam* (Princeton, NJ: Princeton University Press, 2005); Mary Dudziak, *Cold War Civil Rights: Race and the Image of American Democracy* (Princeton, NJ: Princeton University Press, 2002).

93 Kalven, *Worthy Tradition*, 216–227.

94 Ibid., 123–124.

95 Stone, *Perilous Times*, 522.

96 Ibid., 523.

97 Athan Theoharis, *Spying on Americans: Political Surveillance from Hoover to the Huston Plan* (Philadelphia: Temple University Press, 1978), 136.

98 David Cole and James X. Dempsey, *Terrorism and the Constitution: Sacrificing Civil Liberties in the Name of National Security*, 3rd ed. (New York: New Press, 2006), ibook edition, chap. 6, p. 98 of 342. On COINTELPRO in general, see Theoharis, *Spying on Americans*, 136–137.

99 Weiner, *Enemies*, 195–199, 247–248, 271, 274.

100 Theoharis, *Spying on Americans*, 11.

101 Ibid.

102 Jayko, *FBI on Trial*, 10; Weiner, *Enemies*, 329–331.

103 Syd Stapleton to Farrell Dobbs, July 10, 1978, and Marvel Scholl Dobbs to Farrell Dobbs, August 12, 1978, f. 5, box 1, Biographical Material, Farrell Dobbs Papers, WHS.

104 Farrell Dobbs quoted in Jayko, *FBI on Trial*, 284–287.

105 Jayko, *FBI on Trial*, 13–14.

106 Cole and Dempsey, *Terrorism and the Constitution*, ibook, chap. 7, p. 124 of 342; Judge Griesa's August 25, 1986, decision in Jayko, *FBI on Trial*, 33–185. Years of briefings contributed to the delay in Griesa's ruling: see Jayko, *FBI on Trial*, 38.

107 Griesa's decision in Jayko, *FBI on Trial*, 66–67.

108 Jayko, *FBI on Trial*, 15.

109 So too did the internecine party fights Barry Sheppard describes in his memoirs. See Sheppard, *The Party*, 2:125–142, 207–211, 287–288, 299, 322, 328–329.

CODA AND CONCLUSION

1 Jayko, *FBI on Trial*, 26–27, 46–55.

2 Cole and Dempsey, *Terrorism and the Constitution*, ibook, chap. 6, pp. 103 and 104 of 342.

3 Weiner, *Enemies*, 353.

4 Ibid., 355.

5 Ibid., 331–366.

6 Ibid., 365–378.

7 Ibid., 382–398.

8 Cole and Dempsey, *Terrorism and the Constitution*, ibook, chap. 6, pp. 106–107 of 342.

9 Ibid., chap. 8, pp. 138–139 of 342.

10 Ibid., chap. 10, p. 158 of 342.

11 Ibid., chap. 10, p. 158 of 342; Howard Ball, *The USA PATRIOT Act of 2001: Balancing Civil Liberties and National Security* (Denver, CO: ABC Clio, 2004), 17.

12 FBI Amerithrax Investigation, http://fbi.gov/about-us/history/famous-cases/ anthrax-amerithrax/amerithrax-investigation (accessed August 21, 2012).

13 On the appropriateness of such temporary deference to the executive during times of national emergency, see Posner and Vermeule, *Terror in the Balance*, 3–14.

14 Ball, *The USA PATRIOT Act*, 44.

15 Cole and Dempsey, *Terrorism and the Constitution*, ibook, chap. 13, p. 204 of 342; Stone, *Perilous Times*, 539, 552–553.

16 Stone, *Perilous Times*, 539, 553.

17 Mary Dudziak, *War Time: An Idea, Its History, Its Consequences* (New York: Oxford University Press, 2012), 101–105.

18 Stephen J. Schulhofer suggests such safeguards. See Schulhofer, *Rethinking the Patriot Act: Keeping America Safe and Free* (New York: Century Foundation Report, 2005), 84, 119–125.

19 *New York Times*, March 3, 2006, http://www.nytimes.com/2006/03/03/ politics/03patriot.html?_r=1 (accessed October 20, 2012).

20 Cole and Dempsey, *Terrorism and the Constitution*, ibook, chap. 12, pp. 193–194 of 342.

21 Ibid., chap. 12, p. 196 of 342.

22 O'Connor quoted in Schulhofer, *Rethinking the Patriot Act*, 12.

23 Stone, *Perilous Times*, 556.

24 Dudziak, *War Time*, 106.

25 See Francis Biddle, "Civil Rights in Times of Stress," *Bill of Rights Review: A Quarterly* 2, no. 1 (1941): 14.

26 Dudziak, *War Time*, 135.

27 Dudziak distinguishes between the ongoing Cold War (which lasted until 1989) and the easing of the "red-baiting" that accompanied it during the Second Red Scare by the late 1950s; see Dudziak, *War Time*, 77.

INDEX

Page numbers in italics refer to illustrations

House Committee Investigating Un-
American Activities (Dies Committee), 30
House Un-American Activities Committee (HUAC), 200–201, 204, 236n148
Howard, Milton, 79
H.R. 5138 (Smith Bill), 31–42; opposition
to, 33–34, 37–39, 40–41; passage and
signing of, 34, 40. *See also* Smith Act
Hudson, Carlos: as Smith Act defendant,
77, 137, 184, 187, 227n1, 262n6; testimony against, 94, 95, 97, 103

immigrants, 16, 222; and Smith Act provisions, 31, 32, 33–34, 37, 40. *See also*
anti-immigrant sentiment
Immigration and Naturalization Service
(INS), 72, 156, 203, 211
In Defense of Socialism (pamphlet), 142
indictments, 21, 198; for Smith Act trial, 1,
75–81, 97, 127
Industrial Organizer, 83, 84, 88, 110, 141,
149
industrial unionism, 10, 11, 17, 135; Teamsters union and, 12, 45, 230n17
Industrial Worker, 141
Industrial Workers of the World (IWW),
10, 11, 12, 16, 110, 141, 208
informants. *See* FBI informants
International Brotherhood of Teamsters
(IBT), 46, 56, 181, 205; and craft vs.
industrial unionism, 12, 45, 230n17;
Minneapolis locals of, 58, 64, 243n115
(*see also* Local 359; Local 544; Local
574). *See also* Tobin, Daniel
International Labor Defense, 177
internment (Japanese), 42, 224

Jackson, Robert, 80; as attorney general,
42, 51, 72, 153, 259n111; on Supreme
Court, 80, 166, 199, 216, 259n111
Jacobsen, Betty June, 207
Janosco, Bea, 166–67, 178, 179, 189

Janosco, John, 151
Japanese Americans, 42, 224
Johnsen, Harvey M., 161
Johnson, L. Clair, 150–51
Joyce, Matthew M., 156; background of,
22, 107; in trial of WPA strikers, 22, 24
—in Smith Act trial, 88, 94, 134; directed verdicts by, 2, 107–8, 227n5;
instructions to jury by, 132–33;
rulings by, 83, 92, 93, 94, 96, 97,
100, 106–8, 114–15, 117; sentences
imposed by, 136–37
Judge Advocate General's Office, 31–32
jurors (in Smith Act trial), 88, 134–25

Kalven, Harry, Jr., 165, 199–200, 217,
259n114
Karsner, Rose, 176, 177, 178, 182
Kolinski, Frank, 68
Konvitz, Milton, 168
Korean War, 200–201
Korematsu, Fred, 224
Krivitsky, Walter, 35–36
Kuehn, Karl, 174, 188, 193, 227n2; as Smith
Act defendant, 77, 94, 137, 171, 172, 173,
186, 188

labor anti-communism, 3–4, 205; in Local
544, 45–46, 48, 61; and security state,
4, 5, 7
Labor's Non-Partisan League (LNPL), 79
Latimer, Ira, 80
Lehr und Wehr Verein, 26
Lend-Lease Act, 55
Lenin, Vladimir, 77, 90, 130, 160, 182
Lens, Sidney, 213
LeSuer, Arthur, 77–78
letter-writing campaigns, 140, 185
Levi, Edward, 221
Lewis, Denny, 57, 58, 64, 68
Lewis, John L., 15, 57, 59, 113, 151–52
Lewis, Myer, 66
Lewis, Read, 33

Workers Party, 141, 181, 190–92, 206
workers' self defense, 24–25, 115. *See also* Union Defense Guard
Works Progress administration (WPA), 1; 1939 strike against, 1, 9–10, 20–24
World Trade Center attacks (1993 and 2001), 222–23
World War I, 3, 30, 34, 41
World War II, 3, 9, 13; Communist Party and, 3, 35–36, 70, 79, 142; Japanese

internment during, 42, 224; SWP position on, 1, 3, 70, 79, 113–14, 119. *See also* war preparedness program
Woxberg, H. L., 64, 65, 66

Yates v. U.S. (1957), 197, 216–17, 222, 224
Young Socialist Alliance (YSA), 197, 219, 220, 221

Zachary, Roy, 24

ABOUT THE AUTHOR

Donna T. Haverty-Stacke is Associate Professor of History at Hunter College, CUNY, where she teaches courses in U.S. cultural, urban, and labor history. She is director of the Labor and Working-Class History Seminar at Roosevelt House and the author of *America's Forgotten Holiday: May Day and Nationalism, 1867–1960.*